THE CIVILIZATION OF THE AMERICAN INDIAN SERIES

THE SIOUX / *Life and Customs of a Warrior Society*

the Sioux

LIFE AND CUSTOMS OF A WARRIOR / SOCIETY

BY ROYAL B. HASSRICK

In Collaboration with Dorothy Maxwell and Cile M. Bach

UNIVERSITY OF OKLAHOMA PRESS · NORMAN

By Royal B. Hassrick

(In collaboration with Gordon Macgregor and William Henry),
Warriors without Weapons (Chicago, 1946)

(In collaboration with Cile M. Bach), *Building the West*
(Denver, 1955)

Western Heritage (Denver, 1958)

Indian Art of the Americas (Denver, 1960)

(In collaboration with Dorothy Maxwell and Cile M. Bach),
The Sioux: Life and Customs of a Warrior Society

The drawing facing the title page was adapted from a painting entitled
Sioux Battle *by Oscar Howe* (Nazuha Hokshina, "Trader Boy"),
*artist in residence at the University of South Dakota. It is decorative,
not ethnographic, and is used here because of its artistic merit in the
depiction of action.*

International Standard Book Number: 0-8061-0607-7

Library of Congress Catalog Card Number: 64-11331

Copyright 1964 by the University of Oklahoma Press, Publishing Division of the
University. Manufactured in the U.S.A. First edition, 1964; second printing, 1967;
third printing, 1972.

The Sioux: Life and Customs of a Warrior Society is Volume 72 in The Civilization of the American Indian Series.

DEDICATED / *to the thousands of Sioux people living today.*

In her buckskin dress decorated with shining coins, Red Thing That Touches in Walking posed for this oil painting by George Catlin in about 1834.

FOR MANY PEOPLE the Sioux, as warriors and as buffalo hunters,
have become the symbol of all that is Indian—colorful figures endowed with great fortitude and powerful vision. They were the
heroes of the Great Plains in the day of heroes and they were
the villains, too. Properly, they have been the subject of much
writing.

To attempt to describe the ways of a people, the patterns of
their behavior, or the concepts of their imagination, is only less
presumptuous than to try to interpret how their nation functioned.
However, to understand the Sioux, it seems fitting to begin with
their view of the world.

Apparently, the most significant theme in the world of the Sioux
was that man is a minute but integral part of a tremendous universe. This will perhaps be apparent by looking first at the Sioux
concept of the order of things and then at the pattern of the
individual's adaptation to it. Thus the following chapters, from
a description of the Nation to the death of a Sioux patriarch, seek
to show the full range of Sioux life.

The Sioux Indians with whom this book deals call themselves
Lakotas, as distinguished from their relatives the Nakotas, or
Yankton Sioux, and the Dakotas, or Santee Sioux. All of these
groups speak closely related dialects of the Siouan language. However, because the word Sioux has been identified with the Lakotas
in the American mind and because Sioux has become the stereo-
type of all Plains Indian culture, the term is used throughout this
book.

The book attempts to present Sioux life as it was in the era of
its greatest vigor and renown—the brief span of less than fifty

years from about 1830 to 1870. To do this, the observations and records of many informants and writers have been freely drawn upon.

Fortunately, when this book was first projected, there were still living Sioux who remembered the great era of tribal history from their early childhood or from the accounts they had heard from the lips of their parents and grandparents. Among these links with a vanished world are names which occur frequently in this book: Arnold Iron Shell, Leader Charge, Blue Whirlwind, Little Day, High Bald Eagle, and Rattling Blanket Woman. Also, there were those who, though younger, had carefully taken note of the words of their elders and were willing to pass them on. These included James Black Horse and his wife Brings the White Buffalo, Charles Chasing Crane, Jesse Bordeaux, Mabel Standing Soldier, Rose Running Horse, and Mary and Irene Red Shirt.

The book also draws heavily upon accounts of the Sioux by white travelers and traders, and the historical and anthropological treatments of the Sioux written in this century. The result is no one man's idea of what Sioux life was like, but a compound of many opinions, both Indian and non-Indian.

Emphasis is laid in the following chapters on Sioux thought and concept, for men are and become in great measure what they think and want themselves to be. Hence what they conceive and how they interpret and rationalize this conceptualization can give insight into what they really are.

Throughout this book runs the dual theme of self-expression and self-denial. Using the Sioux way of life as a case study, an attempt is made to analyze the apparent conflict between self and selflessness by showing first that the need to resolve the conflict is an essential element of any way of life and then that, when the opportunity to resolve the conflict in one's own way is denied, the very reason for living may be lost.

Self-expression involves the concept of ego-preservation. In its broadest sense it includes the individual's endeavor to seek means of gratification, self-preservation, and ways of overcoming fear, including the fear of death.

Individual, yet gregarious, man has a continuing need to re-adapt his person, his society, and his culture to changes in nature, in society, and in self so as to achieve equilibrium sufficient to maintain life. This continuing and necessary readaptation, how-ever, demands a fundamental conformity, a denial of self, a sac-rifice through selflessness.

The conflict of self and selflessness results in a *Gestalt* of such complexity that a host of adjustment patterns are possible—some of them rather bizarre. Associated with (and often inseparable from) the proposition of self and selflessness is the correlated con-cept of security through change. Security for the individual and the group is an integral aspect of ego-preservation and is often believed to be achievable only by maintaining the *status quo*. Thus, survival is believed by many to depend on strict adherence to religious doctrine, to patterns of family interrelation, or to types of dwelling, all of which are tried and true. Yet security and sur-vival are not synonymous, for the changes operative in an indi-vidual, in his society, in his culture, and in his environment require adaptations and readaptations which must in turn be re-evaluated and reappraised. There appears in the book an underlying thesis exposing the spuriousness of the belief in security solely through *status quo* and bringing to focus the urgency for wholehearted belief in survival through change.

Finally, the book is written in the belief that people—all people, no matter who they are or where and in what time they live—have a strong interest in other peoples. From the telling of the story of a nation there may grow a better understanding, by our-selves and by other peoples, of what we Americans are really like.

CARL BODMER depicted a Dakota woman and an Assiniboine
child, possibly a captive, in this engraving, made in about 1834.
The woman wears a classic example of a married woman's buffalo robe in border and box design. Note that even the child
wears a necklace, earrings, and beaded bracelets.

ACKNOWLEDGMENTS

THIS BOOK OWES ITS COMPLETION to the inspiration and scholarship of many individuals. I am especially indebted to Robert McKennan of Dartmouth College for his forthright encouragement; to Donald Scott, director of the Peabody Museum of Harvard University, for his unequivocal sponsorship; to A. Irving Hallowell of the University of Pennsylvania for his enthusiastic and scholarly mentorship; and to the late Frank G. Speck for his profoundly encompassing insight. Grateful, too, am I for the advice of the late Clark Wissler of the American Museum of Natural History for his generous support of this project, and to the late Scudder Mekeel for his sharing of concepts.

Of the researches and writings of Alice Fletcher, Ella Deloria, J. R. Walker, Clark Wissler, John C. Ewers, Jeanette Mirsky, Frances Densmore, J. O. Dorsey, J. Brown, Luther Standing Bear, and George E. Hyde, I am most appreciative. To them goes recognition for the compilation of significant material essential to the completion of this work.

Special tribute, moreover, is due to the true authors of this book. These are the Sioux men and women whose devotion toward preserving the history of their people and whose patient explanations and meaningful interpretations have given insight to the Sioux way of life. To the late Chief Arnold Iron Shell of Harrington, South Dakota, is owed the gratitude of genuine companionship and true comprehension for faithfully recording the life ways of his people. To the late Chief Leader Charge, of Cut Meat District, goes deep appreciation for his devotion to the careful reporting of the old Sioux way. To Samuel Broken Leg for his precise reporting of former Indian customs, to Mabel Standing Soldier, to Mary and Irene Red Shirt, and to Rose Running Horse are extended thanks for their assistance in clarifying a variety of details of Sioux life. To the late Little Day, I am indebted for her vivacious and ebullient observations of her Sioux childhood. Especially to the late Blue Whirlwind, for her understanding of the woman's role and more especially for her devoted affection, am I most grateful. To Michael Bordeaux and Charles Chasing Crane, my interpreters, are offered my sincere thanks for their patient versatility in translation and their lively companionship in bridging language barriers and social customs toward the goal of recording the observations of their people. Most particularly am I indebted to James Black Horse and his wife Brings the White Buffalo for their encompassing comprehension of the value of recording the Sioux way, and most significantly for their whole-hearted mentorship of the project. Only through their enduring friendship and sustained loyalty could this book have become a reality.

All but three of the line drawings in this book were drawn by me. The details and many objects were given me by informants and are in my original field notes; other objects were in my collection, most of which I have given to the Denver Art Museum, though I still retain a few. The drawings of the rider in battle, of the dog and travois arrangements, and of the horses' heads and bridles were done by my brother, Kenneth Hassrick. I am thankful for his help.

To Barbara Hassrick and Kay Roberts, I owe much tribute for their conscientiousness in typing and retyping, and much comfort for their observations with respect to editorial accuracy.

To Roma McNickle is offered deep appreciation for her valued and compassionate editorial comments. Without her suggestions this work would have suffered.

Lastly, to my collaborators Dorothy Maxwell and Cile M. Bach, I extend heartfelt thanks. Only through Dorothy Maxwell's corroboratory conversations with Sioux descendants and her assistance with the over-all organization of this book has its completion become possible. Only through Cile Bach's able and enthusiastic literary ability to co-ordinate the vast accumulation of field notes and scribblings has the Sioux way found a chance of being told.

No research, however, is without its financial sponsor. To the trustees of the B. G. Royal estate, for money to carry out initial field work, I give grateful appreciation.

Only with the help, advice, and understanding of each one of the foregoing people could this work have been accomplished. Any contribution it may make will be due in major part to their wisdom. This, however, in no way relieves the author of any responsibility for the contents of the work.

ROYAL B. HASSRICK

Lone Star Ranch
Elizabeth, Colorado

TABLE of Contents

Introduction	*page* ix
Acknowledgments	xiii

Part One—Rank and Order

| CHAPTER 1. | The Structure of the Nation | 3 |
| CHAPTER 2. | Morals, Modes, and Manners | 32 |

Part Two—The Warrior

| CHAPTER 3. | Ethnocentrism | 61 |
| CHAPTER 4. | The Scheme of War | 76 |

Part Three—Familiarity and Respect

CHAPTER 5.	The Family	107
CHAPTER 6.	The Sexes	121
CHAPTER 7.	Fun	143

Part Four—The Predators

CHAPTER 8.	Nomadism	171
CHAPTER 9.	The Predators	188
CHAPTER 10.	Production	209

Part Five—Self-Sacrifice

| CHAPTER 11. | The Universe and the Controllers | 245 |

CHAPTER 12. The Vision Quest 266

CHAPTER 13. The Way to Status 296

CHAPTER 14. The Individual and the Sioux Way 310

CHAPTER 15. Epilogue 339

Appendix A—Iron Shell's Winter Count ... 346

Appendix B—Familial Terms and Their Use ... 352

Bibliography 354

Index 361

LIST / *of Illustrations*

Sioux Battle	*frontispiece*
Red Thing That Touches in Walking	viii
A Dakota Woman and an Assiniboine Child	xii
Tokala Meeting-Dance and Election of Officers	2
Big Soldier	55
A Sioux Encampment	56–57
Bull Bear	58
Steps in the Making of a War Bonnet	81
Plan of a Sioux Attack upon the Shoshonis	82
Red Shirt	101
A Painted Sioux Tipi	102–103
White Hawk	104
Rider in Battle; Cedar Block; Big Twisted Flute	127
Flutes; Sticking Together Game	128
Sioux Games	139
Moccasin Guessing Game	140
Cat's Cradles	141
Red Cloud	165
Ear of Corn	166
Running Antelope	167
Iron Shell	168
Little Day's Camp; Wigwam Cover and Shingles; Leader's Wigwam Frame	179
Signpost; Dog and Travois Arrangement	180
Bridles; Halter	181
Hobbles	182
Riding Equipment; Snowshoes	205
Methods of Arrow Release	206

Hunting Equipment   207
Woman Carrying a Load of Wood; Tanning Equipment   208
A Pipe Bag   219
A Shield Cover   220
An Elk Skin Dress   221
A Buffalo-Hide Robe   222
Tipi, Tipi Doors   235
Tipis; Water Bag   236
Backrest; Bed; Painted Tipis   237
Methods of Cooking; Types of Quills; Bladder Bag   238
Methods of Quilling; Painting Equipment   239
Designs for Painted Robes   240
Designs for Painted Robes; Woman's Beaded
     Garments; Wicasa Yatapika's Shirt   241
Man's Legging; War Shields; Beaded Cradle   242

MAPS

1. Sioux Territory, 1680–1963   *pages* 4–5
2. Sioux Territory, *ca.*1850   67

PART ONE / *Rank and Order*

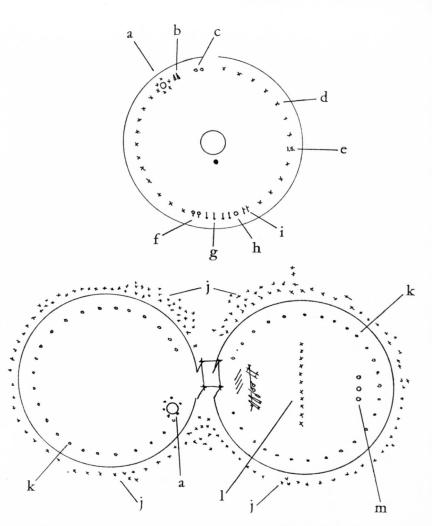

Tokala meeting-dance (*above*) and election of officers (*below*):
a, singers; *b*, Ȧkicitas; *c*, heralds; *d*, other Tokala members; *e*,
Iron Shell; *f*, rattlers; *g*, lance owners; *h*, drummer; *i*, pipe
bearers; *j*, populace; *k*, Tokala members; *l*, eleven candidates;
m, Tokala leaders. (See Chapter 1.)

CHAPTER I

The Structure of the Nation

A CENTURY AGO the Sioux Nation was a great nation. Its realm reached from the Platte River north to the Heart, from the Missouri west to the Big Horn Mountains. The nation was composed of seven major divisions: the Oglala, Sichangu, Miniconjou, Hunkpapa, Sihasapa, Itazipcho, and Oohenonpa. The Oglalas, meaning to "Scatter One's Own," lived to the southwest and were the most populous; the Sichangus or "Burnt Thighs" lived to the southeast of the Oglalas. Now known as the Brulés, they were the next important division in terms of size. The Miniconjous or "Those Who Plant by the Stream" and the Oohenonpas or "Two Boilings," more commonly known as "Two Kettles," lived to the north of the Brulés. The Hunkpapas, "Those Who Camp at the Entrance," the Sihasapas, "Black Feet," and the Itazipchos or "Without Bows" (or, as the early French called them, "Sans Arcs") were smaller divisions which occupied the northern part of the Sioux territory.[1]

In prehistory, these seven divisions of Sioux were possibly a separate group associated with the venerable assembly known as the Seven Council Fires. Although the tribal identity of this early

1 Harry Anderson, "An Investigation of the Early Bands of the Saone Group of Teton Sioux," *Journal of the Washington Academy of Sciences*, Vol. XLVI, No. 3 (1956). D. I. Bushnell, "Tribal Investigations East of the Mississippi," Smithsonian Institution *Miscellaneous Collections*, Vol. LXXXIX, No. 12 (1934). George E. Hyde, *Red Cloud's Folk*. Scudder Mekeel, "A Short History of the Teton-Dakota," *North Dakota Historical Quarterly*, Vol. X, No. 3 (1943). James Mooney, "The Ghost Dance Religion," Bureau of American Ethnology, *Fourteenth Annual Report*, P. 2 (1896). Doan Robinson, "History of the Dakota Sioux Indians," *South Dakota Historical Collections*, Vol. II, No. 2 (1904). John R. Swanton, "Siouan Tribes and the Ohio Valley," *American Anthropologist*, New Series, Vol. XLV, No. 1 (1943).

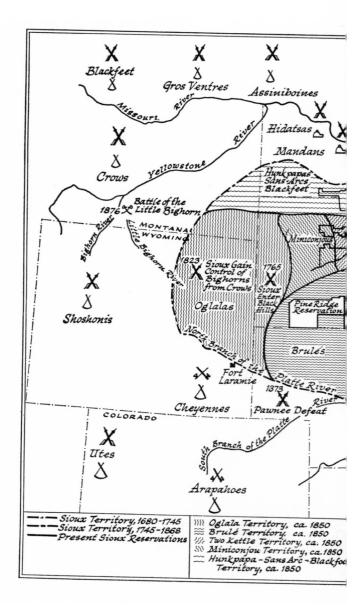

Blackfeet

Gros Ventres

Assiniboines

Missouri River

Hidatsas

Mandans

Crows

Yellowstone River

Hunkpapas
Sans Arcs
Blackfeet

Battle of the
1876 Little Bighorn

MONTANA
WYOMING

Bighorn River

Little Bighorn River

Miniconjous

1823
Sioux Gain
Control of
Bighorns
from Crows

1765
Sioux
Enter
Black
Hills

Pine Ridge
Reservation

Shoshonis

Oglalas

North Branch of the Platte River

Brulés

Fort
Laramie

1373
Pawnee Defeat

River

COLORADO

Cheyennes

Utes

South Branch of the Platte

Arapahoes

- · — Sioux Territory, 1680-1745
- - - Sioux Territory, 1745-1868
——— Present Sioux Reservations

)))) Oglala Territory, ca. 1850
≈≈≈ Brulé Territory, ca. 1850
//// Two Kettle Territory, ca. 1850
\\\\ Miniconjou Territory, ca. 1850
~~~ Hunkpapa – Sans Arc – Blackfoot
          Territory, ca. 1850

Plains Crees

Ojibways

Lake
Superior

Red River

Plains
Ojibways

Mille Lacs
1680

rikaras

Standing Rock
Reservation

1725

Cheyenne
River
Reservation   1735

Yankton Dakotas

Santee-Dakotas
1700

Mississippi

Sioux Meet Lewis & Clark, 1804

Crow Creek
Reservation

rule Reservation

MINNESOTA

ebud
servation

Poncas

Omahas

Iowas

Missouri

Platte River

Pawnees

IOWA
MISSOURI

River

Republican

NEBRASKA
KANSAS

SCALE
0   40   80
MILES

River

River

Shull

X	Nomadic Hunting Tribes	X	Enemies
△	Sedentary Agricultural Tribes.	X	Allies
⌒	Woodland Tribes		

Sioux Territory, 1680–1963

council is almost lost in tradition, its members are believed to have included the Mdewakantons, the Wahpetons, the Wahpekutes, the Sissetons, the Yanktons, the Yanktonais, and the Tetons. Of all of these tribal names, only the terms Teton and Santee (comprising the first four tribes above) persist. The Siouan language was common to all of these people. In the course of years, dialectical differences divided the original group into three distinct entities—the Dakotas, Nakotas, and Lakotas. Nomenclature here becomes difficult in that no group is identified by a single name. The Dakotas were also known as the Santee Sioux; the Nakotas as the Yankton and Yanktonai Sioux; and the Lakotas, with whom this book is concerned, as the Teton Sioux or "Dwellers of the Prairie," the Plains Sioux, and the Western Sioux. It was the Tetons who became the western vanguard of the original Seven Council Fires. The identification of these people becomes even more involved, however, because in early times the Chippewas, threatened on one side by the powerful Iroquois and on the other by the less powerful Seven Council Fires, dubbed the Iroquois "the True Adders" and the Sioux "the Lesser Adders," or "Nadoweisiw-eg." The French, encountering the latter term garbled the Chippewa word ("Nadowe-is-iw," in the singular), transforming it to "Sioux." Thus in anthropological terminology, all three groups—the Dakotas, Nakotas, and Lakotas—properly may be called Sioux. However, in popular nomenclature, the word "Sioux" has become identified with the Tetons, the dashing buffalo hunters of the prairies.

No one recalls when the Seven Councils met. Even among the Tetons, none remember when they themselves assembled as a body. Yet each of the seven Sioux divisions, while independent, sometimes joined others and lived so closely that their distinctions tended to be lost. Thus around 1800 the Two Kettles, the Without Bows, the Blackfeet, and the Hunkpapas probably formed one group known to some as the "Saones," while the Oglalas, the Brulés, and the Miniconjous formed another group and were sometimes referred to as the "Tetons."

As time passed, other relationships developed. New groupings

6

appeared and old ones dissolved, so that after 1850 the Sioux tended to band themselves into four or five rather than two main bodies. Generally, they held separate Sun Dances, possibly joining with one or two other groups with whom they traded. Except during this period of festivity, the divisions spent the year hunting and camping throughout their respective territories. Often two or three of the smaller northern divisions combined their efforts. However, in the minds of the Sioux, there were, regardless of these associations of convenience, seven Sioux divisions. This was the pattern of nature and logically the ideal and proper pattern for a nation.

Ideally, the entire Sioux Nation assembled each summer to hold council. Multitudes of people gathered in a great camp circle to renew acquaintances, to decide matters of national importance, and to give the Sun Dance. This was a period of renewed national unity and celebration. It was no mere assembly of representatives but a congregation of all men.

This annual meeting of the seven divisions symbolized the cohesiveness of the nation. The deliberations and actions of the chief men in council were the epitome of Sioux political thought. The Sun Dance was the ultimate of spiritual expression. Together, at one grand occasion, all the Sioux celebrated.

It was at this convocation that the Wicasa Yatapickas, the four great leaders of the nation, met for deliberation. Selected from among the outstanding headmen of the divisions, theirs was a position of unparalleled honor. Their opinion was paramount, their prestige unsurpassed, their reputation unimpeachable. The dignity of their office was characterized by the quality of their responsibility. It was at this occasion that the four great leaders formulated national policy and formally approved or disapproved actions taken by the headmen of the separate divisions during the past year. At this meeting they endorsed or rejected plans proposed by subordinates. Here they sat in judgment on offenses against national unity and security. They were, in effect, at this one summer session, an exclusive senate with supreme-court authority. Thus, while the Sioux Nation was theoretically governed by the four head chiefs selected from among the headmen of the various divisions, in reality, their position was almost entirely honorific. While their prestige was unexcelled and their authority unsurpassed, they conferred so infrequently that the vast bulk of tribal administration was perforce relegated to the leaders of the separate divisions.

In practice, each division within the Sioux Nation was an autonomous system capable of functioning independently of the tribe. The political organization varied slightly among the divisions, but in general each division was under the authority of four chiefs or Shirt Wearers.

The Sioux knowledge of their past was essentially an unformalized curiosity about their history and origin, factual, traditional, and mythical. The seriousness of their interest was evidenced by the keeping of winter counts, pictorial records of past events, and by the tales and myths which the old men retold every evening after dark.

Factual knowledge of the past was recorded in the winter counts. These records were kept by important individuals, apparently by the headman of each band. They were painted on deerskins, usually in spiral form with the first record at the vortex. Each picture served as a reminder of the most important event of each year.

The years were titled, not numbered. Each was named for one outstanding event, such as the death of a famous man or some startling and unusual phenomenon. Hence, a member of the band might refer to his age by saying, "I was born the year Crow Eagle was lanced."

Iron Shell's count, begun by his great-grandfather, recorded events first among the Miniconjous, later among the Brulés where his father resided.[2] The first recording was referred to as the winter a "Good White Man Came" (1807). The white man shook hands, brought gifts and food for all, and carried with

[2] Arnold Iron Shell preserved in a notebook the winter count which his father, Iron Shell, had kept. A complete and annotated text of this count will be found in Appendix A of the present volume.

8

him a document, but no one among the Sioux knew what he said, for there was no interpreter.

Iron Shell's winter count continued uninterrupted through 1883. Included among the significant events were such happenings as the winter "Little Beaver's Tipi Burned" (1809). This was probably Registre Loisel's trading post on Cedar Island near the mouth of Bad River, then operated by Manuel Lisa. It was very likely burned by the Sioux.

The year 1813 was mentioned as the winter of "A Man with a Gun." A war party of Sioux killed a Pawnee carrying a gun in one hand and a ramrod in the other. This was reported to be the first firearm which this particular band of Sioux had seen.

The following year, "Crushed a Witapahatu's Head," recounts a proposed treaty, according to American Horse, between the Kiowas or Witapahatus and the Sioux. At a council held near Horse Creek at Scotts Bluff, the Sioux became angered by the action of one of the Kiowas and killed him. The Kiowas were living in and about the Black Hills at this time and were expelled shortly thereafter by the Sioux.

Iron Shell's grandfather, a headman among the Miniconjous, died in 1816, the winter "Shot in the Heel Died." The next year reports the death of Bone Bracelet, Shot in the Heel's father, the first keeper of the count.

"Smallpox was a frightening scourge for all the Plains Indians, and the year 1818 was known as "Smallpox." The years 1845 and 1850 were likewise named for the dread disease.

The winter of the "Mature Corn Camp" (1823) notes that the Sioux camped near a cornfield. This probably refers to the attack by Colonel Leavenworth's troop and Sioux forces upon the Arikara villages on August 10, 1823. After the Arikaras' defeat, the Sioux pillaged their corn crops.

On November 12, 1833, there occurred a brilliant meteoric shower, and the year is listed as the winter of the "Shifting Stars." The winter "The Sun Died" refers to the eclipse which occurred on August 7, 1869.

The winter of "Fighting over the Ice" (1836) recalled the

9

battle between the Pawnees and the Sioux on the North Platte River. Battiste Good's winter count states that seven Pawnees were killed.

"Killed Many Broken Arrows" (1837) recounts an incident of intertribal warfare wherein the Wazhazhas, a band of the Brulés, and probably several other groups destroyed a war party of the Broken Arrow people. According to Big Missouri's count, the massacre took place because a member of the Broken Arrow camp stole the wife of a man belonging to another band.

"Stealing Arrows from the Pawnees" (1843) is remarkable because the Sioux recaptured several sacred arrows belonging to the Cheyennes which the Pawnees had previously stolen. The Sioux returned them to the Cheyenne owners, and the two tribes have remained close allies ever since. The Sioux, however, were not successful in returning all the arrows, and one or more still remain in the Pawnees' possession.

"Big Issue" (1851) refers to the first Fort Laramie Treaty at the Platte River. Here government officials dispersed gifts to the Sioux. The next event concerning the government is entitled "Many Deer Came to Make a Treaty." This was in 1865, when General Maynadier treated with the Sioux. The final treaty mentioned in Iron Shell's count, "Went to Make a Treaty," refers to the Sioux's cession of the Black Hills on September 26, 1876.

Iron Shell's last entry (1883) tells of the first Sioux dance lodge made of logs, referring to it as "Red Top Tipi Band Made a Dance Hall."

It is significant to observe that nowhere in the winter count is there mention of battles with the United States Army, not even the Sioux's climactic victory at the Little Bighorn. The count rather strikingly indicates that the Sioux were concerned primarily with their own affairs, and that the wars with the white man, if important, were secondary. References to white men involve traders and treaty-making, matters which did affect their economic and political life. The record indicates that the Sioux conceived as important those events which played a dramatic part in the total pattern—the loss of a great leader, the hardship of a cruel winter, the internal strife caused by wayward individuals. In reality, the winter counts were the Sioux's own history and became valuable to them not merely as a record but as a standard upon which to judge the important matters of life.

Time-reckoning for the Sioux was concerned, however, not only with maintaining a chronicle of the years but with keeping a count of months and days.

According to Iron Shell, the year of thirteen months began in April, and the basis for this was that his father (also named Iron Shell) replaced the moon-counting stick at this time:

> In the evenings, when the moon first rose, Iron Shell made a nick in a long pole he kept by the bed for that purpose. Every night he made another nick, until the moon finally disappeared. Then he said "The Moon Died." There were usually 25 or 26 nicks for each month, for there are three days when the moon cannot be seen. On the other side of the pole, Iron Shell marked a single nick to show the passing of a month.
>
> Iron Shell carried this stick wherever he went. He got a new stick each year, cutting it in the moon of the Birth of Calves.

It is possible to infer that April, the moon of the birth of calves, was associated with the annual renewal of the Sioux's food supply as exemplified in the calving, combined with the termination of the winter. The important thing is that the idea of a year having a beginning or ending was of little matter to the Indian. The winter served as a designation point in a spiraling series, unmarked by any periods in the sequence.

The firm base upon which the Sioux's rather fluid governmental structure rested was the family hunting group or *tiyospe*. It was upon this unit that Sioux organization was structured, for it rendered the nation at once flexible and cohesive. Existence for the Sioux people, as for all mankind, was the vexing combination of individual endeavor and group enterprise. It was harassed by trial and error, frustrated by conservatism, and tortured by change. The degree to which their environment determined their adjustment may be academically debatable, but it is nonetheless pertinent to the Sioux Nation's vigorous development, heady dominance, and tragic decline.

The Sioux, as early as 1700, were hunters of small game and buffalo. Since only small units of population could be supported at any one place under a strictly hunting economy, these people needed to control a wide area of territory, and a nomadic way of life became essential. Sioux society had its foundation in small, close-knit family hunting groups. The leader of such a group was generally the patriarchal family head, a member of the grandparent generation. It was he who guided his sons and sons-in-law in the ways of hunting and warfare. This group, the core of Sioux society, was known as the "tiyospe." It was a clannish group. Loyalties were directed toward the leader, and devotions were toward kin. The family of man, wife, and children, while a biological reality, was not of particular sociological importance. Brothers and sisters were the family of significance. As the sons or daughters of a leader, as the co-operative partners in a closely related team of hunters and warriors, the family survived not so much as a result of marital co-operation as of sibling co-ordination.

The extended family arrangement, wherein a leader—and probably in some instances a partnership of related leaders—directed the undertakings of their mature sons and daughters, had real practicality for the Sioux economy. Such a family tended to ensure the large force of man power necessary for communal hunting and concerted war activity. A solitary man, his wife, and small children would be at an extreme disadvantage in acquiring sufficient meat and in gathering an adequate supply of wild fruits and vegetables to sustain themselves for long periods. In addition, they would be easy prey to marauders.

For the Sioux, a most natural and entirely wholesome pattern evolved. Here people who had grown up together, who knew one another quite intimately, might, if they wished, continue to make their livelihood in an enduring family enterprise.

Little Day, a member of the Brulé Sioux, recalled the camp of her childhood in the 1870's which typified the scheme of all tiyospes. She remembered particularly the summer camp of Meddling Bear just on the edge of the Black Hills, where tipis were set up according to family prestige in a circle. The site and order were prescribed by the four Wakincuzas. These, Little Day pointed out, were the pipe owners, men of recognized authority whose duties were to direct the movements of the camp. In a large encampment, which she recalled as numbering more than thirty tipis, her father, an important member and brother of the leader Red Leaf, camped at the northeastern end of the circle. The tipis known as the "horns" were nearest to the formal eastern entrance of the circle, a location reserved for leading families. Little Day could not remember the names of each household, but she did recall the tipi dwellers on the southeastern side of the circle and the order in which their tipis stood: Red Leaf, her father's brother; Fall, her paternal grandfather; her uncle, Freeze His Feet Off; and another uncle, Owns a Big White Horse. Next along the circle lived How Goes It, her father's cousin, and next to him lived another relative named White Crow. Her maternal grandmother was the only close relative who lived on the opposite horn. In this way grandmother could be near her family even though there was no room on the eastern side. Little Day's family band exemplified the close integration of kinship among the Sioux.

The Sioux family had no beginning and no end. Membership inevitably changed through birth, death, and divorce. Leadership passed from ancient patriarchs to younger men of proven maturity, but the family survived and continued to operate as an entity. An individual might lose his parents or his spouse or his children, but he could scarcely lose his family.

The position of headman was usually hereditary, though eligible sons were chosen on the basis of their war record and generosity. Such leaders were responsible for the well-being of the family. Since the band was an autonomous economic unit, the prestige of a headman depended upon his ability to provide his people with a good livelihood.

The reputation of a headman attracted not only his immediate family but also distant relatives and friends, who might abandon a less capable leader to place their trust in him. As more people clustered around such a man, receiving his gifts of horses and food and following him to bountiful food supplies, his influence spread beyond his family band and his power increased within the tribe.

The headman of the least of bands achieved his position through an extraordinarily complicated system of family status and individual merit. Of supreme importance to his success was his family background. To be a son of renowned parents fostered political aspirations.

The determinants of a "good family" involved many specific factors, ranging from such pragmatic considerations as wealth in horses and success in hunting to such philosophical aspirations as the four great virtues: bravery and fortitude, generosity and wisdom. Further qualifications for family prestige demanded membership in several fraternal societies and the sponsorship of multiple religious ceremonies. Important, too, was possession of supernatural power, achieved through dreams and visions. Born of such a family, one was *ipso facto* a highly honored individual. Other members of the tribe looked up to such a man, and conversely such an individual's behavior was expected to reflect the tribal goal. Thus, while such status had privilege, it also entailed responsibility. This social system had paradoxical and enigmatic overtones. The story of Red Cloud is a striking example.

Red Cloud's achievements were such that he is known as one of the most illustrious American figures in the nineteenth century. His fantastic war record was unexcelled; his brilliance as a headman was unparalleled; and his finesse as a diplomat brought the commissioners of the United States government to capitulate to his terms in the treaty at Fort Laramie in 1868. In spite of this distinguished career, Red Cloud, because of a modest family background, was never able to command the kind of reverence among the Sioux which someone from an important family might have received.

This kind of social situation constituted a paradox. Although rooted in idealism, the concept of status led to a pragmatic self-aggrandizement. The politically ambitious young man, seeking to achieve the position of a leader, made a conspicuous effort to help the weak, the poor, and the old, and also to bring food to the meeting lodge, where the council of elders was sure to observe his generosity.

The young man of high and noble background, the favorite son, the family's pride, did have an ideal pattern set for him, and it was a goal which few men could hope to reach. The final realization of this aspiration was tangible wealth and political power, as well as the intangible rewards exemplified in the four virtues.

So vital was family status, so keyed to the accepted pattern, to the right way of Sioux life, that it was an ideal. Not all men could measure up to it, and it is to be expected that there were those who questioned it as well as those who openly rebelled. But the skeptics, the rebels, and the misfits had outlets which offered either acceptable alternatives within the society or short cuts to recognition. There was, for example, the recalcitrant who lured his family and close friends away from the established band to form a new and independent camp.

For most men, however, the ideal was an acceptable challenge. Paths to success were sufficiently varied that its achievement was more than a standardized procedure. Realization of fame demanded knowledge and a facile handling of the Sioux amenities. Steps toward leadership might include success in hunting, fame as a warrior, power through a vision, membership in a society, presentation of ceremonies, and exhibition of generosity. Each was a step on the way toward acquiring and maintaining status. Each was in and of itself a most demanding, yet rewarding, experience.

As one Indian described it: "There are places for each man. As you go along life, you can work your way up. Some men can get to the top, others never seem to make it. The old men who have been leaders see in the good young men the future leaders and help them raise themselves."

The societies, honorary fraternal clubs devoted to maintaining the well-being of the community and fostering among their members the value of a high reputation, were competitive advocates of the Sioux way. The number of these societies varied among the band groupings, and their importance fluctuated over the years. The Crow Owners might at one time be most popular among the Oglalas, while among the Brulés their membership and influence might be limited, and elsewhere the society might not exist at all. But no matter how large or influential a society might be, each assumed a role in offering its members good fellowship through feasting and dancing.[3]

Essentially there were two kinds of fraternal groups: the policing societies known as the Akicitas, which were open to all able young men; and the civil societies best represented by the Nacas, composed largely of elders and former chiefs. There were among the several Sioux divisions many recognized Akicitas, whose responsibility as police involved maintaining order during camp movements and communal buffalo hunts. In general the leaders of the band appointed one Akicita group as the official police for a single season. Over a period of years the responsibility was awarded to various clubs. This policy offered a competitive goal or honor for which all clubs vied. Badgers, Brave Hearts, Crow Owners, and Kit Foxes all coveted the appointment. The society which was chosen for several seasons achieved a recognition, whereas the unchosen ones might experience a real loss of prestige and even possibly a decline in membership.[4]

Just as the Akicitas found representation among the several Sioux divisions, so did the civil societies. Among the most important was the Naca Ominicia. Members of this group were a kind of congress of patriarchs, including former headmen, famous

[3] Clark Wissler, "Societies and Ceremonial Associations in the Ogalala Division of the Teton-Dakota," American Museum of Natural History *Anthropological Papers*, Vol. XI (1912). Clark Wissler herein presents a classically detailed analysis of the Oglala Akicita societies.

[4] The number of civil and police societies varied from division to division, but among the more important were the following: civil societies—Naca Ominicias or Big Bellies, Ska Yuhas or White Horse Owners, Miwatanis or Tall Ones, and Iyuptalas or Owl Feather Headdresses; police societies—Tokalas or Kit Foxes, Sotka Yuhas or Plain Lance Owners, Irukas or Badgers, Cante Tinzas or Brave Hearts, Kangi Yuhas or Crow Owners, and Wicinskas or White-Marked Ones.

retired hunters and warriors, and distinguished shamans, definitely past their prime and endowed with the pompous proportions of middle age. One observing herald, in a facetious moment when calling them together for a council, proclaimed: "Come, you Big Bellies, to your meeting." Henceforth the Nacas were known to the Sioux by this disparaging tag. Another colloquial title for the group was "Those Who Wear Buffalo Headdresses," later contracted to "The Short Hairs."

In addition to the Nacas, there were other civil groups generally of less importance but reserved for distinguished older personages. One was Ska Yuhas, or the White Horse Owners. There is no indication that the possession of a white horse was a prerequisite of membership; rather, a reputation as a superior hunter was demanded. Another group was the Miwatanis, or Tall Ones.

The separation of societies on the basis of age was fundamental in Sioux culture because of the supreme importance of status, based upon two things: the accomplishment of youth and the wisdom of maturity. This pattern reveals the Sioux recognition of mature leadership, founded upon a profound respect for the aged. It was the dictum of the elders which formulated the political direction of the tribe.

Young men were invited to join policing societies at an early age. Some, like Hollow Horn Bear, became active as early as their sixteenth year. To be invited into the Akicita societies, a boy must usually have been on at least one war party, even if in no greater capacity than that of water boy. He would be considered an even more desirable candidate if he were the member of an outstanding family and had killed an enemy or "gone on the hill" to seek a vision. Youths of low status who had not sought a vision might not be invited until their middle twenties. Individuals could make up for the absence of supernatural power or for a modest family background by an exemplary war record. But a man who had committed murder or adultery, or who amassed wealth by not giving feasts, was not eligible for membership. Neither would a poor hunter or an inept warrior be asked to join. As one informant put it, "Such men just live."

Iron Shell described his initiation to the Kit Foxes:

> I was about nineteen when I joined the Tokalas. When I was chosen, the Tokalas were having a dance. Everyone watched these dances and I was planning to go, but had just returned from guarding the horses. As I was getting ready, two young Tokala officers, the two Whip Bearers, came to our tipi saying, "We have come after you from the Tokala dance. You are to join the Tokalas." I stood up and did not refuse. I finished dressing in my very best way, and went with them without questions.
>
> The Whip Bearers took me to the dance lodge and led me past the Tokalas seated round the sides to the leaders seated at the rear. The two Pipe Bearers sat to the left each holding a long stemmed pipe. Over their knees were their quilled, fringed tobacco bags. To their left were the Drum Bearers and next to them were four Lance Owners. Their lances were really bows wrapped in blue flannel, one end of which was tipped with pointed steel. Four eagle feathers were perched at the top and four were hung from the bow at intervals while the bow string was strung with many tiny down feathers. The two "Keepers of the Rattles" sat next to the "Lance Owners." All of these men wore red face paint and several of them had shaved their heads so that only a roach appeared and a braided scalp lock remained.
>
> It was one of the Pipe Bearers who first spoke saying, "Today we are making you a Tokala. Every time we dance, we want you to be present. Sit down some place."

It was not until the next dance that Iron Shell was formally initiated. His father came with him to assume this responsibility, asking one of the Tokala heralds to announce the occasion:

> My boy has become a Tokala. I wish you to announce to all the people that from now on he is Tokala. But first, report his new name "Changes With." Announce too, that because of this thing, I shall give away a horse.

All three stood in the middle of the dance lodge. The herald then called out to the Tokalas as all the people assembled, "Changes

With is a Tokala." He also called upon a poor old man to come up and receive a horse as token of a father honoring his son. The old man came and symbolically rubbed the father's face by passing his hand downward over his face saying, "Thanks." The father then gave the old man a stick in bond for future payment of a horse.

Iron Shell now was permitted to paint his face red, to roach his hair, to carry out such police duties as the Tokalas were called upon to perform. He must attend all dances and feasts or be subject to beating. Infraction of rules might also call for the destruction of his tipi and belongings by the whip bearers.

As a Kit Fox, Iron Shell had achieved the initial phase in a graded society wherein young men were expected to reach an ideal status for their age group, but could not be criticized for nonmembership in a civil society, reserved for elders. Not only was this important for the particular youth, but it was equally important for the entire family. The father, who sponsored his son at the initiation, then became responsible for making a public acclamation of his son's good fortune; he was also obliged to present a gift in honor of his son's new prestige and his new name. In the father's proclamation, there were overtones of unabashed pride. The son's achievements not only guaranteed the family's continued status but also provided the father with additional merit. The entire family and many friends were generally present and basking in the reflected glory. Lured by the ceremony, the feasting, and the dancing, many tribesmen attended these initiations as interesting and colorful social occasions.

On the day of such an event, the herald of Kit Foxes appeared chanting his proclamation: "Foxes are what I'm calling for—Ghost Head is ready with the food." The hour of these dancing feasts might be any time from noon to midnight, depending entirely on the host's readiness with the banquet. In a culture without clocks, minutes, or hours, time was elastic. Appointments were scheduled in such broad terms as morning, afternoon, or night.

Dances had many variations and were a part of nearly every Akicita gathering. Once when Ghost Head entertained, the Kit

Foxes, it was recalled, decided to dance the "Kick and Scatter the Tobacco Ashes." This could only occur after the members had emptied their pipes many times, thereby accumulating a pile of ashes at least one hand high. This happened only once in a great while. Dancing close around the fire pit with the ashes near by, someone was bound to scatter them, for each dancer tried to force the others into kicking the ashes. The loser was obligated to give a feast of a fat puppy dog for the entire society.

The origins of the Akicita societies have been preserved only by tradition. It is generally believed that most of them were organized as a result of someone's dream. Thus the individual was directed by supernatural beings to form an organization which would promote the best interests of the tribe. Having been given instructions regarding responsibilities of the society, and a set of rules and details for preparing paraphernalia, the recipient of the vision would announce these matters to his close friends. It has been said that Akicita societies might be formed by two close friends or *kolas*, men who had pledged exclusive devotion to one another. It is not unreasonable to assume that one of them, having received a supernatural directive in a dream, would report this to his closest friend. The Kit Foxes were believed to have originated in this way. The other groups, including the Crow Owners, the Badgers, and the Sotka Yuhas or Plain Lance Owners have similar traditions of origin.

It is most probable that the original motive of the Akicita societies was directed to professionalism in war and only later shifted to partial control of civil matters. The visions received by the founders frequently included testing the efficacy of the lance or whip in battle. Thus the official songs often refer to matters of death on the battlefield.

It is recalled that the founder of the Kit Foxes, in relating his vision, described his meeting with a camp where the herald called him, saying, "I have been sent to invite you by one who never runs away in battle, who never turns back from an enemy."[5] He later realized that the camp was not of people but of Kit Foxes.

[5] Wissler, "Societies and Ceremonial Associations," *loc. cit.*

The Kit Foxes' chant was doleful: "I am a Fox. I don't know when I'll be killed, but I'm living as a Fox." So was the challenge of the Brave Hearts: "My friend, whoever flees will not become a member, therefore I hardly live (from one day to the next.)"

The Sotka Yuhas' song when initiating a new member was probably most prophetic: "A Sotka Yuha never returned; he grew up to fight enemies; that's what he was meant to do."

Not only did the visionary precepts and the formal songs of the societies devote themselves to warfare, but the prescribed roles of the officers seemed to demand the most courageous endeavors. Only the bravest men were selected for positions of leadership within the societies. They were harangued regarding their behavior on the battlefield and required to carry and use their lances, their whips, or official paraphernalia in war, and they were often expected to exhibit valor to the point of death. Among the Oglalas, members appointed to the position of lance owners were required on the battlefield to stand by their lance and fight, retreating only if a fellow member removed the lance. Officers of some societies were invested with sashes, which when worn in battle were staked to the ground. As with the lance owners, only a friend could remove the stake. So strict were the requirements of officership that young men were frequently reluctant to accept the honor, knowing that to fulfill the obligations successfully was tantamount to death. The Kit Fox song befits the impending tragedy inherent for all worthy members of the Sioux Akicitas:

> *I am a Fox*
> *I am supposed to die*
> *If there is anything difficult*
> *If there is anything dangerous*
> *That is mine to do.*[6]

In spite of the Akicitas' military emphasis as expressed in their traditional origins, in their formal songs, in their requirements for leadership, an Akicita group rarely went to war as a body. Indi-

[6] *Ibid.*

vidual members went to battle, and frequently several fellow members would join an expedition. Here each would be on trial to sustain his own reputation and that of his particular society. But the societies themselves, while fostering militarism, were charged paradoxically with maintaining civil order.

The reasons for this apparent divergent approach may have explanation in the rapid development which Sioux culture underwent from the late eighteenth to the early nineteenth century.

Ambitious and visionary young men seeking their fortune within a small hunting group, subject constantly to attack by enemies, might well conceive of a close-knit military junta as a means to their personal success. The Sioux people of the 1750's were tiny bands exploring the awesome reaches of the Plains. They were subject to attack by neighboring tribes, some of whom, like the Crees, were equipped with firearms. Others, such as the Arikaras with their great numbers and secure villages, presented a most uncompromising barrier to the westward expansion of the Sioux. And yet to acquire the wealth of the buffalo ground, the Sioux were forced to defend themselves and, more important, to conquer others. It is not inconceivable that young men should group themselves together to meet this challenge. But as the years passed, as the Sioux dramatically conquered and quite easily controlled the heartland of the buffalo range, as they grew wealthy and populous, the need for warrior groups must have been supplanted by a more critical need for civil control. The Sioux, as a nation, became so powerful, so completely the dominant culture in the region, that the urgency for rigidly organized military bodies gave way to a need for crystallized civil authority. And such an adjustment could be functionally realistic since the motivation and goal of nearly every young man continued to be a warrior's career. In a sense, the Sioux culture had so thoroughly indoctrinated its youth that it possessed a standing army without now having to organize one. Rather, it needed internal police to maintain its way of life from within. And the Akicita societies were officially directed toward ensuring this more recent need.

Leadership within the Akicitas, as for example among the Tokalas, was invested in the twelve officers—two pipe bearers, two drummers, four lance owners, two rattlers, and two whippers. The pipe bearers were the counselors in times of discord. It was they who reasoned with members who wished to resign the responsibility of their office; they ordered the whip bearers to discipline members for infraction of rules. The whip bearers struck members who were tardy to dance or failed to attend Tokala meetings. It was they who destroyed the tipis of tribal members who defied the rule against hunting alone during communal buffalo drives.

The officers of the Tokalas, though carrying out specified roles, were considered equal in authority and importance. The twelve men were thought of as leaders, and none took precedence over the others. They were, however, guided and directed in all major decisions by three old men. The three old men were former Tokalas, members of the Nacas, venerable leaders of the tribe. As overseers, they were consulted regarding the selection of new members, their advice was asked about ceremonial ritual, and they rendered their opinions concerning the over-all activities of the society. They were the elders whose mature experience was recognized as valuable to the existence of the club.

Chasing as He Walks, a lance owner, was killed in battle. As was customary, his relatives returned his lance to the Kit Fox society. It was understood that when the camps were in a circle, the Kit Foxes would install new officers to fill this and other vacancies. They would also renew their official paraphernalia. Important personages in the selection procedure were the three old men, who "sat in a secret place" to decide who would be the new officers.

At the center of the camp circle, the society members erected two large tipis facing each other and connected by a covering which formed a corridor. In the tipi toward the west, near the doorway, was prepared a rack on which the societal equipment rested. This was set out in a precise order: two pipes leaned at the southern end of the rack; next hung two rattles; then there were the drumsticks; and finally, the two whips. The four societal lances were thrust in the ground before the rack. When the equipment was thus set up, the three old men arrived to take their places behind the ceremonial rack. Behind them sat the other elders. The rest of the Kit Fox members also were privileged to take their places inside the tipis. So that all the tribesmen might view the installation from the perimeter, the sides of the tipis were rolled up.

When the old men were ready to designate the new officers, the singers seated near the door slowly began the traditional song. "One of the Foxes didn't return, 'Chasing as He Walks' didn't return." To the slow measure of the chant, the three old men rose and danced while uttering dirgelike war cries. After this, two of the old men picked up one of the pipes and carried it to a young man of their choice. They then returned with the young man and seated him in a place reserved for the new pipe bearer. With each appointment, the ceremony was repeated. When all of the new officers had taken their places, one of the three old men instructed them in their duties, telling them to honor their badge of office, to act respectfully, and to be brave in war by aiding their comrades. It was customary to end such a speech with the following lines: "If you get killed, that will be good. For this is the rule."

Should a former officer be so inclined, he too might address the incumbents. Grasping the badge of his office, he proceeded to describe his own exploits and how he was honored and respected, after which the drummers sounded the drums. Then he returned the lance by placing it in the ground in front of the new owner, whereupon the new owner took it. In recounting his coups, the former official thereby charged the new incumbent to maintain the high honor of the office.

The celebration was climaxed by a feast of boiled young puppy. The servers distributed the food. Then they made an offering to the Four Winds, to the Sky and Earth, and placed this offering in the center of the tipi, where the fire pit would be. The servers repeated the offering with a piece of meat, but on the second occasion, placed it in the mouth of the first pipe bearer. The new officer acknowledged this token with the word, "*Kola*," while the server replied, *"How."* The entire membership responded, *"To-kala How."* When each officer had experienced this ritual, the feast began. After the feast, the twelve men formed a procession. Led by the first pipe bearer, they marched in a single file around the camp, punctuating their progress by a series of dances. With each dance, there was a special song. The first of these was received by the founder in a dream and was sung only on these occasions. Translated, it read: "Kind Fox leads out first, it is so: leads out in his holiness; it is so." Another of these songs was "When I start coming around the camp circle, the spectators are coming with a smile. Thus I come joyously."

If the police societies were the proving ground for political aspirants, the chiefs' society, or Naca Ominicia, was the resource of tribal leadership.[7] Qualifications for membership were many and varied. A Naca might be a former headman of one of the bands, a leading shaman of proven integrity and magnetism, or a hunter or warrior whose outstanding career had brought him renown. Then, of course, the elders, recognized for their qualities of bravery and fortitude, wisdom and generosity, were also members of the group.

The Naca Ominicia was, in truth, the real council of the tribe. It was this body which met at the Red Council Lodge at the center of the circle to hear the reports of scouts, to determine whether a tribal hunt should be held, whether camp should be moved, whether war was to be declared or peace was to be made. In this sense, the Naca Ominicia held a true legislative responsibility. It is said that the members acted only in unison, that decisions were reached only with unanimous voice. Here the individual constituted a potent minority with veto power. The group must convince the opposition, mediate and reconcile differences, or acquiesce and forego the decision.

In addition to the Naca's legislative responsibility, its power

---

[7] Hyde, *Red Cloud's Folk;* Luther Standing Bear, *Land of the Spotted Eagle;* Stanley Vestal, *Sitting Bull;* Wissler, "Societies and Ceremonial Associations," *loc. cit.* Each of these authors mentions Sioux governmental organization, although Clark Wissler's report is probably most detailed.

extended to ultimate control of tribal administration, for it was this body who appointed the administrators and executives. Political organization varied within the different bands and underwent changes from time to time. Thus among the Brulés, the Naca Ominicias appointed from among themselves ten Wicasa Itacans. This smaller group of men was actually an executive committee which activated the policies of the larger council. The Wicasa Itacans met in order to interpret and make practical the broad decisions of the Nacas; they were, therefore, generally regarded as the real government.

This pattern of government was repeated in other Sioux divisions, with variations in the numbers of Wicasa Itacans. The Oglalas, for example, named only seven to the smaller executive group. One of the most important responsibilities delegated to the Wicasa Itacans in all divisions was the appointment of the Shirt Wearers. These officials were also chosen from the Naca group. The number might vary from division to division, so that among the Oglalas, four men were appointed, while among the Brulés, two men held the office by appointment. The latter were privileged to chose for themselves two associates.

Shirt Wearers were the official executives of the tribe. As such, they were the voice of the Wicasa Itacans. At their investiture, they were presented with either a blue-and-yellow or a red-and-green painted shirt fringed with hairlocks. It is said that some men might instead be given a solid yellow shirt or one decorated with vertical black stripes; however, the usual shirt had a blue upper half and a yellow lower half, or a red upper half and a green lower half. The colors are said to have symbolized the potency of the supernatural Controllers—blue the Sky, yellow the Rock, red the Sun, and green the Earth. The fringe of the hairlocks represented the people of the tribe for whom the Shirt Wearers were responsible, for they were the owners of the tribe.

The term of office for a Shirt Wearer depended in large measure upon the personal wish of the incumbent. As executive officers, these Wicasas would be called upon continually to decide matters of tribal concern, from reconciling quarrels between individuals and families to negotiating diplomatic relations between foreign nations. The welfare of the people was their primary obligation, and upon them fell the final responsibility for providing bountiful hunting and good campgrounds. Not only were the Shirt Wearers delegated executive authority, but they were supreme counselors.

When a man felt that he was no longer able to fulfill the obligations of the office, it behooved him to train a younger man for the task. In addition to possesssing those personal qualities which might be expressed as compassion and wisdom, generosity and fortitude, the candidate should have undergone four ceremonies—the Hunka, the Ball-throwing or Buffalo Rite, the Ghost-owning, and the Owns a White Buffalo. Because only the well-to-do could afford the performance of these rites, the office of Shirt Wearer was in general limited to the sons of headmen or Wicasas. Hence, the office was in general hereditary in character, for a devoted father endeavored to bestow this high honor upon his son. However, some young men, even though sons of obscure parents, possessed such outstanding qualifications for leadership that the Wicasas recognized them nonetheless. Such was the famous Crazy Horse, son of a shaman.

In the governmental hierarchy of the Sioux, the Wakincuzas or Pipe Owners also held a place of importance. Usually, if not always, they were members of the Naca Ominicia. Although they were appointed by the Nacas, they served under the direction of the Shirt Wearers. The number of Pipe Owners varied in the various tribes; among the Brulés, there were two, among the Oglalas, four.

Each Wakincuza carried a pipe and a pipe bag which were presented to him at the time of appointment as his badge of office. At one time, these highly ornamented bags containing the sacred pipes were reserved for the sole use of the Wakincuzas in fulfilling their ordained responsibility in the "Making of Brothers" or Peace Ceremony. The importance of the pipe as a symbol of prestige was analogous to the hair-fringed shirt reserved for the exclusive use of the Wicasas.

The particular responsibility of the Wakincuzas centered in the organization of all camp moves, including the appointment of the Akicitas or police. They assigned camping locations to the bands and to the individual families. They determined the time and location of the periodic halts and rests. It was also their responsibility to give the order for large tribal hunts and surrounds. As officers of the march, the Wakincuzas walked far in advance of the main body of tribesmen. They directed all of the activities of the Akicitas, who as policemen and soldiers flanked the motley procession, kept it in order, and guarded against possible enemy attack.

Until the middle of the nineteenth century, the over-all national government of the Sioux paralleled that of the divisional governments. Thus the elders of Nacas of the Oglalas, Brulés, Miniconjous, and the others, convening at an annual summer camp, appointed four executives, known as the Wicasa Yatapikas, Supreme Owners of the tribe.

The Supreme Owners were the counterpart, on a national level, of the Wicasas or Shirt Wearers of the tribal divisions. As such, they were the executives of the nation with the same authority and responsibility for national welfare as the Wicasas had within each division. Like the Wicasas, the Wicasa Yatapikas must have been above reproach, must have performed the same series of ceremonies, and must constantly have proved themselves judicious leaders of their people. The last known investiture of Wicasa Yatapikas took place in about 1850. When Iron Shell was so honored, it was the culmination of a well-lived life. As the son of Shot in the Heel, headman among the Miniconjous, he was the leader of the No Mother Band. He had been a brave warrior and captured many horses. He was well-to-do. He had performed the necessary ceremonies for his children and had also provided many gifts to friends and relatives. He was careful to bring meat to the old men who gathered at the Red Council Lodge. The elders recognized his qualities and selected him to give the White Buffalo Ceremony. Then, at a Sun Dance, Iron Shell was ordered to report to the council shade where he was to be installed. The Akicitas had placed two great tipis facing each other in the center of the camp circle. This was done in such a way that one faced east, the other west, and between them was suspended a great dew cloth to form a covered corridor.

The Akicitas then pulled the picket pins from the tipis and rolled up the sides in order that the people might witness the inauguration. Near the center of the tipi to the east was placed a red painted robe.

When the installation was to begin, the Wicasas took their places of honor around the perimeter of the two lodges. Those who were less experienced chose to sit in the western tipi while the men who knew their status to be unexcelled chose the eastern lodge. Nearly two hundred Wicasas filled the tipis as the ceremony began.

Now the Naca Ominicias chose ten men from among themselves to sit in the center of the eastern tipi. It was these ten who were to appoint four individuals to serve as Wicasa Yatapikas or Supreme Owners. When the ten Naca Ominicias had made their decision, they called upon two escorts from among the assembled headmen to bring the candidates before them.

The escorts then proceeded to the western tipi, and standing before Iron Shell, who was seated along the edge, ordered him to rise. Taking him by the arms, they then led him to the eastern tipi and set him on the red robe before the ten Naca Ominicias. The escorts next proceeded to the western tipi and returned first with Great War Leader, then with Eagle Feather Back, and finally with Little Thunder.

When the four men had thus been seated before the ten Nacas, two of the Nacas lectured them in turn, telling them of their responsibilities and their honor. The teachings of the White Buffalo Maiden were reiterated, and the duties attendant to their office were spelled out.

When the four men had been so instructed, each was presented with a pipe and bag, symbol of their office, and each was invested with a hair-fringed shirt and hair-fringed leggings as badges of their exalted position. Upon the inauguration of the four Supreme

Owners, a great feast was held and there was much celebration in the encampments, for here was proof of the solidarity of the Sioux Nation.

Owing to the enormous expanse of territory which the Sioux Nation controlled and the increasing size of their population, involving possibly 15,000 people by 1850, the several divisions were no longer able to meet as one body. The installation of the four Supreme Owners about 1850 may represent the last national gathering the Sioux ever held.

The Sioux were a systematic people. They were organizers and classifiers. As the universe was intricately patterned into hierarchies and divisions, so was the nation. Theirs was a form of government, a political concept which incorporated their flair for logic with the pragmatics of successful group-living in a difficult and dangerous world.

The political organization of the Sioux exemplified the necessity for developing methods of delegation of self to a common effort. Within the *tiyospe*, individual participation and co-operation was rewarded with an effective means for sustenance and protection. Relegation of self to a pattern of leadership which had met requirements of noble birth and special achievement was a recognition of the limitations of the individual. Rigid policing on the part of the Akicitas enforced the principle of individual adaptation to the welfare of the group. Civil and criminal codes were established with appropriate penalties for infraction—the former punished by the Akicitas, the latter by the family of the offended.

Leadership itself imposed serious responsibility through the imposition of obligatory ceremonial accomplishments designed to benefit others. Yet rewards were real and offered for many men opportunities for ego-expression and ego-acclaim. Symbols of trust and authority—the pipe and pipe bag, the hair-fringed shirt —were accorded headmen to differentiate them from the common man, thereby reaffirming the prestige of responsibility in the minds of the populace.

Responsible leadership demanded, however, ability to provide for the people the daily requirements of life as well as protection against dangers. This was fundamental, and leaders who failed to devote their energies toward the common weal were subject to abandonment. For those whose personal lives flaunted the moral codes, discipline from higher authority was possible. Leadership involved a trust and, except for the despots, few leaders dared to shirk it.

The great number of independent bands among the Sioux, while attributable to a hunting economy requiring small, dispersed groupings of men, was also due in part to the reluctance of the people to subject themselves to ineffectual or dominating leadership. It would appear that families and groups of families were constantly separating from parent groups to establish independent camps. The hunting economy undoubtedly fostered a sense of independence and made separation relatively easy, for no one was tied to a permanent village or a localized source of food. Unlike a farming people, the Sioux were free. This freedom, which made possible an individualism that could be daring to the point of recalcitrance, imposed upon the leadership uncertainties for which there was no defense. It may well account for the Sioux's ideal pattern of talking over matters with members who had erred rather than ordering punishment for them, and of obtaining unanimous decision in council matters rather than mere majority action. Imposing the will of a dominant leader or a majority group might succeed only in so offending the individual that he and his adherents would secede.

This impetuous sense of freedom implied an inner security on the part of secessionists. The ready acceptance of change, the ease with which groups splintered from their parent bands, was in reality a key to Sioux survival and dominance. For these people, *status quo* meant less than security, and security meant less than opportunity.

CHAPTER 2

Morals, Modes, and Manners

BRAVERY, FORTITUDE, GENEROSITY, AND WISDOM—these were the virtues which all men were expected to seek. While it was understood that no man could achieve excellence in all of these qualities, it was believed that every man should endeavor to attain something of each. For most, the ideal of bravery, which was the simplest and fairly obvious virtue, was easier to reach; wisdom, most amorphous and complex, was most difficult to acquire. Yet each moral quality constituted a remarkable challenge; each was a goal worthy of accomplishment. Nor were they separate, but rather interdependent. In order to exhibit generosity, for example, bravery and fortitude—conceivably even wisdom—were contributing factors.

"It is better to die on the battlefield than to live to be old" was a maxim of Sioux existence. Of the four great virtues, bravery was foremost for both men and women. To be considered full of courage, to have a strong heart, was an honor of extreme importance and worth great effort. Acclaim was accorded only to those who had proven themselves. These were the daring men who deliberately risked their lives in war, who took chances in battle which could only be called dangerous, who defended themselves against obvious odds. Just as a man might show deliberate courage in fighting the grizzly bear, the most ferocious and relentless of all animals, so might a woman display bravery in killing an enemy, in warding off an attacker, or in protecting her family against any harm. Bravery among women was equally as meritorious and deserving of recognition as it was among men.

Bravery was inculcated on the mind from earliest childhood. It appeared in the stories which old people told, in the rules for

32

behavior which parents preached, and in the games which children played. Bravery was not something heard about but never seen; bravery was a way of being, of acting, of doing. And small boys were guided and encouraged to behave fearlessly. The toddler who struck the prowling dog was cheered by older brothers and sisters, who urged the youngster to beat still harder. This encouragement was believed to aid the child in gaining a conviction of his own courage.

If learning how to practice bravery in childhood involved certain rigors, the development of the concept of unflinching bravery was a practical preparation for Sioux adulthood, when the fine line between life and death was an ominous actuality. To be recognized as brave, an adult must exhibit fearlessness and the battlefield offered outstanding opportunities. Courting death became as important a part of warfare as victory, so much so that acts of valor were classified in a recognized system of war honors. Men who "struck" the enemy were said to have "counted coup," and whether or not the enemy was killed or wounded, the record was not jeopardized. The fact that a man was courageous enough to "touch" an opponent and risk death rather than shoot him from a safer distance showed the caliber of courage which the Sioux pattern prescribed. An individual's position depended in part upon the number of coups he had counted, and those who accumulated a large number were conceded to be men of great renown. Since honest bragging was an accepted characteristic of the Sioux people, each man could expect his rightful acclaim. He was expected to publicize his coups, but it was understood that he would not exaggerate. Coups were either witnessed or publicly sworn to, and those which were witnessed became generally known almost immediately, for they were exciting news. Opportunities for recounting one's exploits were frequent, and it would have been inconceivable for anyone not to announce his success. Humility for the Sioux was an indication of stupidity, evidence of a deficiency of personal conviction. To be able to boast was a sign of success.

In spite of this cultural emphasis on the importance of valor, the Sioux were not necessarily born brave. It was to be expected that for many normal people the demands of convention were exceedingly onerous. Consequently, they developed unusual techniques of self-encouragement, one of which was imitating the growls of the grizzly in times of danger. Battle cries were another example of building morale. Although they were calculated to intimidate the enemy, they were equally effective in reinforcing one's own courage.

Associated with the virtue of bravery was the concept of fortitude. Fortitude implied two things: the endurance of physical discomfort and pain, and the ability to show reserve during periods of emotional stress. Although the quality might be described as stoical, stoicism is not an entirely correct definition for this virtue as experienced in Sioux life. While the term applies to much of the stylized behavior, it is completely contradicted by other accepted modes of expression, when at certain times the tribesmen indulged in emotional release of almost explosive quality. For example, it was expected that an individual taking a sweat bath in a purifying lodge would demonstrate fortitude by competing with the other bathers to see how long he could endure the intense heat. Then, regardless of weather and temperature, it was expected that the bath would be followed by a plunge into the river, even if it meant breaking the ice. It was, on the other hand, perfectly proper for women to wail and moan in wild abandon upon the departure of a war party.

The importance of the quality of fortitude was demonstrated again and again in the social conventions of the Sioux. Men on war missions or hunting expeditions were noted for their ability to suffer wounds unflinchingly, to experience long periods of hunger and exposure. Fortitude dictated the voluntary acceptance of physical pain during burial ceremonies, when the mourners were required to subject themselves to self-inflicted slashings on arms or legs, or to endure the agony of tiny skewers inserted beneath their skin, or to cut off the first joint of their little finger—all in order to show respect for the dead. Fortitude was also expected in the rituals of the Sun Dance. Fasting, stolidly accepting the pain of the skewers thrust through the chest muscles, and dancing for hours upon hours while thus suspended from a thong attached to the Sun Dance pole were prerequisites of manlike behavior.

Vision-seeking also demanded endurance for fasting and praying. In this pursuit, the supplicant, far from the village on a lonely butte or isolated promontory, would experience severe privation in the hope of receiving power from the supernaturals.

These dramatic expressions of fortitude had their counterparts in day-to-day behavior. Here fortitude might well be equated with reserve, might be described as the quality of dignity. Thus the Sioux exhibited a strange forbearing approach in their personal relations. In fact, their enthusiasm appeared so low-keyed as to be close to a personal affront. For example, when old friends met after a long separation, they lightly placed their arms over one another's shoulders in a stylized clasp. Their greetings would be a noncommittal *"How"* or *"How, Kola,"* but this would be the extent of the salutation. There was no further sign of endearment. They also were careful to keep their eyes downcast, because an eye-to-eye glance, even among the closest friends, was a source of keen embarrassment. Exuberance at such a reunion would be considered giddy and unbecoming, an infraction of decorum.

These prescribed rules of reserved behavior were imparted to the Sioux at a very early age. It was expected that young people should not speak their opinion before more mature minds. Rather, children were to sit quietly and absorb knowledge, for respect for elders marked the well-bred person.

Lovers were never to be seen holding hands, and man and wife never showed any affection in public. There is no intimation here that the Sioux failed to know all that is necessary to know about the intimacies of marital affection, but this knowledge could not be bandied about. Any overt expression of affection would be uncouth.

It was this totally unemotional side of Sioux behavior which made the term "stoical" appear so very fitting. The same reserve is carried over into the councils. There the orator was expected to use logic, to employ drama, to speak with authority, accuracy, and—more important—persuasiveness. It was as if he must convince his audience to the point of astonishment or tears, for the Sioux statesman expressed himself in poetic and brilliant phraseology. However, such reactions to the Sioux orations were an impossibility. The Sioux audience expected impassioned speeches but accepted them with complete equanimity. Cheers, hoorays, huzzas, and even applause were unheard of in Sioux gatherings. Such exuberance would be both foolish and gauche. Agreement was accorded the speaker by the stolid assents of *"How"* and reserved nods of approval. Disapproval could be expressed by whispered mutterings or by the rebuttal of another speaker.

In group activities at which both men and women were present in the tipi, the women sat at the left, the men at the right. Properly, women seldom looked directly at the men, but rather, bowing their heads, talked in whispers to their neighbors. Likewise, the men rarely looked at the women and, if the group were being addressed, no one stared at the speaker. Even were he to talk about someone in the audience, that person too sat with bowed head and lowered eyes, like a condemned defendant or a bashful hero. To react by word or deed would have been considered unmanly or unwomanly. To express modesty and reserve was the essence of fortitude.

Another precept of the Sioux was stated frequently by the tribesmen: "A man must help others as much as possible, no matter who, by giving him horses, food or clothing." Generosity was a virtue upon which Sioux society insisted. To accumulate property for its own sake was disgraceful, while to be unable to acquire wealth was merely pitiable. The ownership of things was important only as a means to giving, and blessed was the man who had much to give. The Sioux pattern further required not only that a proffered gift might not be refused but that a return gift, even though a token, should sometime be exchanged.

People made a point of gift-giving, almost upon the least provocation. Young people brought food to their elders' tipis; hunters divided their kill with the aged and infirm; women made gifts for the orphaned and the widowed; sisters honored their brothers with presents of moccasins, or their nieces and nephews with elaborate cradles.

Feasts and parties were given by families to celebrate such important occasions as a son's joining an Akicita society or his return from a successful war party. To these everyone was invited and gifts were exchanged.

Generosity, as one of the four virtues, may have given the individual an understanding of the meaning of wealth. At death, a man's personal property was buried with him, and his best horse, the recognized medium of exchange, was killed. There were no wills and no formal bequests. Distribution of material things took place during one's lifetime. For the group, this sanctioned giving contained a subtly positive end. In describing the responsibility for practicing this virtue, one informant said: "A man must take pity on orphans, the crippled and the old. If you have more than one of anything, you should give it away to help these persons." Beneficence ensured existence for the least able as well as the less fortunate. The result was that, rather than being outright burdens to society, the indigent Sioux actually became necessary vehicles whereby the successful men gained social status. Here was socialism with a vengeance. It meant that, ideally and in reality, no member was to go without. The more one was able to give, the greater his prestige. At the same time, the distribution of wealth for the benefit of all fostered relatively equal economic standards for all members of the tribe. Thus, the Sioux evolved a system which ensured the well-being of all the people by the voluntary and highly rewarding dispersal of property.

Not only was spontaneous and informal gift-giving carried out continually, but innumerable ceremonial occasions were provided which made possible the even more dramatic "giveaway." Here the Sioux crystallized the concept of generosity by institutionalizing large-scale giving.

When girls reached puberty, parents endeavored to display their devotion by making their daughters one of the Buffalo Maidens; a family who had lost a beloved child aspired to "Own a Ghost"; or when parents wished to honor a child, they might give him a new name or perform the Hunka ceremony. An integral part of each of these occasions was the formalized and obligatory giveaway. Families saved up in order to make a good showing, for the more gifts that were given, the deeper was the respect displayed for the person honored. Actually, people vied with one another over who could give the most and the finest presents.

The epitome of the giveaway complex was in "Ghost-owning." For a year the bereaved parents faithfully preserved a lock of their dead child's hair to show their respect. In this interim they underwent rigidly prescribed attendance rites, and also devoted their time, often with the help of relatives, to the accumulation of great stores of clothing, utensils, horses, and even food. At the expiration of the time, amid the final ceremony and feastings, the parents gave to the people assembled everything they had collected throughout the year. Here was "giving till it hurt"; for when everything was distributed the couple would dismantle their tipi and offer it to someone, an act which was followed by the final gesture of removing their clothes and giving them away. Alone, in their nakedness, with neither possession nor dwelling nor food, a man and wife thus displayed before all the Sioux's highest ideal of generosity combined with the utmost in tribute for one beloved. Of course, it was understood that such sacrifice would not go unheeded, or that such generosity would constitute ultimate ruin. Within a short time after the end of the ceremony, either friends or relatives would invite the couple for a meal; and later they would band together to provide clothing, a tipi, and other essentials.

Of the four virtues, wisdom was most intangible and most elusive, for the ingredients of this characteristic were, as for all mankind, ethereal. One can display bravery; one can practice fortitude; with intelligent application and continuous endeavor, one can achieve wealth and exhibit approved generosity. But the endowment of wisdom was above and beyond these attributes. To be sure, it was recognized that a person who achieved renown in one or more of the virtues might well possess the elements of wisdom. Yet, for the Sioux, wisdom implied more than simply intellectual excellence. Wisdom was also dependent upon power—insight received from the supernatural. Wisdom involved the ability to advise others, to arbitrate disputes, to instill confidence as a leader of a war party or as mentor for young men, and finally the exploration of the realms of shamanism. Wisdom meant, in part, getting on well with people and, as a leader, inspiring others. The term "Wicasa" or "Man" was synonymous with wisdom and leadership. Moreover, it signified one who had performed "the four ceremonies": the Hunka, Buffalo-singing, Ghost-owning, and the White Buffalo. Because these men had also the ability to reconcile quarrels, the people, including the leaders, sought them out for advice. Wicasas were men who "seemed to have the power of helping and their word was as if from the Gods." Few were the men who were conceded to merit the title of Wicasa. And in consequence, small was the number of persons who possessed wisdom.

The virtues of Sioux society contained an important, illuminating, and pragmatic dichotomy when applied to women. The ideal female virtues were also four in number and included, as for men, bravery and generosity. But the significant difference in the expected behavior for females was expressed in the last two feminine virtues: truthfulness and childbearing.

Bravery for women was closely equated with fortitude for men. Generosity was expressed in terms of bountifully producing clothing, skillfully preparing foods, and then sharing these products with others. Truthfulness, however, was more a matter of ethics, wherein the individual was expected to acquire this attribute and put it to practice. Devices were even provided for proving veracity. "Biting the knife" was the most common detector; in this test, a suspect could prove his honesty by literally biting a blade before his doubters. Were he a liar, misfortune surely would eventually befall him and the truth would out. "Biting the snake," where a small piece of wood symbolized the snake, was an equally effective test. Men and women did not take such oaths lightly. The disastrous consequences were too awesome and the shame too great. And yet, while truthfulness was expected of both sexes, it is indicative of their fear of the consequences of dishonesty that the Sioux should propose this attribute particularly for women.

The reason for this insistence upon truthfulness among women may have its origin in the injunction against gossip. In a community where most neighbors were relatives, where households lived in extremely close contact, and where village unity was essential to maintaining the economy as well as the mutual defense, the effects of internal dissension and mistrust could well be disastrous. And yet, by the very nature of this social pattern, gossip could germinate and flourish abundantly. For the Sioux were entirely human, and for them there was no topic of conversation more intriguing than that concerned with people.

Gossip, or more properly, "talking about people," had positive consequences. In a group where everyone knew everyone else, the valuable and strong influence of "talk" was an effective control. Everyone talked—young and old, men and women told tales endlessly. This helped maintain a certain *esprit de corps*, reminded people of the right and proper way of life, and by reiterating the mistakes of others the Sioux reinforced the codes of behavior. Equally important, it helped hold in check those who would digress. Albeit, gossip was frowned upon, and one of the highest commendations for a woman was that "she did not tell things."

Not only was there literally no privacy, but in the case of women, no chance of escape. While men could find change from the intensity of human relations in going to war or undertaking solitary hunting trips, women had little opportunity to evade the constant companionship of children, relatives, and neighborly females. The insistence of this group pressure was ever present, only to become intensified when band joined band or the tribe met for its annual camp circle. Living under such constantly rigid surveillance undoubtedly created certain anxieties.

Gossip might well have developed constraint, but it might equally have produced insecurity with respect to social situations and the individual's position with his fellow man. The stoical behavior of the Sioux surely found some of its origin as a result of the gossip pattern.

Certainly nearly everyone was aware of the outward effectiveness which talking produced. It must also have been apparent that rampant, uncontrolled talk resulted in dangerous situations. And it was this awareness which must have created the concept of truth as a virtue. That it should be applied particularly to women is most understandable, in that women were most exposed to gossiping by their constant proximity to people and their confinement to the village.

Bearing children was an attribute which pragmatically expressed the Sioux acceptance of life. There was no confusion about the role of women, for being a mother and rearing a family was the ultimate achievement. As a matter of fact, there seems to have been no other acceptable pattern for feminine existence. Women might become dreamers to practice certain curings and rites associated with childbearing and tipi-building, but these in no way appear to have precluded the role of motherhood. The Sioux so fully comprehended, so thoroughly accepted this natural state that they placed it among the highest virtues. Young women, upon being instructed about the responsibilities of marriage, might have been guided as was Rattling Blanket Woman: "After I was married, my mother told me I wasn't going to go through life without having children; and she told me how to care for them." There was no question of the probability of motherhood; rather, a forthright acceptance of an acknowledged predestined fact.

Formalizing the virtues into groups of four was fitting for people who enjoyed systematizing everything. Yet there were other qualities of feminine personality which were considered essential. Actually, they seem to have been held above the other virtues, and from their human quality, they would appear to have had greater meaning to the people. Industry was one of these qualities; fidelity, the other.

When a girl experienced her first menses, she notified her mother, who took her to a separate wigwam or small tipi. Isolated there for four days, the mother would ceremoniously teach her the art of quill embroidery and moccasin-making. As one old person expressed it, "Even though she has learned quilling before, the girl must quill continuously for four days. If she does this she will be good with the awl; if she does not, she will never be industrious."

Girls who could quill and bead, who knew how to prepare hides, and who were good cooks were recognized as potentially good wives. Parents were proud of a daughter who willingly helped with household chores, and conscientiously minded the smaller children. Here was a young person practicing what the adult world extolled. Such a girl would attract fine young men of the best families, who would bring many gifts and horses as her bride-price; she would bestow honor on her family.

In the same way that men kept war records, so did women keep count of their accomplishments. Ambition to excel was real among females. Accomplishments were recorded by means of dots incised along the handles of the polished elkhorn scraping tools. The dots on one side were black, on the other red. Each black dot represented a tanned robe; each red dot represented ten hides or one tipi. When a woman had completed one hundred robes or ten tipis, she was privileged to place an incised circle at the base of the handle of her scraper.

Contests were occasionally held at which women exhibited their work—moccasins, dresses, storage bags, and the like. Cradles were recognized as the tour de force in female craftsmanship and invariably brought to the maker acclaim and even wealth, since a cradle was equal in value to one horse.

During the Sun Dance camp, or at a time when someone had successfully terminated the year-long Ghost-owning rite, the wife of a man who had undergone this rite might decide to have a quilling contest. Thus it was for Rattling Blanket Woman when the herald announced throughout the village that she was having a quilling party and called all who had quillwork to assemble at the center of the camp.

Here the hostess, Rattling Blanket, placed a decorated cradle—

the epitome of a woman's art—at a spot to represent the door of a lodge. Seated at the opposite side of the imaginary tipi behind an array of handiwork, she awaited her guests. Each came and took her place around the edge of the "lodge," placing their goods before them.

Then Rattling Blanket Woman went from guest to guest and after asking what they had made, gave each a stick for every piece of work, whether or not they had brought it. For work done prior to puberty, the sticks were placed to the left of the maker; for that done after puberty, the sticks were placed to the right. When everyone had received the sticks to which they were entitled, the hostess took by the hand the woman who had the fourth most sticks and led her to a place of honor. She then escorted the woman who had the third most and seated her in front of the first woman chosen, and so on until the winner was placed before all as became her position.

When the women agreed that the one chosen was rightfully winner, others brought food, serving first the four winners in the order of their industry, then passing food to the others. To record the event, marks were placed on the dew cloth or tipi lining of the Red Council Lodge. Small marks were made to represent the work done prior to puberty, larger marks for later work, and over them was the maker's name. Thus Rattling Blanket Woman's ten small marks and four large ones were designated by the drawing of a rattle superimposed upon a blanket with a line extending from it to the marks. This was her "quilling count," and just as a man displayed his war honors in the Red Council Lodge, so a woman displayed her abilities. Since women were in reality the producers of consumption goods, it was fitting that emphasis should be placed upon industry. And to the industrious came not only tangible wealth but prestige.

Being faithful to one's husband was particularly commendable. And fidelity was no mean accomplishment in a society in which, on the one hand, polygamy was an accepted form of marriage and, on the other hand, divorce was a common and comparatively simple procedure.

43

Blue Whirlwind described the implications of fidelity when she said:

A woman who had been married only once and been faithful was considered better than any other. Such a family generally lived to be very old. If the husband should die, the widow would often give a feast, inviting other honorable women to come.

After the feast, each one told the others how faithful she had been, and each bit the knife, for this was a vow. Often other women might attend, to contest the statements, but they too had to bite the knife. If they accused falsely, a curse would befall them. Men never came to these feasts, only women of middle age. In this way, everyone knew who were the most honorable women in camp.

When a woman gave this feast, she could not marry again lest a curse befall her and her family. She had bitten the knife, vowing she would be faithful to her husband.

Should a woman learn from her friends that she was being accused of adultery by gossips, she similarly defended her reputation by preparing a feast. For a herald she chose an old woman who all her life had been faithful to one husband, and she invited all women of comparable virtue to feast at the center of camp.

After the women had gathered, the old woman called upon the men of the village to come and point out from among the gathering any woman with whom they had had sexual relations. Should a man see among them a woman with whom he had been familiar, he would denounce her. In accepting the challenge to accuse, he must swear to it by biting the knife or arrow. A woman so accused of adultery was pelted with filth and buffalo dung and driven from camp.

If the hostess, however, was not so dishonored, she might challenge the gossip to produce the man or bite the knife in his stead. If the gossip failed to do either of these things, it was her reputation that was ruined. The trial was then followed by feasting of the virtuous ones; the spectators were asked to withdraw.

Unmarried women and young men held a contest of virtue with much the same purpose in view. An arrow and a knife were placed beside a small hole in the center of camp, and spectators gathered. The virgins would then walk to the hole, place their hand in it, and bite the knife, followed by the men, who would place their hand in the hole and bite the arrow. Should a man in the crowd see a girl falsely avowing her virginity, he might go to her and throw dirt in her face or loudly state that the feast was being held for virgins, not women.[1]

In a society which accepted polygamy as a man's prerogative, in which by the mere beat of a drum a man might announce the dissolution of his marriage, in a group where men's advances were so insistent that unmarried girls were protected by constant chaperonage even to the extent of wearing chastity belts, the ideal of monogamous virtue at first appears to be out of context. And yet, monogamy was not inconsistent with the Sioux way, possibly if for no other reason than because it was really less bothersome. While the double standard undoubtedly had its male advocates, it certainly must have created difficult and embarrassing situations for the girl and her family. Divorce too meant a certain upheaval, even outside the family circle. It frequently involved emotional tensions through jealousy, retribution, and unrequited love, and not a few divorces ended in murder.

Polygamy, likewise, had its difficulties, and the practice of marrying sisters "because they got on better" suggests that a man with two or more wives was a candidate for marital friction. While the man with two wives might expect them to gather more fruits and wild vegetables, make more moccasins, and even relieve one another of some of the arduousness of daily living, and thereby indirectly aid him in having much to offer at times of feasting and giveaways—at the same time such a husband must provide in double quantity. Because of these considerations, it may have been that those individuals who adhered to a monogamous state of matrimony were also those who made less trouble for themselves and others. If this were so, the Sioux were not unwise in according to women who had remained faithful to one man the title of "most honorable."

That the goals for men and women were characterized by the

[1] Wissler, "Societies and Ceremonial Associations," *loc. cit.*, 77.

several virtues is healthy evidence that the Sioux, though very human, were hardly naïve. For where men imagine ideals, create codes, or advocate manners of behavior, they often seem to do so to channel or redirect drives which, though natural, are thought to be deleterious to the group's welfare. That the goals were accompanied by meaningful rewards is a strong proof that the virtues were well conceived and fit reality for a number of influential people. And it was this compatibility which helped to make the nation so effective and so powerful.

Although the consensus was surely one of upholding the virtues, for digressors there were external sanctions which ensured adherence to custom. The group conscience, though certainly instilled in and part of the minds and feelings of many of the people, was still an ideal. Even among those who comprehended the code and conscientiously endeavored to observe it, there were transgressors. For them, as well as for those who in not believing might disregard or even rebel, corrective techniques were effectively employed. These techniques could not of themselves make the coward brave or the liar truthful, but certain of them had strong influence in making delinquents less menacing.

Most dramatic was the role of the Akicitas in bringing adherence to the rules. Direct and immediate punishment by the police was administered for the infraction of the laws of communal hunting or for evading the line of march when moving camp. These were considered audacious actions, endangering the very lives of everyone. The authority of the Akicitas must certainly have kept in line many who might otherwise have broken the regulations.

The cultural ideals as symbolized in the virtues were philosophical concepts over and above the common codes of behavior. The codes were relative to all facets of life. Some were concerned with mere aspects of etiquette, while others involved the weighty forces of law and jurisprudence. Thus, not only was there the right way of doing things, but conversely there was the wrong and even illegal way.

Etiquette demanded that young people should defer to elders

when speaking, that one should thump on the side of the tipi to announce his arrival rather than burst through the door, that guests should be offered the pipe in proper ceremonial fashion. Etiquette also required that men should sit cross-legged and women should sit with their legs to the side, that when gifts were offered they might not be refused, that one entered a tipi on the right and went out on the left. Modes and manners were legion; there were rules for nearly all occasions. Some of these manners were practiced in habit and carried out by rote. Some were prescribed by common decency; others, by ceremonial convention. All played a part in helping people function together more smoothly.

Within this system of social behavior there were in most cases no marked penalties for the ill-mannered or uncouth. Gossip and ridicule sufficed as punishment. However, certain laws were designed to provide a sense of security in many vital areas of societal existence. They were concerned with the protection of property, marital fidelity, communal hunting rights, and the guarantee of life itself. If these laws were broken, the penalty was severe opprobrium and occasionally outright ostracism.

Thievery was recognized as a heinous offense, and apparently personal property was exposed to view almost continuously since it was inviolate. Property included not only food and clothing but tools and paraphernalia, dogs and horses. The codes against stealing were so completely inculcated, so much an internalized sanction, that offenses were extremely rare, almost nonexistent. Thieving was something that children might do in naïveté or that the incorrigible misfit might attempt in utter stupidity. But no one in his right mind, no one capable of thinking, would ever imagine theft, unless it be in absconding with someone else's wife.

Wife-stealing presented a special and recognizably dramatic problem for the Sioux. To steal a woman was somehow correlated with counting a coup, for in the final consideration, women were not only property but also were conceptualized as the enemy. Among the more conspicuous examples of internal social strife were those episodes brought on by one man's desire for another man's woman.

The Sioux were quite aware of the problems which their accepted double standard for the sexes engendered. They countered by offering the premium of high prestige for wifely fidelity and by dangling the reward of "Wicasa" for men of constancy. Apparently these ideological prizes proved insufficient, for the Sioux devised complementary penalties of a most severe quality. The unfaithful wife, victim though she may have been to the overtures of a compulsive male, might well be subjected to everlasting shame by having her nose cut off. It was her husband's prerogative to disfigure her for life, thereby not only stamping her as immoral but also certainly reducing her chances of attracting another man. As if to add to her chagrin, the husband might very well divorce her too.

On the other hand, men who transgressed the marital code by taking another's wife were most surely liable to expulsion from membership in their Akicita society, together with censure from the elders and headmen. If they were officers in the tribe, they could expect immediate impeachment. These penalties were the price for wife-stealing which any man would normally count on paying. A man must also calculate on a much more definitive consequence. If the woman he stole was the wife of a powerful man or a member of an important family, he must reckon with retaliation from the woman's husband and her brothers. Retribution in the form of death was so frequent that wife-stealing and murder might almost be considered as concomitant in Sioux society.

Yet in spite of the rewards for fidelity and the penalties for infidelity, adultery remained a serious problem to the Sioux. The devices which attempted to mitigate the problem were in the nature of symptom-curing and did not alleviate the source. That the devices were of themselves so dramatic only attests to the seriousness with which wife-stealing was viewed. The convictions of the Sioux on this score were so strong that they believed those who flaunted the moral code deserved penalties to the point of disfigurement and even death.

The taking of another's life was punishable by death, yet pun-

48

ishment was generally the responsibility of the victim's family. For murder was not so much a crime against society as it was a trespass against an individual's person. Retaliation was to be expected, yet it was not inevitable. Some men escaped the consequences almost by sheer personal dominance and austerity. In such a case no one dared seek vengeance.

Such was Bull Bear, a headman among the Oglalas of whom Francis Parkman wrote in the 1840's. Bull Bear's unexcelled war record and his outstanding bravery gave him such overbearing dominance that not only were his decisions in council unquestioned, but he blatantly stole the wives of several men with complete immunity.[2]

Yet even Bull Bear, with all his power, fell victim to the enemies he so readily made. In a quarrel with a headman named Smoke, Bull Bear went into the headman's tipi and challenged him to fight. Smoke, however, declined by remaining motionless and saying nothing. Bull Bear in rage taunted him, calling Smoke a woman, and leaving the lodge, stabbed to death Smoke's favorite horse.

Smoke patiently plotted for many months, and later when the two camps were by chance again together, a quarrel arose between some of the younger men of Smoke's followers and Bull Bear's warriors. Bull Bear, hearing the commotion, ran from his tipi to settle the matter, but almost instantly was shot down by many arrows. Smoke had had his vengeance, and it was said that Red Cloud, among others, had joined in the ruse and possibly was the killer.

Sometimes murders might be vindicated in a matter of days. Escape from the village became the only way to evade the consequences. In some instances, a victim's family might wait years for atonement, only to catch the murderer off guard and thereby settle the feud. Murderers who did survive the wrath of their victim's kinsmen might well be subject to ostracism or have to forfeit their rights and privileges in holding office in societies or in the government. Furthermore, such criminals could look

[2] Hyde, *Red Cloud's Folk*; Francis Parkman, *The Oregon Trail*.

forward to an eternity spent in a kind of hell reserved especially for them and hermaphrodites, outside the camp circle of the ancestors.

As one Sioux patriarch explained it:

When a man kills another, he may stay around the camp, as did Red Around the Face. Some men may run to another camp where they have relatives. Here the family may see such a murderer lurking around the village and ask him why he doesn't join them. But whether a man boldly remains at his own camp or goes to another, his relatives urge him to take a purifying bath and meet with a Wicasa.

By taking a sweat bath, the murderer could hope to purge himself of his crime. If he failed to do so and should eat with his family, he and they too would be liable to serious sickness and even death. A man who failed to so cleanse himself saw the face of his victim not only each time he drank water from the drinking bowl, but dreamt of him each night. No matter how many baths some men took, the murdered man's face would not disappear. Such men could neither drink nor sleep, and often became so emaciated that they died. Should his family eat from his utensils, they too might die, so it was a day of relief when the apparitions no longer appeared.

While the murderer was endeavoring to cleanse himself by means of sweat baths, the family of the criminal took steps to make atonement. It was most common that it fell upon the father to take to the meeting lodge several horses. These he gave in charge of the Headman or some Wicasa whom he held in high esteem. Frequently, the Nacas gathered at the meeting lodge would themselves announce that they too would donate horses.

The Wicasa who had been selected to officiate, then went to the murdered man's father and telling him that everyone was desirous to atone for the murder, escorted him to the meeting lodge.

Here the Wicasa, standing before the two parents, and surrounded by the elders of the camp, presented to the victim's father a ceremonial pipe lit with a buffalo chip. "Take this pipe, and in smoking it, have no ill feeling toward another." After the parent of the murdered man had smoked, he returned the pipe to the Wicasa, who with the same admonition, offered the pipe to the father of the murderer. When both had thus smoked, the Wicasa then called upon the Akicita to collect the horses which the criminal's family and the Nacas had donated. These were brought to the tipi. The Wicasa next placed the murdered man's father on one of the horses, and leading him and the remaining horses back to his home, told the mourning relatives that the Kici yuska pi, The Untying Each Other Ceremony, had been successful. For when two men so smoked the pipe, the revenge was overcome, grief was forgotten, and "they became free."

For lesser civil offenses, the penalties of ostracism and tipi destruction were prescribed, and these judgments, carried out by the group as a whole, were the responsibility of governmental authority. Thus, vengeance and atonement were the family's prerogative; maintaining peace and order was the group's responsibility.

There is possibly no other area of man's activities in which the pattern of approved self-expression is more clearly delineated than in the goals which he creates and in the sanctions which he permits. The Sioux appear to have been obsessed with ideals and no less involved with manners. There was the right thing to do and the correct way to do it.

The four virtues possess interesting implications about the motivations of these people, for they represent a kind of philosophical *modus operandi*. Here was a set of prescribed personality characteristics worthy of attainment in themselves, yet which contained corollary attributes that could bring nothing but good for the group.

While the virtues for men and women were not precisely the same, they may be condensed for analysis as fortitude, generosity, wisdom, and begetting children. In a balance of each quality and its antithesis in a society, the equilibrium is maintained by the cultural ideals of that society.

The antithesis of fortitude is fear—a natural conflict between a drive for self-gratification, recognition, and long-term security against an equally strong urge for self-preservation, pain-avoidance, and short-term security. It is true that gratification and recognition may be accomplished by inverse psychological mechanisms so that exhibition of fear may constitute various types of perverse personality adjustment, including catatonic schizophrenia; conversely, self-preservation and pain-avoidance may become psychologically unrewarding and produce an equally perverse adjustment, including masochism. Actually, the Sioux way led its people to this latter alternative under the guise of bravery. Yet in this pattern, fortitude was the touchstone of individual success, and the psychological norm of personal adjustment was the man of courage thriving on competition. It was this ideal, emulated by many men, that made the Sioux so long invincible.

Generosity, the counterpart of selfishness, imposed a goal which thwarted acquisitiveness. To fulfill the obligatory requirements of giving demanded a continual sacrifice of property—that tangible extension of self. The Sioux pattern made this severance easier by offering a reward in the form of prestige. And it withheld recognition from those who had nothing to give or who owned possessions and failed to share them. For those individuals to whom giving was enjoyable, the Sioux way must have been gratifying. For the miser, there could have been few satisfactions, for there was no honor in being merely rich.

Wisdom, and the related female attribute of truthfulness, might be counterbalanced by ignorance, stupidity, and dishonesty. Wisdom was a virtue which the nation held in highest regard, for the emoluments were self-evident. Wisdom implied more than intelligence, for it was a characteristic which might be attained, in part, by an individual's conscientious endeavor to maintain rapport with his fellow man, his supernatural mentors, and the universe. This was a most difficult achievement, and the reward for its accomplishment was the highest—the exalted position of Wicasa. Wisdom, as conceived by the Sioux, was a way of life. Its attainment meant the fullest denial of self in giving one's personal energies to the well-being of others. This culturally patterned opportunity for socially recognized sacrifice points clearly to the Sioux's ability to instill in the minds of men the psychological value of loosing oneself in an absorbing activity on the one hand, and of turning that activity to the benefit of fellow men through leadership on the other.

Childbearing as an attribute for women was a forthright approach to a nation's faith in its destiny. Here was a wholesome acceptance of a basic drive to which the Sioux accorded honor. Among a people for whom infant mortality was alarmingly real and childbirth itself was fraught with the risk of death, it is not unnatural that such an ideal should be proposed. While the responsibilities of parenthood fell heaviest upon the mother and her female relatives, the male role was not without its burdens, particularly with regard to boys. The Sioux way expected of its adults a willingness and an ability not only to provide the essentials of food, clothing, and shelter to children but to see to their education. This latter responsibility was no mean one, and included training in the techniques of hunting and warfare as well as teaching the *mores* of Sioux life.

That the Sioux should set forth virtues toward which the people should strive—fortitude, generosity, wisdom, and childbearing —gives a clue concerning what they considered essential to national well-being. These were their golden rules, and by them men lived and prospered. However, the virtues also show what the Sioux believed most deleterious—the opposing qualities of fear, selfishness, ignorance, and barrenness. Here was a set of natural proclivities which could destroy a society. There is reason to believe that Sioux character possessed these negative qualities in fair share; otherwise it would have been unnecessary to expostulate upon their counterparts. It is not improbable that life was so awesome, and the demands of the warlike society so frightening, that the bravery-fear conflict became crystallized and an issue made of it. Bravery and fortitude appear to be the virtues about which the Sioux were obsessed, so much so that they produced a reaction to normal fear which involved both masochism and suicide. Nor is it improbable that generosity as expected by the Sioux way was similarly adverse to normal ego-development, or that the Sioux fetish of giving was an overcompensation for an inherently strong sense of possessiveness. On the same basis, however, it would be ridiculous to assume that the Sioux were so lacking in intellect that they made wisdom a virtue, or so barren that they placed having children upon a pedestal. But in the context of their cultural meaning, there is the suggestion that true wisdom and all it implied—living the Sioux way—was so difficult of realization that many men would normally fail to make the effort. If enough individuals were indisposed or unable to accept the ideal as a real one, the very spirit which made Sioux life operative would have no sustenance. The Sioux way was successful only to the extent that enough men believed in it to make it work.

WAHK-TÄ-GE-LI.

Big Soldier, wearing the hair-fringed shirt of the Wicasas together with a peace medal presented by emissaries of the United
States, stood for this portrait by Carl Bodmer in about 1834.

Courtesy Denver Art Museum

IN THIS SIOUX ENCAMPMENT, from an engraving by Carl Bodmer, *ca.*1834, a scaffold burial at the right and another at center
background are plainly visible. The woman at the right of the
group carries her infant in her robe. The man with the pipe wears
a metal disc hair plate headdress.

Courtesy Denver Art Museum

ALFRED JACOB MILLER'S PORTRAIT of Bull Bear, done in 1837, shows this leader adorned in the hair-fringed shirt of the Wicasas, two coup feathers, and a bear claw necklace. The metal pipe-tomahawk may have been a gift from a white trader.

PART TWO / *The Warrior*

CHAPTER 3

Ethnocentrism

THE SIOUX HAD SUCH FAITH in their national destiny that they haughtily dominated the heartland of the Northern Plains for nearly a century. They made no concessions, few alliances, and many enemies. They were hated by many and feared by most, and they boasted of this reputation. They were proud of their superiority and were vigilant in defending it. They conquered relentlessly with a conviction of fortune. They were men among men and a nation among nations.

In the mid-eighteenth century the only people to be found living on the endless grasslands along the shores of the Missouri River were Indians. To the north and south, to the east and west, almost as far as could be imagined, Indians lived. The fact that traders and strange white travelers existed on the fringes of this Indian world in such remote settlements as Augustus Chouteau's trading post in St. Louis or at Michilimackinac was of little or no importance to the Sioux camped in the wooded bottom lands along the streams. The focus of their world was centered in themselves and in other tribes of red men.

By 1750 the Sioux society was already on the threshold of an efficient adjustment which was to remain comparatively unchanged for almost a century. A nomadic hunting society, secure in the midst of the buffalo range, they were aggressively independent and economically successful. Their existence depended upon the buffalo and they knew it. From its carcass they got food, from its bones they made tools, from its hide they made clothing and tipis. They hunted the buffalo whenever and wherever they could, and they made unwritten laws to protect their economy. Because the buffalo wandered from grazing land to grazing land, the Sioux adjusted their life to follow the herds. They had small lodges of skins stretched over poles which could be moved on a moment's notice, and they had trained their dogs as beasts of burden to drag their equipment. Very recently they had acquired the horse and were also, by this time, modestly well supplied with firearms. They were discovering a way of life—a way of life which was yet to be crystallized. Nevertheless, in spite of its fluidity, it contained elements of a pattern which was later to become symbolic of one of the most colorful and dynamic societies in North America.

The Sioux had not always enjoyed such power as they possessed in the mid-eighteenth century. On the contrary, in 1650, living about the Mille Lacs region of what is now Minnesota, they were a woodland people, composed of small bands, surrounded by tribes of superior strength.[1] The men tracked deer and small game in the forests; the women, working in canoes up and down the lakes and streams, gathered wild rice. Some of the women may have raised small fields of corn. Occasionally, too, the Sioux hunters must have climaxed their hunting forays by the capture of a buffalo, which at this period ranged as far east as the Appalachians. The value of the bison as an economic resource was immediately apparent. Here was an animal capable of providing not only abundant food but also material for shelter and clothing in a proportion unmatched by other forest creatures. Experience revealed that the herds of bison were more plentiful to the south and west. The lure of this hunting wealth gave impetus for a Sioux migration.

The exodus from the Mille Lacs region was quickened by other compelling circumstances. It was at this time that the Crees, traditional enemies of the Sioux, were being supplied with firearms

---

[1] Bushnell, "Tribal Investigations," *loc. cit.*; Mekeel, "A Short History," *loc. cit.*; Robinson, "History of the Dakotas," *loc. cit.* The westward migration of the Sioux is subject to much speculation and some historic evidence. However, it is believed that the northwestward movement of the Iroquois around the time of the arrival of Columbus split the Siouan-speaking peoples dwelling in the Ohio Valley. The Dakotas, Nakotas, and Lakotas represent that part of the separation which moved northwest. By the end of the first half of the seventeenth century these people were to be found in the Mississippi Valley west of the Mille Lacs.

by the French. The Assiniboines, formerly a part of the Yank-tonai Sioux, had also joined forces with the Crees to challenge their Sioux cousins, the Saones. One story goes that the dispute between the Assiniboines and the Yanktonais arose between two women who quarreled over the division of a buffalo, but others say that the secession occurred as a result of the seduction of a woman. In any case, the Assiniboines were thenceforth known to the Sioux as Rebels.

The threat of these enemy forces possessed of firearms, against the Sioux who had few if any guns, coupled with the lure of plentiful bison, provided a forceful incentive for migration. However, the coveted territory to the south and west was at this time in no sense a no man's land. On the contrary, the Omahas and Iowas were well established in the western area and claimed a vast territory as their hunting ground. It must have been quite evident to the Sioux elders that a certain amount of conquest would be involved. For a group of people deliberately to enter another nation's domain presupposes at least a degree of internal assurance, if not outright audacity. The Sioux seem to have possessed that assurance as early as the mid-seventeenth century.

Specific reference to the Sioux in 1680 by Father Louis Hennepin, Robert Cavelier de la Salle's Recollect missionary, placed them west of the Mississippi River in the vicinity of the Sauk Rapids and to the west. Pierre Charles Le Sueur, the French fur trader, met the Sioux in 1700 in south central Minnesota on the Blue Earth River, although he described their territory as lying between the upper Mississippi and Missouri rivers. According to this French explorer, the Sioux then had one thousand lodges. They no longer used canoes but rather hunted buffalo on the prairie. They lived in skin tipis, smoked a great deal, practiced polygamy, and were excellent marksmen. By 1722 a French trader named Pachot placed the Sioux eighty leagues west of the Falls of St. Anthony or near the headwaters of the Minnesota River.

Despite these meager records, it is evident that the Sioux, representing what might be termed the advance guard of the other

Siouan speakers, were gradually drifting from the headwaters of the Mississippi to settle around the shores of Big Stone Lake and Lake Traverse in southwestern Minnesota. Pressure from the Santee Dakotas, themselves escaping the onslaughts of the Crees to the northeast, combined with the necessity of parrying the Iowas and Omahas to the south and the Assiniboines to the north, made this Big Stone Lake area a logically safer locality. The Sioux, however, were not entirely victims of circumstance, for it would seem that they were as much enticed by the plentiful game as they were indirectly pushed by the Chippewas.

Thus by 1700, according to Le Sueur, the Sioux had relinquished their former characteristic woodland customs to become bona fide nomadic buffalo hunters. This adjustment they had apparently made in the space of only fifty years. To be sure, the shift from a woodland hunting and gathering economy was far less drastic a change than the transition of the Cheyennes and Crows from agriculture to nomadic hunting. To the Sioux, the new way of life was different in degree, not in kind.

The brothers La Vérendrye met Indians whom they called Gens de la Flèche Collée or Prairie Sioux, on April 9, 1743, some fifty miles north of what is now Pierre, South Dakota. In the twenty-one years since Pachot's statement, the Sioux had moved west to the east bank of the Missouri River, having dispelled the Omahas between the Sioux River and the James.

Within the hundred years following 1650, the Sioux reached the western shores of the Missouri River. They had found refuge from the firearms of the Crees and assured themselves a kind of economic security in the buffalo. If they had ever practiced agriculture, all traces of a farming economy had vanished. Their life in this period was entirely adjusted to following the buffalo. Their small portable tipis could be carried on the travois which the dogs dragged. They made no pottery, which would certainly be broken in moving, but rather cooked their food in buffalo paunches by dropping in hot stones to make the water boil. They stored their belongings in rawhide parfleches and spent their lives living out of leather cases. Cradles for babies were made to be carried, and, even in camp, the infants were as likely as not to be hung in their carriers from handy posts. Everything the Sioux owned was movable, and nearly everything they did was conditioned by nomadism.

In the summer they met with other Sioux bands. They pitched their tipis in a circle, each band in its proper place. There they visited and conferred on matters of importance, celebrated, and held religious worship. Once a year the Sioux gathered in this way to re-establish their bond of kinship and unity.

With the coming of fall, the Sioux dispersed. Small groups scattered themselves here and there over the plains in search of game. Frequently several of these groups, each under a separate headman, moved and camped together, partly as protection against their enemies, partly because of congeniality. Together they might build a buffalo pound at the base of a cliff in the hope that they might entice a great herd into their trap and thereby have an abundance of meat for the winter. Or they might plan a large war party against the Arikaras or Omahas and through their boldness not only gain for themselves honor through touching coups but secure for their nation a certain respect among their neighbors. By 1750 they had waged a long and bitter war with the Iowas and Omahas, and they were eventually successful in driving their enemies from a coveted territory, and in reducing them to a state where they no longer proved a menace.

In 1775–76 the Sioux winter count claimed discovery of the Black Hills, and by 1805 it showed that the Sioux had overcome both the Kiowas and the Cheyennes. Captain Jonathan Carver, of the Provincial Troops in America in 1766, corroborated these advances when he said that he met Sioux about two hundred miles from the mouth of the Minnesota, in the vicinity of Big Stone Lake and Lake Traverse. This indicated that the entire eastern portion of South Dakota, south to Pipestone Quarries, as well as an undetermined part of the state including the Black Hills, was now controlled by these people. Rapid as this western expansion may at first sight appear, Carver's information significantly shows that the eastern exodus of the Sioux was a comparatively slow one.

Likewise, the population must have been rather large in order to maintain a semblance of communication and unity over so great an area.

However, the strategic position along the Missouri River in 1775 was occupied by the Arikaras. Unquestionably, the Sioux were handicapped in their mass settlement west of the river by this powerful menace. In spite of the fact that the Arikaras' sedentary community may have been considered as merely an island to be avoided, it was an ominous threat to the Sioux expansion. Powerful and safe in great stockaded villages, the Arikara confederacy could boast of perhaps twenty thousand persons. These agriculturalists, living in several permanent towns along the Missouri, sat warm in their earth lodges during the winter, cultivated their fields in the summer, and hunted bison in between times. In the land which they controlled there was a wealth of buffalo.

Jealous of these resources, the Sioux made forays across the Missouri. They hunted buffalo in the Arikara lands; they stole corn and squash from the enemy's fields; they counted coups on these powerful people. These surreptitious acts of hostility were strangely counterbalanced by periodic gestures of peaceful trade between the two tribes. Sioux frequently negotiated for Arikara produce in exchange for firearms, horses, or furs. They would preface these commercial transactions by offering the pipe of peace to Arikara leaders.

Nevertheless, whether as enemies or friends, the Arikaras were a barrier which stood in the way of Sioux destiny. The Sioux knew this and knew the struggles, the dangers, the hardships which conquest entailed. Possibly they knew too something of the rewards for the conqueror, the penalties for the conquered. Knowing these things, the Sioux deliberately made war on the Arikaras, and in 1792 they inflicted a crushing defeat on their enemies, driving them to the north between the Grand and Cannonball rivers. Thus the Missouri Valley and the western portion of South Dakota were under unchallenged Sioux control.

The ultimate triumph of the Sioux over the Arikaras and Omahas was facilitated by the fact that both of the latter tribes

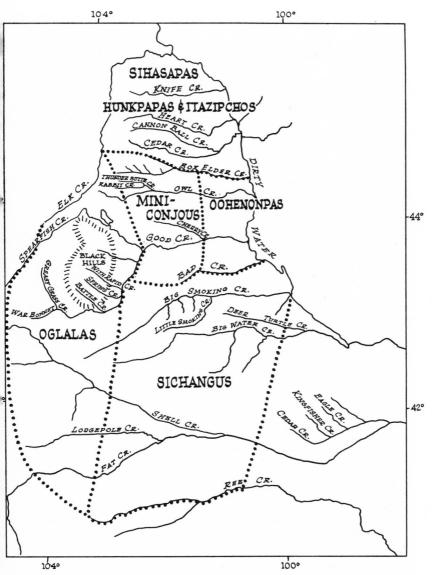

Sioux Territory, *ca.* 1850, showing areas controlled by the various tribal divisions and Sioux names for the rivers.

had been afflicted with a succession of smallpox epidemics. In urban societies, where the virulent plague was transmitted rapidly and widely, the ranks of the tribes were badly decimated, making them more vulnerable to the attacking Sioux.

In 1804, Lewis and Clark found the Sioux divisions on both sides of the Missouri: 300 warrior Brulés along the Teton and White rivers, 150 Oglalas inhabiting both sides of the Missouri south of the Cheyenne River, and 200 warrior Miniconjous on both sides of the Missouri above the Cheyenne. In the thirty-eight years since Carver's visit, the Sioux had completely relinquished their eastern territory in favor of the Missouri River Valley and its tributaries.

Further expansion was achieved by a victory over the Crows in 1822–23. The encounters took place west of the Black Hills, where the triumphant Sioux gained possession of present eastern Wyoming, south to the North Platte. Except for a possible north-south extension west of the Missouri River, Sioux territory remained relatively static throughout the remainder of the nineteenth century.

In their new environment the Sioux found economic security and a refuge from their rifle-shooting enemies. From the barren, wind-swept highlands they could obtain the basis of their livelihood and still remain camped in the sheltering timbered lands that bordered the rivers and the streams.

They were careful to preserve their independence and political autonomy for their bands and for the tribe as a whole. On occasion, they formed tenuous alliances with their relatives, the Yankton Sioux. They met with them periodically to ensure that unity but remained separate and, to a large measure, aloof of all entanglements. With the Saones to the immediate north, the Oglalas, Brulés, and Miniconjous retained close affinity, yet even so, their respective movements were relatively self-determined.

In this period, the Sioux are a good example of a self-reliant, self-determined society. Motivated partly by a drive for conquest, aggrandizement, and wealth which might lead to greater comfort and security, and partly by fear of the consequences of domination—if not annihilation—at the hands of a powerful enemy, they had foresaken their home for a new life in an unknown land. And yet they so tenaciously held to the patterns of their previous existence that the new Plains environment affected them surprisingly little. Like many men, they tried to mold their environment to their preconceived ideas of how life should be lived, and in this they were amazingly successful.

No matter how well the Sioux may have fit their new Plains environment to a woodland hunting culture, they experienced at about this time a set of stimuli of marked significance—the horse and the gun.

Information concerning when the Sioux first received firearms is scant and vague. There is indication that some men were equipped as early as 1700, but the number undoubtedly was so small as to have proved comparatively ineffectual in combat with the Crees's greater supply of weapons. Small supplies of firearms, however, had been received from the French traders and even from the village tribes along the Missouri. Jean Baptiste Truteau, the French trader, in 1794 noted the fear in which the Sioux were held because they had guns. Yet Lewis and Clark in 1804 noted that the Tetons were "badly armed with fusees." The numbers, too, were apparently small, for Zebulon Pike in 1805 estimated that only about 5 per cent of the men carried such weapons. However, possession of firearms was a definite advantage, and it was fortuitous for the Sioux that simultaneously they were increasing their supply of firearms and enjoying the advantages of an expanding supply of horses.

The early muzzle-loading matchlocks, flintlocks, and caplocks were of little effective value for horsemen, but toward the latter part of the nineteenth century, the introduction of breech-loading repeating rifles made the Sioux warrior the world's most renowned cavalryman.

The horse, reintroduced to the New World by the Spaniards, appeared on the central Plains during the middle of the eighteenth century. The exact date at which the Sioux first obtained the animal has not been determined. Certainly it was no later than

69

1742 and probably earlier. In any event, the effect of the horse upon the Indian culture was catalytic.

The use to which the Indians put the horse, and more particularly the manner in which the Indians adapted it to their needs, suggests the stability of their culture. The fact that they called it "sacred dog" or "mystery dog" is in itself important, because their conception of it as a kind of dog presupposed its use and value.

To the Indian here was an animal able not only to do the work of dogs but also to carry a rider. Men mounted on horseback could bring under their control much wider areas of land than had ever before been possible. Now buffalo could be surrounded and driven with greater ease and more assurance of success. In battle, the horse offered an ideal conveyance for attack as well as an excellent means of escape. As a result of these undisputed advantages, the Sioux, like many of their neighbors, made the horse their medium of exchange. As a symbol of wealth, as a beast of burden, and as a conveyance for the hunter and warrior, the horse was incorporated into the tribe's system of living with a maximum of effectiveness. Instead of producing a social upheaval, the horse was accorded an honored place.

With the advent of this animal, the Sioux did not cease hunting bison, nor did they abandon their nomadism; they did not curtail their drive for conquest or their custom of counting coup; they did not alter their pattern of camping in the wooded creek bottoms or their plan of camping in a circle during their annual gettogethers. In effect, they made relatively few concessions. What they did do was to accentuate their cultural pattern by fitting the horse into an existing scheme and building various refinements and elaborations upon it. Actually they became more nomadic, more mindful of conquest, more wealthy in terms of consumption goods and in relation to their environment. With the acceptance of the horse, their culture flourished.

By 1800, some fifty years after the introduction of the horse and a scant eight years after the destruction of the Arikaras, the Sioux may be considered to have established the ultimate pattern of their culture. The cast of their existence was set. By this date they were firmly entrenched in the center of the buffalo range; they had fully exploited the advantages of the horse. Undoubtedly they had made their reputation as a warlike nation something to be reckoned with. Their life was already specialized toward nomadism and war. They were in their ascendancy.

To characterize the Sioux as anything less than vainglorious would be inaccurate. Their arrogance was born of successful conquest. Within the comparatively short period of approximately one hundred years, they had overcome such powerful enemy tribes as the Omahas and Poncas, the Arikaras, the Cheyennes, and the Kiowas. They could hardly help being aware of their great power. The Sioux were far more than aware: they were overbearing in their vanity.

In meeting a group of Sioux on their way up the Missouri River in 1804, Lewis and Clark were bluntly exposed to the opportunistic chicanery of this tribe. William Clark complained that after having presented medals and whisky to the chiefs Black Buffalo and Partisan Walker and other Sioux men of importance, the Indians became "very insolent both in words and gestures (pretending drunkenness and staggering against me) declaring I should not go on. Stating he had not received sufficient presents from us, his gestures were of such a personal nature I felt myself compelled to draw my sword."

The tension of this encounter reached the point where the Indians drew their bows and, surrounding Clark, treated him in a very rough and insolent manner. As Clark's men appeared in force, the Sioux removed themselves to confer, and when Clark offered his hand to Black Buffalo and Partisan Walker, they refused it. The meeting ended with Clark returning to his boat in what he termed "a bad humor."[2]

This seemingly unprincipled display of self-assertion was part and parcel of the Sioux point of view. National destiny was paramount, and any device which promised a chance of securing control and dominance of a situation was the prevailing *modus oper-*

[2] Bernard De Voto, editor, *The Journals of Lewis and Clark*, 35.

andi. Although personal integrity was expected between Sioux and Sioux, for the tribe, national integrity involved deceit and treachery. What appears as a paradox, wherein honesty is demanded among fellow men and dishonesty is commended for outsiders, was in fact the accepted code among all Plains Indians. The Sioux also expected treachery and deceit on the part of their neighbors; they assumed that their enemies were as devoted to the cause of tribal power as they were themselves. The Sioux had no illusions on this score. To fail to gain the upper hand was to court defeat and probable death. Plains Indians were never naïve enough to expect quarter.

As if to impress upon themselves a constantly positive attitude toward their national fortune, vanity was crystallized in exhibitionism at home and abroad. Risk in battle, to the extreme of overtly courting death, was recognized as among the highest of achievements. Such action was accorded high honor and widespread fame. Prestige and influence accrued to the brave in heart. At home, such a man might be given a position of great responsibility. To a neighboring tribe, his name and presence might mean the turning point in battle or the successful accomplishment in treaty-making or trading. Therefore, to assume the boastful attitude, to be self-assertive to the point of overbearance, was the keynote of individual and national survival.

To exhibitionism was added an aura of violence. Like the Plains country where they lived, with its driving blizzards and deadening cold, with its high winds, torrential cloudbursts, and deafening thunderstorms, with the brilliance of its sunny days, with the sharp bleakness of its buttes and mountains, the Sioux appear to have been a people of severe extremes. To kill an enemy was not enough; often he must be mutilated. To force an enemy tribe into submission was not sufficient; it must be driven from the territory. This violent approach was found within the patterns of in-group adjustment too. The penalties of disfigurement for infidelity, of tipi and property destruction for infraction of hunting regulations, are examples of the severity of Sioux disposition. Whether in the games of the children or in the self-torture of the vision seekers in the Sun Dance, the Sioux mania was evident. As opposed to the quiet of peace-loving men, these were an audacious people for whom boldness was a primary virtue. The Sioux were not troubled by an ambivalence in their dealings with nations; their sole objective was a straightforward aggrandizement through impassioned action. They expected self-assertion of themselves and of others.

Such emphasis upon the extreme suggests that the Sioux may have been victims of a vicious circle, wherein maintaining such a fever-pitched approach actually was a mechanism for bolstering the individual's ego. There is no evidence that some men have inherently greater or lesser proclivities for courage. In fact there is certainly a hint that the less courageous Sioux were obliged to reinforce their personalities in order to sustain the tribal tempo. While it is very true that the Sioux were not mere pompous bluffers, the fact that any people should have to resort to public displays of their fortitude and courage not only indicates an underlying fear that their true merit would not be fully recognized but also shows that through repeated assertions of a fact, an individual as well as a group may remain thoroughly convinced of it. While the Sioux may not have been consciously aware of these factors, their effectiveness sustained the nation for a long period of time.

Systematized autosuggestion seemed to elicit a kind of faith in the Sioux's own national destiny. They were a people convinced of their superiority. When that attitude became threatened, they had already developed mechanistic patterns which were ample for reassuring themselves. The Sioux truly experienced a faith in their way of life; for them, success bred success. They called themselves "Lakotas," "The Men." While many groups have characterized themselves as "The People," for the Sioux there was acknowledged justification. This unswerving faith in themselves became a kind of fantastic ethnocentrism wherein the universe revolved around their own tribal "world view" and their ambition. They were egoists and proud of it, yet paradoxically they could ill afford any other attitude. The Sioux pattern of existence had become so compulsively ingrained in violent self-assertion that there was no turning back. Each success, each victory, each conquest required renewed enthusiasm. Crescendo followed crescendo in a compounding spiral of action. Yet its climax was never really reached. The collapse of Sioux society came not through an inherent weakness in the system or a failure of the people to meet the demands of their universe. Rather the course of the denouement struck from beyond anything the Indians could possibly foresee or conceivably control. It came in the form of the white conquerors, so unbelievably powerful, so overwhelming in numbers that even the Sioux's most desperate defense was of no avail.

The ethnocentric exhilaration which the Sioux enjoyed represented a brilliant faith in themselves as a group. Here was national self-expression with a vengeance, and from the record of their success, it paid off handsomely. It was a flamboyant example of ego-inflation which, while not hollow, demanded constant priming. And the Sioux code was admirably designed to keep it primed. Any sacrifices, including life itself, were worth the price, for the Sioux way was a compounding of gratification upon gratification. If an example of the principle of survival through change need be made, the Sioux were that example par excellence. From a meager group eking out a paltry existence in the lake region of Minnesota, driven west from their homelands to the rigors of the awesome plains, faring with a paucity of firearms and even without the horse, the Sioux experienced little of what might be considered security. Opportunism was their only chance, and their very existence depended upon it. Change of a drastic nature was evidently thrust upon them, and their eventual good fortune is testimony of their acceptance of it. Possibly they had little choice, but other nations have vanished in the face of far less odds, while the Sioux appeared to have flourished. Blessed by the happy cirstances of acquiring the gun and horse almost simultaneously—and then finding themselves fortuitously located in the heart of the northern buffalo range—their way of life burst into magnificence. But this was not without effort and a fair share of insight. Other nations might have done the same—only the Sioux did it so brilliantly. These were men ready for change, anxious for improvement, with little to lose and much to gain. Survival was elemental while security was unknown. Their daring acceptance of a new way made existence certain, while their flexibility enabled them to prosper.

CHAPTER 4 / *The Scheme of War*

CONQUEST WAS THE KEYNOTE of the nineteenth-century Sioux nationalism. The economy was based not only upon the successful exploitation of the buffalo but also upon the predatory capturing of enemy property, particularly horses. The conquering of men was synonymous with survival, for there was no middle course. Independence was not a philosophical ideal but rather a practical method for maintaining the Sioux way. It was sustained by what superficially appeared as an opportunistic greed. Sioux society was so pragmatically conceived that it could function in no other manner.

The scheme of war was in reality a societal contrivance which ensured security through aggression. The scheme contained many interrelated factors, among which were role, prestige, and wealth, self-defense through retaliation, and economic power through military strength. Each reacted upon the other in a kind of complementary fashion to create a neat interacting whole.

The role of men was so completely directed toward warfare that it actually took precedence over the much more fundamental activity of procuring food through hunting. That such a condition should have existed indicates the ease with which the Sioux could sustain themselves on the buffalo, particularly after the introduction of the horse and firearms. Living in the center of the buffalo range, these hunters were actually so rich in spoils of the chase that they could afford the luxury of almost continual aggressive warfare and place those accomplished in it in high esteem.

While hardly humdrum, hunting was scarcely so glamorous as the battlefield. There were no honors for the successful hunter beyond the economic well-being of his household. He might be acclaimed for his success and his providence, recognized as worthy of respect, and even reach the position of Naca; but he could not be considered in quite the same exalted category with an outstanding warrior. For it was the warriors who were the heroes.

At a very early age, boys were taught to handle bows and arrows. They played arduous games of the roughest character and frequently simulated the exigencies of the battlefield. They chose sides and fought mock wars.

By the time a boy had reached adolescence, it was not unusual that he should have been invited to act as a water-boy for a war party. Here under the protection of experienced adults, and likely under the guidance of a close and familiar relative, the boy became not only a kind of mascot for the expedition but also a symbol of the coming generation. While his responsibilities were suited to his youth, they were nonetheless deemed essential, for no well-planned and bona fide mission was complete without a water-boy to attend the needs of the veterans. He was as much a part of the team as the Wolf Dreamer or the War Leader himself.

Almost without exception, adolescents prepared themselves for warfare. So enthusiastic, so bent on achieving renown and credit were the youth that, rather than having to urge sons to join a party, the problem facing parents seems to have been one of curbing ebullience. The reluctance on the part of adults to see their young men go to war seemed to create a double challenge. Escaping the authority and protection of the parental world was as important as meeting the enemy. Young men often planned their parties in secret, carried surreptitious invitations to one another and, once prepared, invariably left the village under darkness. These were young men out to seek their fortune. By leaving at night, they would evade the chance of parental prohibition and, equally important, relieve the family of making a decision with respect to the inevitable. And the family of young men undoubtedly underwent most ambivalent reactions at this time. While female relatives were accustomed to weep and wail when it was learned that their men had left for war, the fathers surely must have taken pride in their sons' initiative. Nor could the women, in the last analysis, draw comfort from their tearful despair, for the males whom they were conditioned to respect were the all-daring warriors, not the stay-at-homes.

Headmen, as well as parents, were incessantly confronted with the embarrassment of being unable to restrain their young warriors. "Head Chiefs are generally opposed to the young men going to war, but cannot control soldiers."[1]

The pattern of heroics was so institutionalized that reason, whether for individual well-being or group self-interest, was submerged by the obsession that war itself was the purpose of life.

For the Sioux, there were so many seemingly obvious values for war that the idea of peace was confined to that of mere truce. For the individual, warfare meant an opportunity to acquire property. Capturing horses from the enemy was the direct way to attain wealth and influence. Warfare also meant a sure road to prestige and leadership. Men with the most impressive record of war honors were to be reckoned with in matters of state.

Warfare also implied ensuring the economic base of Sioux society, for only in protecting and expanding the territory in which the buffalo were most plentiful could the Sioux expect to retain an unparalleled national wealth. That their territory was coveted, that their wealth in horses was desirable, were apparent beyond doubt, for the Sioux were as subject to attack and pillage by their enemies as their enemies were exposed to the plunderings of the Sioux.

The Pawnees, hunting buffalo along the south banks of the Platte River in the summer of 1873, experienced the determination of the Sioux to discourage incipient encroachment of their domain. Here one thousand Sioux warriors routed the trespassers, and in one of the last intertribal wars, killed nearly two hundred of their enemies—men, women, and children.[2]

The Kiowas, living in the protected hunting haven of the Black Hills in about 1775, were boldly driven from their stronghold by

[1] Esther Goldfrank, "Historic Change and Social Character," *American Anthropologist*, New Series, Vol. XLV, No. 1 (1943), 79.

[2] Hyde, *Red Cloud's Folk*, 202.

the Sioux, who had decided it was worth taking. And so completely did the Sioux incorporate the Black Hills that they affectionately called the region their "Meat Pack."

Less dramatic than offensive warfare on a large national scale where hosts of tribal warriors battled one another was the incessant marauding of little groups of men. The Sioux were constantly vigilant against the small enemy team who planned to capture horses or scalp a single victim. Defensive warfare was a matter of continual concern. Enemies were on all sides and would travel far to gain honor and wealth for themselves, for they were as deligent in preserving their national honor and bolstering their standard of wealth as were the Sioux. Even during large encampments, where by dint of numbers one might expect security, calculating enemies were a constant threat. The excitement and confusion offered an excellent opportunity to waylay an unsuspecting bystander or capture a not-too-well-guarded horse. Protecting the women and children was a day-in and day-out responsibility. There were no periods of universal peace; there were no nights when an attack might not occur. People were cautioned not to wander far from camp, especially after dark. Herds of horses were carefully watched over, and valuable war horses were picketed close to the owner's tipi. Men always slept with their weapons beside them, and it is said that children were trained not to cry lest the noise attract enemies. A Sioux village was an armed camp ever ready for siege. Only during great blizzards or prolonged periods of intense cold might the people feel secure against attack. The wise old men at one time set forth what they conceived to be the "Four Most Difficult Things of Life." Among them was for a small family hunting party to be attacked by the enemy. Alone on the plains, their men few, and inevitably scattered for effective hunting, a tiny group of women and children was easy prey to a wandering war party. There was such a small hope of defense that annihilation was inevitable. The old men's conclusion in conceding this as "difficult" implied well the hopelessness of the tragedy.

The Sioux way of life by 1830, though most successfully fitted to its natural environment, was by no means a self-sufficient system. The economy, based so heavily on consumption, could be maintained only by constant exploitation. The Sioux were aware of this. As a nation, the Sioux became greedy and arrogant; the pattern of their life wholeheartedly accepted war and fostered it. They jealously guarded their wealth, boisterously proclaimed their independence. War was the fuel for keeping a vicious circle in motion.

As a nation and as people, the Sioux had faith in their system; they were convinced of its inherent right. The exhibitionism of the individual, like the vanity of his group, proudly expounded the glory of the Sioux. Their basic ethnocentrism sustained a national unity which expressed itself in terms of both personal role and status in the societal pattern as well as in the reputation which the tribe held among their friends and enemies.

The ideal male role was adjusted to risk, violence, and self-assertion. To court danger and tempt death, to risk self to an extent almost beyond reason, were prerogatives of success. To boast and brag of one's daring and one's achievements were the accepted rewards for the successful.

Retaliation, defense, conquest, and booty were among the primary motivating causes of Sioux warfare. By 1830 war was so woven within the entire fabric of life, so essential for its successful operation, its patterns so ingrained and accepted, that the idea of individual war honors was already crystallized. Thus, in addition to such personal motives as security, revenge, and wealth as warfare satisfied, gaining honors became an end in itself. For a predatory society, this development was indeed a positive step.

Retaliatory and defensive warfare were undoubtedly the earliest forms; the need for conquest and piracy grew with the later development of the Sioux life pattern. Retaliatory warfare may have had its foundation in simple eye-for-eye retribution. A man was killed by the enemy while hunting; the victim's family thereby suffered an irreplaceable loss; some kind of satisfaction, if only emotional, must be had. Responsibility for righting this wrong

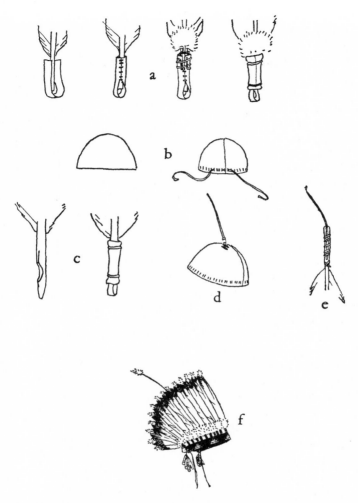

Steps in the making of a war bonnet: *a*, feather wrapping; *b*, cap construction; *c*, cutting quills of plume and wrappings; *d*, cap with plume; *e*, hawk feather attachments; *f*, finished war bonnet. (See Chapters 4 and 10.)

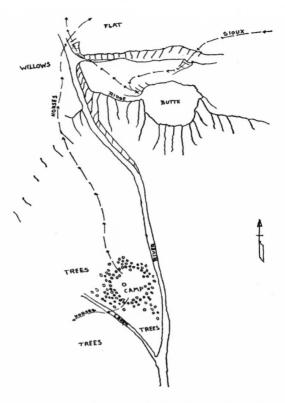

Plan of a Sioux attack upon the Shoshonis. (See Chapter 4.)

was initiated not by the group but by the family, who in turn might expect support from other members of the tribe. While it was not considered the duty of the group to retaliate, since acts of aggression against members were a personal feud, actually the enduring hostilities between nations of Indians was frequently occasioned by such acts against individuals. On the Plains, nations at peace were careful not to harm each other's members; among nations at war the reverse of this was the rule.

Shot-in-the-Heel's son, Holy Circle, had been killed in war with the Shoshoni. His body was abandoned on the battlefield, for it was good to be left in enemy territory. Iron Shell, his brother, now a Big Belly and retired from the Ska Yuhas determined to avenge this death by arranging a wacekiyapi or worship. Here were invited the members of Holy Circle's military society, the Sotka Yuha, for the purpose of showing their respect. And it was here that Runs-Him, considered by Shot-in-the-Heel to be the bravest of all Sotka Yuhas, pledged himself to avenge the death of his fraternity brother, thereby relieving Iron Shell of any responsibility.

A few days after the worship, Runs-Him gave a feast inviting the members of the Sotka Yuha. Runs-Him was organizing a war party of which he would be Blotahunka or war leader. The next day the men made preparations, gathering moccasins and packing saddle bags. Much equipment was needed for a war party. In saddle bags they put their best leggings, their bone breast plates, their otter skin braid wraps and their bladder food bags containing pemmican. Feathered war bonnets in their rawhide cases or protective head-dresses placed and packed in the saddle bags were hung from the pommel. They also brought new make-up kits packed with elk grease and paint, a porcupine tail brush, their pipes and pipe bags and a buffalo horn drinking cup or a carved wooden bowl. And in addition to their bow and arrows, they might bring a shield or lance, a whip or club. The owners of the Sotka Yuha carried whips or feathered lances, the badges of their office. Some men carried dew clothes to sleep on; others took only their robes.

As each man was ready, he went to Runs-Him's tipi, the Blota-hunka riding a saddle horse and leading his war horse. By noon, about thirty men had gathered. Without procession or ceremony, the Sotka Yuhas left the village. But through their tears, the wailing women might see them going to the mountain country of the Shoshoni far to the west.

The war party moved casually—they took their time for they did not want to tire their running horses, which they rode only in battle. They found a flat camping spot by a bend in the creek where they could keep watch of their horses and get a good sleep. After watering their animals, they picketed their saddle horses and left their race horses to graze. They didn't post guards for they were still in Sioux country, but throughout the night one or another of the men would be up checking. Each was trained to be a light sleeper—to be awakened at the least sound.

At dawn the camp arose and when all the horses were gathered and the saddle horses readied, the men ate. When the meal of pemmican was finished, they mounted their horses and rode leisurely until noon, stopping near a stream for water. Here a couple of the men who definitely hoped to count coup went over a nearby hill and returned shortly, dressed in their battle regalia and singing the Sotka Yuha's song. One of them walked up to a young man who had been on only a few war parties and punched him with his lance. Everyone laughed heartily for they knew this hardened fighter was joking with an inexperienced man—this was to show him what a real warrior would do. As the other men laughed and ate, these fellows paraded back and forth singing: "I'm going into battle. I'll use my horse more in battle. I'll prove my horse is better than the enemies'. I will run their horses down."

Then they returned to the hill to change their clothes, having left in the minds of their fellow-men the knowledge that they would stand their ground no matter what the odds.

When the noon meal was finished, the journey continued, but the route now kept to the lowlands and wooded draws. When it was necessary to cross the barren flats, they approached slowly, carefully surveying the countryside in all directions before proceeding.

A small herd of buffalo was sighted, and after the area was thoroughly scouted for enemies, the Blotahunka, to conserve food, selected one of the good hunters to kill a buffalo, saying: "You better take one arrow." In this way the others knew the best man had been chosen and that if he failed to kill with that one arrow he would be shamed before them—that someone else would be appointed on the next occasion. The hunter took his arrow and slowly rode his war horse bareback toward the herd. When he had studied the situation and had chosen his mark, holding his reins in his mouth, he galloped into the buffalo herd. His horse, trained to run close beside the fleeing beasts, made the hunter's work easier. Aiming his arrow at the heart of a fat buffalo cow, he killed the beast with deftness and surety. With one arrow he had assured the party of a supply of meat as well as proving his reputation as a marksman.

The others then rode down hooting and howling to help butcher. In the heat of the sun and work, some men had made wreaths of sage or red grass, others wore strips of buckskin. One suggested they have soup and upon the Blotahunka's approval, they carefully removed the paunch. When the meat was cut and the delicacies removed— the tongue, liver and kidney—they headed for a creek. Some men began heating stones while others stretched the paunch over four crotched sticks and filled the paunch with water. When the stones were hot, one of the cooks carried them to the paunch on a forked stick. After about ten stones had been thrown into the water, it began to boil and then strips of meat were dropped in to cook.

While the soup was being made, the man chosen as the Blotahunka's helper gathered leaves and branches for his leader's place— the others gathered their own material. When the soup was ready, the war leader's helper fed him such choice tid-bits as the center section of the tongue, using a forked stick. After Runs-Him, the Blotahunka, had been ceremonially fed, the others ate the long strips of meat by holding one end of it in their teeth, the other end in their fingers and cutting off each mouthful, close to their lips, with the aid of their knife. When they finished the meat, they filled the cups and bowls with soup.

They traveled only a short way after this feast, stopping before twilight to sleep, for they were in enemy country now. Later, after nightfall, they got up and resumed their journey. If an enemy had spied them, making their camp, and had gone for help, when the help returned and surrounded the spot they would find no one there. The Sioux, following the lowlands, would travel several miles before turning in for the night.

The party had been in enemy territory several days now and one evening, Runs-Him, the Blotahunka, sent two scouts ahead. The scouts rode in the ravines toward a great ridge and leaving their horses in the thickets, climbed on foot to the top, their buckskin head-covering hiding the blackness of their hair. They must be able to tell, from meagre signs, the evidence of large or small war parties in the area. The fortune of the mission depended in large measure upon the adequacy of their reports—theirs was an assignment of responsibility.

The scouts returned shortly after dawn in a quick but unhurried manner which indicated that nothing startling had been observed. Nevertheless, Runs-Him, the Blotahunka filled his pipe, offering it first to the Four Winds, the Earth and the Sky, presented it to the scouts. Their smoking was a vow to tell the truth, in the same way as the Blotahunka's vow before the Nacas when the party would reach home.

As a result of the report that no enemy nor danger was present, the Blotahunka ordered the group to move on. Each night scouts were ordered to go upon the hill. At dawn of the third day the two who were chosen as scouts hurried into camp and after proper ceremony reported a medium sized camp at the forks of two distant creeks. For this, each would be entitled to a scout feather. This was the end of the journey—this is what they had come for.

Now the men dressed in their finest regalia. Some wore fine buckskin shirts and leggings, others quilled arm bands or bone breast plates. While most men dressed in their finest costume, for this was the way to die in battle, some however wore only moccasins and breech clouts. Each man prepared his wotawe or amulet, and painted himself and his horse according to wotawe's sacred formulae. Those who owned war bonnets put them on and while all bonnets were not wotawes, the power of the eagle endowed any bonnet with a certain protective quality. The lance owners took out their otter skins and feather trailers and put them on their lances. Some put feathers in their horse's manes and tails, some tied up the tails with red flannel.

When everyone was dressed, they assembled again for the scouts to go over in detail the locations and directions of the camp. The plan was to enter the village at daybreak, run off the horses and retreat. When they were chased, they would turn and put up a fight. To enter a camp at dawn was daring, but they were avenging Holy Circle's death. When each man knew the plan, when everything was ready, the warriors, one at a time, rode a short distance and blowing an eagle wing whistle besought Wakan Tanka and their special supernatural helper for help saying: "If I am successful I will give you a robe as an offering, for this is the greatest." Holding up his right hand the warrior sang to the west, then to the other directions, then he returned.

When nightfall came, the war party broke camp and headed toward a large butte leaving the two youngest members to mind the horses. Usually boys of ten or twelve years were left behind to keep the camp, but in this party all the men were experienced warriors, and since no boys had been invited, those left behind had to be chosen either because they were young or because their horses were poor.

The butte was about a mile from the village, some fourteen miles away from the Sioux base of operations. They led their horses up to the butte and waited. Just before dawn each man took from the pouch on his wotawe a pinch of medicine, offering it first to the Four Winds, the Sky and the Earth, he then placed a pinch in his horse's mouth and nose to make him long-winded. He then rubbed medicine in the eyes and forehead of his horse and down his mane to the tip of his tail. If the prescription called for it, he placed a pinch in his own mouth, around his eyes, in his nose or in his hair. After the medicine was administered, the men led their horses about so that they might urinate, for this helped prevent them from getting colic and enabled them to hold out. Geldings were considered to have the greatest endurance; some mares were considered good; stallions had no sustaining qualities.

At daybreak, the Sioux watched the Shoshoni turn their horses out to graze, leaving only a few picketed within the village. The herd ran along the river to drink and then headed north to the flats. As the last of the horses were leaving the water, the Sioux rode down among the willows and drove the stragglers toward the flats where they surrounded the herd and headed northeast to their camp. Two men, however, hung back as rear guards to discover what move the enemy would make. When they saw the Shoshoni warriors, they rode up to their party to report.

They then rode to their rendezvous where Runs-Him, the Blota-hunka, gave orders for the two guards to ride ahead toward the northeast with the saddle horses and the stolen herd. Over one hundred Shoshoni ponies had been captured. Loping their war horses on the high ground, the main Sioux party followed slowly in the same direction. It was their hope that the Shoshonis in galloping to overtake them would wind their horses. When the Shoshonis came within shooting range, the Sioux urged their horses just enough to make the enemy spend their arrows. In the chase, many Shoshoni warriors dropped back, their ponies being exhausted. When the Shoshoni ranks had thinned to about the same size as the Sioux, the Blotahunka suddenly ordered his men to turn. Each man made a short quick circle; leaning behind his horse to serve as a shield, each shot an arrow as he raced forward. After a very short distance, the riders shot a second arrow and wheeled their ponies in retreat. This manoeuver stopped the Shoshonis merely temporarily and it was only after the third turn that the pursuers became the pursued. Immediately the Blotahunka shot the nearest Shoshoni. As he clung to his horse the Sioux leader hit him with his lance of office, knocking him from his horse and counting a first coup. Next he hit the horse to make it his. Then he returned to the fallen victim to scalp him. As the others rode on, each intent upon striking a first coup, another Shoshoni fell.

Some of the Shoshonis made for an embankment while others scattered, heading for home. The Sioux claimed twenty killed. When the chase was over and all but those behind the embankment had escaped, the Sioux rode out of range. Here the Blotahunka decided that they should return home. They had killed enemy and captured horses—and men protected by a bank were hard to deal with.

The Sioux rode over the battlefield and touching the fallen enemy divided coups among them. Nearly every man got a first coup—the war leader was entitled to two.

They rode toward home slowly for they were not afraid, joyfully for they had lost no one, proudly for they had avenged Holy Circle's death.

The next day they divided the horses, yet those horses struck in battle were not included in the sharing. As they rode they worked red paint and grease into the scalps they had taken and tied them to long poles.

When they finally neared home, they camped for the night, sending scouts forward to locate the village. At dawn the next day, stripped of their clothes, their faces blackened and bodies painted, waving their scalps from poles, and yelling, they charged into the camp. Runs-Him, the Blotahunka, led the first pony he captured and carried two scalps. As they circled the center they cried out their names, saying: "I made a kill and took their horses." The second time around they trotted slowly so that people might recognize them and some were singing: "I promised to get his horses, too." The Blotahunka then mounted the horse he was leading and holding up the other scalp rode around twice more, alone.

When Runs-Him, the war leader, reached the center of the camp he called out to Shot-in-the-Heel saying: "This is the hair of your Society brother; take this horse for this is his horse. Ride this horse and blacken your face and put on your best clothes."

The warriors gathered outside the meeting lodge where their friends and relatives embraced them. Then one of the Nacas offered a pipe to the Four Winds, the Earth and the Sky, presented it first to the war leader and then to the other warriors. "Runs-Him," said the Naca to the war leader, "I am going to ask you a question. You must tell the truth, you must not tell lies, for in lying a curse will befall you. Therefore, tell the truth." It was unnecessary for Runs-Him to bite a knife, for he was talking through the pipe. In a clear voice he told the gathering what had occurred and when finished, he asked the others if this were true. They concurred.

"You have done a good deed," said the Naca as the people cried, "Thanks, thanks." At this the men's sisters and female cousins ran up to take the scalp sticks for the victory dance. The men rode off to get the ponies left behind the hill.

Shot-in-the-Heel dressed and blackened his face and walked over to where the women were dancing with the scalps. Mounting his pony, he rode about and as he waved the scalp he called, "This is my son." Then as he danced with the women everyone knew that his mourning was over, and that his son had come back in the form of a scalp.

During the day many feasts of jerked tongue, pemmican and young dog were given in honor of the victorious warriors, horses were distributed by the men to their sisters and other female relatives who visited the tipi bringing with them halters. During the feasting the warriors were given quilled moccasins and other handcrafts which their sisters had been making for them in their absence.

In the evening, parents of the men might give clothes and horses in their sons' honor.

The "Dance Until Morning Dance"—a drawn-out scalp dance— began this night to last for four nights. Here the young girls of the camp joined while men who had won coups sang. Everyone black- ened his face. Each night the feasting was supplied by one of the warriors or his family. While the men slept during the day time the sisters gave away pieces of rawhide and soft buckskin for moc- casins, often cutting up the family's painted packing cases so that all who asked might have enough for a pair.

On the fifth day the camp returned to normal. The death of Holy Circle had been vindicated."[3]

Taking a scalp was closely associated with the retaliatory as- pect of warfare, but scalping implied a much more involved con- cept than a simple eye-for-eye desire for vengeance. For the scalp was a badge of honor, a sign of victory, and a symbol of life itself all in one. Scalping was no mere bloodthirsty act of the savage mind but a ritualistic necessity for men who believed that the human spirit was somehow in and of human hair.

The locks of hair embellishing the Wakincusa's shirt in reality represented the people of the tribe for whom the wearer was responsible. Bereaved parents wishing to honor a child who had died kept a lock of his hair to celebrate the Ghost-owning Cere- mony. And so when a warrior presented a scalp to a relative of some man who had died in battle, he gave not a gruesome trophy but the very spirit of the fallen warrior, and thereby symbolically the spiritual essence of the lost relative.

Not all war parties were so successful as the Holy Circle cam- paign. Some ended in complete tragedy with the death of all con- cerned; others failed in that no enemies were killed, no coups counted. Men returning from such an operation entered the camp almost secretly under cover of darkness in order to hide their shame. The Sioux accorded no credit for an attempt that ended in failure; it was only success that merited acclaim.

[3] Arnold Iron Shell, informant.

The origin of the various Akicita societies, who served as police to enforce order in the camp, seems to have been the assurance of individual success in battle.[4] A man who had received certain rules and regalia from his supernatural mentor, often through a dream, would invite two or three young men to test this new medicine. Upon proof of its efficacy after several successful forays, they might decide to invite others to form a fraternal organization. Officers would be appointed, uniforms distributed, songs learned, and all would be expected to stand by their comrades in any emergency. They joined because they were warriors. Their hope was to outshine other such organizations in feats of bravery and in number of coups. Young men and boys who early had shown initiative and daring were sought out as candidates for membership. They acted as a body both in war and as camp police. In a large battle they would vie with members of other societies to win acclaim.

The fact that the Akicita societies, without exception, were founded upon the desire to be successful in war, yet also functioned in a civil capacity, suggests that the need for civil control must have been contemporary with their origin. This need may have first occurred with the development of the communal buffalo drive and the Sioux's earliest conquest of the Plains. Here were groups of young men exhibiting strong traits of valiancy and fraternal cohesiveness, factors which could be put to good use by civil authorities in controlling the populace during periods of extreme tension.

Retaliation and defense, though important aspects for preserving the *status quo* of Sioux society, were secondary to and considered separate from horse-stealing. Raiding enemy villages was the foundation upon which the economic system rested—it was the key to individual success and group wealth. War honors and warrior societies were the mechanisms through which the piracy operated and flourished.

The significance of the horse to Sioux society and culture cannot be overemphasized. The characterization of many of the

---

[4] Wissler, "Societies and Ceremonial Associations," *loc. cit.*, 13.

Plains Indian peoples as the "Horse Indians" is no misnomer. By 1800 the Sioux undoubtedly were not only conscientious in their attempts to procure these animals but were already assiduously adapting them to their needs. But more than this, the horse was directly responsible for a revitalization of Sioux cultural values. Such a change was inherent in their acceptance of the horse, for in welcoming an obviously improved means of securing a livelihood, they unwittingly fell heir to a variety of consequences.

The high value of the horse, and particularly the status value of possessing many horses, acted as stimulus upon the entire war pattern. A new reason for war had suddenly appeared. As the horse became incorporated into the Sioux way of life, the need became more and more significant. An economic race with keen competition was developed, and it must be kept in motion if the new security were to be maintained. War made this possible.

Ghost Head's almost classic description of primitive military strategy illustrates something of the ingenuity, the planning, and the techniques required for the successful raiding party. Having dreamed of the Wolf—patron of warriors—Ghost Head possessed the ultimate qualification for success: supernatural power!

> When I went on war parties I always took a wolf-hide, bow and arrows and enemy clothing. When I wanted to go I'd tell two or three friends who might want to go with me—the smaller the group the better, for a little number is harder to detect. I also told my father, but I never told my mother for she would worry. For this reason I never had moccasins made especially for a trip, as many others did; rather, I always kept some on hand. We would start early in the morning. Usually the other men would be waiting outside my tipi for they knew that I stopped for nothing and would go on alone. As soon as I came out we would start, for I didn't want my mother to worry. This time I planned that we would go to the Crows.
>
> After we had walked three or four days we stopped at dawn by a creek for the men to make tobacco offerings to the wolves. Some vowed they would feed all the Wolf Dreamers, if they returned. While they did this, I took my wolf-skin to a nearby hill and facing

the Four Winds, called and cried to the wolves, asking them the whereabouts of the enemy.

When I returned from the hill, we smoked and then I told the men what I had learned—how many days away the enemy was, how large their camp was, whether we would meet an enemy war party and how many men were in it.

As the enemy was far away, we could hunt deer and small game, yet as we kept on I went ahead to scout and hunt, meeting the men later. There I had ready a deer or antelope for them, having first made sure there was no danger.

When we finally got into enemy territory we remained close together. There was no more hunting. As we came closer, I tried to locate the enemy, for since they were equally alert, it was safest to know where they were before they knew of us. When the wind was from the north, we stayed on the south side. This rule was observed for all Four Winds. At night the smell of fire or tobacco smoke, or the sound of a snorting horse was a sure sign of the enemy. These were things the wolves taught me. If in this way I might have detected an enemy war party, I would scout their position from across creek and report this to my men. If the enemy party had been small enough that we could have overcome them, I would have given instructions as to the best way of attacking, for I had seen the position. Such attacks must be made before daybreak lest the enemy should move out. However, on horse-stealing trips we rarely ever attacked a war party, but rather went around them. Our purpose was to capture horses.

Our plan was to reach the Crow village at night and spend the next day surveying the camp from a hill. Here we would decide upon the best plan. This we did.

When evening came, I put on the Crow clothing which I had got from earlier battles, and started alone for the village. Had it been a Shoshoni camp I would have worn Shoshoni clothing so that I would have smelled like a Shoshoni and painted my face and fixed my hair so that I would not be noticed. However, I always wore my wolf skin around my waist, tightly under my belt.

To enter the Crow camp, it was necessary to wait until someone had gone out between the tipis and then I entered through the same passage. In this way, the people inside the tipis, thinking that whoever left had returned, were not suspicious. In this summer camp, the tipis were placed close together and at night many horses were left to wander within the circle. Saddle and pack horses were picketed outside the circle, but the best horses were generally picketed at the tipi door inside the camp. To enter any enemy town, it was necessary to walk boldly—to walk as if you belonged there and were going some place.

In going about a camp, I was careful never to study a horse. Frequently one or two men would be lying in the grass waiting for such thieves and therefore it was necessary to look from the sides of your eye so that these men would not be suspicious. When one of them spoke to me, I only nodded, for it was unwise to make a remark. Rather, I kept on walking so no one would talk with me and pretended I was busy carrying something beneath my robe.

In this way I walked around the entire Crow camp looking at the best horses, for I was trying to spot one of the fast horses I had seen in a previous battle. I acted as if I were going toward the Dance —there seemed always to be dancing at the Crow village—but then turned off looking for horses. This may have taken an hour or more, because I tried to recognize the fast horses—the first four or five that chased us the last time we raided the Crow camp.

I had learned that when a man kept peeping at his horse from his tipi, or when he lay in the grass nearby, that this was the sign of a good horse. The Crows put feathers in the manes and tails of their best ponies and this was a good sign too.

Finally I left, leaving the camp in the same way I had entered, for I knew the land better. When I had gone a safe distance I hurried to the others, running all the way. Here I told them everything—where the good horses were, where the largest herd was located. Each man then decided what horse to take, for I told them about each one. Then I removed the Crow clothing and put on my own clothing. Then we left—still in the evening darkness, for an enemy can't chase far in the dark. They are afraid of being waylaid, while we could ride hard on trails we had already picked out. We entered the Crow camp one at a time; the man whose horse was farthest from where we entered proceeded first. While it was important to walk boldly, we, nonetheless, covered our heads with our robes to hide our wotawe feathers.

When I was inside the circle, I passed by my horse to see just where the picket was and whether anyone was lying in wait. Since no one was there, I returned casually and cut the halter near the picket so that I might use it for a bridle. Then I walked on. When the pony had moved off a little, I painted his white markings with dirt or charcoal, so that he was less easily recognizable. After this was done, I walked back and forth gently shoving him toward the main camp opening. When we were about half way to the entrance, I climbed on him and rode him slowly to the entrance. In this way, should the owner pass by looking for him, he would not recognize him. After I got the horse close to the entrance, I dismounted and tied the halter to his leg so that I could see how the others were making out.

The man whose horse was nearest the entrance had already gone, so I went to discover how the next fellow was faring. He was having trouble, because someone was keeping watch of the horse. I then helped him out by throwing a stone at the guard. The guard jumped up angrily asking why I threw stones at him and I laughed and threw another stone. The Crow, wanting to know who was joking with him, got up and then I ran off toward the dancing. Before I got there, however, I cut off toward my horse, for I now knew my friend could get his. This was risky, but it worked.

When I returned to my horse, I drove him toward the camp opening and deliberately chased him through as if I were someone who had just come in and wanted to turn my horse out for a while to graze. As usual, there were a couple of Crow men standing guard there to see that no good horses strayed, so to fool them I turned around and hurried again toward the center.

Before I got to the center of camp, I turned toward the tipis. While most men preferred not to pass a lighted tipi when leaving an enemy camp, if I found one in which a woman was sitting alone I would use this as an exit. [It is possible that Ghost Head assumed that a woman would be less likely to demand knowledge of a passer-by since she would be unarmed, and further in leaving by a lighted tipi he reduced any appearance of suspicion by the sheer boldness of the act.]

When outside the ring of tipis, I returned to the entrance through which I came and cautiously began shoving my horse away. Then mounting him I rode back to our meeting place to join the others. From here we rode away from the camp and away from home.

The next night we agreed to return to the same camp in search of more horses. I was still looking for a fast buckskin horse, but arrived too late. The dances were breaking up so there was not time to find it. This time we had to give up and started for home, each riding a horse. We traveled all night and all the next day toward home. Then that night I went on the hill to learn from the wolves if any enemies were near. I was told by the wolves that an enemy war party was going south, about a day's journey ahead. I told my friends that they could go after them if they wished, but that I was going hunting. Then we slept, lying on our halter ropes so the horses would not wander. The next day the others went home. I left them here and I went hunting for I enjoyed bringing back an enemy horse packed with meat.

The basis of the war honor system was the coup—originally awarded for the striking of an enemy. It appears that later coups were granted for other acts of bravery and daring. A man's reputation depended upon the number of points he could accumulate, and competition for them was intense.

A system of graduated points was evolved wherein the first man to touch an enemy was awarded a first coup or "direct hit," and the right to wear a golden eagle feather upright at the rear of his head. The second to touch the same enemy was entitled to wear an eagle feather tilted to the left. The third won the right to wear an eagle feather horizontally, while the fourth and last could wear a buzzard feather hung vertically. The last three feathers were known as "count feathers." Thus four men killing four enemies might, by dividing, each win four coups. Coups were granted for the touching of a man, woman, or child. Credit was given for touching, not killing, an adversary, except in hand-to-hand combat. It was the daring required of close contact for which the honor was given. Thus an individual might mortally wound a man with an arrow yet gain no coup because four of his fellow Sioux literally beat him to the touch. To count coup, one might use his hand, his bow, his lance, or certain societal paraphernalia like rattles or whips. All coups must be witnessed and later sworn to. To have an enemy count coup on oneself was a misfortune and a dishonor.

Coups were also recognized for other brave and warlike acts. Killing an adversary in hand-to-hand battle permitted the victor to paint a red hand on his clothing or upon his horse. Saving a friend in battle entitled a man to paint a cross on his clothing, and if the benefactor rode his friend to safety on the back of his horse, he might wear a double cross. Coups might be indicated by painting vertical stripes on leggings; red stripes indicated that the wearer had been wounded. Coup feathers dyed red also signified wounds; notched feathers showed the owner's horse to have been wounded.

Scouts who were successful in sighting an enemy were awarded coups. A black feather ripped down the center with the tip remaining was their badge.

Coups were given for the stealing of horses. As such, there existed double incentive, for the man not only gained credit toward his war record but a tangible economic asset as well. Here bravery for bravery's sake was not only an end but a means. Horse hoofs, painted on a coup feather or upon leggings or on a man's horse, indicated the number taken, while each hoof mark was colored to represent the color of the horse. A man's prowess and wealth were shown by the wearing of a miniature rope and moccasin at his belt to signify his capture of ten or more horses; the rope alone was worn when less than ten horses were brought back.

The symbols for coups varied among the Sioux divisions, and individual badges were occasionally honored. Thus, High Bald Eagle carried a small wooden knife, painted red, on the end of his walking stick. A lock of horse hair to indicate the Pawnees whom he had killed was attached to the knife.

The prestige pattern and the economic system were the essence of coup-counting and war honors. The incentive for war honors themselves—the credit given for bravery—suggests that these features may actually have been institutionalized as a mechanism to prevent flinching in situations of extreme danger. However, the overemphasis upon valor and fortitude; the rivalry; the high credit awarded for touching as opposed to killing; the reputation accorded those who went so far as to stake themselves in battle, yet who were well assured of escape through the high credit given their savior—these evidences of the Sioux's concern with national exhibitionism and the importance of war show that they were literally victims of a cultural pattern which had gone beyond the limits of natural endurance. It is likely that they credited bravery and flaunted danger to cover an innate normal fear.

Anything less than a bravery in battle was cowardice. But this was a cultural ideal which only a few men fully lived up to. The fact that bravery was an ideal, that it was expected of men, that it was institutionalized, and that it was the basis of prestige suggest that the role played by war in maintaining Sioux existence had become so vital that it was essential to the continuance of the total system. The point of view that it was good to die in battle expressed the psychological burden which such a pattern might place upon the individual. The dependence placed upon shamans for the preparation of protective war medicine or wotawes, and the reputation and following enjoyed by the dreamers whose wotawes were proven, point to the helplessness of the individual fully to cope with the required pattern. Successful competition demanded not only natural fortitude but supernatural power. The demands of the society were beyond the normal proclivities of its members.

That the pattern was effective and the individual's valor was real is proven by the qualitatively high value expressed by their adversaries, including the United States cavalry, and the historical incidents which record their national conquest and expansion and later valiant defense.

Great social position was accorded the holder of many coups, and one's status was further assured by the number of horses which one accumulated. Certain rights such as cutting down the Sun Dance pole or piercing children's ears for wearing earrings were reserved for men who had struck coup, and with these rights frequently went the honorarium of a horse. Nevertheless, a great war record was not sufficient prerogative to ensure political recognition and a position of authority in later life. A good record was a stepping stone, a prerequisite for later responsibility, but not an assurance. Generosity, kindness, and social position were equally necessary qualifications.

The role of the warrior was tuned to the exhibitionistic character of Sioux adjustment. Here the individual could give vent to proclivities for excessiveness before all men. He could gamble his life against the enemy's bravest, and no matter what the outcome—life or death—he won. His masochistic tendencies found reward in failure (if he were killed, he was acclaimed a hero), while his vanity was sustained in success (if he returned, he was steeped in glory). War was an all-pervading contest against himself, his fellow men, and his adversaries.

On the battlefield the Sioux ideally tried to outshine everyone. He was a show-off, and the better job he made of it, the greater his reputation. That he may have paid dearly for protective medicine was no discredit, and that a supernatural helper guarded his every move did not lessen his claim. He was expected to ridicule those who were less aggressive—his lack of feeling for others was the essence of sportsmanship. There were rules and codes of chivalry. A champion was one who adhered to the regulations and excelled. He wore little badges and won special favors.

He was respected if in getting more coups than anyone else he later blatantly proclaimed his own ability. When he took a scalp he gave it to his women, who sang his glory while dancing with the scalp suspended from a pole. He took every opportunity to count his coups—at dances and at ceremonies he proclaimed his worth. He welcomed the chance to paint his exploits on someone's tipi lining. He did this because congratulation-of-self at the expense of others was a virtue, modesty a vice.

In the Sioux way, war made self-expression veritably synonymous with self-denial. War became a device to bargain life against death in a most daring fashion. The stakes were high and the risks great, for unless a man were emotionally set to assume the full implications of selflessness, he might not fully enjoy the exhilaration of the culturally touted and socially accepted form of self-expression. Not only must the warrior risk life in order to win it, but the very spoils of war were in themselves valuable only when expended. Thus the economics of war were dovetailed into the practical aspects of self-denial, and the truly meaningful rewards were the tangible dividends of prestige and fame through the individual's advocacy of the Sioux way.

While war maintained the *status quo* through risk, it demanded on the part of the people stark acceptance or sacrifice. For some men, war may have constituted an escape, but there is little information which would lead to this conclusion with regard to a majority of the warriors. For the victim's relatives and friends, there was no escape—only the need for an adjustment to the reality of sudden death and loss of a loved one. In a sense, Sioux security and aggrandizement through competitive aggression was as expensive as it was heartbreaking. But then, man has not yet devised a way of life which does away with the need for war. For the Sioux, peace was a counterpart of war—both realities, both desirable, and both worthy of man's endeavor.

RED SHIRT posed for this formal portrait by W. H. Jackson in the 1880's. While wearing the latest white man's vest and shirt, Red Shirt adheres to tradition with his hair style and dentalium shell choker.

Courtesy Denver Art Museum

THE DRAMATICALLY IMPRESSIVE CHARACTER of the painted Sioux tipi, bearing the exploits of warriors, is clearly evident in this early photograph, *ca.*1890.

W. H. JACKSON photographed White Hawk in the 1880's wearing a dentalium shell choker. Her hair style is typical for Sioux women, but her dress, shawl, and earrings are introduced items.

Courtesy Denver Art Museum

PART THREE / *Familiarity and Respect*

CHAPTER 5 / *The Family*

THE SIOUX CODE prescribed that behavior between persons should be governed by the principles of familiarity and respect. And among persons who were related, these aspects of behavior were intensified into joking and avoidance. The principles upon which the kinship system operated and upon which family members based their behavior were ones of age and sex influenced by descent and proximity of relationship. Functioning of these concepts to ensure a cohesive, workable society, wherein members endeavored to foster harmony and avoid conflict, was directly correlated with the Sioux notion of family and the system of reckoning kinship.

The *tiyospe*, a group of individuals banded together under a common leader and often related through descent or marriage to the patriarch, was the ancient and important core of Sioux society. Through the able guidance of an experienced and dependable elder, small groups of people co-operated in hunting and in war; in carrying out the daily chores of homemaking, rearing children, celebrating, and worshiping; in caring for the aged; and in burying the dead. To accomplish all of these successfully, the *tiyospe* was of necessity an intensely cohesive organization. In general, the *tiyospe* was composed of members of one or more families, and because interrelation of family members was subject to a patterned system, the *tiyospe* itself was imbued with a sense of order.

The Sioux conceived the family as an ever-living yet ever-changing entity. As a body of individuals related through descent, it was enduring. Membership was a matter of consanguinity where each person reckoned his affiliation with respect to lineage of grandparents and parents, and with relatives—uncles and aunts, brothers, sisters, and cousins. While the individual might literally choose between belonging to his father's or his mother's family, he was, nevertheless, a member of both families. And the matter of choice was a comparatively simple one. Boys generally associated themselves with their father's family; girls, with their mother's. Affiliation, however, was further governed by residence. If one grew up in the proximity of one's mother's family, matrilocal aspects influenced loyalties. However, if a child was reared among his father's people, then relations with that family might be expected to be stronger. Actually, while there were no rigid rules for family membership, there were definite provisions for affiliation, so that rarely was anyone left in a nebulous status.

While the *tiyospe* was the primary self-sufficient unit of Sioux society, the conjugal family of man and wife was the smallest recognized group. Even for a man with several wives and possibly many children, the family was still a relatively small and dependent body in no way capable of maintaining its food supply or of assuring its own defense. Rather, it carried out its activities as part of the larger *tiyospe* with which it was associated.

Young married couples might live briefly with one or the other's parents, but this was inconvenient and for any length of time unworkable, because of the avoidance taboo among parents- and children-in-law. A wife might not look at or address her father-in-law, and similarly, a husband was prohibited from any familiarity with his mother-in-law. This was as difficult for a daughter-in-law residing with her husband's people as for a man living with his wife's family. As a result, a young couple was usually given a tipi to be pitched in front of one or the other parents-in-law's lodges, where they might enjoy the proximity of their family without the embarrassingly difficult situations occasioned by the taboo.

"Sometimes there were several of these young married couples' tipis in a camp. Placed before their parents lodges, the camp circle looked as though it were two rows deep."

Sioux custom required that no man marry a girl with whom

he had a common grandparent. Thus brothers, sisters, and cousins were prohibited from entering into a connubial relationship. Ideally, a man should choose a wife from outside his kinship group, and in such a lineal system as the Sioux devised, wherein descent was traced from common progenitors through as many generations as memory would permit, it followed that persons of the same band were in general related and thus might not marry. Within the great divisions, however, such as the Hunkpapas or Without Bows or Brulés, a man might well expect to find a spouse.

Leader Charge, headman of the Cut Meat Band, said: "As a Miniconjou, my father, Red Eagle, might have married a girl from his division, but it was better to marry into the Brulés or the Oglalas. My mother, his wife, Sitting Eagle, was a Brulé."

While the conjugal family of man and wife was subject to dissolution by divorce or death, the family of lineal and collateral relatives was permanent. An individual remained responsible to these relatives during his lifetime, regardless of his marital status or his residence. The high respect which brothers and sisters held for one another continued throughout life and was constantly reinforced by acts of generosity and signs of affection. It was for her brother, not her husband, that a woman made moccasins. It was for her brother's and sister's children, not her own and her husband's children, that a woman made cradles. And a brother, by the same token, brought scalps honoring his mother and sister, not his wife.

When the warriors returned from the warpath, "the men's sisters or cousins came over to take the scalp sticks. If a man had no sister, who ranked first, he would give the scalp stick to his cousin, who ranked second, or next to his mother, who ranked third, and finally to his wife, who ranked fourth."

In the event of divorce, the wife returned to her family, while the husband returned to his. The woman might set up her tipi near her parents, or move in with them or with a sister. It became the duty of her male relatives to provide her with food and shelter.

Children of broken homes did not present an especially serious problem. Generally the children, provided they had reached the age of five or six, were permitted to decide with whom they would live; girls tended to go with their mothers while boys remained with their fathers. Grandparents often took the custody of children, particularly in the case of a parent's death, and this arrangement imposed no very severe upheaval. Usually the grandmother had already been acting as nursemaid for her children's offspring.

Of family membership Blue Whirlwind said: "My son, like his father, belonged to the Miniconjou and was named Rejoicing Over His Horse, in honor of his grandfather's successful war parties. My daughter Brings the Horse belonged to my camp, the Brulé. Sometimes a father was very fond of a daughter and might take her into his camp. Should a man think a lot of all of his daughters, he will consider them all of his camp. But when a woman wishes to claim a girl for her camp, she has the first say."

Because of the wide range of possible relatives within the family, orphans were a rarity. Even at the loss of both parents, the grandparents or the brothers or sisters of the parents were commonly available to accept the responsibility for rearing the child. While children belonged first to their parents, it is true, the clannish character of the lineal family was so pronounced that in times of crisis its members were quick to assume the upbringing of the orphan.

In addition to those brothers and sisters acquired through the accident of birth, one might obtain other close relatives through a variety of techniques of adoption.

Formal adoption was customary under certain circumstances, though it generally did not involve orphans as such. Rather, it served as a procedure for replacing a child previously lost through death. In such cases, if a person should find either a child or adult who in some way reminded him of his former offspring, he might request the right to adopt the person and thereby assume the duties and obligations of a parent. If the proposal was agreeable to all concerned, the foster parent prepared a feast and publicly announced the new relationship by giving a horse to the parents and performing a giveaway honoring the child, as well as bestowing upon him the name of his predecessor.

Some adoptions like the *hunkas* were highly formalized relationships in which the status of the family was a motivating element. Others, wherein a family might take under its wing an orphaned child or acquire a youngster to fill the place of one previously lost through death, were simple acts of paternal devotion in which public announcement was the only formality. The relationship of *kolas*, however, was the most informal, yet close-knit, of any of the adoptive patterns.

The word *kola* literally means nothing more than friend, and is commonly used in speaking to convey that idea. One may say "*How, kola*," when greeting anyone, for it is a term of warm good will. While among the Sioux, as for all of mankind, the concepts of friend and friendship may actually involve subtleties within a complex range of amity, the relationship of *kola* represented the epitome of esteem and affection.

Young men frequently, as an outgrowth of childhood friendships, informally agreed to become *kolas*, to join one another as partners in all undertakings, to share material belongings for their mutual benefit. In hunting and in war they would remain inseparable, assisting the other to the limit of death. This Damon-and-Pythias relationship might include joining the same clubs and attending together the same dances. Frequently they married sisters, and since they were expected to share equally in all things, they in some instances may have exchanged wives. *Kolas* were recognized as able teams, as loyal associates. It was considered good to be a *kola*.

Captives, especially children, were commonly adopted into the family of the captor and underwent ceremonial adoption similar to that carried out in the child-replacing rite. Captive women might properly be adopted through marriage to their captor, although frequently they were given their wish in the matter. Should they reject this proposal, it was considered only proper to return them to their people. It goes without saying that men rarely took a female captive without the hope that she would make an attractive wife. Otherwise, the difficulty and danger of bringing a woman into the tribal circle would not be worth it. It frequently fell to married couples to care for their aging and widowed parents. Rarely was there a household not supporting one such old person. Because of the avoidance problem, generally only the wife's father or the husband's mother, or relatives in a similar classification where avoidance was less strict, lived with the couple. The complete avoidance taboo between the elderly woman and her son-in-law was so strict that, were a wife's mother to live with the couple, even the most commonplace daily living would have been nigh impossible. This same difficulty would have been experienced were the husband's father to dwell in the household of his daughter-in-law.

Grandparents played an important child-rearing role, for these older people fulfilled the capacity of nursemaid for their married children. These were the constant, and often stabilizing companions for the very young, and the part they played may have been quite influential in creating Siouan cosmology. The term "grandparent" used in referring to the supernaturals may have been a direct outgrowth of the older generation's kindly dominance.

Not all aged parents could expect to seek shelter in their children's home. So strong was the avoidance taboo that if the wife's mother had no son to whom she might go, she must camp alone. It became her daughter's responsibility to assist her economically, and frequently she pitched her tipi next to her daughter's to enjoy her company and to care for her children. But living with her daughter was completely impractical.

Some old people, unwanted or without relatives, had no place to go. These were forced to live alone at the edge of the encampment. Here they were given food and supplies by the generous young men who thereby gained prestige. They became the recipients of the wealthy man's spare horse at name-giving ceremonies, and as wards of the society, they were the basis for moralistic myths, and the foundation for the philanthropist's prestige.

But at best theirs was a tragic lot, too often filled with insecurity and despair.

Still worse was the fate of some old people whose care their children found such an odious liability that they were simply abandoned. As the camp moved away, the indigent one was left in his tipi with enough food and firewood to last several days. While the practice was socially frowned upon, it was nonetheless a very real cultural pattern.

Once Iron Shell, as headman, was among the last to leave the old village site during a move to a summer camp location. As he and his family proceeded they came to a forlornly ancient woman sitting alone with food and water near by. "What is the reason you sit here, Grandmother?" the headman inquired.

"I'm old and worthless," replied the old woman. "My son can no longer care for me, so I shall sit here to die."

"But that is not right," said Iron Shell. Arranging her upon a travois with her meager bundles, he made her a member of his procession.

When Iron Shell's party reached the new camping site, he led the old woman on the travois to her son's lodge. It was a poor family, for they possessed only one horse. Iron Shell called upon the son, saying, "Here is your mother." And pointing to the horse and travois, he said, "Here is a horse for her. Don't you ever again leave her like that." And the son was glad. As long as the old woman lived, the son dragged his mother from camp to camp.

To learn the required and accepted terms of relationship and modes of behavior toward relatives was expected of everyone. The list of terms could be learned by rote, but the application of them was more difficult, and was the foundation for the correct functioning of Sioux society and the basis for social conventions.

Children grew up within the framework of the conjugal home of parents and brothers and sisters—a home with its setting among the wider family of grandparents, uncles, aunts, and cousins. Such an environment demanded that children learn the correct terms of address and the proper modes of behavior for those lineal as well as collateral relatives who were members of the *tiyospe*. Because of the bilateral nature of the Sioux family, the child's knowledge of his father's or mother's family depended upon which family he lived with. In either instance, the need for learning terminology and behavior patterns was ever present and early acquired. The terms which needed to be learned and used in addressing members of one's family were many and rather complicated. They included the usual designations of mother and father, uncle and aunt, sister and brother, son and daughter, nephew and niece, and grandparent and grandchild, and the intricacies of in-law terms. Matters were complicated by the Sioux system of calling one's father's brother "father," and his sister "aunt," whereas one's mother's sister was referred to as "mother" and her brother as "uncle." There were terms for older and younger brothers and sisters, and proper designations for one's children depending upon the order of their birth. While the Sioux system was complicated, it was logical and worked well, for it was patterned upon the way in which the people believed the family should operate.[1]

The proper behavior pattern was governed by principles of familiarity and respect, reciprocity of action, sex differentiation, and generation. In other words, the individual adjusted his actions toward others first in accordance with the degree of familiarity or respect which the other's status demanded; second, with reference to the way in which the other person behaved toward him; thirdly, with regard to the sex of the other, including the sex of the person through whom the relationship existed; and fourth, in relation to the generation to which the other belonged, whether senior, peer, or junior.

In this system respect was correlated with seniority and famil-

[1] Royal B. Hassrick, "Teton Dakota Kinship System," *American Anthropologist*, New Series, Vol. XLVI, No. 3 (1944); Alexander Lesser, "Some Aspects of Siouan Kinship," *International Congress of Americanists*, Vol. XXIII (1928), 563–71; Jeanette Mirsky, "The Dakota," in Margaret Mead, *Co-operation and Competition among Primitive Peoples*, 382; J. R. Walker, "Ogalala Kinship Terms," *American Anthropologist*, New Series, Vol. XVI (1914). Each of these authors gives descriptions of terminological structure. For a detailed statement of the terminology and the patterns of behavior which needed to be learned and used in addressing member's of one's family, refer to Appendix B of the present volume.

iarity with peership, each being conditioned upon relative age or generation. Avoidance and joking on the other hand were associated with sex.

Familiarity and respect were the foundation upon which the kinship system operated. In practice, there was nothing haphazard or complicated; the rules provided clear-cut gradations of behavior, ranging from the joking relationship representing friendly and intimate familiarity to complete avoidance as an expression of highest reserve and respect. Toward one's sister-in-law a boisterously friendly and intimate joking relationship was expected; toward one's mother-in-law complete avoidance was the rule.

Between these poles there were gradations of proper behavior, including the dignified expression of love expected between man and wife. Here the consummation of their sexual life and the responsibility of children involved deep ties. The role of husband as head man in his family—as provider in some instances to more than one wife—made the relationship subject to complexities for which no precise behavior prescription was set forth.

Tenderness and affection characterized the correct expression between parents and children. The behavior toward anyone called "mother" or "father" should be one of love colored by respect. One loved and respected one's parents; one loved and cherished one's children. The relation between grandparent and grandchild was the same, though often more gentle and open.

A man showed toward his "brother" the deepest love and devotion, and he exhibited a like but somewhat less intense bond toward a male "cousin." A woman likewise showed a strong devotion toward her "sister," and slightly less toward her female "cousin."

Reserve and respect were the accepted modes of behavior for all persons called "uncle" and "aunt" and "nephew" and "niece." The influence of the sex difference of the common relative—in the case of a man, his mother; in that of a woman, her father—combined with the strangeness engendered by collateral relatives were factors calling for this reserve in contrast to the more open tenderness and affection enjoyed by parents and children. Nephews and nieces patterned their reactions on the basis of reciprocity. Partial avoidance—which made it improper to look directly at the other person, or to speak except under most urgent conditions —was required for all persons whom a man called "sister," "female cousin," or "father-in-law." Similarly, a woman should avoid her "brothers," "male cousins," and "mother-in-law."

Complete avoidance was demanded between "sons" and "mothers-in-law" and between "daughters" and "fathers-in-law." Not only must they not look at one another, but they might not speak. In an exceptional situation wherein communication became essential, a brief conversation might be carried on through a go-between, but this would indeed constitute an emergency. The effect of the prohibition was to reduce materially the chances of mother-in-law problems among the Sioux.

The bilateral nature of the Sioux kinship system involved the necessity of an especially strong sense of consanguine unity on the part of lineal and collateral family members. The lineal family of grandfather, father, and son, with their male blood brothers as collaterals, was the basis of the *tiyospe* and band organization. Here interactions could and must remain deepest, yet most spontaneous. Here true love and respect prevailed so that the relationships were less intensified by differences in generation or sex than were the affinial ones occasioned by marriage. In a sense, a lineal and collateral family might be thought of as a clan of males, who brought in women as instruments for maintaining the lineage, or conversely as a female tribe which acquired husbands to sire their children. But among the Sioux each sex, man and wife, carried equal weight in reckoning relationship, so that the system was bilaterally or equally balanced.

The differentiations based upon one's generation had their roots in the lineal family, and these patterns were transferred to affinial relationships. Interactions involving the different generations within the lineal and collateral family served as a factor for control by the older generations and accounted in part for the respect pattern. Thus fathers and mothers loved their children but commanded obedience. Grandparents and grandchildren reacted toward one another in a similar manner, yet because of the skip in their generations, the element of control was less intense.

The canon of respect, however, was markedly intensified between all lineal and collateral relatives through the principle of sex differentiation. Therefore, where an individual of the younger generation was related to two related individuals of the older generation, his treatment of them depended upon whether the senior individuals were of the same or different sexes. Thus uncles and nephews had less spontaneous interactions because of the uncle's strong respect behavior toward his sister—a sibling of the opposite sex, who was also his nephew's mother. Likewise, uncle-and-niece, aunt-and-nephew, and aunt-and-niece relationships were governed by this sexual demarcation.

When the two senior relatives were of the same sex, the member of the younger generation reacted toward them as they reacted toward each other, only exhibiting additional respect in deference to their generation. Thus a son reacted toward his father's brother as he reacted toward his father, without any extra show of respect due to the sex difference. The case was the same with a woman in relation to her mother's side.

Where there was no generational difference, lineal and collateral relatives—that is, brothers and sisters, parallel- and cross-cousins—showed patterns determined by sex difference combined with the slight feeling of distance shown between collateral relatives. Members of the same sex showed the strongest amount of affection with the least amount of constraint. Thus brothers were bound to one another as loyal friends, and sisters were devoted to one another in tender and open attachment. Members of the opposite sex showed the same strong affection but tempered it with a high degree of reserve and respect. Hence brothers and sisters maintained the strongest feelings of attachment, yet expressed their respect by not looking directly at one another or carrying on lengthy conversations. Because of their close relationship, they could not marry, and the respect pattern was an effective control.

Upon marriage, the spouse acquired an additional set of affinial relatives—his wife's people, in the case of a man; her husband's, in the case of a woman. These affinial relatives held a new place for the individual. They were strangers to be held at a distance. Interactions between individuals in this affinial relationship reached the two extremes of familiarity and respect—joking among brothers- and sisters-in-law, complete avoidance between children and parents-in-law. The terms used in addressing one another and the correct reaction patterns were transmutations from the lineal configuration and the generational differentiations.

Where there was a difference in generation between affinial relatives, respect became so pronounced as to become avoidance. Sons and fathers-in-law, daughters and mothers-in-law must take care to keep themselves at a distance, never to look directly at one another, and to avoid speaking. When affinial relatives differed in both generation and sex, respect was to be shown by the most pronounced form: complete avoidance.

When there was no generational difference between affinial relatives, then there was the most pronounced type of familiarity: joking. These affinial relatives—brothers- and sisters-in-law—seem to have presented a new problem which might have endangered the operation of the system, but by formalizing the natural pattern of reaction, the Sioux resolved the ambiguity of the relationship. Thus members of the same sex were placed in the category of siblings and cousins, which again limited the possibility of tension between two persons—husband and brother-in-law—both of whom were in dominant and close relationship with a common relative—the husband's wife and the brother-in-law's sister. To relieve any possible tensions, brothers-in-law must publicly exhibit their congeniality to ensure their continued, if not sometimes superficial, good will.

Members of the opposite sex, brothers- and sisters-in-law, also indulged in strong joking, the most pronounced form of familiarity aside from the connubial relationship. The practice of the levirate, which made it customary for a man to marry his deceased brother's wife, and the sororate, the practice of marrying a wife's sister, justified as well as intensified this joking relation-ship. Since affinial relatives of the opposite sex—brothers- and sis-ters-in-law—might well become spouses, joking decreased the ten-sion over possible premature or illicit sex relations on the one hand, and made for an easy transition, in the event of marriage, to a connubial relationship on the other.

The framework of kinship within which the Sioux patterned their interpersonal relationship imposed definite methods for as-suring group well-being. Security for the young was especially assured by the existence of a cohesive extended family. Children then became the responsibility of many people. For adults, too, this sense of belonging was not wanting, for the individual was rarely independent but rather a participating member of a team of close-knit relatives—part of a family with no beginning and no end. Home was not so much one's own lodge but rather one's village, and the *tiyospe*, the asssembled tipis of one's family, might be likened to an airy dwelling with many rooms. In addition to the intimacy of association which family life provided, the pat-terns of interaction, in being so definite as to be rigid, imposed cer-tain procedures which made for special conviviality as well as for studied formality. Here were codes of behavior devised to reduce tensions, and conversely, to promote harmony. By conforming to the etiquette, the individual could find an automatic sense of se-curity, wherein the need to choose was reduced to a minimum and the chance of social *faux pas* was equally minimized. Conse-quently, existence within such a formalized family system as the Sioux devised could only imply devotion of self to the welfare of others. Members were a cog in a wheel, working first in relation to the common good and secondly for themselves. There were obligations not only for parents and grandparents toward their children and grandchildren but for aunts and uncles toward their nieces and nephews. There were obligations for brother toward brother, sister toward sister—no individual was without responsi-bility. The success of the *tiyospe* was dependent upon the co-hesive functioning of its members, and the kinship system was ideally suited to implementing it.

The stylization of Sioux behavior suggests in what awe the people held social dissension. The Sioux had wrapped themselves with protective devices to meet almost every conceivable exigency—devices which appear so stultifying and restrictive that personal expression, in group relations, would seem to have been hampered to the point of constriction. It is true that the studied stoicism, the careful reaction in interpersonal affairs characterized the Sioux people's approach to life.

CHAPTER 6

The Sexes

MARRIAGE FOR THE SIOUX, as for so many peoples, was a complex of what might be termed an agreement between families and a concurrence between partners. In some instances, to be sure, parental agreement amounted to contrivance, but more frequently it became a matter of acceptance, primarily because the Sioux man actively courted the girl of his choice. When family opposition was strong, elopement invariably brought acquiescence. That the Sioux man was conditioned to consider woman as an adversary molded and colored the marriage pattern in some dramatic and rather heady ways. Premarital relations between the sexes, though by no means condoned by the family or parents, were nonetheless not uncommon. And to the young man who was successful went the commendation of his peers. Not only did this become a matter of conversation, but it was worthy to be counted as a coup upon his private, if not his public, record.

Nor was the attitude that premarital intercourse constituted an achievement a mere applause for antisocial behavior. Rather, it was a recognition of the very attributes which men should possess —in this case concerned with sex, in contrast to the hunt or war. Here was a form of subversive aggression which society feared, which families abhorred. Together they constructed rewards for chastity and defenses to ensure it—rewards and defenses of such stature and firmness that the young man who dared challenge the value placed upon feminine virtue was probably as calculatingly bold as he was impetuously amorous.

Virtue and chastity for women were more than mere prudery. The Sioux often discussed sex deviation and liberties in rather direct and ribald fashion, condemned transgressors publicly, and on occasion penalized them with social ostracism and physical disfigurement. They also set such a high standard for women that those who achieved it were accorded significant status and respect; in a sense they attained a goddess-like quality. And it is probably true that the boastful young man, confronted with the implications of this image, might well have subverted his physical and immediate ambitions to a long-term psychic and social gain.

It is possibly surprising, in light of the dual standard with respect to sex, that the Sioux failed to consider prostitution. But there is no evidence that it entered their lives—probably for several good reasons. In a war-directed society, men were at a premium, and conversely women were plentiful. In a close-knit society wherein the reputations of all women were known and ideally all were placed upon a pedestal, there was little opportunity for a man to attempt to satisfy secretly or consistently his sexual aggression without public disapproval. Finally, in a way of life where goods and horses were the only medium of exchange, there was no "money" in prostitution. And under such circumstances, even a mistress could not be maintained. The entire matter, however, for the Sioux, was not only unheard-of but unnecessary, for they could enjoy the complications of polygamy rather than the hollow despair of prostitution or the keeping of a mistress. Morever, divorce was a comparatively simple method of disposing of one woman for another.

Young people were prepared for marriage and family responsibilities at a rather early age. In addition to the instructions which children received in matters of personal hygiene, homemaking, and child care, opportunities for surreptitious observations of sexual matters were ever present when the family lived in a tipi. Even little people's games such as the Packing Game, First Love, and Elope involved playing as make-believe lovers and parents.

As children reached adolescence, parents advised their children about matters of sex and marriage. Ideally, instruction for girls assumed a very serious and pragmatic character. The attributes for a young woman to emulate, as explained by an old Sioux informant, required that "a good girl should remain single until she was well prepared for marriage. A girl who was respected was one who was taught by her mother quilling and beading and who said nothing to courters until she found the right man. Rather she sat around making leggings and when young men came to see her, she was silent."

While it fell upon the mother to instill these ideas by teaching and lengthy talk, were the girl to attain a respected position within the group, it was her brothers, referred to as *hakatakus*, who served as guardians, watching and protecting her from the advances of other men. A perfect girl was an asset, socially and economically; proud was the family who reared one. Blessed was the husband who married one.

"If some young man ran off with a girl but didn't marry her and she returned and then perhaps ran off again, such a girl we called Witkowin or 'Crazy Woman.' " According to one Sioux informant, "Witkowins died young, for some reason."

The ideal pattern was explained and upheld with lectures, undoubtedly coupled with some intimate and indeed personal advice by the older female members of the family, particularly if the older members were only a little older. Discussions, analyses, and interpretations of sex were common among young people, and probably consisted of as much fact as any such sessions ever do. The instruction, moreover, was complemented by such formalities as the Buffalo Ceremony and the Ball-throwing Rite, at which a shaman, enlisting the aid of the supernaturals, officiated, and which all people were invited to attend.

This was public announcement that one's daughter had reached womanhood, that she was now preparing for marriage, and that she was ready to be courted. At this coming-out party the girl was introduced in a manner which would do honor to her and justice to her family's social position. Here was an opportunity to display generosity in behalf of womanhood, and parents endeavored to make the most of it.

Ceremony and instruction in the proper behavior for young women were not considered sufficient of themselves to guarantee virtue and honor. In a system which recognized one role for women and another for men, the Sioux family was not so naïve as to leave matters entirely to the moral fortitude of a sweet young thing designed for mating, or solely to the gods, among whom the evil ones were ever present. The imponderables were too numerous to expose a girl's reputation to chance. The chastity belt resolved this problem; in lieu of a belt, the girl's legs were tied together at night. This device, of course, did not preclude the possibility of a clandestine affair with a man in the brush away from camp, but constant chaperonage by an older female relative, combined with the real danger of enemy ambush against anyone leaving the proximity of the camp, certainly limited the chance of a girl's losing her virginity in this way. Since young men were known to have rolled up the side of a tipi in order to sleep with a woman, and in the presence of her sleeping family to have been successful in coitus, the protective belt was as widely an accepted measure of security to the family as it was an annoyingly uncomfortable mechanism to the young wearers. There is no evidence that all girls were obliged to endure the discomfort of a chastity belt, for it is probable that some were of such stuff that their own principles adequately fortified them against masculine tempters. But the fact that the Sioux maintained the custom of strict chaperonage and resorted to the chastity belt is strong evidence that occurrences of premarital sex relations presented a dangerous threat to the ideal of feminine virtue and family honor.

That some individuals, rather than facing the consequences of having an illegitimate child, resorted to induced sterility or possibly to abortion is indicated by the following observation:

> Big Crow, a man who had dreamt of both the Buffalo and the Elk, gave girls medicine that would stop them from giving birth, but they could never have babies afterwards. Roan Horse's sister and a friend once ate some of his medicine just for fun. But Big Crow, whose medicine they stole, would not withdraw the power because he was angry. So neither girl ever had any children.

Courting for young people was a relatively stereotyped affair. A young man, wishing to meet and talk to a young woman, could follow the prescribed procedure of meeting the girl of his choice in front of the tipi. There he might enfold the girl in his robe, and together, with heads covered from view, they might converse privately in public. Such formal courting generally took place in the darkness of evening, yet a meeting before a tipi with families going and coming, curious children romping near by, or an ever-present chaperone at hand, was hardly conducive to gay companionship or intimacy. A popular girl might expect to have several young men awaiting their turn to embrace her beneath the robe, but a stag line of arduous young men could scarcely be confused with a quiet date. A girl might refuse the embrace of a man, or cut it short in favor of a more pleasing companion, so that while the courting custom gave the girl a certain control of the situation, it also protected her very well. This was the formal, dignified Sioux design for love-making—a most reserved, a most restricted kind of courtship. But this was the Sioux way.

Young people, in reality, had little opportunity for getting to know one another. Chance meetings, brief conversations, formal courting beneath the blanket were situations from which could develop only the most superficial sort of mutual understanding. What young people could learn of one another depended in large measure upon indirect information received from friends and conveyed by family confidants of the opposite sex. While such information could be reasonably accurate in a small community where everyone knew everyone else, courtship among members of the same band was perforce infrequent because of the close relationship and the consequent prohibition of affairs between family members. Only when many bands came together for the great summer conclaves or when several joined for the winter encampments did courtship flourish.

To succeed in winning a girl's heart, young men not only endeavored to make themselves attractive in grooming and dress but enlisted the aid of the gods. Brushed hair, plucked beard, perfumed grease, finely tanned robe, carefully quilled moccasins, white shell earrings—each became an element in masculine sex appeal. There were, of course, young men far more adept at presenting themselves favorably than others. The Sioux had their dandies and their louts. But no matter what advantage the fop might possess, or under what handicap the clod might function, each was careful to make use of the powers of the supernatural.

Shamans, skilled in preparing love potions, in making magical flutes, and in giving prescriptions for their proper use, found a source of income in abetting the sex drive. Medicine designed to give a young man power over young women was available from such men as the Elk and Buffalo Dreamers. Most efficacious was the flute. Such was the "Big Twisted Flute," a flageolet of cedar, decorated with the effigy of a horse, most ardent of all animal lovers. These were fashioned by able shaman-craftsmen who had dreamed of the Buffalo. The flute itself, however, was effective only when accompanied by the magical music of love. This music was composed by the shaman according to instructions received in a dream, and was conveyed as an essential part of the sale of a flute. Having mastered the music appropriate for love-making, a young man would play a magic tune to entice the girl of his choice. If properly executed, the music was irresistible. According to Leader Charge:

> Some flutes were so powerful that a girl, hearing the melody, would become so nervous that she would leave her tipi and follow it.
> Many flutes had such power that if a man should touch a woman with it, she became so entranced that she would go with her lover anywhere. Frequently he would escort her to the Shaman who made it. Here the Shaman would blow the smoke of herbs in the woman's face and give her medicine to revive her. When she realized where she was, she considered herself a married woman. Such a marriage was looked upon as an elopement.

For such marriages, a bride's price might or might not be paid, but a forward-looking young man usually arranged to give horses and gifts to the girl's family in order that he might be regarded as a reputable person.

Sioux marriages were generally planned, if not by the couple, then by their relatives. The degree of calculation might vary from

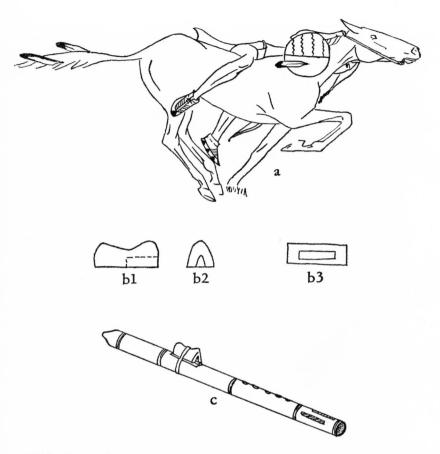

a, Rider in battle, "drawing out arrows." (See Chapter 4.) *b1*,
Cedar block, side view; *b2*, cedar block, front view; *b3*, cedar
block, lead cover; *c*, Big Twisted Flute. (See Chapter 6.)

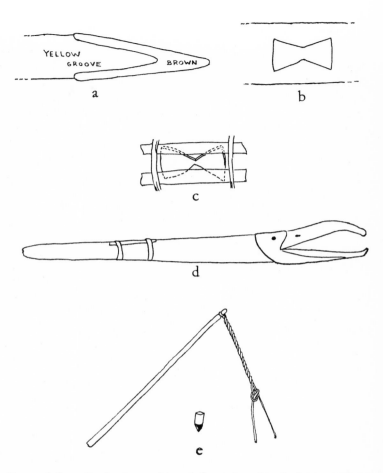

a, Base of flute beak; *b*, section of flute showing hole; *c*, split-feather reeds; *d*, Elk flute. (See Chapter 6.) *e*, Sticking Together Game. (See Chapter 7.)

a hasty rationalization by the lovers to a premeditated design by the parents. Even marriages made in a Sioux heaven had to be lived on a Sioux earth. Impetuous young lovers must, of necessity, have reckoned with the realities of rigorous social and economic factors, for there was no possible vacuum of social isolation or economic independence in which unapproved love could survive.

Contractural marriages—those arranged by parents—were the commonly accepted form. Although they may represent an early type, parentally planned marriages possibly began to give way to those by individual choice when the introduction of horses brought about greater mobility.

Lovers desiring to be married announced their intentions to their close relatives. In the happy event that their families were mutually agreed upon the propriety of the match, arrangements were immediately set in motion. The formal proposal was carried by a close friend or a brother of the boy, properly to the girl's brother or to some male standing in a similarly close relationship to her. It was between these young men that the details of the bride-price were determined, and it was the girl's male relatives, the *hakatakus*, to whom the fee was paid. It was understood that the greater the young woman's social position, the higher the price—a value that might range from one to many horses.

As an example of a proper marriage, Iron Shell related the following rather timeless incident:

> There was this young man who wished to marry a girl. He went over and talked to her several times asking her to run off with him, but she refused. Finally, he asked her if there was any possible way that he might marry her. She told him to go home and tell his family to make a feast and that she would ask her parents.
>
> So the young man went home and told his people, urging them that they must give a feast if he were to win the girl. His family agreed and took several fine horses over to her Hakataku, and then they took clothes to the girl.
>
> When the day of the feast came, the Hakataku put the girl on one of the saddle horses the boy's parents had given them and led her over to the tipi of her bridegroom's parents. Many people came to

the feast, but there was no speech. This form of marriage is known as "Wiyan he cinacaqupi." "He wanted that girl, so they gave her to him."

With her new tipi pitched at a close but respectful distance from the home of her parents-in-law, the bride was ready to set up housekeeping. A honeymoon would have been impossible in light of the ever-constant warfare; it would also have been considered a childish confusion of marriage with elopement. As a wife, the bride now became a contributing member of her husband's family, a new and important asset to the common weal. She would learn to work closely with her husband's sisters and female relatives, and to banter with her brother-in-law. Her relationship with his mother would be warm yet reserved, while with his father she would exhibit a silent and uncommunicative respect due his generation and sex. Overnight the Sioux attempted to transform the bride from a wistfully enchanting Buffalo Woman to a responsible, mature, and dignified matron.

For those brides who joined their own parents' camp—and this was quite possible in Sioux society—the matter of adjustment to marriage was more simple. In-laws were not a problem to be reckoned with. All a bride had confronting her were the chores of cooking, fire-keeping, bed-making, house-cleaning, entertaining guests, and attending to the whims of a relatively strange man called a husband. Willingness on the part of women to carry out these duties went far to making a marriage successful, and a successful marriage among the Sioux was accorded high and enviable honor. Thus, the marriage partners enjoyed not only the private gratifications of wholesome companionship but all the approbation of their fellow men.

The truth of this is suggested partly by the premium placed upon successful marriage and more spectacularly by the utter ease of divorce. Divorce was so simple that all a man needed to do was publicly to "beat the drum" and announce that he had thrown away his woman. This was not a matter of disavowing his wife, for no vows were involved. Marriage was not sanctified, but rather it was an agreement of the moment, a bargain to which both parties paid a set price for a commodity "as is." If the marriage worked, it worked because it was mutually satisfactory to the partners and their families; if it failed, it was the partners' affair and the family must needs adjust. But this family adjustment was by nature not a catastrophe simply because the sustaining element of Sioux society was the family itself, not the conjugal relationship of man and wife. When a marriage worked, the Sioux were quick to bestow high honor and acclaim: when it failed, they were compassionate enough to withhold condemnation.

The causes of divorce were obvious and simple: laziness and infidelity. As Leader Charge explained it:

> If a man has a very lazy wife, he will wait until his Akicita society has a dance. Here he will ask for a drum stick and hitting the drum once, he will announce, "Whoever wants her can have her, come get her, I don't want her any more." Often in her jealousy, a wife so divorced will try to stab her husband. If she cannot do this, she will go to the place he keeps his horses and stab his favorite one.
>
> If a man has a wife who is unfaithful, he will order her to take the tipi down and get out. Then he will take his belongings to his parents and she will go to hers. Women so divorced become witkowin, crazy women who are morally wild.

Women, too, might divorce men:

> Sometimes men leave their families to go around with other women, until their wives finally leave. They always argue as to who should have the custody of the children, but if one is nursing an infant, they can't take that one from her. The women usually get the children.

Divorce constituted only one escape from incompatibility. It was, in essence, a forewarning of the disintegration of the Sioux family system. Divorce was intended to eliminate conflict in the hope of securing community well-being. As if to neutralize the potential insidiousness of divorce in a society fostering the dual standard for the sexes, the Sioux permitted a man to have more than one wife at a time. Rather than disregarding the masculine desire to possess not one but several women, the Sioux took advantage of it. Polygamy was recognized as an acceptable adjustment for those men whose desire was not satisfied by a single spouse. And as such, this acceptance reduced one of the incipient causes of divorce, since the "other woman" was placed in the positive role of "another woman."

"A man could marry any number of women—it mattered only if he could support them. Some women could be bought cheaply; for others one had to pay a great deal."

A man might marry as many as six wives, although this was unusual since the matter of supporting this many wives, in two or more tipis, created, if nothing else, a discouragingly heavy economic responsibility. Men desiring plural marriage generally contented themselves with two wives, frequently marrying a younger sister of their first mate.

Polygamy for the Sioux in no way implied a lower status for women or inferred any jeopardy of their rights. In many instances it was the woman who suggested that her husband take a younger wife, realizing that this would relieve her of some of the housekeeping burdens while giving her added status as the senior spouse of a well-to-do man. For it was common knowledge that only the wealthy could afford more than one wife.

The sororate, wherein men married sisters, had the advantage of bringing together in a connubial family two women who were bound together by lineal ties as well as by early and close friendships. Moreover, it reinforced the consanguine family. Here the influence of the woman's branch literally outweighed that of her husband's, and in those cases where the residence was established matrilocally, the cohesive character of the females' family-band was intensified. Plural marriage in such a setting meant to the family the addition of a responsible, able-bodied male, the proper and fitting role of the brother-in-law.

Polygamy appears to have been expected, though not obligatory, only in one situation. At the death of one's brother, a man was counted upon to marry his widow. In those cases where the living brother was already married or where the deceased had been polygamously married, thus leaving more than one widow, plural marriage became inevitable. It would be unreasonable to believe that every man jumped at the opportunity of marrying his brother's widow; probably many men dreaded the thought of outliving their brothers. Actually, while the levirate was practiced, it probably functioned only upon mutual agreement and was not a binding responsibility.

Of particular concern to the Sioux with regard to sex was the male transvestite whom they called *"winkte."* While the *winkte* was not abhorred, he was surely feared. Here were males who, unable to compete as men in the rigorous hunting and war system, found escape by adopting the female role. Dressed as women, and following the feminine pursuits of tanning and quilling, they lived in their own tipis at the edge of the camp circle—the area relegated to ancient widows and orphans.

That the Sioux were so forthright in the handling of their transvestites speaks well for their awareness of the problem. *Winktes,* though accorded a place in Sioux society, were marked by a kind of ostracism. In wearing women's clothes, they became an object of disdain, for in the councils of men, to be referred to as having the "heart of a woman" was the height of derision. *Winktes* not only possessed women's hearts but dressed and acted as women. Nevertheless, the homosexual held his own, if not with honor at least with sufferance.

Homosexuality among the Sioux is in part ascribable to the extreme demands placed upon males to compete successfully. But this in itself is not sufficient reason, for it follows that either the majority of men would have rebelled against the demands, and the demands would have been modified, or improbably the reverse: that a majority of men would have turned to *winktes.* Rather, the role of the *winkte* suggests that certain Sioux boys were victims either of actual biological homosexuality or of parental overprotection. In a warring society which well might deprive children of their fathers through premature death, and which undoubtedly brought heartbreak and loneliness to many a wife, it would only be natural that some mothers would endeavor to protect their young sons from what might be considered the senseless dangers of aggressive warfare. Even the games which boys played were excessively rough and brutal. Designed to steel them to the conditions of battle, the games also must have rather definitely separated the brave boys from the sissies. There can be little question that the Sioux had their mama's boys; the system was a natural for producing them. That some of the more sensitive, the more determined, and/or the more perverted eventually became *winktes* is then quite understandable.

Parental fear that one's son might become involved with perversion is evident in the warning which Iron Shell gave his son:

> My father told me the way to go and what to do until I was married—among these things was to leave the winktes alone. A winkte is a man who dreams that by living as a woman, he will live a long life. This he may dream when he is a young boy, but later when he becomes a man, he will come out one day with a dress. Then he will do woman's work and live like a woman. These men are good shamans and go about calling one another sister. Each has his own tipi, for after men have had sexual relations with them, their parents put up a tipi for them. If a man goes to a winkte and treats him as you would a woman, something serious will befall him. When the winkte dies, and after you have died, you will regret your relationship, for you will suffer when you reach the land beyond. Here you will not live in the main circle, but away with the murderers suffering, for here the winktes will torture you.

The degree of perversion was unquestionably a variable one since some men must have associated with bona fide *winktes* without themselves becoming one. Even for such individuals, the censure was great.

Since the true transvestite was accorded his sanction through having received instruction in a dream, the *winkte* was recognized as Wakan. He might have certain curative powers; certainly his right to grant private or secret names to children was conceived as a supernatural prerogative.

Blue Whirlwind commented:

> There is a belief that if a winkte is asked to name a child, the child

will grow up without sickness. My grandson was given the name
Iron Horse when he was three days old by a winkte, and I gave
him a horse.

Fathers will go to the winkte and flirt with him. Whatever the
winkte says will become the secret name and this he will name the
child. Winkte names are often unmentionable and therefore are
not often used. Girls never had winkte names.

Winktes possessed ability to tan and quill, possibly supernaturally inspired, and it was generally conceded that they excelled
women in this work. Pieces produced by them were highly desirable, entirely marketable, and frequently cherished as master-
pieces.

The role and status of the *winkte* suggests an ambivalent attitude on the part of the Sioux. The *winkte* was held in awesome
respect on the one hand and in disdainful fear on the other. Conceivably, the attitude may have represented an antagonistically
aggressive reaction by the average male because of his own unrequited heterosexual urges.

Lesbianism seems to have played a much less obvious part in
the life of the Sioux. Certain dream instructions given to young
women—in particular, the Double Woman's Appearance—hint at
a kind of sanction for female perversion. Rattling Blanket Woman,
for example, underwent a true choice situation during her dream
experience, and selected, albeit unwittingly, the role of wife and
mother in opposition to a career of professional craftsmanship and
suggested spinsterhood. And yet there exists no record of old
maids among the Sioux. Furthermore, there seem to be no examples of female inversion, and the role of women within the
society appears to obviate the development of any meaningful
causes.

If Sioux men considered women as adversaries, as foes to be
conquered and quelled, Sioux women were no less straightforward
in their opinion of men as dangerous predators. This innate hostility assumed several overt forms, yet it was generally sublimated
for the smooth functioning of the group.

Male and female conflict was expressed clearly in the young

men's reckoning of coup for accomplishing coitus and, contrari-wise, in the young women's resorting to the use of the chastity belt. A husband's hostility toward an unfaithful wife was sadis-tically exhibited by his right to cut off the tip of her nose. Such a disfigurement not only marked his wrath upon her for life and surely reduced her attractiveness to other men, but it made per-manently public the male's position of dominance and authority.

That such dramatic signs of conflict should have existed sug-gests an innate distrust between the sexes for which both were undoubtedly accountable. One's expression of this distrust was found in public gatherings. Although quite probably for such alleged reasons as conviviality, men and women literally sat in opposing areas. Wives did not join their husbands; brothers, their sisters; or boys, their sweethearts. All the men met in one camp, as it were; all the women, in another.

If a dance were given, the men danced or the women danced. In those instances where the participation of both sexes was re-quired, the sexes danced in separate areas, either one on one side and the other on the other, or they formed two distinct lines, one of women, the other of men. Only in the Night Dance, an occasion for formal courting, did men and women join as partners. When food was served, the men ate first, followed by the women and children. Even in the comparative privacy of one's tipi, the woman waited upon the man and ate only after he had finished.

That women were inherently dangerous was further exempli-fied by the dread in which they were held by men during the menstrual periods. At such times women moved to tiny segrega-tion huts away from the tipi. There they were brought food and water, generally by female companions, and there they remained until menstruation ceased. It was during such times that sacred objects and men's war paraphernalia were especially subject to contamination, so that they took the precaution of moving the women a safe distance away. Women, even under normal physi-cal conditions, were a sufficiently corrupting influence that for them to touch a man's medicine or equipment was to defile it. Likewise, success in major undertakings—whether seeking a vision, performing a ceremony, or going on the warpath—required a period of abstinence from intercourse with one's wife, generally for a preceding period of four days.

This male and female hostility appears to find its roots in an unresolved masculine fear. That Sioux men, as did men among other groups, should believe women to have been potentially dangerous is understandable; but that they should have conceived women to possess the power to destroy through defilement the very objects upon which their own achievements and the masculinity of their role were dependent indicates how deep-seated was their fear. Whatever were the circumstances which led to the male attitude toward women, they must have been traumatic enough that there was crystallized a premise which both sexes unquestionably accepted. It could be that fear grew from the very real enervation concomitant with being in love and from the physical weakening consequent upon sustained sexual intercourse. This latter could readily be a frightening factor to a people whose existence rested in large measure upon the superior physical alertness of its males.

Sioux men, having conceded that their women were to be feared, were themselves victims of a rationalization in thinking of the females as defilers. The pattern suggests a kind of masochism through self-denial. It is doubtful that the Sioux women would have imposed upon themselves the unpleasantness of isolation in a miserable hut, or the notion that as a sex they were contaminators. Yet whatever its origins, the concept was accepted by both sexes, and it created a conflict which permeated all relationships in the Sioux system.

In the dual standard under which the Sioux operated, it would appear that it was the women who experienced the rewards of self-denial. The vigilance of the chaperon and the discomfort of the chastity belt are evidence of the culturally imposed denial which was considered essential for the girl's well-being. Ostracism to an outside hut during menstrual periods could hardly be thought of as delightfully self-expressive or ego-inspiring, and the loss of one's nose for a transgression of the sexual code must have imposed a rather horrifying disfigurement both physically and psychologically. In fact, the dual pattern would seem to have been designed to guarantee a selflessness among women as a means of building male ego. For if the women were easy victims, the men were selfish bullies. Yet it may be that the hostility which men held for females was symptomatic of a deep-seated resentment toward females because of either their inability or their unwillingness to fully satisfy the male sexual urge. Men may have felt justified in sadistically imposing a pattern of self-denial on women which would compare to the sacrifices demanded by their own role. Naturally, neither of these possible causative factors were recognized by the Sioux, but they do represent the stuff of which men endeavor to maintain an equilibrium—often in a bizarre fashion and at a high cost. Here the balance of self-against-self was weighed between male and female in what would seem a difficult and a not-too-happy situation.

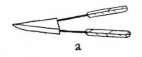

a

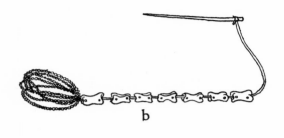

b

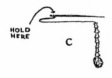

HOLD
HERE

c

HOLD
HERE

d

a, *Hotana cute*; *b*, Using Hoofs; *c*, Shoot for the Side; *d*, Whirl
and Shoot. (See Chapter 7.)

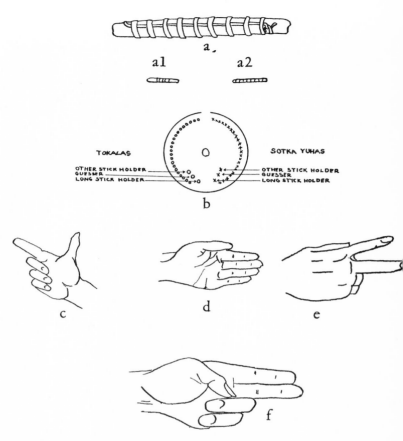

Moccasin Guessing Game: *a*, guessing stick; *a1*, Tokala stick; *a2*, Sotka Yuha stick; *b*, diagram of Moccasin Guessing Game between Tokalas and Sotka Yuhas; *c*, both outside hands; *d*, both center hands; *e*, outside of one hand, inside of other—or both left hands; *f*, outside of one hand, inside of other—or both right hands. (See Chapter 7.)

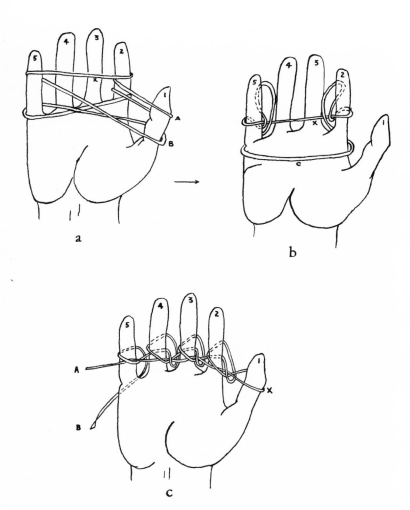

Cat's Cradles: *a*, remove A and B. Put 3 and 4 through resulting opening or ABX; *b*, pull C; *c*, lift X from 1. Pull A. (See Chapter 7.)

CHAPTER 7 / *Fun*

GAMES FOR THE SIOUX frequently were contrived life-situations in miniature. They ran the gamut from the more complex diversion of the Moccasin Game enjoyed by adults to the raucously rough Swing-kicking Game played by young boys. Fun and sport in the most lusty sense were the byword of these people, and as if the game were not enough, they added wagers with high stakes to intensify the sport. The Sioux were thoroughgoing gamblers, and scarcely a game was played without bets.

There were games for children, sports for young men and women, and pastimes for adults. There were winter games and summer games, there were little games for twosomes, and great contests for teams. The diversity was extraordinary.

Children's winter games included ice-sliding, where the boy who slid farthest might win a wooden top; or the Sticking-together Game, where boys and girls whipped their tops on the ice and forced them together to see which would outbump and outspin the other. There was sledding on bowed buffalo ribs, and in very cold weather, sheets of rawhide were used. There was Throwing It In, played along a bank at the edge of the ice. In a little semicircle were made five holes into which tops might drop. Two boys, whipping the tops toward the holes, gave the final lashes from a distance of about six feet. If the top went into the center hole, the game was won. However, if a boy made any one hole and his opponent none, this also counted as a win. Some boys became so skillful that they could hit almost any hole which they aimed for. The winner received a top each time he won, and the game could continue until one of the boys exhausted his supply of tops. Sometimes darkness overtook the contestants so they would *"kiganakapi"* or "postpone the finish" until some later time.

Hotana cute, another game, required a carved triangular rib bone to which were attached two straight gooseberry sticks tipped with a bird's tail feather. Equipped with these tiny winged sleds, men would challenge one another to see who could bounce theirs from the ice to make it glide the greatest distance. This took much practice, and boys waited until achieving finesse before attempting wagers. It was also considered helpful to *"wageumasakti the Hotana cute,"* or "get it in condition so that it would soar."

The Buffalo Horn Game, using a short feathered stick tipped with the end of a buffalo horn, and the Sliding Wood Game, employing a four-to- six-foot shaft hurled somewhat in the manner of a javelin, were played under much the same rules as *Hotana cute*.

Team games for boys were of a rough-and-ready nature, designed to offer excitement and fun as well as to encourage toughness and physical endurance. The Fire-throwing Game was one such sport. Teams of boys would prepare piles of brush, placing them about fifty yards apart. After lighting the brush, each boy would pick out several flaming sticks and advance upon the opposing team with the object of surrounding its fiery stronghold. Attacking in close formation helped prevent teammates from striking one another, though each party might hurl the sparkling brands at the other. If neither team should retreat, but meet in the center, they would strike at one another amidst smoke and sparks. A veteran of many fire-throwing games once explained: "In close fighting after you have hit an enemy two or three times, your torch goes out. Then you get your share until his stick dies out."

"Throw at Each Other with Mud" was a slightly more gentle spring pastime where teams of boys attacked with mud balls which they threw from the tips of short springy sticks. Each boy carried several sticks and an arsenal of mud as he advanced. "It certainly hurt when you got hit, so you must duck and throw as you attack." Sometimes live coals were imbedded in the mud balls to add zest to the game.

The Buffalo-Hunt Game made no claim to gentleness but required dexterity as well as fortitude. "Here a boy was chosen who was brave and could stand a lot of collisions." He was supplied with a five-foot stick, to which was attached a large cactus leaf from which the center had been cut to represent the buffalo's heart. As the "buffalo" walked about holding his green, prickly heart before him, the hunters tried to pierce the heart with their bows and arrows:

If the hunters missed, he chased them a little with the cactus, but if an arrow went through the heart, he chased the hunter until he poked him with the cactus, and then off to stick another. The place to strike was on the buttocks; some boys grunted, but others hollered. When the buffalo tired, the game was over. But since some of the needles were deeply penetrated, there were always quite a few boys who stayed awhile picking out thorns. Little fellows would often back out when they saw that a fast running buffalo was to come up.

The Swing-kicking Game took first place as a rugged conditioner, and there was no pretense at horseplay. Here two rows of boys faced each other, each holding his robe over his left arm. The game was begun only after the formality of the stock question, "Shall we grab them by the hair and knee them in the face until they bleed?" Then using their robes as a shield, they all kicked at their opponents, endeavoring to upset them. There seem to have been no rules, for the boys attacked whoever was closest, often two boys jumping one. Kicking from behind the knees was a good way of throwing an opponent, and once down he was grabbed at the temples with both hands and kneed in the face.

Once released, the bloody victims would fight on, kicking and kneeing and bleeding until they could fight no longer. The game was over when one side retreated or someone yelled "Let us stop."

As Iron Shell explained, "Some boys got badly hurt, but afterwards we would talk and laugh about it. Very seldom did any fellow get angry."

During the winter, girls and young women enjoyed a variant of tenpins called "Doing the Sliding." Here two opponents, seated on bunches of willow, faced one another on the ice about fourteen feet apart. Behind each player were collected such stakes as porcupine quills, earrings, or necklaces. In front of each player was stood a little red stick called "smoking." Then with a ball made from pipestone or granite, no larger than a prairie chicken's egg, each took her turn trying to hit the opponent's "smoke." If the first player missed, she must forfeit one of her stakes; if she hit, she received another free turn. After five turns, her opponent tried her skill, and this continued until one or the other had lost all her stakes.

Women also played a variation of the Sliding-Wood Game, while teen-age girls, when they could entice a victim, had fun at Throwing One Up Like a Ball. For this prank four girls would grab the corners of a robe and then ask a little boy to come play with them, requesting him to stand in the center of the robe. When the girls jerked the corners over their heads, the child was thrown high in the air, and when they pulled the robe from side to side, he was rolled and tossed about relentlessly. Most frequently, the boy's G string broke and his breechcloth fell off. Then with a final throw, the girls left him and everyone laughed at his misfortune. "Many times the boys were pretty embarrassed, since nearly every time their G strings broke or came undone. Some little boys would never do it again, and those that did wore two G strings. Sometimes boys wouldn't look at the girls after this."

One of the most enticing games for women was Shooting Dice with a Basket. For this, a small basket woven of willow shoots or sometimes of shredded cattail leaves, measuring eight inches in diameter and six inches in depth, was commonly used to toss the dice. The dice were three pairs of plum seeds: one pair contained the image of a buffalo, the second pair had a swallow, while the third pair was painted black.

Scoring was reckoned by the combinations of dice. Should the pair of buffalo turn up combined with the reverse side of the remaining four dice, this counted ten points. Should all reverse sides turn up, the player won thirty-two sticks and all the stakes. The variety of combinations offered a complex of scoring so that Shooting Dice with a Basket was a delight to play.

Young men played Knocking the Ball or shinny, generally in the spring. These games were often occasions for much excitement and much betting for the entire encampment. Sides were selected—often the north side against the south—and representatives of the initiating side called "Those who tie things together as they go" rode first to the opposing side to collect the stakes. When the representatives had returned to their own side, those who wished to bet looked over the collection of roaches, jewelry, and clothing and, seeing something that they wished, tied their bet to it. The riders determined whether or not the stakes were of equal value. When all the bets were matched, someone was chosen to watch over them while they were stored in the meeting lodge.

Now the players prepared themselves, stripping off their robes and leggings, unbraiding their hair, and painting their faces. The goals were two tipis at the opposite sides of the camp. The south team tried to strike the north tipi with the ball; the north team attacked the south tipi. Standing in the center of the camp circle, each man with a bent ash shinny stick, the teams waited for the referee to throw up among them a small leather ball.

The rules required that no one might touch the ball with his hands, but it was permissible to kick it. There were no boundaries, so the game was often played far afield in the hope of wearing out the opponents. Passing the ball to teammates was customary, and often several lined up near the goal to win a point. After one team "hit the tipi," all would yell and cheer while the ball was returned to the center of the circle for the next running. At the close of each point, the teams exchanged goals. Games were won by the team scoring two out of three points. After the game, those on the winning team who had wagered went to the meeting lodge and picked up what they had bet together with the article tied to it.

Women played shinny under the same rules as men, except that they used longer sticks which they held in both hands. If one hit a picket pin on the tipi goal, her team was forthwith declared the winner of the game. In choosing sides, neither men nor women seemed concerned about equality of numbers—skill and team-work appear to have been more important than mere mass.

A pastime enjoyed by young and old of both sexes—in fact one of the few games played by men and women together—was Using Hoofs, a real test of dexterity. Six metatarsal bones of a deer, each with four holes at the side and equipped with loops of beads, were strung on a deerskin string knotted at one end, fastened to a bone or wooden pin at the other. The object was to swing the bones in prescribed sequence upon the pin.

When a team of women challenged a team of men, they would kneel on opposite sides of a tipi, each side holding ten sticks to-gether with the objects they intended to wager. The man chosen to begin knelt before his men with the pin pointing toward the women's side. His task was to swing the bones up and pierce the first one with the pin. For accomplishing this he won one stick from the opponents. If he pierced it again, he won another stick, and if he stabbed the hole at the side of the bone, he won all ten counters. When he had won ten sticks, his female opponent had to purchase them back from him with some object she had brought as her wager. When the man missed, he threw the game to his opponent and she tried to make the first bone. Generally the game seesawed back and forth until one side had lost its ten sticks and had to buy them back again.

Next, they might agree to Shoot for the Side, and after shoring the string, they attempted to pin one of the remaining five bones, receiving a point for any one which they pierced, and ten points for side holes. When this obstacle had gone the rounds, they would Shoot for the Katydid—the little bug that tells you that buffalo are near by singing *ptewoyoka*—the number-six bone. Finally, they would Shoot for the Loop, and if one was successful in running it through one string of beads, he got two sticks, if all five loops, he got ten.

Other variations included Whirl and Shoot and Shoot without Holding. When these had been mastered, the entire sequence might be repeated, this time with the left hand. And it was understood that left-handers would now use the right hand.

Most popular during the long winter nights was the Moccasin Game played between teams of young men, often chosen from among the Akicita societies. A match played between the Tokalas and Sotka Yuhas typified the contest:

On one side of the meeting tipi sat the Tokalas, on the other the Sotkas. Some one was selected to collect the bets from the Sotkas, which were then displayed to the members of the opposing team who then selected the article they wished by tying it to their own wager. Then the pairs of articles were placed in a pile at the rear of the tipi.

The Sotkas were attended by four singers as were the Tokalas, each with a hand drum. The Sotka chosen to play first, a brave warrior, was given a stick wrapped with red buckskin and small enough to be concealed in the hand. These little sticks were made by Dreamers to be invisible. When the warrior stood in front of his team, the Sotka drummers sang a short song while he danced. At the end of the song, he told of his exploits and then, turning, selected one of his teammates to serve as the guesser. In addition to the guesser, each team had a keeper of seven long sticks to be used as tallies.

Kneeling before their team, the warrior and guesser now faced the Tokala's guesser and warrior. The Sotka warrior then shuffled a little stick between his hands hidden beneath his robe, then thrust them out with a waving motion with forefinger pointing toward his opponents as the other fingers hid the stick. All the while the drummers sang a song, slowly as he shuffled the stick but with increased tempo just as he extended his arms. The Tokala guesser watched his opponent intensely and with a sign indicated in which of the warrior's hands the little stick was hidden. The Tokala guesser then rose and took the little stick from the Sotka as well as one tally stick from the keeper.

By guessing correctly, the Tokalas had won the preliminary round and were now entitled to be first to have a pair of men as hiders of the stick. The Tokala guesser consequently selected two of his members, each with one little stick, to kneel before the Sotka's guesser while he himself retired.

The Tokala drummers now began to sing and then with a sharp increase in tempo, the Tokala hiders drew out their arms, waving them in all directions, while the Sotka guesser carefully watched. With all the fingers of his right hand extended, he then pointed at the Tokalas, to indicate that the hidden sticks were in the outside hands of his opponents. This was incorrect, since both were in the center hands, with the result the Sotkas lost two tally sticks. Properly he should have made a slicing motion to indicate their hiding place.

Again the Tokalas hid their sticks, the singers chanted, the arms began to wave, and the guesser signalled his choice of the right hands by extending the first and second fingers of his left hand toward his opponents. This was correct and the Sotkas won one tally stick and the right to hide the sticks. Missing a guess cost two tallies, winning a guess won only one. The next pair of Sotka hiders of the stick included a man of exemplary skill who was able magically to throw the hidden stick from one hand to the other, thereby, completely confounding the Tokala guesser. So successful was the powerful Sotka that the Tokalas lost many sticks and finally replaced their guesser with a man of more insight, who luckily outguessed the Sotka star.

And so the game continued, each team rotating guessers and hiders until suddenly a Tokala guesser, renowned for his power and insight, removed one of his moccasins and began beating it upon the ground. As the Sotka hiders of the stick were waving their arms and attempting to magically shoot the stick unseen from one hand to the other, the Tokala guesser mysteriously stole one of the little sticks. The Sotka hiders were dumbfounded, for they could not imagine where their stick had gone. But then with a guttural clearing of his throat, the Tokala guesser triumphantly drew from his moccasin the missing piece, which he casually threw back to the Sotkas. The game was automatically a victory for the Tokalas, who congratulated their champion and picked up their winnings.

The number of Sioux games was manifold. Marksmanship contests such as Shot at Bound Grass played on horseback or See Who Shoots the Farthest were games of skill which boys played continuously. Little children played at moving camp and house-keeping, using tiny tipis and horses fashioned from dried mud, or follow-the-leader in a little game called "Kick My Tail Off." Girls and women experimented with a variety of cat's cradles or string figures, while boys made out of box elder popguns which shot wads of chewed ash bark. These were considered excellent weapons in sham battle. Men enjoyed the Rawhide Hoop Game, trying to pierce a rolling hoop with five-foot spears; this was also called the "Rolling Game."

There were many variations in scoring the more complicated pastimes such as the Moccasin Game. In general, by awarding only half the number of points for winning or beating an opponent and thereby doubling the points for defeating him, skill was expected while ineptitude was heavily penalized.

In wagering, winners took all, and among adults, stakes might include such valuable articles as horses, or such important possessions as wives. Betting was more than an addition of spice to amusement; it was part and parcel of the fun.[1]

If the games were miniature life situations, they were also means of self-assertion within prescribed situations. Aggression against one's associates could be expressed without harming group solidarity. Games were thus a culturally acceptable device for taming aggression, and had the additional value of teaching physical dexterity and mental alertness. That the Sioux played for stakes—and for such high stakes—indicates the intensity of the conflict between self-expression and self-denial. Here the successfully assertive individual took all, the loser forfeited all. The arms of the scale were far apart, and the degree of balance was great indeed. It was as if the Sioux desired to live either in highest exultation or in lowest despondency.

Jokes, too, were part of Sioux fun. Old men whiling away their

---

[1] Stewart Culin, "Games of the North American Indians," Bureau of American Ethnology *Annual Report* (1907). The author has compiled a valuable collection of American Indian games in which many Sioux games are described.

time in the Red Council Lodge amused themselves with stories of pranksters and fools.

There was the young man who had dreamt he must act contrariwise—a Heyoka—who wore only a buffalo tail tied over his shoulder and a worn out tipi top as a robe. In the bitterness of a winter night, he made his way barefooted through the snow to his grandmother's for lodging. He slept uncovered and shivering at first, while his grandmother tended the fire trying to warm him. As the wood supply was growing lower and the old woman became more and more fatigued, she finally said, "Grandson, I can't stand this any longer, take this heavy robe to warm yourself." But because of his perversity, he became even colder under the winter robe and by morning the supply of wood was exhausted. This man became known as "Cold Clown."

There was another Heyoka named Running Horse whose sister owned a pair of earrings made from the white curved shells of dentalium. Dentalium shells had only recently been introduced among the people and were considered highly valuable. "Sister, I have just come from the encampment up the river and saw some straight dentalium. You ought to have yours straightened too." In order to be fashionable the sister agreed. He then removed her earrings and placing them on a flat piece of wood, tried to straighten them with a granite cherry pounder. But since all dentalium shells are naturally brittle as they are curved, each one was broken until the earrings were ruined. From this time on Running Horse was known as "Shell Straightener."

Later, Shell Straightener's sister proudly made a pair of handsome red moccasins to honor her brother. When he next appeared, she said to him "Hohan," "wear them." It was an extremely hot afternoon, but when he returned to his tipi, he immediately built a large fire. Then he put his new moccasins in the fire, and waiting with a stick, poked them now and then. His mother happened to drop by and seeing the blazing fire asked him what on earth he was doing. "Oh," he replied, "Sister gave me these fine moccasins and told me to "Wohan," "Cook them." Whereupon his mother became very angry telling him he knew less than nothing.

Once Shell Straightener was chasing buffalo in the company of his father, who seeing his son was not yet prepared to shoot yelled at him, "You better take off your robe to shoot at it." Immediately Shell Straightener reined in his horse, and as the buffalo escaped, he dismounted and laying his robe on the ground shot it full of holes.

Rattling Blanket Woman related an amusing incident about the time when early one morning a herd of buffalo ran into camp:

> Everyone got their bows and jumped upon their horses. One man was late in rising, yet he too climbed into his clothes and mounted his horse. As he caught up with the herd and began to shoot, he noticed his sleeves kept catching in the bow string. He turned to look, only to find he was wearing his wife's dress and that the bulge was high in the air over his back. And everyone laughed. When he reached home he took off that dress and hit his wife with the bulge.

The repertoire included dozens of such tales.[2] Everyone enjoyed their telling, for this was Sioux humor—limited almost entirely to the simplest of punning and rather harmless contrariness. There were no riddles, no complex situations, no mistaken identities—rather, the most elemental sort of wit.

Traditions, too, were an integral part of Sioux storytelling. Never concerned with chronological accuracy, the Indians related in legendary form past events of interest and importance. Storytelling was a seasonal avocation, essentially reserved for the long winter nights. The nomadic tempo of Sioux life came to a halt during the mid-winter when the people settled in semipermanent villages among the protected wooded stream bottoms. Major hunting expeditions and large-scale camp movements were impractical in the cold season. Well supplied with provisions obtained from the great autumn hunt, the Sioux could then relax. This was a time of leisure.

The stories which old people told around the fire before bed-

---

[2] Ella Deloria, "Dakota Texts," American Ethnological Society *Publications*, Vol. XIV (1932). J. R. Walker, "The Sun Dance and Other Ceremonies of the Ogalala Division of the Teton Dakota," American Museum of Natural History *Anthropological Papers*, Vol. XVI, Pt. 2 (1917); Clark Wissler, "The Whirlwind and the Elk in the Mythology of the Dakota," *Journal of American Folk-Lore*, Vol. XVIII (1905). The foregoing authors have recorded many myths and tales in the Sioux repertoire.

time were generally anecdotal, and when related, they were frequently qualified by such phrases as "It is said" or "They say."
Brings the Buffalo Girl told the story of "The Woman Who Lived with the Wolves":

There was a young woman who fought with her husband and ran away. It was winter, but she walked out upon the plains without stopping. After about two days she had consumed all the food she had brought, but since she wanted no one to find her, she continued, tired and very weak as she was.

Finally, as darkness approached, she came to a hill. This she climbed so that no one would look for her there. When she reached the top she discovered a cave. She crawled in, but she was so tired she could not go to sleep. At last she dozed, but later awoke. She felt warmer now and as she put her hand out, she felt something soft and furry. However, she was very tired and went back to sleep.

Early in the morning she awoke, and found herself among a den of wolves. There were several wolves and one which was very large spoke to her saying, "Don't be afraid, we are your friends. We will not harm you." Then she knew she was safe.

She told the wolves how hungry she was and the great wolf again spoke, telling her that they would bring her food. Then the wolves left the cave and soon they returned bringing with them a piece of fresh deer meat. This she ate raw for she was so hungry.

This young woman stayed with the wolves for nearly two years. The wolves hunted for her, bringing her meat which she cooked. She even put up drying racks and made dried meat and by adding berries she made pemmican. She tanned hides and made herself dresses, and stored her food in parfleches, for the wolves brought her all she required.

Then after a while the great wolf said that it was time for her to return. Nearby was a herd of wild horses, and he told the woman that if she would run with the horses for two days, she would find herself near her people and she might then return to them. The wolf warned her, however, that the stallions would try to force her to stay with them, but this she must not do, for she would be captured in any case.

So the young woman left the wolves and went with the horses as she had been instructed. The stallions tried to detain her, as she had been warned, but instead of refusing their attentions, she continued to run with the herd. She refused to return to her people, but rather allowed her clothes to become soiled and her hair to be snarled and tousled. She could run as fast as any of the horses and kept up with them very well.

One day some hunters were out and spied the herd of wild horses. They ran back to their camp and notified the others. The men got ready and soon left camp to capture the horses. They chased the herd on their running horses and as they tried to surround them, they noticed a strange animal in their midst. They chased the herd a great distance, but the woman kept up with the horses so that the hunters could not tell what she was. Finally the horses tired and the hunters were able to surround them. Here they lassoed several of them and roped the young woman too. When they caught her, she struggled as strongly as any of the horses, pulling and trying to escape. But the men held her, and eventually brought her back to camp along with the horses they had captured.

When it was discovered who she really was, her relatives took charge of her. They combed her hair and put on clean clothes, but they had to constantly watch her, for she was not tame. It was a long time before she quieted down. The woman lived to be very old and she was known as "Cave Woman."

Tales and myths were passed down from one generation to another almost word for word, with changes due primarily to faulty memory. While they were often considered *chunkaka*, a term expressing credulity, myths recounted the traditions of the supernaturals; in essence, they were the religious history of the Sioux.

Although several versions of the Iktomi myth occur, the narratives have a common denominator in prankish supernaturalism, which the following, summarized from the Ella Deloria collections, so well conveys:

Iktomi was traveling when he heard singing. This made Iktomi want to sing and dance too, but he could not tell where the music was coming from. Finally, after searching about, he realized that it came from a buffalo skull lying near by. As he came closer, he could see through the eye of the skull that the mice were having a great dance, and he called to them, asking if he could join them. However, not waiting to be invited, he pushed his head into the skull, whereupon the frightened mice fled in terror. Then Iktomi tried to remove his head from the skull, but he could not. Iktomi was very forlorn with the skull stuck to his head, so he went to a rock and beat the skull upon it until it broke away. But in doing this Iktomi so bruised his head that he was very sick and dizzy for a long time afterward.

The repertoire of Sioux stories, amounting to several score, is surprisingly large when it is realized that they were retained only in the memory. Many were quite lengthy and involved, containing tidbits of humor and examples of amusing situations, both real and imaginary.

Songs and the playing of musical instruments, while often entities of themselves, when accompanied by dancing were nearly always an integral part of some activity, usually either ceremonial or celebrative. The primary musical instruments were the drum and the rattle, although flutes and whistles were employed in the Sun Dance, on the battlefield, or in love-making. Most significant was the human voice, and songs accompanied by drumming formed the basis of Sioux music.

Dances of a more or less social nature were held by warriors and their female relatives in celebrating victories, by women honoring their own virtue, and by soldiers exhibiting their prowess. Mixed dancing between men and women was confined to the Night Dance, a formal party culminating with a feast.

The seemingly endless monotony, the insistent repetition of minor variations on a theme, and the relentlessly entrancing character of the Indian dance are well portrayed in this stylized courting dance to which newlywed couples were also invited. Held throughout the summer evenings in a large tipi near the center of the camp circle, the Night Dance was quite popular. Young women dressed in their finest deerskin gowns joined men adorned in handsome paint and tinkling deer-hoof sashes. "It was nice, for even the spectators dressed up and it was good to see them walking around camp."

As the people gathered, a fire was built in the center of the lodge, and the sides were rolled up so that the onlookers might also enjoy the party. Near the fire were two paunch kettles in each of which was placed a butchered puppy, the hostess' gift to the group. The girls entered and sat on the south side of the tipi, and the boys went to the opposite side. The singers arranged themselves to the north of the door near the men and sang songs as the dancers entered. At the west end of the tipi sat a boy and girl, chosen by the men to act as honorary chaperones, while two other young men were selected to be servers.

When all the guests had at last assembled, the girls arose and, walking over to the boy's side, chose a partner by kicking the sole of his moccasin. Together they formed a line about the tipi, with the girls at the right side of the boys. When the singing began, each dancer grasped his partner by the belt, and with bent knees, two-stepped in a gently rocking gait clockwise around the fire to the rhythmic beating of the drums.

After they had danced for several minutes, the singers stopped as if to recess, but immediately started again; this continued until they had completed the four parts essential to all songs. When the fourth section had been sung, an intermission followed while the dancers took their places to rest. When the music started again, the men got up and selected their partners from among the girls.

After several intermissions, the singers might decide upon Circling the Kettle. Then the two servers arose and danced before the girls; each server chose a partner, and the four formed a line, with the last girl chosen standing to the right. Now they danced as before around the fire, but the girl to the right picked a partner as she passed the boys' side. When these five dancers reached the girls, the fifth in line (a boy) chose a girl and so on until everyone was dancing. When each new dancer was chosen, the singers changed songs, whereupon the dancers all swung about face and danced the other way. When all were dancing the singers again changed the song, and the dancers moved in single file. When the tempo was momentarily increased, the boys turned around and grasped their partner's right hand with theirs, shaking them in front of their faces, for this was the "Hitting-Each-Other-in-the-Face Dance." Again this was done in intervals of four, after which an intermission was called.

When the singing once again commenced, the servers, carrying wooden bowls, arose and went to one of the kettles, where they probed for the puppy's head and a piece of meat. When their bowls were filled, they danced with them towards the girls' side. The server carrying the head offered it to the young woman who had cooked the puppies and supplied the feast, while the server carrying the meat gave it to the girl of his choice. Then the two girls got up and, dancing with the bowls toward the men, kicked their chosen partner on the foot; then the girls turned around and danced back to their side of the tipi. As the boys approached, the girls faced about, offering the bowls to them. But as the boys reached for them, the girls withdrew, dancing backward toward their side. This they did four times, and on the fourth attempt, the boys finally got the bowls.

Then the servers danced again to the kettles. There they filled bowls for all the men and then danced over to present them with the food. When each boy had his bowl, they all arose, and dancing toward the girls, four times offered them the bowls. When the girls had finally received their food, the servers distributed bowls to the men.

In the center of the lodge, the servers now placed four bowls—one containing the other puppy's head, one his forefeet, one his hind feet, and the fourth his tail. Four warriors were then chosen to sit in the center, and the first chosen was entitled to the puppy's head, while the last one chosen might relish the tail.

When everyone had finished eating, the warriors each stood and chose a girl. Facing one another as the singers chanted, the partners danced toward each other, met in the center, and danced back. This they did four times, but as they danced forward they sang, while the singers only drummed. As they danced backward they were silent, while the singers sang and drummed. When the fourth part was completed, the first chosen warrior asked the drummer to hit the drum so that he might count a coup. After his recitation of bravery, he made a small gift to one of the on-looking children. Each of the warriors in turn told of an exploit and gave a gift to someone in the crowd.

When the warriors had finished recounting their warlike deeds, the hostess arose and presented to the boy whom she had selected to receive the first puppy's head a quilled hair ornament for his adornment.

When these formalities were completed, the singers once again began and the dance continued. As the evening wore on and the time drew late, the couple chosen as honorary chaperones eventually arose and, amid the other dancers, themselves danced out of the tipi. This was the sign that the dance was over. The girls filed out the doorway to their awaiting mothers; the boys drifted about the camp before going home. This was a Night Dance—a formal social ball for the Sioux.

Scalp Dances were held for warriors to celebrate victories, and the men were joined by their mothers and sisters, who held the hair-trophies aloft on poles as they danced. A wide number of honoring songs were customarily sung, most of which were composed for the occasion in recognition of the accomplishments of the men concerned.[3] Such dances were generally held in the open at the center of camp, with the men's steps mimicking birds and animals and warlike pantomimes in the center, while the women quietly side-stepped to the drum beat in a semicircular line facing the center. Men frequently dressed in imitation of some animal, often wearing a showy bustle with feathered horns and painted skin trailers. Though the women wore their finest dresses, they made no attempt to simulate the world of nature. In the Scalp Dance, black face-paint was worn by all as the symbol of victory.

Among men, a good dancer was one who kept his body crouched and his chest up, his knees bent, but his head high occasionally looking from side to side. He must be quick with his feet, careful to place them with assurance whether shifting sideways or stepping out.

[3] Frances Densmore, "Teton Sioux Music," Bureau of American Ethnology, *Bulletin No. 61* (1918). This student of native music has recorded several such honoring songs in her important treatise.

In those sacred dances performed by such shamans as the Buffalo Dreamers to exhibit their powers or test their medicines, the dancers dressed as the buffalo and imitated the animal's actions. Here the steps became much more ponderous than those expressed at less esoteric affairs such as might be given by an Akicita society, where men would imitate the actions of the prairie chicken or hawk.

The Winyan Tapika, or Good Woman's Dance, was also held throughout the year, but was confined only to those women who had had dreams which were believed instrumental in aiding them to remain morally upright and pure.

The warrior societies held dances throughout the year, and each prided itself on the individual character of its dance form. Dances were announced by the camp herald, who told who was giving the dance and where it would be held. Many of the societies invited two or four young women who were highly respected to sing with the men. This was indeed an honor, for which the girl's father expressed his gratitude by giving away a horse to some needy individual. Such girls became members of the clubs and were called "Tokalas" or "Badger Earrings" and were expected to be present at all dances.

The social dances of the Sioux appear to have contained little if any of the compulsive magic which characterized their religious dances. While members of the Akicita societies wore their official paraphernalia and well might imitate the steps of some favorite bird or animal associate, the intensity of the mysticism, the transference of the individual to the being of the animal appear not to have been the motivating factor. Nor were the dancers elaborately regimentized, but rather they performed as individuals, expressing their personality through antics, special steps, and even characteristic paint and attire.

Drums, as the most important musical instrument, were made with care and patience. From a green willow pole, about the diameter of his wrist, the craftsman fashioned with a knife a thin, flat piece approximately three and one-half feet in length and three inches wide. This he bent to form a circle, with one end tapered in order to make the overflap as flush as possible, and he cut three parallel grooves around the entire frame. He then tied three strings of buckskin around the frame, placing them within the grooves, and after shaping the frame to a perfect circle, hung it up to dry.

After two or three days of drying, the frame was ready to have the head applied. First, however, the craftsman cut into the wooden frame a series of small holes, each about two finger-widths apart, and fashioned a number of tiny pegs to correspond to the number of holes. Then over the frame he laid a piece of wet untanned deerskin, which had been soaked long enough to become thoroughly pliant and was large enough to encase the sides of the frame, overlapping the base about an inch. When this was adjusted, he cut a thin strip of the rawhide from the perimeter of the skin. This would be used to lace the head firmly. Finally, along the border of the head he cut a series of holes through which was to be threaded the rawhide lace. Now the drum was ready for assembling. Placing the frame over the skin, the drum-maker pulled the edges of the head over the sides of the frame and began threading the lace through the holes. When the lacing was completed, he drew the rawhide thread as tightly as possible and then tied the ends of the thread into a knot. Next, with an awl, he punched holes through the skin at the side of the frame at points corresponding to the holes which he had already cut in the wood, and inserted the little pegs which he had previously prepared. Finally, he took two strips of rawhide and, securing them at four equidistant points at the back of the drum, formed a crosspiece of leather to serve as a handgrip.

Dreamers might paint symbolic devices upon their drums, though in general most drums were undecorated. Large doubleheaded drums, cut from hollowed logs and suspended from the ground by four decorated sticks, were used for public ceremonies and dances. Around such a drum four men could sit comfortably and sing.

A drum-beater was made by covering the end of a short stick with a deerskin pad, and especially among the warrior societies these beaters were often decorated with porcupine quillwork. Often before they were played, drums were warmed—frequently over a fire—in order to give them a richer, more sonorous tone which was considered preferable to a higher pitch. Most men owned drums, and in the evenings the encampment would be filled with the quiet drumbeat of men amusing themselves with song.

Rattles were generally made of deer hide, first soaked and filled with sand to dry, then equipped with a wooden handle filled with pebbles collected from an anthill and decorated with an eagle down feather. Similarly, the buffalo scrotum made an excellent rattle, while the "Medicine Melon" found near the "White Mountains" along the Platte River was fragile and short-lived, but of good tone. A stick wrapped with deerskin, to which was attached, in rows, the cut claws of a deer, was used as a rattle, especially by Heyoka Dreamers. Rattles were most frequently carried by dancers and employed by shamans in curing the sick.

Flutes were considered especially Wakan and full of power, and their making was reserved to Dreamers. The smallest was the eagle-bone whistle, quite often decorated with quills and eagle down, and worn suspended from the neck, especially by warriors and men performing the Sun Dance. The Elk Dreamer or the Dreamer of the Double Woman made and carried a flageolet which could produce one sharp note. These were long tubular flutes of ash, the lower end carved, shaped, and painted to portray a crane's head with opened beak. Even this one note, if played in accordance to magical instructions, was believed to have influence over women.

The Big Twisted Flute, however, made by men who had dreamed of the Buffalo, was by far the most elaborate and versatile. Carved of two grooved cedar halves glued together and bound by thin rawhide lashings, the flute was equipped with five finger holes and an air vent covered with an adjustable block for changing pitch in the shape of a headless horse, and was decorated with red at the interior of each orifice. Phallic in form and color and bearing the carved body of the horse, the Big Twisted Flute was the dangerously powerful instrument of love. Only, however, when supplied with magic music, were flutes to be feared. Otherwise, they might be played by men in the privacy of their tipis for the enjoyment of themselves and friends. It was pleasant to hear the flute's sound in the evenings as old men reminisced with love songs.

The plaintive minor key and the lilting, whistling tone imbued the music of the flute with an erotically esoteric significance. Flutes were expensive and when supplied with the magic formula for love, the Dreamer could expect to receive for his fee a fine horse. Highly valued and much respected, the Big Twisted Flute was the Sioux's highest musical achievement.

THOUGH ACKNOWLEDGED by many as the possessor of more coups than any other Sioux, Red Cloud posed for this portrait by W. H. Jackson wearing only one feather. His hair-fringed shirt is a badge of his office, while the bone breastplate, a popular item of adornment, was manufactured in the East for the Indian trade.

Courtesy Denver Art Museum

EAR OF CORN sat for this portrait by W. H. Jackson wearing a stroud dress embellished with elk teeth and a beaded necklace.

Courtesy Denver Art Museum

THE THREE COUP FEATHERS, the hair-fringed shirt, and the peace
medal show Running Antelope to have been a dignitary. The fur
braid wraps and dentalium shell earrings terminating in abalone
shell pendants were popular among men even at the time of this
photograph by W. H. Jackson.

Courtesy Denver Art Museum

WEARING the hair-fringed shirt of his office and a Washington medal presented to his father, Iron Shell sat for this photograph in 1936.

PART FOUR / *The Predators*

CHAPTER 8 / *Nomadism*

THE OLD MEN of the Sioux spent many of their evenings philosophizing at the Red Council Lodge in the center of the camp. They came to the conclusion that of the four important things in life, food was the foremost. This was to acknowledge their dependence upon their chief source of food and other material needs: the buffalo. Because this great animal roamed the Plains, the Sioux found nomadism the only way of life. Indeed, the buffalo conditioned countless facets of daily life and thought among the Sioux.

The location of their settlements was almost solely determined by the proximity of sizable buffalo herds. While a camp might remain at a site for many weeks or possibly for as long as a couple of months if supplies of meat were plentiful and caches full, permanence was not important in itself. On the contrary, economic wealth depended upon temporary residence, and to that end Indian culture was directed. Theirs was a nomadic existence. The portable skin tipis, the travois, the leather containers, the willow back-rests which could be rolled into small bundles, the cradles adapted for easy transport—all indicate how the material culture was focused toward mobility. They had nothing which could not be carried by a person, dog, or horse. What food and clothing they did not store in soft leather bags or in decorated rawhide parfleches they tied in bundles.

They had no pottery but rather boiled their food by dropping hot stones into a buffalo paunch filled with water and supported by four sticks. Water they kept in a skin bag suspended from a stout pole. To grind fruits and dried vegetables, grains, and meats, the women used a small quartzite pestle and granite mortar or a stone-headed maul; the entire set would not weigh ten pounds.

They grew no vegetables and, unlike their neighboring enemies the Crows, cultivated no tobacco. The few things suggesting permanent locale—small bark-covered wigwams into which some families moved to protect their hide tipi covers from rotting during spring rains, and the caches of seeds and dried fruits and vegetables—in no manner tied the owners to a fixed spot. Food in well-hidden caches would keep for many months; when it was needed, the owners would return to claim it.

Their willingness to move, however, did not mean that the Sioux found no attachment to the land. There were favorite places to camp, to have Sun Dances, to locate their winter villages. People held nostalgic memories of particular sites, and for them returning was like a home-coming. Nevertheless, they were essentially a restless people. They liked the excitement and disciplined pattern of moving camp, of seeing and experiencing the new, of testing the unknown in the hope of greater security. Indeed, to live as they did, they had to love change, for success hinged upon mobility.

Moving camp was an undertaking which involved co-ordination of the entire group. The Nacas, the civil authorities of the tribe, made the decision of when and where to go. The Wakincuzas, "The Ones Who Decide," having chosen from among the several soldier societies one to act as police, would officially lead the procession.

Upon the instruction of the Wakincuzas, the herald sang the announcement throughout the camp. Families began dismantling their lodges and packing their belongings on the travois and horses. An entire village could be on the move within fifteen minutes. The pattern of movement was not haphazard; each family or household had a more or less permanent position, so that in moving, those whose lodge site was nearest to the direction of march started first.

The plan of march was likewise systematically determined. Far in the lead were three or four scouts, fanned out to the flanks. Directly ahead of the main body were the Wakincuzas, who officially carried the fire. To the sides and rear were the police, whose duty was to keep the people in order. No one was permitted to pass before the Wakincuzas, to wander off to hunt, or to linger behind. The penalties for disobeying were severe. A man who deliberately left the line of march was subject to a beating and the possible destruction of his tipi and belongings at the hands of the Akicita. The rear of the caravan was likewise protected by scouts.

During the day stops were made at the discretion of the leaders. Despite the number of horses available, many people traveled on foot, and time was taken out to adjust the packs, to rest, to eat. An average day's march might cover as much as twenty-five miles; under pressure bands could travel over fifty miles in a day.

The Wakincuzas chose the campsite. When a likely spot was found, the leaders formally smoked the pipe and announced their decision through the herald. Then the people began making camp, the women placing their tipis in the order in which the family had marched, each tipi with its doorway facing east.

Sites were chosen which afforded a good water supply, ample wood, grazing and forage for horses, protection from wind, and security from enemies. Level, wooded bottom lands cradled by bluffs or ridges were sought. The forested Black Hills were ideal for winter camping; the Sioux were a woodland people who had moved to the Plains, and the Black Hills were homelike. Once a year, however, they camped on the high ground, or flats, pitching their tipis in a great circle which had an entrance to the east. There they held their Sun Dance.

With the exception of the summer Sun Dance camp, when the tipis were placed in a strictly circular arrangement, the village plan was an informal assemblage of lodges, with the location of tipis determined by family relationship, position in the previous village site, and geographical configuration. Relatives tended to live near one another, and, when a new household was set up, the owners were at liberty to place their lodges where they chose. Generally, a young married couple put their tipi close to one of their parents' homes. Such an addition did little to upset the scheme of camp movement. Similarly, trees and the configuration of land, while making a formal camp circle impossible, did not destroy the ease and order in which a village might be moved.

The philosophy of the Sioux regarding the consumption of natural resources was aptly stated by Iron Shell when he said, "Such things as cherries and even buffalo don't stay around long and the people must get them when they can." Whenever a herd of bison approached camp, tribal hunts were immediately organized to ensure a sustained supply of meat. Moreover, whenever a family's own supply became low, they themselves would organize a hunt. Such *tates*, or family hunting parties, were continually leaving the main body of the villages in search of food. The Sioux economy was dependent on the movements of the bison, the all-important product.

An economy based on the buffalo was little affected by changes of season, yet certain natural phenomena and associated activities were recognized. The summer months—Moon of Strawberries (May), Moon of the Ripe Juneberries (June), Cherry Ripening Moon (July), and Moon of the Ripe Plums (August)—were each named for a vegetable product utilized by the Sioux.

Some months were named for universal factors, such as the Moon of the Yellow Leaves (September) and the Moon of Falling Leaves (October). Other names hold particular reference to a Northern hunting people and add insight to their adjustment to that way of life. So it was with the Moon of the Hairless Calves, for when cows were butchered in November, the fetus was found to be still without hair.

Midwinter months were given such definitive terms as Moon of Frost in the Tipi (December) or Tree Popping Moon (January, when frigid temperatures caused trees to split with a resounding noise). Sore Eyes Moon referred to snow-blindness suffered in February. March was the Moon when the Grain Comes Up.

April, the Moon of the Birth of Calves and the year's beginning, found the Sioux still encamped in their winter quarters within the timbered draws. During this time the small family hunting parties continued to leave the main camp as they had done throughout the winter, depending on their needs. It is probable that in the spring the Sioux had as great a supply of deer, elk, and antelope as of buffalo. The spring months heralded the sugar season, when men and women tapped the box elder tree for its sap. Horse-breaking of yearlings and two-year-olds began, and stallions not suitable for spring breeding were castrated. This too was the time of foaling, though little attention was given to the mares. During the spring months some of the people moved into wig-wams lest the drizzling rains rot the less durable tipis. This was the time of year when tipis were repaired or renewed, from new hides collected during the fall and winter. Leggings and mocca-sins were made from the "smoked tops," and smoking of hides began in the warm weather. The clubs put on dances, and vision-seeking began now, to last until cold weather.

In May, the Moon of the Thunderstorms or Ripening Straw-berries, the bands moved from their winter settlements to higher ground. This movement was traditional and not entirely the result of necessity. They changed because they liked to do so. If food was low, a hunt was planned to coincide with this migration.

Throughout the early summer months, family hunts were still carried out, and raiding parties were continuous. Individuals pro-cured game for their households; women were busy gathering early vegetables. Parfleches and robes were painted while the weather was bright and warm, and sweet-smelling leaves were gathered and preserved, especially during the Moon of the Ripe June Berries. Tribal hunts were organized when a herd of buffalo was sighted, but it was the policy to kill only a limited number since the meat might spoil before it could be prepared and con-sumed. This was the time of the year when the animals fattened.

The major part of the summer, on the contrary, was given over to the preparation and execution of ceremonial affairs. It was the season of celebration: vision-seeking and cult performances, so-cietal elections, and female virtue feasts. The Sun Dance, held in the Cherry Ripening Moon, served as the climax of the ceremonial season. Afterward, Naca and Ska Yuha meetings decided the course of fall events.

At the termination of the festival season, the fall hunt was immediately organized. The fact that the name *tate* was given to this activity shows that it was a recognized component of the economic cycle. There was no formalized communal hunt, as such. Rather the breakup of the great camp circle occurred before the individual bands set out. It was among these local bands that communal hunting took place.

The autumn was a busy time of year. Women were gathering vegetables and nuts and drying meats in preparation for approaching winter. Men hunted seriously so that the supply might be adequate, occasionally burning the range to force buffalo to come nearer the hunting camps. "Fall is the time we hunt the most," is the way one informant put it. When the season drew to a close, caches were prepared as winter insurance.

As the bands moved from place to place during the hunting season, young men occasionally planned war parties, agreeing to rejoin the camp at a predetermined location. In the event that the main camp should be unable to wait for the return of the warriors, the headman saw to it that a signpost was set up for them. This post was usually fashioned from the shoulder blade of a buffalo, and tied to a stick, it was pointed in the direction the camp was moving. The shoulder blade was marked with hoofmarks, a drawing of a travois, and the name of the headman in pictographic form. In this way, the bands knew where one another were.

When the first heavy snows began to fall, usually in early December, the camps gathered at a predetermined place to decide upon the permanent winter campsite, and from December until March or April the Indians remained in the sheltering wooded hollows near rivers or in the Black Hills, close to supplies of firewood. This was the season when men made bows and arrows and needed tools. *Tates* and individual huntsmen would go searching if their supplies were low. Severe winters brought starvation, and it was during such times that rose berries, acorns, horses, and hide scrappings were eaten. Stories of cannibalism have their setting in winter.

No matter how strongly the Sioux may have been inclined toward a nomadic hunting life, its success was originally dependent upon the dog as a beast of burden. Without this animal as an aid in moving belongings and supplies an itinerant hunting people could scarcely have survived amid the vastness of the Great Plains. The original westward migration of the Sioux in the seventeenth century was accomplished with only the benefit of the dog. As early as 1660, according to the Frenchmen Pierre Esprit Radisson and Jean Baptiste des Grosseliers, the Sioux were still planting corn. Yet they must have depended heavily upon the buffalo to have already acquired the title of the "Nation of Beef."[1] Hunting excursions undoubtedly were made to the west—a practice which such farming people as the Mandans and Arikaras continued to carry on throughout the nineteenth century. Here was an incipient nomadism in the form of hunting expeditions carried out only with the aid of the dog. In fact, the peopling of the entire plains was thus accomplished by the Cheyennes and Arapahoes, the Crows, and probably the Blackfeet. All these tribes gave up a farming economy in favor of moving west to hunt buffalo.

It was, therefore, the dog which played the key role in the early migration onto the plains. The dog dragged the tipi poles and carried the burdens. Harnesses were fashioned and travois built which made him an effective aid to transportation. When the horse was introduced, the Sioux simply transferred the dog's burdens to the larger animal.

Even after the advent of the horse, however, the dog continued to play a role in Sioux existence. In moving camp, the dog was still harnessed to a travois loaded with packing bags and equipment. During the berry season, he was employed to drag home the harvest. Moreover, puppies continued to be a delicacy for feasts, and dogs were standard playmates for Sioux children.

Little Day described the part played by dogs in daily life:

> When I went berry picking, I always went with Rattling, and we always took a dog with a travois. This was a big, black male, for males are stronger for pulling a travois. We called him "Long Face" because his face was so long. Nearly everyone had a travois dog.
>
> We picked cherries and plums and gooseberries in a draw not far from camp. The dog followed us, and we carried deerskin bags. We

[1] *Voyages of Pierre Esprit Radisson.*

wore the bags as an apron and picked gooseberries and plums into them. The cherries we picked by hand, bending the tree down and picking the fruit into a calf skin we had placed on the ground. After we had picked the cherries, we called the dog, "Wey, wey, wey," and when he came up, we loaded our bags of fruit on the travois.

Then we went to the plum bushes and spread our calf hides and picked plums into them. We filled one bag with plums and the rest we put in one of the hides. We had no room for gooseberries that day, so we loaded the plums and went home.

The Sioux had a variety of dogs; large animals about the size of a husky were preferred for working, while a smaller type was kept for eating. Dogs ranged in color from blacks to grayish browns, with pointed faces and sharp ears, giving them a coyote-like appearance. Dogs were tolerated but not loved by adults. When caught trying to steal meat from the drying racks, they were beaten with sticks unmercifully by the women. As puppies, however, they were fondled, fed, and even nursed, should their mother die, with meat juices from an improvised deerskin bottle-bag fashioned with a nipple. Puppies were taken from their mothers and weaned when a month or two old. At this time the women "put two fingers in their mouths to stretch their throats" and fed them soups.

Again according to Little Day:

We had a dog house in back of our tipi. It was something like a sweat lodge, though about three feet in diameter. It was covered with hay over which sod was placed, and a short passage-way covered with sticks and sod was the entrance. Inside was a matting of grass. My mother made this house, though nearly every family had one made the same way.

Mother built this house for a female with five puppies. This was not a travois dog, just an ordinary dog whose puppies we ate when they reached about three months. That's about the main reason we kept those dogs.

Dogs served also as protection. Travois dogs slept near the door inside the tipi and were trained to bark at strange noises. "By

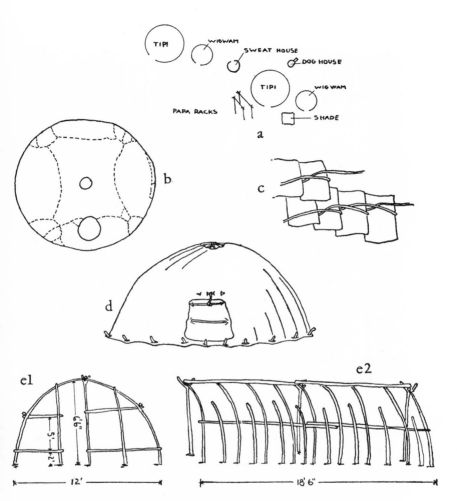

a, Little Day's camp; *b*, wigwam cover; *c*, bark shingles for wigwams; *d*, Little Day's wigwam; *e1*, Leader Charge's wigwam frame, front view; *e2*, Leader Charge's wigwam frame, side view. (See Chapter 8.)

a, Signpost; *b*, dog and travois arrangement. (See Chapter 8.)

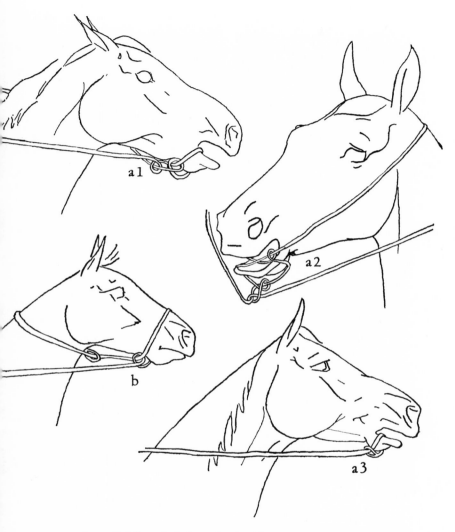

a1, *a2*, and *a3*, Bridles; *b*, halter for breaking. (See Chapter 8.)

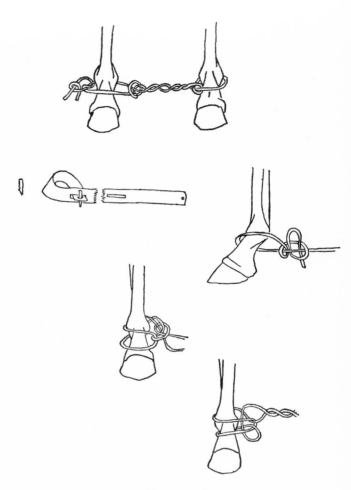

Hobbles. (See Chapter 8.)

going 'sst,' they would stop barking, yet you had to hit them to make them stop annoying visitors." From the comments of old Sioux informants, their dogs were as charming as anyone's.

The advent of the horse among the Sioux must have been an occasion of joyous wonderment. Here was an animal that could do the work of dogs but do it far more effectively. His size and strength meant that he could drag much larger travois and transport much heavier burdens. As if this were not enough, this wonderful beast could carry a rider, thereby making a man more fleet than human minds had imagined. Truly, the horse was Wakan. Thus they called it the "sacred dog."

To this hunting people whose existence depended upon game, particularly the buffalo, the horse gave assurance of a bountiful supply. The horse was so efficient that not only was greater security forthcoming, but actual overabundance and wealth was possible. Consequently the Sioux became as dependent upon the horse as upon the buffalo.

On the other hand, the advent of the horse gave rise to problems of cultural values. The horse was more than a mere convenience; it possessed the attributes of supernatural potency, analogous to "medicine." Thus owning a horse in a real sense gave a man the same advantage as personal medicine, in hunting and in war. Yet the horse was tangible property, the accumulation of which ran counter to the enforced co-operative pattern; the accumulation of intangible property, power, was the prerequisite for successful fulfillment of role. This scheme required some modification in order to admit the horse.

The Sioux partially resolved this problem by the provision that a man's position was determined not by the number of horses he owned but by the number he could afford to give away in return for goods or services or prestige. Yet the importance and value of possessions was not and could not be held in check. The increasing number of horses that became available, and the invigorating effect which the horse had upon the economy, created a surplus and a momentum for which the existing system was not prepared. Now affluence and wealth became realities, and it was not unnatural that the horse, as the visible means and cause of this upswing, should become the symbol of wealth and the medium of exchange. Big tipis or many wives or elaborate clothes might be indications of wealth, but the direct and indirect means of attaining these was the horse.

Thus the man with the fastest horse was in a position to kill more buffalo than someone with a slower mount—and in securing for himself an abundance he immediately assumed a position different from the less fortunate. Likewise, a family equipped with superior animals was assured of a greater supply than was a family whose herd was inadequate or inferior. Furthermore, a string of horses enabled the owner to move more belongings with greater ease than could a man with only one horse.

These assets when coupled with the horse's durability made him an excellent medium of exchange. To the Indian all important goods and services were valued in relation to the horse. The price of a wife, of a shield, of having one's children's ears pierced, or of a war bonnet, was generally one horse. Therefore, the larger the number of horses owned by one man, the easier was the path to economic security and social position.

If one of the effects of the horse was to create both group and individual wealth, a corollary of this change was the increase of individualism. Personal wealth could be and was distributed, and the strong demand for the horse intensified the value of property. The ability to give away more than someone else was evidence of individual or family superiority. Now, not only could the owner of many horses present material proof and valuable offerings to the less well-to-do in substantiation of his claims, but the comfort and luxury offered by the horse were rewards in themselves.[2]

A large herd of horses was not easy to acquire. Horses were not

[2] Francis Haines, "Where Did the Plains Indians Get Their Horses?" *American Anthropologist*, New Series, Vol. XL (1938), 112–17; Francis Haines, "The Northward Spread of Horses among the Plains Indians," *American Anthropologist*, New Series Vol. XL (1938), 429–37; Clark Wissler, "Influence of the Horse in the Development of the Plains Culture," *American Anthropologist*, New Series, Vol. VI (1914).

successfully bred, though attempts were made to increase herds by rudimentary surveillance and control. The chief methods by which stock were replenished were by capturing wild horses or by stealing them from other tribes. But stealing was much easier than capture. The number of wild horses until the turn of the nineteenth century is estimated to have been small, and the capture of even one horse required much skill and considerable luck. In stealing horses, the Indian could hope to secure several at one time. He was also reasonably sure of getting one that had been broken, and he was certain to receive both economic benefit and social prestige if his mission were successful. Social prestige might be incentive enough to send a man on a horse-stealing party, for in capturing an animal in this fashion, he was entitled to a coup, or war honor. The accumulation of such coups was the key to social and political success.

The Sioux method of breaking a horse was quick, ruthless, and effective. Ideally, colts were not trained until they were three years old. Younger colts, it was believed, could be broken more easily, but older colts proved stronger and better disciplined. Boys, however, often trained yearlings, and oddly enough, such young animals were considered to become especially long-winded and good runners.

A horse to be broken was first choked down with a noose about his neck while one man sat on its head. When the horse was well secured around the neck by two or three men at the end of a long rope, the man on his head jumped off, being careful to avoid the horse's kicking feet. Immediately the horse would spring up, and the men held to the rope allowing the animal to fight. As the horse battled the rope, the men gradually led him to the camp circle. Here the men wound the rope several times around the horse's legs and jerking suddenly, threw it to the ground. Quickly one of the men jumped on him as the others tied his front feet together and then secured these to the horse's left hind leg. When the horse was freed to rise, it was thrown by its hobble again and again. This ordeal lasted for whatever time it took to exhaust the animal.

When the horse was finally so tired that it lay upon the ground, too weak to struggle, the men thumped him lightly over his body and especially over his neck and ears and back. After tapping him thoroughly, they threw a robe over the animal's back. The horse generally bucked and jumped trying to throw off the robe, but being hobbled, fell again and again in its struggle. When the horse could no longer muster strength enough to throw off the robe, one of the men approached and gently jumped upon his back. Then the rider carefully placed a halter over his mouth. When it became evident that the animal was adjusted to the halter and rider, the others again tapped and patted and smoothed the horse's body. Then, with caution, the hobbling ropes were released, and the horse trotted off bearing his rider. To accomplish this pacification might take all day; some especially mean horses required two days to train. But in any case, the Sioux's method was effective enough to gain for them some of the world's best-trained, fastest, and most enduring horses.

The most valuable pony was the gelding race horse. The horse that could outrun all others was an indisputable asset. So highly prized was such an animal that its owner kept it under the closest guard, even picketing it at the tipi door. Some ponies became famous throughout the plains. Warriors took special note of such animals and actually made expeditions in the hope of capturing this or that renowned one. Race horses were given special care and treatment and used only when actually needed. Thus a man would ride a saddle horse on the war party and lead his race horse until the attack was made. The Sioux would sprinkle their race horses daily with cold water in the belief that this gave the horses additional stamina.

The admitted superiority of geldings not only was instrumental in the development of castration techniques but added a touch of additional finesse to the horse-stealing pattern. Particular tribute was given to the man who stole a picketed gelding.

Economic security for these nomadic people was founded upon the principle of quick adaptation to changing circumstances. Willingness to move one's dwelling presupposed acceptance of the transitory character of their basic food supply. And yet the Sioux were careful to plan their movements in accordance with the natural cycle. They arranged to be near the ripening rose berries at harvesttime, to be near groves of box elders when the spring sap was running. They had favorite places to pitch their camps. They found order in the nature of things and applied it in a routine of living. For in spite of their acceptance of change, they desired security. Though opportunistic, they were creatures of habit, and they did not seek change for change's sake alone.

CHAPTER 9 / *The Predators*

THE WAY OF LIFE OF THE SIOUX can best be characterized as predatory. Their well-being depended upon their ability as hunters of game and as gatherers of wild fruits and vegetables. There was absolutely no agriculture and, with the exception of the horse and dog, no domestication or husbandry. In this respect, the economy of the Sioux was essentially one of consumption.

Ranging the grasslands were vast herds of buffalo and scattered droves of antelope. Coyotes and gray wolves prowled the high grounds; hawks and golden eagles soared above. This land where rivers and streams almost without exception cut their courses deep to meander through alluvial plains and river benches, where stands of pine bordered the ridges, and cottonwoods and box elders clustered in the moist lowlands, produced an amazingly wide variety of wildlife. Deer, elk, porcupines, beaver, duck, and magpie all were common. The Indian hunter, in search of his daily food supply, did not overlook this wealth. In fact, it was as much through the familiarity with and utilization of this woodland environment as through the exploitation of the buffalo that the permanent existence of a hunting people on the plains was possible.

Despite the fact that often great numbers of animals could be taken at one time, hunting was a continuing responsibility and an arduous chore. Hunting was not sport, it was work; it was not a diversion, it was a persistent and a very real business. Success required skill, endurance, and a knowledge of the ways of animals. A good hunter enjoyed a good life; a poor hunter not only suffered want and discomfort and deprivation, he endured ridicule and pity for his poverty.

188

As former woodland hunters, the Sioux naturally realized the importance of the bison to their economy and tapped that resource to its fullest extent. By doing so, they assured themselves a more secure, and at times even an abundant, life. But they also realized that the bison in all its numbers could not alone support them. The deer produced meat which they considered better food than buffalo meat, and deer hide was recognized as more desirable for clothing.

It was only natural that as hunters the Sioux should employ methods and expect results consistent with their earlier existence in the forest lands of the northeast. It was only natural, too, that their settlements should have been located close to water and therefore within the woods. Only for their ceremonial camps in midsummer did they venture to settle upon the high ground. Their reliance upon a forestlike environment was evident in nearly every facet of the production economy: for their clothing, their tools, their weapons, and in some cases their shelters, they drew heavily upon the timbered areas. Their dependence upon this modified woodland environment may have accounted for their determination to wrest the Black Hills country, which they later called their "meat pack," from the Kiowas, the Cheyennes, and the Crows.

There is every reason to believe that the Sioux, or any hunting people, could not have survived the rigors of the plains without the buffalo, and there is good reason to believe that population by hunting groups could not have existed without the horse. These factors, however, do not suggest that the horse and the buffalo together were sufficient to support a large-scale hunting economy —the retention of a woodland way of life was equally important.

The Sioux divided hunting into two categories: the *tate* or family hunt and the *wani-sapa* or communal buffalo drive. Both of of these were supplemented by the individual's daily hunting occasioned by a need for food or by his desire, for instance, to capture a bird to secure a coveted feather for a costume. Sometimes a man would hunt for the sheer love of it; at other times

189

he might go out just to be doing something. In addition to this daily hunting, the surprise appearance of game further augmented the supply obtained through the *tates* and the *wani-sapas*. The bear, startled by berry pickers, the badgers uncovered by rabbbit hunters, the prairie chicken's nest exposed by a playing child, even buffalo wandering into a sleeping camp, formed a part of lucky happenstance in the lives of a hunting people.

Late in the summer when the ceremonial camp broke up, groups of families or bands dispersed at *tates* throughout the region for the fall hunt. This was the season for collecting winter stores. There was little formal organization during this period, for while the band was under the supervision of the headman and possibly other civil authorities, including the policing society, the dispersal of families into small, effective hunting units prevented stringent surveillance. Each unit was on its own until it joined the main tribal body at a predetermined village site in the early winter.

Men usually hunted in pairs as members of a small family group. Teamwork was advantageous in heading off animals and covering their retreats, though some men preferred to hunt alone. Success demanded keen knowledge of animal habits.

When hunting deer, it is often well to climb a ridge to spy a herd. When deer are discovered, it is necessary to decide the best way of attack, being certain the wind blows against you, and how to keep under cover, for if deer are in the open they are difficult to kill.

Often it is necessary to crawl to the nearest point for a good shot. Some men removed their moccasins, for they could stalk more quietly and believed this brought good luck. When stalking, a man must choose his course, hold his breath, and walk very slowly. By placing his toes down first and then putting his weight on his heels, and taking only a couple of steps at a time, he could be sure no noise had been made.

Before shooting, the first animal to be killed is picked out. Then when ready and in position, the first arrow is shot at the first animal, the next at the second and there may be time for a third, but after that, the others are out of range. Now is the time to butcher.

Deer are the most sensitive of all animals and hence the hardest to kill. Therefore, the hunter needs to be most careful when hunting them.[1]

Occasionally a hunter would find deer grazing near a steep, high bank, whereupon an entire herd might be cornered and killed. Often this was possible in the badlands where erosion had cut the land into a maze of sharp cliffs.

Sometimes several hunters ran antelope or deer into snowdrifts, circling them into a creek where the snow was deep and soft. When hunting in the snow, men wore high-ankled moccasins. Some used wooden snowshoes, and others tied to their feet sheets of rawhide which had been frozen after wetting.

The off-wind approach, the surprise attack followed by a quick succession of shots, the wolf- or deerskin disguise, the waylaying of animals along their trails were all part of the technique. Except for the buffalo drive, hunting was done on foot, the horse being tethered at a distance to be used as a pack bearer. Proper stalking was essential, for making a kill was as dependent upon stealth as upon the accurate aiming of an arrow. A pen around a known feeding spot, a noose hidden at a deer trail, a blade concealed in a piece of meat to catch a mink or fox who would unknowingly cut its tongue and thereby bleed to death—each was a useful device to capture game.

The One Horn, a Miniconjou headman, was famous for his ability to run down on foot a fleeing buffalo and kill it with his bow and arrow. Such an accomplishment, of course, was a feat of personal stamina and not a common hunting technique.[2]

"For bear and larger game," according to Iron Shell, "men propped up large logs on a stick to which bait was tied as lure. Sometimes these deadfalls missed."

Kit foxes and other small animals such as raccoons and badgers

[1] Colonel Richard Dodge, *Our Wild Indians*, 420. This nineteenth-century military observer stated that the Plains Indian would "grasp five to ten arrows in his left hand, and discharge them so rapidly that the last will be on its flight before the first has touched the ground, and with such force that each would mortally wound a man at twenty to thirty yards."

[2] George Catlin, *North American Indians*, 237.

were often trapped in narrow pens. Here a stockade about two by three feet was built of six to seven sticks set up in a palisade with a narrow opening at one side. Two forked poles about six feet tall were set at each end of the enclosure, and a heavy rawhide rope was strung taut between them. From this a green log about two feet in length and ten inches in diameter was suspended horizontally with a slip knot, and to the log was firmly tied a piece of fat. When the fox entered the trap and jumped up to pull down the bait, the string holding the log slipped loose, and in falling it dealt the animal a deadly blow.

Small game, birds, and fish were not spared by these hunting people, for many of them were considered important supplements for a varied diet. Bands of boys hunted rabbits, surrounding them in great droves and killing them by throwing specially designed "rabbit sticks" or short heavy clubs.

"Red squirrels," one Sioux explained, "were killed with bows and arrows for they lived in trees. The old women liked to boil them until they became very soft so they would not have to chew. Old women also tanned the hides, and when they got enough together, they made little robes on which to sit to smoke their pipes."

Prairie dogs were shot. Beaver were smoked from their holes and then clubbed to death. Women who found a den of porcupines would dig and probe with sticks to twist and tangle the fur and then quickly drag the animals out so they might be killed with clubs. Wolves and coyotes, skunks and muskrats were important prey. A man named Kicks-Up-Dirt was even known to have killed and eaten six bobcats.

Iron Shell described the lore of several animals as follows:

> The badger is very strong. When a man kills a badger, if he turns it on its back, cuts open it chest and carefully removes its insides so that no blood is lost, when the blood thickens, by looking in the hunter can see his image. Should he see himself as he is, he knows he will die young. But if he sees himself as an old man with white hair, he cries, "Hye, hye" thanking the spirits. Now he knows he can risk getting many coup and will live long to die with a cane in his hand.

Some hunters were so nimble they could kill a badger by jumping on its back with both feet. Others never could do this, but instead landed on the badger's chest, for badgers turn over quickly. These men got badly bitten.

In winter, if a man found raccoon tracks at the foot of a hollow tree, he would put hay and sticks in the hole, stuffing them in, set fire to it and wait.

When the smoke appears, either the racoon will fall down through the fire, dead and half-cooked, or will climb out the upper hole and jump. When he lands, he can be killed with a club.

Birds were rarely shot but rather clubbed, and occasionally they were snared and trapped.

To catch snow birds, we took several horse hairs with nooses at one end and tied them to a stick, about six inches apart. This we laid on a bare spot of earth from which the snow had blown away. Then from a distance we waited to watch a flock settle. When one little bird would fly up, he would get caught and as we approached the others would fly, but several would catch their feet in the tiny nooses. Snow birds were good boiled or roasted on coals.

Hunting with a *wismahi yeyapi* or "sending-arrow" was excellent for ducks and geese at a great distance in the center of a lake, for sending-arrows went farther than regular arrows shot from a bow. These special arrows were made about six inches longer than standard ones, with a notch cut midway along the shaft. To a four-foot ash whipstick was attached a three-foot string, knotted at the end. By placing the arrow on the ground behind the hunter with the knot in the notch, the hunter lashed the whipstick over his head, thus sending the arrow forward, high in the air, where it was released. Some men became very skillful at this.

Prairie chickens were shot. When a nest was discovered, it was taken home, eggs and all, for both meat and eggs were favorite foods. The eggs were boiled, never eaten raw, while the chickens might be boiled or roasted. The eggs of most birds were collected and relished—duck, crane, pigeon, meadowlark, even magpie and owl. The goose egg, however, was considered by some to cause carbuncles and was therefore shunned. Screech owls and whippoorwills were caught after approaching them slowly with outstretched arms. By making fists and placing the thumbs through the index and third fingers, and then pointing the thumbs at the bird's eye, the men blinded the bird and then suddenly grabbed it by the neck.

Skill, knowledge, and diligence were not regarded as sufficient attributes in themselves to guarantee success in hunting. There must be an understanding of the animals, and a recognition of their spiritual qualities as well. The nations of animals, in permitting their members to be taken by the Sioux, demanded respect and specific propitiation in return. The animals' demands were generally brought to the Sioux in visions.

To a degree, all animals were sacred, and because of their Wakan character, religious rites were an accepted prelude to hunting. The Sioux philosophy which conceived man as an integral part of nature, yet dependent upon animals for power because of their supernatural affiliation, made propitiation all important. As such, there was no joy in killing; instead, a sense of gravity prevailed. Hunting was a serious and mystical business—a combination of skill, organization, and power obtained from the supernaturals.

Respect for animals meant that a pipe should be smoked prior to hunting, symbolizing man's supplication. Propitiation involved an offering of thanks at the kill and later small bits of meat at the meal. As one informant explained, "When eating, one should put a piece of meat aside for the spirit, holding it up and then throwing it away saying, 'Recognize this, Ghost, so that I may become the owner of something good.' " Men who failed at hunting generally ascribed their misfortune to some mistake or omission in these obligations.

In addition to the rituals prescribed by animals and accepted by all Sioux, certain individual action might be taken to assure success. The hunter might obtain advice and power from the supernaturals by seeking a vision, or he might indirectly request such help through a shaman. Ghost Head, a man of renowned ability, was able to foretell the success or failure of his missions by daily referring to a cliff upon which signs appeared to him. In hunting, no known trick or device, secular or otherwise, was overlooked.

Eagle-hunting was a particularly sacred and uniquely virile undertaking. Iron Shell's recounting of it is especially revealing:

In the fall of the year, men went to the mountains to hunt eagles. So it was that Struck-in-Face and his friends set their camp in a secluded, wooded area at a safe distance from the treeless promontory where the trapping was to take place. At camp the men set up their tipi and built a purifying lodge.

At the chosen spot on the ridge, the men marked out a rectangle about six feet long and two feet wide with the axis north and south and then marking squares, cut them with their knives and carefully removed the sod to one side. Then with their knives they began to dig a pit, loading the earth into a robe with the mountain sheep horn spoons they had brought with them. The loads of loose dirt were then carried away from the pit to be piled here and there to simulate gopher hills. When the pit had been dug to the depth of three feet, Struck-in-the-Face placed a nest of sage at the south end of the pit. Next they placed a row of poles across the top to serve as beams, leaving an opening, however, at the north end large enough to allow Struck-in-the-Face to climb in later. A rawhide rope was then stretched over each side, covering the beam ends and secured with stakes to make the roof firm. Finally the men replaced the sod and brought other bunches of grass to plant around the opening in order to camouflage the trap.

When the trap was completed, Struck-in-the-Face prepared an altar in his tipi, placing behind the fire pit an offering stick and ten tiny tobacco offerings, each hung from a small stick. These could not be disturbed, nor while he was hunting the eagle would the people touch them or make a noise.

Long before dawn on the following day, Struck-in-the-Face went to the purifying lodge and took a sweat bath. Then he and a companion went to the trap carrying with them a dismembered carcass of a jack rabbit. After Struck-in-the-Face had climbed into the pit, his helper adjusted the camouflage, set the bait securely and left. Now Struck-in-the-Face, lying on his back in the trap, awaited the eagles.

Late in the morning, the first eagle appeared, soaring high above the ridge. Struck-in-the-Face waited for some time while the great bird wheeled and glided over and about the area, then gradually, almost warily, it floated down to alight near the hidden hunter. Then, as if with determination, it walked over the trap and began tearing at bits of the lure. Suddenly, Struck-in-the-Face thrust out his hands and grabbing the eagle by the legs, pulled the screaming, struggling bird down into the pit. Then dexterously wringing its neck, Struck-in-the-Face placed the eagle on the bed of sage at the foot of the trap.

By sundown, Struck-in-the-Face had caught three eagles. He had been fortunate, for many eagles had been flying that day. He now left the trap, and with his eagles went to the purifying lodge. Placing the birds in a row to the left of the pit, he took a bath in propitiation, for this was the custom when one killed an eagle.

Men trapped for crows and magpie in a similar manner, by concealing themselves in clumps of small pines and covering themselves with pine bows to which were tied a piece of fat. When the birds alighted, the hunters caught their legs and wrung their necks.

Boys often kept crows for pets, and many were taught to speak, often calling people by name as they passed by. Once a pet crow went to Claw's tipi and said, "Claw, you had better start crying." Answering, Claw said, "Crow, why don't you cry?" but Claw's wife died soon after this.

Boys made pets of young hawks, coyotes, skunks, and badgers, but the animals ran away when they were full grown. Young eagles were also kept, generally until autumn, when they were killed and the feathers removed. Hawks, too, were kept for their feathers; they were never trained for falconry.

Fishing was done with a bone hook tied to a long line of sinew attached to the end of a willow pole. Grasshoppers were considered good bait for trout and redfins.

According to an old informant:

Suckers never bit when we fished for them, so we used spears. These were made from forked poles about six feet long, with four barbed-like notches on the inside of each sharpened prong. If you missed the fish with the prong, it was certain to be caught by the center barbs. We also caught suckers in another way by attaching a noose of rawhide to the end of a pole. Then putting the loop in the water, we carefully slipped it over the fish's head past his gills. By jerking very rapidly, we often caught a sucker.

Beginning downstream and working up toward a waterfall, two persons with a large piece of hide, through which many small holes had been punched, could expect to seine many fish. With one person on each side of the bank, they progressed upstream with their sievelike skin, netting fish from the pools as they went. This was recognized as a good method for assuring a large catch, if the falls were high enough to prevent the fish from escaping.

Men cooked fish in a small pit lined with leaves. Over these leaves the cleaned fish were laid. They were covered with a row of sticks, and above them were placed more leaves. Finally a thin layer of earth was spread level with the surface of the surrounding ground. Then a large fire was built over the pit. When it burned down to a few remaining coals, the earth and leaves and sticks were removed, leaving the fish thoroughly baked in their leafy oven. Then setting a place of leaves, the men put the fish before them, peeled off the skins, and enjoyed a meal. Fish that were brought home were preferably boiled. Fish were cleaned but not scaled, for the skins peeled off more easily after cooking.

Turtles and tortoises were captured by hand, the latter in the early morning as they came out to drink the dew. These were boiled for soups, and their meat was considered a delicacy.

The effectiveness of the individual hunter in maintaining an adequate supply of meat and raw materials was determined by the fact that the fall hunt was carried out by the individual, or at most by teams of two or three men. However, the society could not support itself by the individual efforts of single hunters; group action and co-operation were necessary. The *wani-sapa*, or buffalo surround, attests to this, for a successful drive insured a winter's supply of food. And this insurance was necessary to existence on the plains.

The communal hunt or *wani-sapa* was by far the most spectacular and certainly the most efficient method of securing game in quantity. It was a group activity, formalized by religious and political jurisdiction. Unlike the informal *tate* instigated by a family head and carried out in a variety of ways depending on the animal to be hunted, the *wani-sapa* was a tribal matter deserving the co-operation of nearly every member, accepted and sanctioned by the highest authorities, and used solely to secure buffalo.

The character of the *wani-sapa* itself shows the systematic proclivities of the Sioux in action. The hunt was organized under the authority of Nacas who, as part of their responsibility in deciding tribal matters, held meetings to consider the adequacy of the food supply. Their decision to hold a hunt usually was occasioned by lack of meat, but occasionally it was based on advice from a shaman who had seen game in a dream.

When the need for food was critical, a shaman might be asked to assume tribal control in conjunction with the civil authorities. A Buffalo Dreamer thus rendering his services underwent a sweat bath in order to commune with his supernatural helper and receive instructions. He then announced whether or not he could be successful, and if not, another shaman was asked to take over. A shaman convinced of success prescribed certain rituals and offerings for the people to give his Helper. He then directed a ceremony, usually an imitative buffalo dance, again purified himself in the sweat bath, formally predicted the manner in which the buffalo would appear or where they would be found, and outlined further ceremonial procedures. Once the buffalo were sighted, the civil authorities assumed control.

The decision to hold a hunt was rarely postponed to the point of imminent starvation, and only in the case of potential famine were the Dreamers called upon. The buffalo were sufficiently plentiful and the methods of securing them effective enough that famines, though real, were not common.

The headmen were responsible for maintaining an adequate food supply, and the Nacas frequently held meetings to discuss the need for a hunt. On occasion they invited members of the Ska Yuha, an organization of elders recognized for their former abilities as hunters, to join in their deliberations.

Upon a decision to hold a hunt, the Nacas chose two young men of unquestioned integrity as chief of the scouts "to go upon the hill." Summoned to the council lodge by the herald, they were given instructions concerning their search for the buffalo. The first to be chosen was the leader. The honor of being elected as chief of the scouts enabled one's parents to perform a giveaway in their son's name. There was set up in the center of the camp circle a pole which represented an enemy, or buffalo, and a coup-striking contest followed. A man of high standing who had been a scout and had counted coups was chosen to start off the scouts amid dancing and singing. Upon leaving camp, the leader assumed control of the scouts, directing the searchers and instructing them to report.

After the scouts set out, the camp was often moved in the direction they had taken. When those who had "gone upon the hill" returned without finding buffalo, they entered camp in the manner of an unsuccessful war party—secretly and without ado. If their mission had been successful, however, they announced their approach by riding a horse back and forth along a ridge or hill to a distance approximating the area occupied by the herd they had sighted. They then rode to the *tiyo-tipi*. Here an altar was prepared with sweet grass, buffalo chips, and pipe. An Itacan offered the consecrated pipe to the scouts and to the gathered Nacas in ceremonial manner, for smoking the pipe here was a vow which demanded the truth. When the smoking was finished, the scouts were asked to report. The herald then made public that a hunt was to begin, and the warrior society responsible for police duty for the season reported to the *tiyo-tipi* to receive any special instructions. If the camp was to move, they saw to it that no one strayed, lest the herd of buffalo be disturbed. While the police were in direct control of the camp, the ultimate direction was generally vested in the Ska Yuhas or White Horse Owners. And it was these elders who decided the best method for carrying out the hunt.

The hunters were under the direction of experienced huntsmen. The plan of attack was discussed after the party had come in sight of the herd. Great precaution was used lest the animals become frightened and run off before the parties were ready and united. Plans varied according to the terrain, but a few were standard practice. Most common was the two-group surround. Here the hunters divided into two sections, and at a given signal, "*Hoka he*," from the chosen leader, each hunter charged on horseback, the two groups converging upon the bewildered herd. From the time of the signal each man was on his own, racing his horse at the herd to kill as many fat bison as possible. Stragglers contented themselves with the smaller animals, or merely tied the tail of some swifter hunter's kill, thus indicating their claim to some of the meat. The old men and young boys in charge of the pack horses brought up the rear to assist in butchering and in packing the kill. Each hunter carried arrows painted in a fashion peculiar to his choice; each arrow, therefore, served as a label indicating the owner. At the conclusion of the hunt individuals would return to claim their kill. Disputes over rightful ownership occasionally occurred and were settled either by the Akicita or by the leader of the hunt. Those individuals who had been completely unsuccessful in killing any animals and instead had tied the tail of someone else's kill might now make claim of their interest. The hunter was given first choice but might not deny meat to the less fortunate. Certain individuals were known as "tail tiers," but such a reputation was not to be envied.

Running buffalo, and occasionally antelope, over a cliff's edge was an effective method for securing large quantities of meat. Certain selected individuals were sent out to drive the animals. In addition one person—a Buffalo Caller—went out to entice the herd toward the cliff. The role of Buffalo Caller not only involved complete understanding of the animal's habits but demanded the utmost of endurance and skill. Dressed as a buffalo, the Caller through his antics and mimicry must gently urge, cajole, and entice the leaders of the herd toward him and the cliff. Men, women, and children had their duties too. At the head of the cliff, and extending on the plain like the arms of a great V, stretching possibly a mile or more in distance, men and women were stationed at intervals. In some cases, where the cliff was used often for driving buffalo, these stations were marked by piles of rocks. As the caller was successful in luring the buffalo toward the apex of the V and the animals were well within these wings, the people at the most distant stations would arise and wave their robes to frighten the buffalo forward. When the buffalo became sufficiently alarmed they would stampede, and the caller, whose work was thereby successfully accomplished, would rush to the edge of the cliff to seek protection at the side. The leading buffalo, increasingly confined toward the apex of the V by the stationed people, would eventually come to the cliff and with his followers be hurled to death by the stampeding animals behind. Frequently corrals were built at the bottom of the cliff where men would club and stone the animals who had survived the fall.

Division of spoils was based upon the assumption that all members of the group, having contributed to the united effort, were entitled to a share of the meat. Certain individuals, because of their age or special talent in regard to the hunt, were entitled to either choice or first portions. The Caller would be among these individuals. The distribution was again under the jurisdiction of the hunt leaders and the Akicita, but the solution was often simplified by the custom of endeavoring to kill only such meat as was needed. The possibility of gaining personal prestige was limited, except to the leaders and the police. It is probable that this method of taking animals was dying out during the nineteenth century because of the increased mobility afforded to the Indians by the horse.

The same principle of surround was employed when animals, particularly buffalo and antelope whose habit was to herd, were driven into snowbanks during winter. Horses were of little value in deep, drifting snow; snowshoes were used instead. Here again the hunters used bow, arrow, and spear.

The significance of the surround was that large numbers could be taken. An abundance and in some cases an overabundance of meat, hides, and other raw materials were essential to the Sioux, for there were those stark occasions when the buffalo would seemingly disappear and starvation and want would follow. The surround was necessary as insurance against just such emergencies, and if upon occasion some animals were wasted, that was only a natural consequence of oversupply. Even more significant, however, was the fact that the surround was a group enterprise involving a strict policing system and a communal distribution to the benefit of everyone.

Upon the conclusion of the hunt, policing duties were terminated except for punishment of the offenders. It was the Akicitas' prerogative to destroy a man's belongings, even the tipi in which he lived if they saw fit, and to flog him if his crime merited it. However, when the offender publicly showed regret, remorse, and humility, the Akicitas would frequently reinstate his property through the collection of things like those they had destroyed. An arrogant offender seldom experienced such mercy.

The procuring of meat and game was the primary basis of the Sioux's consumption economy. The Sioux were meat eaters. But if meat was the staple, plant foods were valued supplements.

From the time when the earliest fruits ripened in the summer to the last of the rose berries in winter, women busied themselves collecting vegetables. Berry-picking was a family affair, generally the job of young unmarried girls and old women. Picking-aprons were worn by some, while others picked into their upheld skirts. For fruit like buffalo berries, cherries, or gooseberries, which grew on bushes, the picker placed a small hide beneath the bush and dropped the harvest onto it. The supply could then be transferred to skin bags. The women usually brought a dog and travois to transport the harvest.

Root vegetables like wild potatoes and turnips were dug with a stick. Men were not exempt from gathering vegetables. When an abundance was discovered, a husband and wife might pick together so that the greatest possible amount could be preserved before spoilage occurred. In treading for arrowleaf berries, the depth and danger of the water frequently forced the harvesting job upon the men, who tossed the fruit to their women standing on the bank.

The Sioux women so thoroughly surveyed the potentials of native plant life that literally no source of food was overlooked. Indeed, it was a common practice for the old women to probe new campsites in search of a mouse's cache of dried beans. Moreover, for each vegetable product there were specific methods of preservation and use. As a Sioux woman expressed it:

> Timpsila or Prairie Turnips ripened when the Sahiyela or timpsila flower had bloomed and withered. Prairie turnips were good boiled and mixed with fat.
>
> To store them, we cut the tops off with our teeth and removed the skin leaving the meat and roots exposed. Then, after braiding the roots to form a long strand, we dried them over the papa drying rack. As they were needed, we cut turnips off and boiled them with fat.
>
> Wild onions were larger and sweeter than turnips. It was time to pick them when the prairie grass was thickest. Mixed with meat, either fresh or jerked, onions were extremely good.
>
> Wicagnaska or gooseberries ripened in mid-summer. These were dried and packed in parfleches and were used to make gooseberry mush. And gooseberry mush was the finest of all.
>
> From the cactus we gathered the red tops or fruit and often brought them home, worked them around in a deerskin bag to remove all the thorns. Next we crushed them with a pestle and mortar in a rawhide bowl in much the same way we pounded cherries, and placed them in rows to dry. From this, we made mush, sometimes adding a little fat.
>
> We women did all the berry picking while the men sat around.

Among the important spring foods were strawberries, Cheyenne turnips, wild turnips, and Juneberries. Later in the season potatoes, artichokes, and cherries were harvested. Plums and fungi were relished during the autumn; later, rose berries and acorns were collected.

Certain foods such as cactus fruit and acorns required special treatment. Acorns were first roasted in a bed of coals. When they popped from the bed, they were collected, boiled, dried, and crushed with a cherry pounder. Mixed with fat, the acorn stored well and made an excellent mush.

And yet, in this teeming land of plentitude, abundance was matched from time to time by scarcity.

"When there was no food, and the children began to cry, we put up a hide and scraped it. These scrapings we boiled to make soup for the children, and we ate it too."

Confident in their ability as exploiters of the natural environment, the Sioux enjoyed a sense of economic security to which their wealth was attestation. Firmly established in the heart of the northern buffalo range, their position made them even more stable, for the seasonal north and south migrations of the herds crossing and recrossing the Sioux territory brought this tribe into much more frequent contact with the animals than were the Indians living on the periphery or at the extremities of the range. This abundance and reliance upon one resource held the key not only to the temporary success of the Sioux but also to their ultimate ruin. With a sort of blind overconfidence, they closed their minds to any other economy. So successful were they that there was no reason to consider alternatives such as agriculture. Like the gambler in a winning streak, they believed they had hit upon an infallible system.

By 1850 the Sioux had become proficient plunderers. Their men devoted their lives to maintaining the nation's effectiveness; their women labored to utilize and embellish the wealth. Teton society and Sioux culture during the mid-nineteenth century were efficiently wealthy.

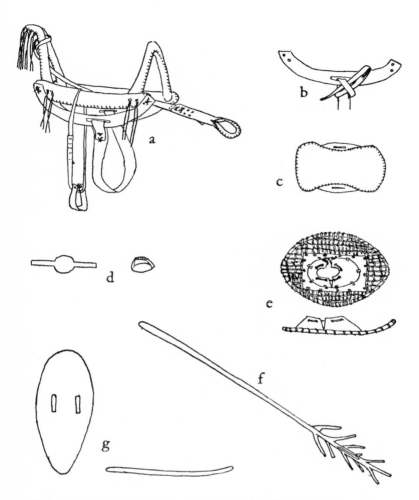

a, Woman's saddle; *b*, girth; *c*, man's pad saddle; *d*, stirrup. (See Chapter 8.) *e*, Rawhide snowshoe; *f*, snowshoe pole; *g*, wooden snowshoe. (See Chapter 9.)

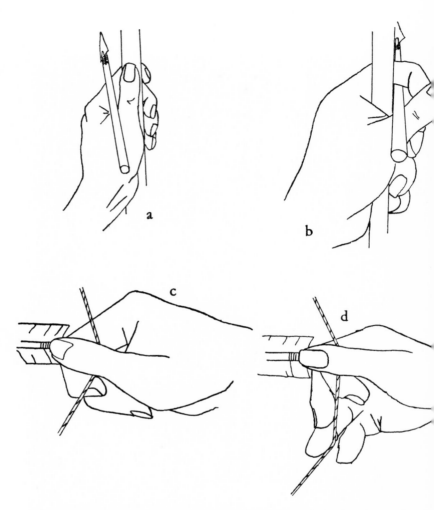

Methods of arrow release: *a*, laying it over; *b*, laying it on the inside; *c*, Iron Shell's method; *d*, Leader Charge's method. (See Chapter 9.)

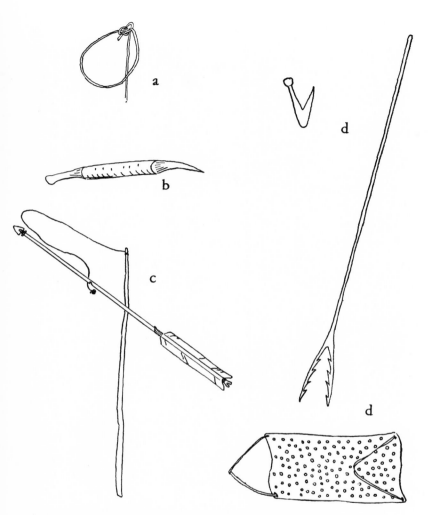

a, Noose; *b*, rabbit stick; *c*, "sending-arrow"; *d*, fishing equipment. (See Chapter 9.)

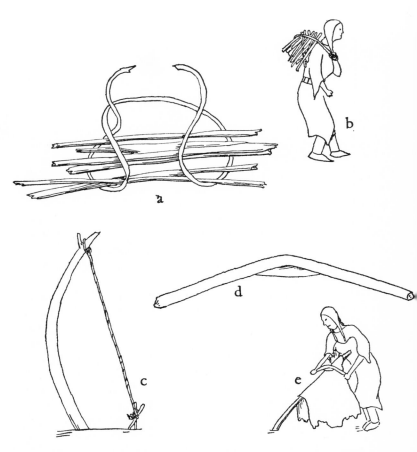

a, Load of wood; *b*, woman carrying wood; *c*, hide-rubber; *d*, dehairer; *e*, woman using dehairer. (See Chapter 10.)

CHAPTER 10

Production

THE SIOUX DIRECTED THEIR EFFORTS toward a complete and systematic exploitation of their natural environment. So rich and abundant was nature that production of food was unnecessary and, in fact, unthought-of. The produce of the farms—corn, beans, and squash—could be had by trade with such neighboring village tribes as the Omahas or Arikaras. And if the Sioux had nothing to trade, they would plunder. They were hunters first, gatherers second, and farmers never!

Not being farmers, the Sioux returned nothing to nature. Nor did they attempt to maintain or to increase the resources upon which they depended. In this situation they were luckier than some other nations whose livelihood was conditioned on a nonreplaceable resource. The bison at least were self-perpetuating. The Sioux could hardly have foreseen the end of the buffalo, for they understood the concept of depletion no better than the white hunters who later killed off the great herds.

Yet, though they did nothing to increase the economic base, the Sioux did engage in production which made it possible to utilize this base more effectively. This was the manufacture of clothing, shelter, and other artifacts which were well adapted to the environment and to the nomadic life that was necessary for following the buffalo.

Sioux production was intricately interwoven with the roles of individuals, and there was involved a definite division of labor, a division that was largely determined by the abilities and limitations of the groups of workers. Manufacture of articles of shelter, of clothing, of war and the hunt, of religion, of amusement, and of personal adornment was carried on by nearly every adult member of the group. But definite limitations were placed upon the making of certain articles, depending upon one's sex and sometimes upon one's age. Proficiency and specialization were often relegated to a few individuals who gained acclaim and frequently some wealth. The duties of each member were consequently prescribed within a range of limits, and though individuals enjoyed a freedom of expression and a freedom of choice within the limit of their role, few were bold enough to trespass into an activity not in accordance with the pattern.

In addition to cooking and drying meat supplied by her husband or brothers, the woman gathered wild berries and dug roots, kept the water bag filled, and provided wood for the fire. Manufacture of clothing included not only sewing and decoration but tanning the hides of which all clothing was made. Women also tanned hides to make tipis. When the camp moved, it was the women who packed the goods, took the tipi down, and put it up again when the new village site was reached.

The making of a tipi suggests something of the effort involved in one sphere of a woman's activities. This was no casual undertaking and careful planning was needed. First an adequate supply of hides must be accumulated, for even a small tipi required seven hides, while larger ones contained as many as twelve to eighteen. At the same time, gifts and food had to be collected for helpers, since no one made her tipi alone.

Preparing a buffalo hide was a strenuous and tedious task that demanded strength, skill, and patience. The first step was the removal of the flesh and gristle by staking the hide out and scraping away the tissue with a chisellike implement fashioned from bone and tipped with a blade. Stooping over the skin, the woman pulled the blade toward her, removing the particles. The hide was then allowed to dry in the sun, perhaps for several days, before being scraped to an even thickness with a short, hoe-like tool. The hide was then turned over to remove the hair, a process usually carried out with the scraper. At this point the raw hide was stiff and hard. After soaking in water for about two days, the hide became soft and pliable and was ready for final curing.

Mixtures of brains, liver, fats, and sometimes red grass were rubbed thoroughly into the skin, and then allowed to dry. Next the skin was stretched and finally worked back and forth over a twisted rawhide thong to completely break down the tissue. Though minor variations in technique might be employed, tanning was a tedious process that might take one woman as much as ten days.

Cutting the hides to the proper pattern for the size of the tipi desired was a task to be supervised by a woman who had not only experience but high moral qualities. Two White Buffalo was recognized as such a woman and was consequently frequently invited first to feast, and if she accepted, requested to supervise and sew on the flaps. Otherwise, the tipi when erected would fill with smoke. "Wicked women's sewing makes the smoke go back in the tipi."

In preparing the pattern for an average-sized tipi, stakes were placed in the ground to form a large, irregular triangle of approximately a forty-five degree angle. One served as the center of a radius, and at a distance of twelve feet a second stake was placed. The third stake was located at a point about thirteen feet from the first stake and eighteen feet from the second stake. This triangular figure was equal to one-half the tipi and approximately a quarter-section of a full circle. Four hides, from which the legs were trimmed, were then sewn together to fill the lower area of the triangle and so placed that the tails were at the bottom while the heads were toward the top. A fifth hide was used to fill the upper area or apex of the triangle. The trimmed legs were used to fill in or patch the spaces wherever they might occur. This process was then repeated for the remaining half of the tipi, thereby utilizing five more hides. This was referred to as a "four-width" tipi since four hides were sewn in a row to form one-half of the base. A finished tipi made to these dimensions had a radius at the base of about eleven feet.

The tipi was then folded in half and laid between the stakes so that the fold lay along a line from the top stake to the second stake (or shorter distance), while the two front sides lay along a line from the top stake to the third stake (or greater distance).

By using a piece of dark clay as a marker and by attaching a rope to the top stake and extending it to the second stake, a radius could be swung and marked to determine the bottom or perimeter of the tipi. From the line between the top stake and the third stake, the correct line for the front of the tipi was marked and then trimmed accordingly. When this was completed the door was cut and the buttonholed piece for securing the pins was attached. Finally the smoke flaps were sewn. This was done by Two White Buffalo, at least one hide being reserved for this. It took three women about four days to sew a ten- to twelve-hide tipi.

A well-appointed tipi required additional embellishment with "tipi front quills." These dangles, made of short strips of rawhide wrapped with brightly colored porcupine quills to which were attached horsetails, feathers, or tiny cones fashioned from tin, hung in two rows down the front. In addition, four quilled or beaded discs with horsetails hung from their center might be attached to the tipi to the height of a man's head and at equal intervals.

A "dew cloth" made of hides fastened to the lodgepoles around the inside of the tipi to shoulder height served as an insulator and kept out the dew. Frequently the owner invited young men to paint their war records upon the lining. Men so requested were glad to do this for it gave them the opportunity to display their exploits and receive a free meal.

Erecting the tipi was a skill which every woman must know. Lodgepoles of pine, though sometimes cut and peeled by the men, were set up by the women. Fifteen to twenty feet high, and extremely heavy, the poles must be well secured in case of wind and storm. Three main poles were first set up as foundation, usually secured with a guy rope to a stake driven into the earth at a point approximately in the center of the tipi. The remaining poles were then placed in the crotch formed by the junction of the main poles. The exact position of the poles was adjusted after the cover was placed, forming an ellipse rather than a perfect circle so that the front of the tipi was steeper than the rear. It took two women to set a tipi, while a small girl was held up to insert the front pins. Proper and frequent adjustment of the smoke flaps in relation to the direction of the wind was necessary to prevent smoking and ensure a correct draft. A door, made by stretching a hide over a U-shaped willow frame, covered the small entrance.

The tipi, as well as its furnishings, was so perfectly adapted to the nomadic requirements of Sioux life and so ingeniously designed with respect to the physical nature of the plains environment that it can rightfully be called a masterpiece of architecture. When a camp had to be moved on short notice to follow the ranging bison herds, the tipi could be struck, packed, and its furnishings and contents loaded on the horse travois in less than fifteen minutes. In making camp, two experienced women could raise a tipi and be ready for housekeeping within an hour or so. Such speed spoke well not only for the women's proficiency but for the designer's understanding of efficiency in construction.

In addition to portability, the tipi's shape made it a most fitting dwelling for the severe cold of the plains winter. The reduction of air volume at the top of the lodge because of its conical shape in effect reduced the amount of heat required to warm the lower living space. Consequently, even when temperatures fell below zero, the tipi remained entirely comfortable. The dew cloth created an air space that reduced heat loss in the winter and kept the dwelling cool in the summer. In very hot weather, the picket pins could be removed and the sides rolled up to provide cross ventilation of cool air. It is, therefore, no misstatement to say that the Plains Indian comfortably lived within a chimney during the winter and under a parasol during the summer.

A well-run household involved a definite arrangement of furnishings with ample space for pleasant living as well as for storage and cooking. Beds of folded buffalo robes were placed away from the door at intervals around the perimeter of the tipi. The place of honor opposite the door at the back of the lodge was sometimes reserved for the master, although often he and his wife slept nearer the entrance to the south. Back rests of willow rods supported by tripods were placed at the head and foot of the owner's bed. Parfleches and soft leather storage bags containing foods, utensils, and clothing were stacked along the dew cloth between the beds. On a forked pole to the left of the door hung the water bag. Firewood was stored just outside the door. From the tipi poles, or from the tripods supporting the back rests, the man might hang his painted bonnet case and his medicine pouch. Shields were hung from a forked pole at the rear of the tipi.

The fire pit was placed directly behind the door, about one-third the distance from front to back of the tipi and directly under the opening of the flaps. This made the area in back of the fire pit much more commodious and gave ample room for the altar which was located behind the fireplace. The remainder of the floor, carpeted with buffalo robes with the hair side up, was pleasant to walk upon. Some families tied cut deer hoofs and later tiny bells to the tipi tightening rope. When the wind blew, music filled the tipi.

The Sioux dwelling not only was comfortable and pleasant throughout the year but was in its way quite handsome. Decorated on the exterior with its four medallions and rows of quilled pendants paralleling the entrance, frequently painted with bold symbols and animal figures belonging to the husband, and topped by a spiral of graceful lodgepoles extending from the apex often tipped with long white or red deerskin streamers or a scalp which airily fluttered in the breeze, the tipi had a certain quality of magic. Inside, the daylight filtered through the skin cover and gave a translucent effect to everything. The dew cloth embroidered in horizontal stripes of quilling served as a handsome background for the painted back rests and decorated packing cases. The rich brown of the buffalo rugs softened and contrasted the brighter wall area, which in turn gave a feeling of spaciousness.

In theory, the tipi belonged to the woman—it was her property and her responsibility. As if to crystallize this concept, the dwelling was thought of as a woman and names for various parts were generally feminine. The flaps, for example, were "woman's arms." In practice, however, the woman was not sole proprietor. Her husband exercised certain rights and assumed certain responsibilities. The size of the tipi depended as much upon the husband's ability to obtain skins as upon the wife's ability to prepare them. A good hunter or a successful horse thief was able to accumulate more hides and thereby afford a bigger lodge. As one man expressed it, "The men with the fastest horses lived in the biggest tipis."

Certain of the decoration was also determined by the husband. Shamans painted representations of their visions or supernatural helpers upon the cover. Those who had dreamed of elk, for example, painted their tipi yellow and emblazoned a lone elk at the rear. Men who had dreamed of the buffalo were known as "Those who live in black tipis."

Moreover, the husband's interest in the tipi was symbolized by the fact that it might be destroyed by the Akicita if he failed to conduct himself properly on a hunt. That the property of one person should suffer destruction for the action of another was reconcilable within the societal pattern. The husband, as theoretical owner of his wife, became as responsible for her property as for his own. A good husband proved his worth by accumulating and caring for property, both his wife's and his own, in order that it might sometime be given away. He was a sort of trustee. When he jeopardized any of it, he not only weakened his economic position but seriously strained his family life and opened himself to anguish as well as disgrace. The man was the head of the house—its success or failure depended upon him. Unfortunate was the individual who lived with his wife's people, for he was a "buried man."

But the tipi was the center of the household, and this center was the woman's domain. It was here that she cooked the family's meals; it was here that she made the family's clothing; it was here that she gave birth to and nurtured the family's children.

When a man brought deer to camp, it was the woman's task to butcher. With the carcass, the hunter brought the heart, liver, kidneys, and pancreas bundled in the paunch which he had previously inverted and cleaned with grass. A matriarch described the preparation of meat:

Rattling Tipi first cut off the front legs close to the ribs, next the rear legs and then removed the takoan, the great sinew running over the backbone from rump to shoulder. The takoan contained the tampco, a delicate section of deliciously tender meat. With this removed, she then split the carcass along one side of the backbone and next cut each half just below the ribs making four pieces. The neck and the head were last to be removed, and the remaining hind quarter she hung from a forked pole near the door.

The following morning, Rattling Tipi prepared the quarter for drying. Carefully cutting thin strips, which stretched to an arm's length and were about three hands wide, she struck three dowels of sun flower stalk crosswise on each strip, one at the middle and one at each end. When all the strips of meat were ready, she took them outside and placed them over the drying rack, a long pole supported by two sturdy forked poles.

Racks were made high enough to prevent the dogs from jumping up and stealing the meat. Boys would sometimes tie a knife to a stick, cut the meat from the pole and run away with it. Then we had to take a whip after them and thrash them if we could catch them, and we whipped them hard. Girls never did this for girls didn't steal—they knew what happened to the boys when they were caught. But the dogs were really more meddlesome than the boys.

Magpies often pecked the meat along the pole so that it broke in two and fell to the ground. If we failed to see this in time, the dogs made a feast.

When the flies were too thick, we hung the meat inside over a rawhide rope stretched between several lodge poles. By putting wet sticks over the fire to make it smoke, the flies would stay away. When it rained, we dried meat inside but it took much longer. In sunny weather it took about three days to thoroughly dry and when one side was dried it had to be turned over. As the meat dried, the shrinking often caused the sticks to bend and break, so they were thrown away. When the meat was hard it was ready to be cut up into papapuze [dried jerked meat] and stored.

Before storing, papapuze had to be folded to fit a parfleche. The meat was folded on a piece of deerskin and another skin was placed over it, upon which the woman tramped to flatten the meat with her weight. When it was thoroughly compressed, the dried meat was placed in a parfleche and stored at the edge of the tipi. Pieces were cut off and cooked as needed.

Women prepared papapuze in a variety of ways. Sometimes it was broiled by placing a piece the size of a hand on coals, which had been spread with a stick. Slices of papapuze might also be boiled in a paunch kettle. Filled with water into which heated stones were dropped with a forked stick, the buffalo's stomach was supported at the corners with sticks to make a serviceable cooking pot. Six hot stones about the size of the fist were usually sufficient to bring the water to a boil. Paunch boiling was generally done outside in both summer and winter. Sharpened sticks were used to remove the meat. "Boiled meat was always best, for there was soup to go with it."

Broiled papapuze was the basis for making *wakpapi* or pemmican. After the meat had been cooked on the coals, water was sprinkled on it. Then with a granite meat pounder, the papapuze was pulverized in a rawhide bowl where it was mixed with bits of fat to taste. The pemmican was next fashioned into patties which could be eaten immediately or, being quite dry, stored well, especially when frozen.

Dried cherries and grapes, crushed with pits and seeds, were commonly mixed with pemmican. These, too, might be stored, either as patties in a paunch bag or frozen during the winter. Pemmican made from buffalo meat was considered the most desirable.

Meat was also roasted, especially large cuts such as the ribs. These were suspended by a cord from a tripod placed over the fire so that the meat hung several inches above the coals. By using the extended end of the skewer as a handle, the meat could be swung and turned as it roasted.

Many foods were eaten raw. Fresh fruits in season, such as

strawberries and grapes, were consumed with relish. The liver and kidneys of all game were especially delectable when uncooked. Boiling, however, was the most popular form of food preparation. The buffalo's brains, the gristle about the nostrils, and the tongue were boiled and recognized as particular delicacies. Roasted buffalo hump was also a favorite, while soup made from the hoofs or the tail were thoroughly enjoyed. No part of the animal was overlooked. The Sioux were most fond of boiled unborn calves. The lung and pancreas were especially good. Intestines turned inside out, cleaned and filled with strips of meat, were tied at intervals to form sausages. Boiled, and then cut between the ties so that meat and juices could be sucked from the hot sausage, "Crow guts" were a gourmet's feast.

Seasoning for soups and broths was rare and limited largely to peppermint leaves. Salt was scraped from the edges of dried buffalo wallows and stored in deerskin paunches, but was so scarce that most women did not consider it a condiment and it was therefore not in general use. Honey was considered poisonous by some, while box-elder sap was occasionally mixed with chokeberries in making mush.

The role of the woman as cook, tailor, housekeeper, and nursemaid was generally complicated and yet made less arduous by the actual size of the family. The average household might consist of a man and his wife, possibly his widowed mother, and his several children. Conceivably his oldest son and daughter-in-law might live with them. In such a family, the wife would have the help of the mother-in-law, daughter-in-law, and her own daughters. The daughter-in-law would be of particular help in doing many of the tasks. Co-operative work was the rule.

Ideally, every woman was expected to be accomplished in all the female arts, but the goal was nearly impossible to attain. What the average woman did possess through her girlhood rearing was a practical training in nearly all domestic arts. Her skill and her incentive would do much in determining her competency, and her efficiency in one or more phases might eventually be acclaimed by the community.

A PIPE BAG decorated with porcupine quill embroidery and quill-wrapped fringe, from about 1870.

Courtesy Denver Art Museum

A PAINTED SHIELD COVER encasing shield, from about 1860.

Courtesy Denver Art Museum

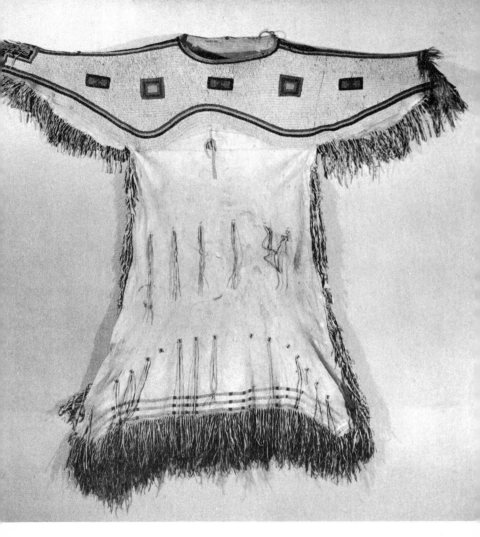

THE YOKE of this elk skin dress, from about 1865, is decorated
with seed beads.

Courtesy Denver Art Museum

THIS SHAMAN's wearing robe of buffalo hide, from about 1860, has a black and white painted design against a completely red background. Since the hair was left on this robe, it was meant to be worn in winter.

Those few individuals who so outshone others in some particular accomplishment became specialists. Women who had dreamed of the Double Woman or Deer Woman, a being who appeared in a vision as a human but disappeared as a deer, were famous for their ability to do porcupine quillwork. It is said that a woman who first dreamed of the Double Woman taught quilling to the people, having learned the art herself in her vision. She had set up a tipi and asked that a porcupine be brought to her. Alone she sorted and dyed the quills and later chose a helper to aid her in quilling a robe. When it was completed she held a feast, inviting all Dreamers to contest.[1]

Quilling was probably the highest attainment in the female arts. Unlike tanning, which required much brawn, quilling demanded delicate dexterity. The Sioux woman graded her quills into four sizes and stored them in bladder pouches according to size and color. By boiling roots or berries, she obtained various colors and hues. Blue Whirlwind derived red from the snakeberry root, yellow from huckleberry root, and a purplish black from the fox grape. Green dye was secured from an unknown root, it is said, and later she got blue from a clay obtained through trade.[2] She soaked the white quills briefly in water before immersing them in the dye. She allowed them to remain in the dye only a short time lest the core of the quill be worked out. When the color was satisfactory, she placed the quills on a piece of bark in the sun to dry.

In quilling, the Sioux woman first softened about six quills in her mouth, with the points extending just beyond the corner of her lips.

In decorating moccasins, the woman marked two guidelines on the hair side of the skin with the point of her awl. At the heel she punched two holes parallel to the surface of the skin and the guidelines. Through these holes she ran pointed sinew threads, tying

[1] Wissler, "Societies and Ceremonial Associations," *loc. cit.*

[2] Carrie A. Lyford, *Quill and Beadwork of the Western Sioux.* Information obtained by this author discloses that red dye was obtained from buffalo berries and squawberries, yellow from sunflowers, and black from wild grapes and hickory nuts.

a knot in the end of each to hold them fast. All sinew sewing was done through the surface of the hide so that no stitching was visible from the underside. Next she would tie a long strand of sinew to a little stick and secure the stick by stepping on it or by placing it in her moccasin. She tied the loose end of the sinew to the upper thread already attached at the point of the knot. The thread of sinew stretched to her foot acted as a guide for the upper line forming the top of the strip of quillwork.

After the quill was split and the butt flattened over the side of the overgrown nails of her thumb and forefinger, it was laid under the lower sinew at the starting point and turned over tightly. Then a stitch was taken with the sinew exactly the width of the flattened quill and secured by a half-hitch or loop stitch. The quill was then turned under the lower thread and a similar stitch was taken, and so on, with new quills spliced in until the desired length was reached. Two quills might be used alternately from upper and lower threads. When opposing colors were used, a pleasing plaited effect was had. This stitch, the most widely used, was called "quilling with tied sinew," but the same effect could be had by the use of parallel rows of stitches without the tied sinew.

At least nine different quilling techniques were employed, all having special names and many reserved for specific tasks. Thus, the quilling of the rawhide fringe of a pipe bag involved a wrapping technique; the embellishing of a pipestem required plaiting. Fine lines for use in narrow designs, called "one-awl quilling," were produced with only one thread around which the quills were twisted. Before the advent of beads, porcupine and occasionally bird quills were the primary sources of decoration.[3] The women decorated men's shirts and leggings with bands of quillwork applied to long removable strips of leather. They ornamented the handles of war clubs; they striped their soft leather bags with rows of red quills. Probably the most significant art, except for the adornment of baby carriers, was the decoration of robes. A woman

---

[3] *Ibid.*; Wissler, "Societies and Ceremonial Associations," *loc. cit.*, 93. Wissler suggests that bird quills were used in decoration. Unlike the Cheyennes, the Sioux appear not to have used dyed cornhusks for decorative purposes.

was credited highly for each robe she produced because the women who first taught the art embroidered a robe.

One of the most essential and indeed most decorative articles of clothing was the robe. The most desirable robe was one made from the skin of a two-year-old female buffalo, for its size as well as its texture was best suited for wearing. For winter use, the hair was left on, but for summer wear robes were dehaired and sometimes scraped thinner in order to be lighter in weight. Fine robes to be worn for dress and special occasions were decorated with painted geometric designs or with embroidery of porcupine quills.

In painting a robe, Roan Horse Woman's sister used colored earths ground in a tiny stone mortar and stored in small deerskin pouches. Red paint was made by heating a yellow rocklike substance, while black was obtained from very dark earth or charcoal. Though some women mixed their paints with a watery glue made from boiled hide scrapings, others apparently used only water. Roan Horse Woman's palette consisted of reds, ochers, yellows, dark browns, and blacks. Blues were a relatively modern color, and green too was only recently introduced among the Sioux. Using a creasing stick on the stretched and dampened hide, she stood over the hide and marked first the outline of the border. With tiny brushes made from the sharpened end of the porous rib of the buffalo, she dipped into the tortoise-shell paint cups the color she desired to use in the border. When the border was completely filled in, she began to work on the central portion, creasing the outlines first and then coloring. In frescoe-like technique, she kept the robe damp while painting. Sizing the painting with the cut end of a cactus leaf or glue helped to preserve it, and moreover, sizing had the pleasing effect of outlining the designs in white.

Certain painted designs were reserved for women's use. The buffalo was most popular, while a design in the form of two facing E's each with four bars was also worn. Older men wore the "shield" or "Black bonnet," while robes containing paintings of men and horses showing exploits were apparently very rare.

Both men and women wore the spider web, while solid yellow robes were apparently worn only by Heyokas. Robes decorated with porcupine quills, most commonly in a series of red horizontal stripes, were worn mostly by women and children. Frequently unmarried women's robes were embellished with a row of medallions and pendants across the bottom. Young unmarried men often wore robes with horizontal bands of quilling with four large medallions, the first medallion being placed at the left or head of the hide.

Robes were worn in various ways, but fashion demanded the head of the buffalo be worn to the left. Young men often wore their robes over their heads, while older men placed one end under their right arm and held it with their left hand, leaving the right arm free. Women wore their robes over both shoulders, though they also might wear them over their heads.

In certain instances the decorative designs on robes identified the status of the wearer. The design designated the sex and to a degree the age, and apparently also whether the wearer was married or single. All clothing, as a matter of fact, served, in addition to its decorative, protective function, to differentiate one kind of person from another.

The proper attire for women consisted of a dress fashioned from two elk skins, knee-length leggings, and moccasins. For everyday wear, these garments were naturally utilitarian and unadorned.

For formal occasions the Sioux women vied with one another for elegance. The yokes of dresses were heavily embellished with rows of elk teeth or quilled embroidery, and in later times with dentalium shells and beads. Around their waists they wore leather belts bearing geometric designs. Leggings and moccasins, too, were ornamented with colored quills and later with beads. Styles in dress changed slowly, but the fastidious woman prided herself on the workmanship and individuality of her wardrobe.

Some of the designs and geometric figures used in the decoration of clothing "belonged" to certain families and were handed down from mother to daughter. Some of them were believed to

226

have been received in dreams. Most of the designs were given names, such as "tripe" for checkerboard, "star" for a Maltese cross, and "mountains" for a stepped pyramidal form. Naming the designs did not necessarily imply symbolism as such, for often they were employed simply for their decorative value with no intent to convey meaning.

Certain designs, however, did possess symbolic implications. Some indicated an event in the owner's life, such as colored hoof-marks on men's leggings to represent the number and color of horses captured. The "spider web" design and the "dragonfly" in the form of a patriarchal cross implied kinship with Thunder, and hence became protective in character. Those who had dreamed of the Double Woman or were Heyokas often used swallows on their clothing.

Male apparel consisted of an undecorated leather breechcloth and moccasins. Leggings, reaching from the ankle and covering the thigh, were tied to a decorated belt or simple leather G string. It appears that poncho-like shirts of deerskin were worn by only a few men for daily use. Decorated shirts, bearing two quilled bands extending down the arms and two over the shoulders as well as quilled neckpieces in medallion, square, or triangular shapes at the throat and nape, were reserved for members of the Big Bellies and possibly some Akicita officers, as a badge of station. Painted shirts were worn only by the Wicasas, with the upper half being blue and the lower yellow, or the upper red and the lower green. Some Wicasas, it is said, might prefer an all yellow shirt or one bearing vertical green stripes. Locks of hair fringed the sleeves of the shirts to symbolize the people in their charge. Wicasa Yatapikas, in addition to the shirt, were entitled to wear hair-fringed leggings as a sign of their greater responsibility.

The Sioux also wore such ornaments as earrings of dentalium shells, quilled armlets, gorgets of mussel shell carved in button-like form, necklaces of bear claws, beaded chokers, and quilled braid wrappings. Men often fastened to their hair a trail of silver trade discs attached to a long leather band. Each of these fashionable devices was worn to embellish the person. Certain ornaments were worn in a manner to signify status. Young girls who had not yet reached maturity wore their hair braids down the back tied with pendants, whereas those who had reached puberty wore their braids over the shoulder. Young unmarried men wore tied to their scalp locks a band of quilling surmounted by two feathers from which hung a lock of horse hair reaching below the shoulder blades.

People sought out the women who could do intricate quilling, who made handsome cradles, who best wove a buffalo-hair rope. There were good beaders and poor beaders, good tanners and poor ones, and there was a market for well and beautifully made articles. Specialists could demand a high price in goods for their work, and they also received approbation and prestige.

The division of labor among the sexes was a co-operatively designed arrangement wherein each sex did that work for which they believed they were best suited. That women's work involved the labors of tanning, carrying wood, and on occasion bearing burdens in no way inferred a low status. Evidence to the contrary is offered by the high position of women among the Sioux, the values placed upon virtue, upon child-bearing, and upon industry and craftsmanship.

The woman's role in Sioux life was manifest in her capacity to make and maintain the essentials of daily living. Her quilling and painting were the tribe's primary art expression, and it was essentially geometric in form. Triangles, rectangles, and circles in various and—in later times—complex patterns dominated the field.

The man's interest in the production economy was devoted to the tools of hunting, war, and religion—the very facets of life for which he assumed responsibility. It was his duty to manufacture bows and arrows, bowls of wood, spoons of horn, spears, shields, drums, and rattles. He was early taught how to make weapons and how to use them. He learned that only men could touch shields and such sacred things, that a woman's touch contaminated and destroyed their efficacy.

Making arrows was an art which every man should know, but the work of a skilled craftsman was always in demand. Various woods were used for making shafts but gooseberry was preferred; cherry and Juneberry were alternatives. These were cut in the winter and stored in bunches.

In making an arrow, the man first shaped the nock with a knife, then cut the shaft to the desired length. Arrows were measured from the elbow to the tip of the little finger, plus the length of that finger. The slot for the point was cut next.

Smoothing was done by twisting and pulling the shaft through a hole formed by two pieces of grooved sandstone held firmly in the hand. When the arrow was sanded, it was run through a straightener—a flat bone in which there was a hole large enough to allow the arrow to fit loosely.

After the arrow was considered to be smooth and straight, several zigzag lightning lines were cut in the shaft to give it speed and make it true. Then with earth colors mixed with saliva, two or three bands were painted below the nock to serve as identifying marks.

The feathers of the turkey buzzard and wild turkey were most frequently used to feather arrows. These were split shafts or quills, flattened and cut to the proper length, usually about six inches, with about one inch of the feather's rachis extending at each end. Three such split feathers were secured to each arrow with a wrapping of fine sinew. The arrow-maker held one end of the sinew thread in his mouth and by slowly turning the arrow with his hands, wrapped the thread around the feather and arrow.

When the ends nearest the nock were secured, glue made from boiled buffalo hoofs or the hide from the neck and jaw was applied beneath each feather's shaft.

After the shafts were glued, the lower ends of the feathers were wrapped to the arrow, and glue was applied to both wrappings. They were trimmed to about half an inch at the forward end, to about one inch at the rear.

As white men came among the Sioux, points were made from

skillets secured in trade. These were cut with steel tools and sharpened with files. Their shapes, however, closely approximated earlier forms chipped from stone. Although three shapes appear to have been most common, their uses in hunting or war were interchangeable.

Blunt pointed arrows for birds were made the same length, but had only two feathers. The points were carved first.

Points were glued into the groove cut in the arrow shaft and secured by a wrapping of sinew.

The Sioux considered ash to be the finest bow wood. A tree about the size of the forearm was cut in the fall and over a period of two weeks carved down to shape as it was dried near the fire. The finished shaping was begun at the grip, the ends being tapered afterward, and the bow was cut to a length approximating the height of the owner's waist. During the making it was tested periodically by bending over the knee. The width and thickness of the bow depended on the grip of the man who would use it. The ends were tapered to the thickness of the little finger, and notches were cut to hold the bowstring—two at one end, one at the other. The maker frequently painted his bow either blue or yellow. Sometimes the two were combined—the back being blue, the front yellow.

Bowstrings were made from the sinew found below the buffalo's shoulder. This was shredded and then soaked. Two strands of sinew were placed together on the naked thigh, and a third piece was placed slightly below. All three were rolled together with the palm, and pieces were added as the rolling continued to make a cord of interlocked strands about three times the length of the bow. This cord was then folded in thirds and twisted to form a three-ply bowstring. When the twisting was complete, the string was stretched and put out to dry, with the ends tied to prevent unraveling.

The bowstring was fastened to the single notched end of the bow by a loop; then it was tied to the other end. By tightening the knot at this end, the bow was brought to proper tautness and then tested. A bow was never left taut except when in use.

Sinew-backed bows, to which were glued three to five layers of sinew, were made slightly shorter than one-piece bows, but were known to be harder hitting.

Bows and arrows were kept in bow cases and quivers made from a buffalo hide tanned with the hair on. Otter and bobcat quivers were also highly prized.

The manufacture of tools and weapons was time-consuming and often tedious. Their making required a knowledge of raw materials and their properties and an understanding of the use to which the tool was to be put. Crooked arrows and weak bows were of no value for they invited failure. Anyone, however, who possessed sufficient skill and patience could become a proficient toolmaker. Thus a fine workman could supplement his wealth by making wooden bowls, war clubs, spears, and occasionally pipes, flutes, rattles, drums, and even feathered bonnets. Since the making of these articles in many cases involved nothing esoteric, the field was open.

On the other hand, the value of certain articles depended solely upon their possession of supernatural potency. Their effectiveness was determined by impartation of certain esoteric power. They were *wotawes* or medicine. Only a Dreamer who had received help from his spiritual mentor or guardian could impart this power to objects and make *wotawes*. In many instances the number and range of articles which a Dreamer could consecrate was limited. Many things, such as flutes, rattles, feathers, headdresses and war bonnets might be medicine, but certain articles like shields and love flutes were always medicine and made only by Dreamers.

White Horse, who had dreamed of both Thunder and Deer, made a shield for a young man in the following manner. He bent a hoop of light wood large enough to cover his chest to serve as a pattern. Then cutting the breast from a buffalo bull's hide, he soaked it in boiling water to shrink it, placing it outside the tipi. When satisfied with its thickness he brought it inside and cut it to the measurement of his hoop, allowing the distance of three fingers extra. Next he cut holes around the perimeter, and folding the excess over the wooden hoop, he laced it with a rawhide thong, adjusting the lacing as it dried. Before the shield was dry, however, he painted the face green and over this he painted a blue spider-web design. When the painting was finished he punched four holes in the inner corners of the web and inserted four sticks. The shield was then ready to be hung in the sun. By adjusting the lacing while drying, White Horse was able to bend the shield to give it a convex shape. When dry, the sticks were removed and four eagle feathers were hung from each by a thong. On the back a shoulder strap of buckskin one finger wide was attached. Shields were worn over the shoulder or around the neck either in front or in back. When White Horse finished, the man for whom he had made it prepared a sweat house, under the roof of which the shield was placed. During the ceremony which followed, White Horse told of his dreams, of who gave him power to make shields. He then prescribed the rules of the shield: that it must be hung outside to the rear of the tipi on a forked stick, and that it must be kept in a pouch covered with buckskin to protect it from rain. This must be done as long as any woman in the tipi had not yet reached menopause. Further, the owner was instructed not to touch the shield after he had had sexual relations with a woman—until purifying himself either with a sweat bath or by bathing thoroughly in a stream and drying himself with sage.

Frequently instructions explained the symbolism. Thus High Bald Eagle was told that the hawk was placed in the center of his shield so that when charging, he would not turn away; that the four feathers represented four enemies; and that when one enemy was killed, he must paint one feather red. He was told that four feathers were put on the shield as an incentive for him to gain four coups. Instructions usually included a prescription for applying war paint, the necessity for making vows prior to battle, and for fulfilling the vow by sweat baths and offerings after battle.

When White Horse had completed his instructions, he and the owner left the sweat lodge and, mounting horses, rode naked around the camp blowing eagle-wing whistles and displaying the shield. They returned to the sweat lodge to dress, and the owner then took his shield home and hung it up according to the rules. He then returned to White Horse's lodge and gave him a horse, a price which they had previously agreed upon.

White Horse made three more such shields and received a horse in payment for each. None of the four owners of these shields were ever wounded in battle.

Not all shields were so expensive, nor were they all so effective. A Dreamer might make a shield for his own use, but he must follow the rules just as strictly as one who had purchased a shield. While all shields were embellished with protective designs, there were various methods of construction in vogue. The most common type of shield consisted of a thickened disc of rawhide, upon which might be painted symbolic devices, the whole then encased with a soft deerskin cover containing magical painting and mystical trappings.[4]

In addition to shields, Dreamers made love flutes, small bundles containing medicine, and various forms of headdresses, each with its prescribed rules and price. Since no one man had received power to make all types of medicine, Dreamers utilized the services of other Dreamers. However, the number of Dreamers versed in any one specialty was small, and therefore there might be only one or two individuals within even a large band capable of making effective love flutes or shields. So long as his medicines were strong, such an individual held a fortunate position.

• The articles the Sioux produced, their clothing, utensils, weapons, even their dwellings and their furnishings, constituted a forceful and in a way dramatic art expression. Art was an integral part of everything they made. As embellishment on a shirt, as decoration on a cradle, as design on a parfleche, color, form, and balance were harmoniously expressed. Moreover, the form of objects exhibited the Sioux's devotion to artistic achievement. A feathered war bonnet, a ceremonial pipe, the tipi, all encompassed

---

[4] Clark Wissler, "Some Protective Designs of the Dakotas," *American Museum of Natural History Anthropological Papers*, Vol. I, Pt. 2 (1907). This author's analysis of protective designs used among the Sioux is an important contribution to the subject of native belief.

the essential elements of true design and sound color use. Among the Sioux, everyone was an artist.

Certain techniques were reserved for women, and men had their specialties. But for some things such as pipes, joint effort of both men and women was required, the man for carving the wooden stem and bowl, the woman for decorating the stem with quillwork. Because everyone contributed to the art of the Sioux, it was a truly national expression.

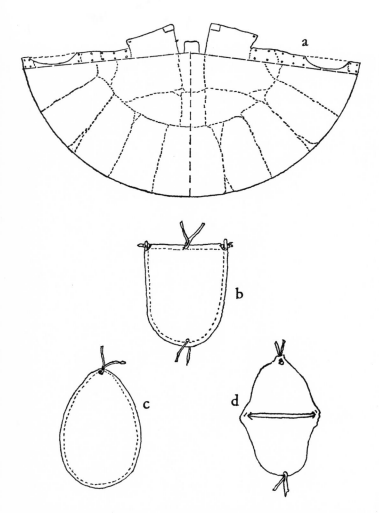

a, Five-width tipi; *b*, Little Day's tipi door (U-shaped over a
bent rod); *c*, tipi door (oval-shaped over hoop); *d*, tipi door
(simple skin with stick-stretcher). (See Chapter 10.)

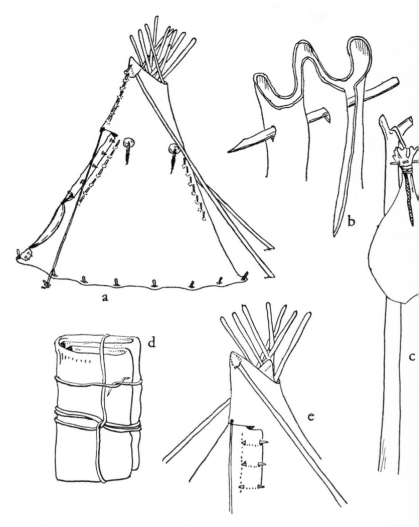

a, Typical small tipi; *b*, detail of neck of water bag; *c*, water bag suspended from pole; *d*, folded tipi; *e*, tipi flaps closed against the wind. (See Chapter 10.)

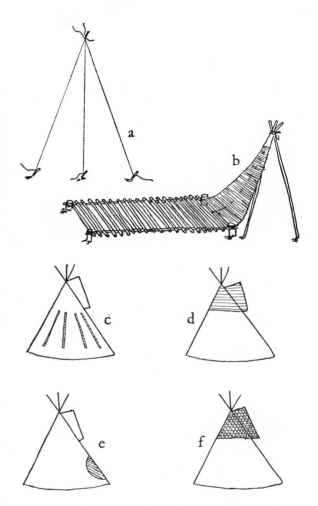

a, String frame for constructing backrest; *b*, bed and backrest.
Painted tipis: *c*, Blue Stripe; *d*, Red Top; *e*, Red Door; *f*, Black
Top. (See Chapter 10.)

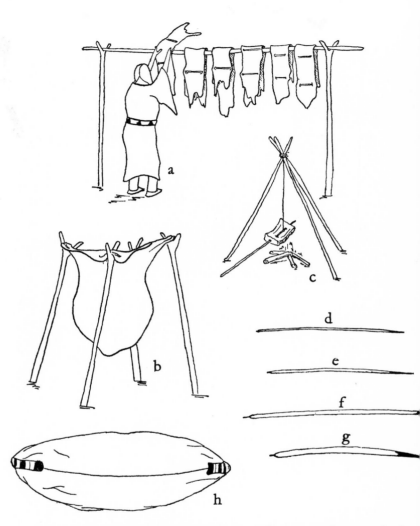

a, Woman hanging up papapuze; *b*, cooking paunch; *c*, method of cooking ribs. Types of quills: *d*, "small and long"; *e*, "quilling work"; *f*, "big quill"; *g*, "from the tail." *h*, Bladder bag. (See Chapter 10.)

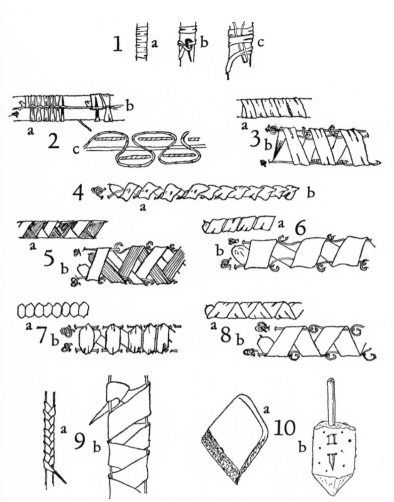

Quilling fringe: *1a*, complete; *1b*, tying the quill; *1c*, sinew loop tie. Tipi "front quill": *2a*, complete; *2b*, method of starting; *2c*, side view. Quilling with tied sinew: *3a*, complete; *3b*, method. One-awl quilling: *4a*, method; *4b*, complete. Two-quill quilling: *5a*, complete; *5b*, method. Quilling without tied sinew: *6a*, complete; *6b*, method. Stitching quilling: *7a*, complete; *7b*, method. Zigzag quilling: *8a*, complete; *8b*, method. Pipestem quilling: *9a*, complete; *9b*, method. Painting equipment: *10a*, bone brush; *10b*, cactus-leaf brush. (See Chapter 10.)

Designs for painted robes: *a*, old woman's; *b*, married woman's; *c*, spider; *d*, girl's; *e* and *f*, woman's. (See Chapter 10.)

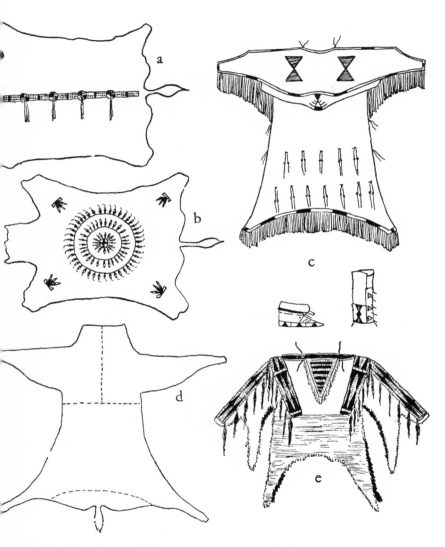

Designs for painted robes: *a*, young man's; *b*, man's. *c*, Woman's
beaded garments—dress, left moccasin, and left legging. *d* and
e, Wicasa Yatapika's shirt. (See Chapter 10.)

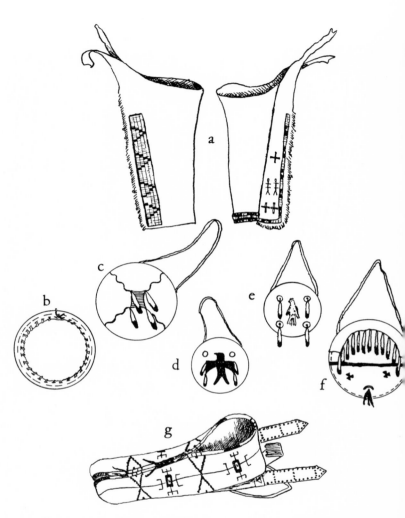

a, Man's legging. War shields: *b*, rear view of White Horse's shield; *c*, front view of White Horse's shield; *d*, swallow shield; *e*, High Bald Eagle's shield; *f*, buffalo shield with deerskin cover. (See Chapter 10.) *g*, Beaded "horse cradle" or cradleboard. (See Chapter 14.)

PART FIVE / *Self-sacrifice*

CHAPTER 11

The Universe and the Controllers

THERE WAS, AND IS, and will be Wakan Tanka, the Great Mystery. He is one yet many. He is the Chief God, the Great Spirit, the Creator, and the Executive. He is the Gods both Superior and Associate and He is the Gods-Kindred, both the Subordinate and the Gods-like. He is the good and evil gods, the visible and invisible, the physical and immaterial, for He is all in one.

The gods had no beginning and they will have no ending. Some are before others; some are related as parent and child. Yet the gods have no mother or father, for anything that has birth will have death. Since the gods were created, not born, they will not die. Mankind cannot fully understand these things, for they are of the Great Mystery.[1]

Had it been recorded in writing, rather than transmitted verbally from generation to generation, the above statement would parallel passages of the Bible, the Koran, or the Mahabharata. For the concept of one god, embodied in the Great Mystery and endowed with multiple manifestations, is basic to the religious philosophy of the Sioux.

For the Sioux, a reverent acceptance of man's rightful place presupposed an understanding of the universe. Knowledge and interpretation of natural forces became the science of living essential to the very existence of the individual. The more comprehensive and in tune the understanding, the more forthright was

[1] Walker, "The Sun Dance and Other Ceremonies," *loc. cit.* Walker's pioneering and penetrating researches have made possible an understanding of Sioux philosophic concepts rarely paralleled in ethnographic investigations. This conceptualization of Sioux cosmology is a paraphrase of his report, and the analysis which follows owes much to his insight.

the person's direction, the more assured his adjustment. Among the Sioux, this search for understanding was a national concept. It did not result in skepticism but led to the development of highly systematic beliefs in the universal forces and the supernatural. Science and religion were not separate—they were one. Candid acknowledgment that these concepts did not fully answer all the questions which man's curiosity and wonder are capable of posing, that certain truths were beyond human comprehension and must be accepted on faith, shows the maturity of Sioux thinking, the subtlety of Sioux theology.

For these perceptive philosophers, the controllers of the universe were the universe. Wakan Tanka, as the all-pervasive force, was eminent among gods. His being, as good and evil, was divisible. As good, his was a four-part being, divisible and again divisible into sixteen gods. He thereby incorporated not only all the significant elements of the universe of which the Sioux were aware but also those elements which they knew they did not understand. Such a comprehensive cosmology, encompassing the emotional and physical needs of mankind in close relation to his environment, gave the Sioux people a framework within which they could carry out their activities with a sense of security in a very insecure world.

As visible and invisible, as material and immaterial, as human and as animal, the gods embodied all manifestations of nature. There was no conflict in this idea that the deities could be represented as a force, as an object, and as a being. The wondrous power of the Controllers was in and of all things. Man, too, was an integral, functioning part. Thus, man possessing the quality of Gods, a Spirit, a Ghost, a Spirit-like, and a Potency, was himself closely associated with the Great Mystery. That the gods themselves should assume the attributes of humans, including their foibles, substantiated the interrelationship of the universe through parable. For the Sioux, any concept which denied or minimized the cohesiveness of this system would have been as naïve as it was unreal.

The hierarchy of the Sioux gods was a complex one. The all-encompassing Wakan Tanka was conceived of in various graded levels of manifestation and was identified with each. In these various aspects, the number four was supremely important; and the idea of "many-in-one" is repeated again and again. For example, the supreme Wakan Tanka is endowed with four titles. He was the Chief God, the Great Spirit, the Creator, and the Executive. Next in the descending order there were the four Superior Gods: Inyan, the Rock; Maka, the Earth; Skan, the Sky; and Wi, the Sun. Each of these had a special area of responsibility in the order of the universe. Inyan was the ancestor of all gods and all things; he was also the advocate of authority and the patron of the arts. Maka, who followed Inyan as the protector of the household, was believed to be the mother of all living things. Skan, who was the source of all force and power, sat in judgment on all gods and all spirits; and Wi, though last of the Superior Gods, ranked first among them as the all-powerful Great God, defender of bravery, fortitude, generosity, and fidelity.

The Superior Gods were in turn followed by the Associate Gods. Even as Wakan Tanka was identified with each of the Superior Gods, so did the Superiors become identified with their Associates. Thus within this overlapping identity, one within another, the Associate or counterpart of Sun was Hanwi, the Moon. Thought by some theologians to be the wife of Sun, Hanwi set the time for important undertakings. Tate, the Wind, serving as the associate of Sky, controlled the seasons and admitted spirits to the Spirit Trail. Whope, the associate of the Earth, the daughter of the Sun and Moon, was known as the Beautiful One. She served as the Great Mediator and as patron of harmony and pleasure. Inyan, the Rock, claimed as his associate Wakinyan, the Winged. Possessed of the voice of thunder with a glance of lightning, Wakinyan was patron of cleanliness.

The Gods-Kindred appeared at the next level of importance in this coterie of divine beings. They were the issue of the Superior or Associate Gods, and as such were frequently called the Subordinate Gods. Again numbering four, this group included the Buffalo, the Bear, the Four Winds, and the Whirlwind.

The Wanalapi, or Gods-like, who formed still another division within this system, might be described as abstract philosophical concepts. They included the Spirit, the Ghost, the Spirit-like, and the Potency.

Taken together, these four major groupings—the Superior Gods, the Associates, the Subordinate or Gods-Kindred, and the Gods-like were the benevolent aspects of the Great Mystery—sixteen in one, yet only one.

The complexity of this idea of interlocking individualism and simultaneous multiplicity was compounded at every level of this cosmic hierarchy. For example, the Stars were regarded as supernatural people of the sky and at the same time as an aspect of the Sky God. Likewise, the Buffalo played a double role in the Sioux saga—as People of the Sun and also as manifestations of the Sun God.

All these benevolent powers had their counterparts in theology. The evil gods were many, and they also had definite status and rank, but with few exceptions, each was independent of the other.

Iya, the chief of all evil, was personified by the cyclone. Lesser gods in the demon group included monsters, water spirits, forest dwellers, goblins, evil mannequins, and various noxious things. Iktomi, the first son of Rock, known as the Trickster, was a deposed god. Somewhat similar in concept to the Christian Lucifer, he played an important role in many of the cosmic legends. Other important figures in this category of evil spirits included Waziya, the Old Man; his wife Wakanaka, the Witch; and their daughter Anog-Ite, the Double-faced Woman.

Such, then, was the Sioux cosmology—a dual concept of good and evil powers controlling the universe long before the origin of man. These conflicting spirits were the Controllers. The actual creation myth was clothed in intricate saga and legend which involved, as an important aspect, the punishment of erring gods.

The creation story began long, long ago when Waziya, the Old Man, lived beneath the earth with his wife Wakanaka. Their daughter Ite grew to be the most beautiful of women, thereby captivating the attentions of one of the Associates—Tate, the Wind

God. Though not a goddess, Ite became the wife of Tate, who lived at the entrance of the Spirit Trail. She bore Tate four sons, quadruplets—the North, the West, the East, and the South Winds. The first born, North Wind, became cruel and surly. Hence his father Tate took from him his birthright, giving it to the boisterous second son, the West Wind. Thus, the order of winds became West, North, East, and South.

Affiliated by the marriage of his daughter with the prestige of the benevolent spirits, Waziya became dissatisfied; he yearned to have the power of the true gods. Iktomi, the Trickster, always anxious to foment discontent and to promote ridicule, bargained not only with Waziya but also with Wakanka and Ite, promising the parents great power and the daughter a talisman for even greater beauty, if they would assist him in making others ridiculous. He tantalized Ite even more with the prediction that her enhanced beauty would rival that of the Goddess Hanwi, the Moon, who was the pledged wife of the great Sun God Wi. All three conspirators agreed to Iktomi's bargain.

Possessed of a charm, Ite became more and more conscious of her beauty, less and less devoted to the welfare of her sons, the Four Winds. At this time, Sun saw Ite, and struck by her incredible beauty, the god forgot his wife Hanwi and invited Ite to sit beside him at the feast of the gods. When the time for the feast came, Ite arrived early. Finding the place next to Sun's vacant, she took it. Sun was pleased. When Moon finally arrived, she saw her seat usurped, and she was so ashamed that she hid her face from the laughing people, covering it with a robe. And Iktomi, the perpetrator of this event, outlaughed everyone. After the feast Skan, the Sky God and judge of all the gods, called council. He asked for the stories of Wi, the Sun, who had forsaken his wife; of Ite, who had dared to usurp the place of a goddess; of Wakanka and Waziya, who had coveted godlike powers; and of Iktomi, the arch-schemer. Then Skan passed judgment.

Sun was to forego the comfort of his wife Moon; he was to rule only in the day, allowing Moon to hold sway at night. Whenever they were together, Moon would always cover her face in shame. The sentence for Ite was even more severe. In condemnation of her vanity and ambition, of her negligence of maternal and connubial duties, she would give premature birth to her next son who would be unlike all other children, and her children would not live with her but with their father, Tate. Furthermore, it was decreed that she would return to the world and live without friends. Still more, although she would remain the most beautiful of women, only half of her would be so. The other half would be so horribly ugly that people would be terrified at the sight of her. Henceforth she would be called Anog-Ite, the Double-faced Woman.

Wakanka and Waziya were to be banished to the edge of the world until they could learn to do good for young children and old people. They too were to be named for their misconduct. Wakanka would be called the Witch and Waziya the Old Man or Wizard.

Iktomi also was subjected to banishment. He was to go to the edge of the world, where he was to remain forever friendless. The malicious Iktomi accepted the judgment with his usual jeering smugness, reminding Skan that he had still the birds and animals with whom he could fraternize and upon whom he could continue to play pranks.

Tate, condemned for his indiscretion, and suffering from the absence of his banished wife, was instructed to raise his children properly and to do a woman's work. Thus he lived alone with his four sons, the Winds, and his fifth son little Yumni the Whirlwind, in their home beyond the pines in the land of the ghosts. Each day his sons traveled over the world according to his instructions.

The principal characters in this debacle of deities appear again as central figures in the myths of creation and origin. It was Tate and his family who served as an impetus to the creation of the world. The legend is a charming one. One day, as the Four Winds were on their tours away from home, a shining object appeared outside of Tate's tipi. Tate looked out and saw a lovely young woman, beautifully dressed. Tate asked her who she was and whence she came. She replied that she came from the Star People, that her father was Sun, her mother Moon, and that she had been sent to the world to find friends. She also told him that her name was Whope. When the Four Winds and Whirlwind returned home, they were surprised to find that their father had taken a woman. But after Whope had prepared for each of them their favorite meal, and no matter how much they ate, their plates remained full, they realized that she was supernaturally endowed. When they learned that their father treated her not as a wife but as a daughter, she was welcomed to their lodge.

Soon each brother wanted Whope as his woman and vied with one another in showing favors. Tate decided to hold a feast, to which all the gods should be invited. At this feast Tate honored his guest with presents. Many told stories of their power and there was much dancing. Then the gods asked Tate how they might please him. He told them that if they honored his daughter Whope, he himself would be pleased.

Then they asked Whope what it was that she desired. Whope arose and stood by Okaga, the South Wind, who folded his robe around her. "I want a tipi for Okaga and myself, a place for him and his brothers." So her wish was granted and Whope became Okaga's wife. And then, as a present for the couple, the gods made for them the world and all there is in it.

The banished Waziya and his family were also involved in the Sioux creation legends, which show both appealing naïveté and philosophical reflection. As recalled by the venerable leaders of the Sioux, the story begins when the only people on earth were Waziya the Wizard, Wakanka his wife, their daughter Anog-Ite, and the Trickster Iktomi. Iktomi grew tired of playing pranks on birds and animals; he reveled in their misfortunes, but they showed no shame. So Iktomi in his boredom turned to Anog-Ite, asking her what she most desired. She told him that she wished to be among her own people. Iktomi then asked her how he might achieve this end, promising meanwhile that if she would tell him, he would never resort to tricks and pranks again.

Anog-Ite explained that if her people tasted meat and learned about clothes and tipis, they would want such things and come to where they could be had. With these instructions, Iktomi then went to the wolves, seeking their aid in bringing mankind to earth. Again in return for their help, Iktomi swore to abandon his perennial pranks. The wolves agreed to this, and Iktomi instructed them to drive moose and deer and bear to Anog-Ite's tipi, where she would prepare food, clothing, and tipis to entice mankind.

Then Iktomi gave to one of the wolves a pack, which Anog-Ite had prepared, containing tasty meat and fancy clothing for a man and a woman. He then directed the animal to take the pack to the entrance of the cave which opened into the world. The wolf did as instructed, and when it saw a strong and brave young man apart from the others, it presented the pack, telling the young man to taste the meat and advising him and his wife to wear the clothing. The wolf told the young man that the people also should be allowed to taste the food and see the clothing, and that there were many such good things as these on earth. The young man Tokahe, "The First One," was pleased to do this, for now he would be considered a leader. When the people tasted the meat and saw the clothes which Tokahe and his wife wore, they were envious and asked how they, too, might obtain such things. The old man of the group then directed that three brave men accompany Tokahe to find out where such good things came from and to prove that Tokahe was truthful.

The four men set out and, led by the wolf, entered the world from the cave. They were led to a lake where Anog-Ite had pitched her tipi. She appeared to Tokahe and his companions as a beautiful young woman. Iktomi appeared as a handsome young man. The four young men were shown much game which Iktomi had previously arranged with the wolves to have driven past. Anog-Ite gave them many tasty foods and many presents of fine clothing for them and for their people. Iktomi told them that he and his wife were really very old, but by eating this earthly food they remained young and attractive.

When the four young men returned through the cave to their

people, they described what they had seen. But an old woman, skeptical of such wonders, cautioned them to be wary. The people argued, some wishing to go with Tokahe, others saying that he was a wizard. When Tokahe offered to lead any who wished to follow him up to the earth, the chief warned them that whoever ventured through the cave to the earth would never find the way back. Nonetheless six men and their wives and children joined Tokahe, and they left the underworld guided by a wolf. When they reached the earth it was strange. They became lost and tired, hungry and thirsty. Their children cried. Anog-Ite appeared and tried to comfort them, but they saw the horrible side of her face and ran in terror. Iktomi appeared in his true form and laughed at their misery. And their leader Tokahe was ashamed.

The revelation of Iktomi's terrifying falsity and of Anog-Ite's shattering ugliness was then alleviated by the appearance of Waziya the Old Man and Wakanka the Witch, who according to the prophecy at the time of their banishment had come to understand the qualities of mercy and tenderness. They appeared to Tokahe and his followers, bringing food and drink. They led the disheartened group to the land of the pines, to the world of the Ghosts. They showed them how to hunt, to make clothing and lodges, and how to live as men now do. Thus Tokahe and his followers were the first people on earth. Their descendants are the Sioux.

To these Sioux and to the generations of Sioux that followed, mankind was but an infinitesimal part of a stupendous and mysterious universe. They knew this implicitly and accepted it. Life on earth was too rigorous, too dangerous, too ephemeral to allow them the luxurious delusion that man was exalted. The forces of nature were so real, so close, and so great that disregard of their omnipotence was inconceivable. Rather, reverence and gratitude that man was permitted to exist in the midst of such an awesome world were the logical and realistic foundations of Sioux belief.

In spite of this innate grasp of a complex and awe-inspiring universe, the Sioux, as individuals, made little pretense to a total understanding. This knowledge and interpretation was reserved for the special few, the shamans, the Wicasa Wakan or Holy Men. Versed and trained in the knowledge of the universe, able to establish a rapport between themselves and the Controllers, these Holy Men had the responsibility of interpreting the macrocosm to the people and of giving advice on proper conduct. The shaman's perception of the powerful Controllers was simultaneously humble, acute, intimate, and familiar.

It was essential for him to know that the Sun as all-powerful chief reigned over the Spirit World, the world itself, and the world beneath the world. He knew that the Sky as the source of all power provided each man with a Spirit or personality, a Ghost or vitality, a Spirit-like or essence, and a Potency or power. The shaman also understood that at the time of death Sky judged man's Spirit upon the testimony of the Ghost. Likewise the Holy Men of the Sioux cherished the sagas of the Earth and the Rock, as All Mother and All Father, the protectors of all things, alive and inanimate.

It was equally important that the shaman be versed in the ways of the Associate Gods, knowing Whope, the Beautiful One, as defender of chastity; Hanwi, the Moon, as antagonist of Anog-Ite; and Tate, the Wind, as guardian of the Spirit Trail, who admitted those which Skan, the Sky, judged worthy. The shaman knew also all the legendary traditions. He knew that a man who beheld Wakinyan as the Thunderbird—or saw in a dream such of his helpers as the swallow, the lizard, the snowbird, or the nighthawk—thereby became a clown for life.

A complete understanding of the attributes of the many subordinate gods, Tatanka, Hunonpa, Tatetob, and Yumi, was also expected of the shaman. It was necessary that he recognize Tatanka, the Buffalo, as the patron of generosity, industry, fecundity, and ceremonies as well as the special overseer of the successful hunter. He sought out Hunonpa, the Bear, as the patron of wisdom and medicine. His knowledge of Tatetob, the Four Winds, revealed the god as one yet four: West, North, East, and South, controllers of the weather and the directions. He knew that

Yumni, the Whirlwind, was taught all the games by Whope and consequently served as the patron both of these and of courtship. Inheritors of all tribal legend, the shamans were filled with poetic lore. They understood that the Gods-like dwelt in all things, that they were the *nagi* or personality, the *niya* or vitality, the *nagila* or essence, and the *sicun* or power. Each of these philosophical concepts was made tangible and real through the interpretations of the Holy Men.

While the *sicun*, or powers of good, were greater than those of evil, the powers of the evil gods had also to be reckoned with. Iya, the master of all malevolence, was a monster who ate animals and men; his foul breath brought disease. Gnaske, the Crazy Buffalo, was the patron of wrongdoing and might bring insanity or paralysis. The Unktehi captured men and transformed them into beasts; the Nini Watu were maggots which could cause aches, pains, suffering, and putrefaction. The Gica caused accidents, while the Can Oti made men lose their directions.

It was necessary also that the shaman be familiar with the symbolic attributes and the proper ceremonial procedure for each god. He knew, for example, that the colors red, blue, green, and yellow signified the Sun, the Sky, the Earth, and the Rock. Black, an indication of intense devotion, might also represent evil forces. A red forked zigzag represented Wakinyan, the Thunderbird.

Keeper of a vast treasury of tribal memories and lore, the shaman also knew that fire embodied the power of the Sun, while mysterious things exhibited the power of the Sky. He was aware that anything which grew from the earth could possess the power of the Earth, while anything with the hardness of stone could be endowed with the power of the Rock. The smoke of tobacco or sweet grass was the tangible force of Whope's harmonious meditation. Sage smoke could drive away certain evil forces. The buffalo skull or any other part of the animal contained the power of Tatanka, the Buffalo. Strange and unusual things could possess the power of the Bear.

Cosmic analysis was also the province of the shaman. He understood the beginnings of things, that Skan, the Sky, caused the world to be made in fours, with the four classes of Gods, Superior, then Associate, Subordinate, and finally the Spirits. Above the earth were four elements: the Sun, the Moon, the Sky, and the Stars. There were four directions: West, North, East, and South. Time was composed of four parts: day, night, month, and year. There were four parts to all plants: roots, stem, leaves, and fruit. There were four classes of animals: crawling, flying, four-legged, and two-legged. Finally, man's life was divided into four phases: infancy, childhood, maturity, and old age. The shaman interpreted these concepts and instructed men to carry out their activities in sets of four.

As Skan caused the world to be made in fours, so he caused it to be made in rounds. The sun, the moon, the earth, and the sky are round. The day, the night, the moon, and the year circle the sky. The four winds circle the edge of the world. The bodies of animals and the stems of plants are round. Everything in nature, save the rock, is round. Therefore the circle was, for the Sioux, a sacred symbol and could indicate the universe, the sun, time, or direction, depending upon its particular form and color.

So great was the magnitude, so tremendous the power, so complex the ways of the Controllers, that man reverently searched for knowledge and understanding which would permit him to exist in this awesome presence. Prayer and supplication, through ritual and ceremony, expressing worship and entreaty were the only effective ways of ensuring life on this earth. The consequence of disregard or of ignorance was misery and death.

The rituals and ceremonies, therefore, were patterned to the realities of the universe. They varied with the particular Controllers and their attributes. Thus, the Sun, as Chief of the Controllers, was honored by the most impressive and encompassing of the ceremonies—the Sun Dance. Other Controllers were worshipped in ways appropriate to them, and the details of these rituals were adhered to assiduously. Failure to propitiate correctly could be as disastrous as omission of atonement. Accuracy and perfection in any undertaking could constitute the difference between success and failure and even life and death. And in no undertaking did man dare forget to honor and worship the Controllers.[2] Again to the shaman fell the responsibility for a knowledge of the ceremonies and performance of the rituals. Through his role as spiritual mentor, the shaman was the people's wise and faithful counselor in all such awesome matters. As intercessor between the deities and men, the shaman spoke an occult language. Guardian of the nation's devotion and integrity, the Sioux shaman was a member of a respected and revered priesthood. The theology demanded theologians.

Many, many years after Tokahe led the first men through the cave to the upper world, and many years after the Sioux had become experienced and accustomed to life on earth, a mysteriously wonderful event occurred. The Goddess Whope visited earth. The story of this visitation, one of the most beautiful episodes in Sioux mythology, is the origin of many of the moral premises of Sioux society, as well as of the symbolic ceremonies which expressed these recognized moralities. It was as if the Controllers, observing the affairs of men, and the manner in which they conducted themselves, decided that the time had come to show mankind more of the marvels of their power and thereby reinforce the Sioux's awareness of the relationship between man and the gods.

As told by Iron Shell, the story begins:

> And so it was, to two young men who had been sent by the council of the Sans Arc division to scout for buffalo, there appeared a most beautiful woman dressed in the most lovely clothes. And on her back she carried a bundle. So pale and shining was her countenance, so perfect was her figure, that the two men were amazed.
>
> As they beheld her, she spoke to them saying, "I am of the Buffalo People. I have been sent to this earth to talk with your people. You have, now, an important duty to perform, an important message to carry to them.

[2] Alice Fletcher, "Indian Ceremonies," Peabody Museum of American Archaeology and Ethnology *Report*, Vol. XVI (1884), 260–333; James O. Dorsey, "A Study of Siouan Cults," Bureau of American Ethnology *Annual Report*, (1890). Additional details of theological symbols may be found in the works of these authors.

"Go to your leader and tell him to have a council tipi set up in the center of the village. Have the door of the tipi, like the entrance of the village, face the east. Have sage spread at the place of honor. Behind the fireplace soften the earth and shape it in the form of a square and to the rear of this place a buffalo skull. And behind the skull build a small rack. I have matters of great consequence to tell your people. I shall be at the village at dawn."

As she spoke, one of the men, struck by her charm, lusted for her and when she had finished speaking, in spite of his companion's protests, he attempted to seduce her. Immediately a crash of thunder was heard and a cloud enveloped them. Gradually, as the cloud vanished, the remaining scout beheld the beautiful woman standing unmolested while at her feet lay only a skeleton. She then directed the remaining young man to return to his village and report her message to his people.

When the scout returned to the camp he told the headman, Buffalo Who Walks Standing Upright, what he had witnessed and gave him the message as he had been ordered. The people were much alarmed by the story of the missing scout and much excited by the prospect of so mysterious a visitor. It was announced that special preparations were to be made for welcoming this stranger. Everything was made ready according to her instruction. An escort of virtuous young men was chosen to lead her through the village to the special tipi. By daybreak, a great assembly of people had gathered around the council tipi to await her arrival.

When the sun rose from the east, the beautiful woman appeared. She was dressed as she had been when first seen by the scouts, but instead of a pack, in her right hand she carried a pipe stem, in her left a red pipe bowl. She walked slowly through the entrance of the village toward the council tipi. In a stately manner she entered it, and circling to the left of the door, she sat down in the place of honor. When she was seated, the leader welcomed her.

The leader told the people how fortunate they were that Wakan Tanka had sent them this beautiful woman whom they would accept as a sister. Then he spoke to the beautiful one, telling her that her brothers and sisters were ready to hear her message.

Arising and holding the pipe, the Beautiful Woman, it is said, first addressed everyone. She told them that the Wakan Tanka was pleased with the Sioux, that she, as a representative of the Buffalo

People, was proud to be their sister. She told them that because they had been faithful and reverent, and had preserved good against evil and harmony against discord, the Sioux had been chosen to receive the pipe which she held in behalf of all mankind. The pipe was to be the symbol of peace and should be used as such between men and nations. Smoking the pipe was to be a bond of good faith, and a Shaman smoking the pipe shall be in communion with the Wakan Tanka.

Then she addressed the women as her sisters, saying that in life they do bear great difficulties and sorrow, but in their kindness they comfort others in time of trouble and grief. By giving birth to children, by clothing and feeding them, and by being faithful as wives, they maintain the family. The Wakan Tanka have planned it so and are with them in sorrow and grief.

Next she spoke to the children, as little brothers and sisters, who should respect their parents who love them and have made many sacrifices so that only good would come to them.

To the men, she spoke as a sister. She told them that all things upon which they depend come from the Earth, the Sky, and the Four Winds. The pipe she held was to be be used to offer sacrifices and prayers to the Wakan Tanka for all the blessings of life—and that it was to be offered daily. She told them to be kind and loving to women and children, for they are weak.

Finally, speaking to the leader, she explained how to care for the pipe, for as headman it was his duty to respect and protect it, since through the pipe the nation lived. As a sacred instrument of preservation it should be used in times of war, famine, sickness or any other need. She instructed Buffalo Who Walks Standing Upright in the proper use of the pipe and it is said she promised the Sioux that in time seven sacred ceremonies would be revealed to them which they were to practice: Purification, Vision Seeking, the Sun Dance, the Ball Throwing, Making a Buffalo Woman, Making as Brothers, and Owning a Ghost.

She visited with the Sioux four days and before leaving, she told the leader that the Wakan Tanka were pleased by the way he had conducted this meeting, and that she was honored to be his sister.

Then taking a buffalo chip, she lit the pipe, and offered it first to Sky, then Earth, then to Four Winds, she smoked a puff and passed it to the leader. When he had smoked a puff, she announced that her mission was finished and laying the pipe against the rack, she left the tipi unescorted.

As she went from the tipi she turned to the left, walking slowly. She left the village and then, while everyone watched her disappear, she was transformed into a white buffalo calf. In this way, Whope, the daughter of the Sun and Moon had returned to the earth to teach mankind. She was known to all as The Beautiful One, and to the Shamans as Whope.[3]

For ten generations the descendants of Buffalo Who Walks Standing Upright have cared for the Calf Pipe in behalf of the Sioux Nation. They have performed the ceremonies attendant to it with ritualistic precision.

The red catlinite bowl is carved in the form of an inverted T, whose arms are winged-like and whose bowl is a diamond-shape spool. Though it is polished, it contains no decorative incising. Two holes appear near the top of the inner wing, and a thong containing two blue beads is tied to the outer hole. The Calf Pipe, wrapped in buffalo calf wool, is kept in red flannel. To the wooden stem are attached a pendant fan of red eagle feathers and four small scalps. The stem is encased in several bird skins.

Together with the pipe are other accouterments, including three ornate carved wooden paddles for ceremonially handling coals of fire and a pipe tamper decorated with porcupine quilling. Each of these is contained in a bundle of many wrappings which daily is placed on a tripod, in the mornings to face the Sun from the east, in the afternoons to face the Sun from the west. Only on such important occasions as famine, plague, or in pledging peace is the Calf Pipe removed from its bundle. Few men, even among the Sioux, have ever beheld it.[4]

[3] Joseph Epes Brown, *The Sacred Pipe: Black Elk's Account of the Seven Rites of the Oglala Sioux;* Densmore, "Teton Sioux Music," *loc. cit.;* George Owen Dorsey, "Legend of the Teton Sioux Medicine Pipe," *Journal of American Folk-Lore,* Vol. XIX (1906). Several variations of the legend of the White Buffalo Maiden have been collected, and can be found in the writings of the foregoing authors.

[4] Sidney J. Thomas, "A Sioux Medicine Bundle," *American Anthropologist,* New Series, Vol. XLIII (1941).

Since the bringing of the Calf Pipe, men have fashioned many replicas in order to carry out the teachings of The Beautiful One. The Pipe, when smoked in communion, not only symbolizes peace but serves as a tangible medium for soliciting aid from and communicating directly with The Beautiful One. As mediator between gods and man, she transformed her power to the smoke of tobacco through the pipe. When a shaman smokes the pipe in propitiation, the God himself holds communion with him.

The characteristic patterns of Sioux theology involved several aspects of a profound and fundamental philosophy. The cosmology represented a system of great complexity and logical integration. The rank and order of the universal forces was a carefully conceived organization which explained not only how the world operated but mankind's role in relation to it. It boldly combined a vital animism with anthropomorphism and frankly acknowledged a polytheism controlled by a single, all-pervasive power—the Great Mystery.

Many aspects of Sioux theology warrant interpretation. Their concept of the macrocosm reveals their drive to comprehend the unknown. The variety of avenues indicates their ingenuity.

Conceiving the source of infinite power, Wakan Tanka, as a single yet divisible deity is not in itself monotheism. In fact, Sioux theology made no pretense of belief in one God alone. On the contrary, it successfully encompassed the idea of a single omniscient, omnipresent deity with that of a vast complexity of interrelated gods. To each were assigned specific attributes and powers, some for good and others for evil.

It can be argued that the Sioux mind conceived the cosmology, attributed qualities to their gods, and then worshipped those benevolent deities through supplication and entreaty in order to preserve themselves against the evil forces which they had likewise conjured. Certainly the Sioux were forthright in ascribing human qualities to their gods, yet giving them nonforms. It can also be argued, however, that the Sioux, in observing the awesomeness of the natural forces, and in experiencing the interaction of the beneficial and deleterious effects, interpreted those phenomena in

terms of an orderly universe. Certainly, the Sioux no more created the forces of generation or destruction than a scientist creates
matter. Yet this did not preclude their ability to interpret those
forces, and in a very real sense, use them for their own benefit. For
who is to say that the power of lightning, symbolically transferred
in representational form upon a buffalo-hide shield, cannot make
the bearer impervious to arrows? Until the advent of parapsy-
chology such a sequence would have been considered a scientific
impossibility and relegated to mere magic.

On the other hand, the Sioux were surely a party to the forces
of good and evil as are all men. They placed their idea of good
upon a pedestal and deified it. They prayed to it to protect themselves from harm. Good was equated with the four virtues, with
those attitudes and actions which fostered self-preservation by
satisfying physical and emotional needs and avoiding pain. Evil
became the antithesis of good and was associated with harm-pro-
ducing factors, including breaches of the code and personal ex-
cesses which jeopardized the well-being of others.

The Oedipean nature of the White Buffalo Maiden legend may
owe part of its origin to the masculine character of the society.
The role of the two male scouts, one representing greed and lust
and the other respect and temperance, typifies the dual nature of
the Sioux character. The White Buffalo Maiden symbolized not
only the mother but more significantly the sister, and she characterized herself as such. In her was embodied the female kin toward
whom males must sublimate the sex drive under penalty of death.
Conversely, she became the protector of women against the lust
of men. That the sex act carried such strong taboo dramatizes the
conflict under which the Sioux male existed, and suggests the
origin of the double standard. The need for symbolizing such
restrictive association for a related female seems to have found
compensation in the attitude that unrelated females were the natural target for male seduction. Such women were fair game. The
lustful hunter was destroyed not so much for his uncontrollable
lust as for his breach of a taboo and his commission of a sacrilege.

That the Sioux chose for their tutelary deity a woman, rather than a man, indicates their concern to revere feminine qualities. That the Buffalo Maiden was, in fact, the Goddess Whope, wife of Okaga the South Wind, enforced the proposition that the Sioux savior was completely and wholesomely feminine. She firmly established a rigid yet healthy realistic sexual pattern to which both its men and its women could subscribe, and which they could respect.

The occurrence of such a divine figure among any people may be due in large part to a critical need for reform that the people themselves cannot effect. The code of behavior which the Buffalo Maiden brought suggests the social crises which the Sioux at one time faced. Among these, peace among fellow men and nations was paramount, and Whope carried with her not only the word but the effective ritual.

The Maiden is said to have come to earth among men over ten generations ago. At this time, the Sioux were engaged in a losing struggle with the powerful Chippewas, a struggle which gave every indication of unequivocal defeat. Supernatural aid took the form not of a secret and powerful weapon or a political trump but of an effective code and symbol of peace—the pipe. Such aid would make it possible for the Sioux to accept defeat. On the other hand, it might so raise their morale that they would rally to sustain themselves.

Peace on earth was no more possible for the Sioux than for other men, for tragically, as among so many peoples, peace for the Sioux meant that rival nations should see the light through Sioux eyes. Actually, peace for the Sioux was a series of interludes between wars—a highly desirable state of affairs, but by no means the sole state. In this, however, the Sioux appear to have been less confused by their supernatural aid than have other nations, for they acknowledged that man's capability for peace goes hand in hand with his zest for war.

Furthermore, the Sioux goddess brought her people a code of behavior, a set of commandments which included interpretive information which explained the commands. Interestingly, they appear to have been phrased in the positive "Be kind to women, for they are weak," rather than in the familiar "Thou shalt not—" without explanation. That such commands should have been forthcoming at all seems to indicate an internal moral problem among the Sioux at the time. Their external crises may have accentuated social stress. The Sioux were fortunate in being able to welcome an additional and new set of values which equipped them for survival when destruction was imminent.

Sioux religion was more than a mere hierarchy of Controllers who governed the world and man. It was a moral system. It declared that good outweighed evil. It set forth virtues which were to be emulated and penalties for disregarding them. It did this by parables, by commandments, and by acts. Moreover, Sioux religion was vital. The appearance on earth of the deity in the form of Whope, The Beautiful One—who set forth moral codes, reiterated the humanness of the Controllers, and instructed the people in the mysteries of ceremony—was a concrete testimony to the living quality of Sioux belief. That the Controllers should send as representative a goddess of virtue to teach mankind revealed the tender quality of their religious morality.

Obviously, Sioux religion possessed characteristics which have counterparts in other religions. It contained certain fundamental precepts common to universal philosophy, for no one group of people has ever had a corner on truth. Not only was the system pragmatic in the recognition of man's capacity for rationality, but it was deeply spiritual in the acknowledgment of man's capacity for faith. It answered many profound questions for man. Yet it left unanswered others equally profound. It forthrightly gave the Sioux something to believe in that was greater than man himself and thereby rendered a source of emotional security, inspiration, and code of behavior. The Sioux religion permeated man's every action, his every living moment. He was of it and it was of him.

Sioux theology hypothecated a universe which not only permitted but expected human self-expression. Means for his self-gratification were offered by supernatural instruction in hunting, lodge-building, and the making of clothes. By providing instruction for ceremonial acts of gratitude, the theology sponsored ample avenues for ego-development and expected men to avail themselves of those opportunities. Sioux religion acknowledged the need for emotional as well as physical security. Such security was an objective of Whope's visit and of the daily ministrations of a priesthood versed in the ways of the universal forces. The mechanisms for overcoming fear were manifold and included supernatural guardians and elaborate rituals, protective symbols, and human spirits. Fear of death was mitigated in a variety of ways: the undying quality of the supernaturals, the close relationship of man with the supernaturals, the concept that man's spirit was capable of attaining life after death.

Conversely, Sioux religion demanded self-denial to a surprisingly high degree. The examples of self-indulgence and their consequent penalties which the gods themselves experienced were vivid reminders of the danger of uncontrolled gratification. The codes and moral precepts which were drawn from cosmological hypothesis and from the later divine teachings were rigid indeed. They required that men keep constant vigil on themselves, lest misfortune, sickness, or death should befall. Not only did the religion provide lessons and penalties for those who would disregard the precept of self-control, but it seemed to add further dangers in the form of evil forces which tested man's fortitude or brought him suffering.

Sioux cosmology, recognizing the conflict of self and selflessness, appears to have set extremely firm boundaries upon its people, with an emphasis upon ego-control. This viewpoint is suggested by the number of possibilities for self-expression which were channeled toward ceremonial supplication and gratitude, coupled with the severity of the penalties for ego-indulgence.

A century ago this was the universe in which the Sioux lived. This was the rank and order of things supernatural. To understand how the Sioux adjusted themselves as mortals to the realm of the Controllers, to know how they fitted themselves to universal forces as a nation and as individuals during the period of their prosperity, is akin to solving a riddle. For the ways of men and the pattern of their living, if not secret, are complex.

CHAPTER 12

The Vision Quest

THE SIOUX BELIEVED that man could not succeed without power. But with power, almost anything was possible.

Power was conceived as a force emanating from the supernatural with which man might be endowed. To a few men it came naturally with little effort. To others it came only after rigorous supplication and search. But to most men it never came.

Wakan Tanka, the Great Mystery, was all-pervasive and omnipotent. His energy, however, was disseminated to a myriad of lesser supernaturals who found embodiment in many living things, especially birds and animals. The eagle, the hawk, the swallow, the elk, the deer, and the buffalo—each was a possessor of a specified power; each was representative of some particular deity. Many, if not all, animals and birds were so endowed—some for good; some for evil. It was through these intermediaries, if not from Wakan Tanka, that man received potency, for the power which animals possessed was often specific and transferrable, so that man could be a recipient. Man himself was relatively helpless, endowed by nature only with his own limited *sicun*, or spiritual power. The qualities which the animals possessed were valuable and often necessary complements which men sought through the aid of shamans in order to live more effectively.

The Sioux, in attempting to understand their place in nature, separated themselves from it to such a degree that in a sense they stood apart. Aware, however, that their very existence was dependent upon the natural environment, they sought to gain rapport to an extent that was almost compulsive. Once having accepted the proposition that they stood alone amid the universe, different from the plants and animals and subject to the buffetings of physical forces, they seem to have been driven to fit themselves intellectually into its realms. The lengths to which they went in order to secure this adjustment were as ingenious as they were dramatic.

Their interpretation of the universe comprised of a complex hierarchy of powerful deities or Controllers from which all forces emanated, including life as conceived in the *sicun,* the spiritual power imparted by Skan, signifies the Sioux's telling need for clearly understanding the meaning of their place. Recognizing with humility the wondrous mysteries of life, they revered their gods with solemnity and awe. Perhaps the Sioux were unable to put themselves on a par with animals. At least, they were unwilling to do so. They deliberately placed themselves upon a lower plane with respect to rapport with the universe and its Controllers. With complete devotion, the Sioux appealed to the animals as emissaries in tune with the gods for guidance and help in all matters and endeavored to ensure the affinity through offerings, fetishes, and imitative dances.[1]

In reality, the Sioux may have been envious of animals, whom they unconsciously felt to have a more efficient ecological adjustment. In any case, their relationship with the animal world was defined, crystallized, and functional.

Only those who were most pure in body and spirit might achieve communication with the Controllers. In order, therefore, to prepare the individual for communion with the supernatural, the rite of purification by sweat bath was practiced.

Properly, a shaman should officiate, for purification was a Wakan undertaking. A dome-shaped frame was fashioned from willow poles, much as a small wigwam was constructed. Over the willow frame, robes were placed in such a manner that the lodge would be airtight. Near the center a small pit or *iniowaspe* was dug to serve as a receptacle for the heated stones, while around

---

[1] Densmore, "Teton Sioux Music," *loc. cit.;* James O. Dorsey, "A Study of Siouan Cults," *loc. cit.;* Walker, "The Sun Dance and Other Ceremonies," *loc. cit.* A thorough reading of each of these works will give the reader a good analysis of the impartation of power.

267

the floor of the lodge was spread a blanket of sage. Purification lodges were so located that the entrance faced toward the east. The earth which was removed from the *iniowaspe* was made into a little mound about two paces distant from the entrance and just in front of the pile of rocks and firewood where the stones were to be heated. This mound was called *hanbelachia* or the vision hill. Between the vision hill and the *iniowaspe* the earth was cleared to form a path known as the *smoothed trail*. The *iniowaspe*, the *hanbelachia*, and the smoothed trail represented in symbolic minia- ture the vision quest.

Offerings of red flannel strips or of tobacco tied in tiny bundles were attached to sticks and placed to the west of the hill, or fastened beneath the robes at the ceiling of the lodge. The sacred pipe to be used was placed upon the hill, with the stem facing the east.

Those who were to purify themselves with a sweat bath re- moved their clothing upon entering the lodge, carrying only a spray of sage to cover themselves. A helper remained outside to attend the fire, refill the pipe as needed, and carry the heated stones to the entrance of the lodge on a forked stick. From here he passed them in to the shaman in charge, who placed them in the pit.

When all was in readiness, the helper passed in the first four stones, if this were to be a sixteen-stone bath. As they were laid in the pit, one of the participants might touch the pipestem to the stone. After the stones were in place, the man who held the pipe passed it to the shaman, who would say, "All my relatives—living and deceased" or "All winged things," depending upon the char- acter of his dream instruction. Then the pipe was passed around so that each participant might smoke. This was done four times. When the tobacco was consumed, the Dreamer gave the pipe to the helper, who refilled it before returning it to the *hanbelachia*.

Now the Dreamer took his mountain-sheep-horn spoon and, dipping it into the paunch of water at his side, flicked water upon the heated rocks. Great clouds of steam filled the lodge. This he did four times. Then he might sing songs believed to be pleasing to his supernatural helpers and efficacious in securing purification for his clients. These should be sung in sets of four. Meanwhile, the client and other participants prayed for assistance while they wiped themselves with bits of sage. When someone felt that he could no longer endure the smothering effects of the vapor, he might cry out, "All my relatives," whereupon the Dreamer would say, "Open up."

When he had again smoked the pipe four times around, four more stones were brought in, the lodge was closed, and the ritual of purification by steam was again undertaken. Often the heat became so intense that spots or areas of men's bodies seemed painfully burned. It was found however, that by chewing a bit of sage and spitting it upon the affected area, it became cool. Such areas were believed to be where impurities were lodged, and the combination of steam and sage operated to release those impurities. To ensure the effectiveness of the sweat bath, it was carried out in four parts. Four times the pipe was smoked; four times the water was sprinkled upon the hot rocks; four times the shaman sang during each session. It was correct to do things in series of fours.

When the purification rite was completed, tiny hoofmarks of the Dreamer's supernatural animal helper would often be visible upon the symbolic *hanbelachia*. And should the sweat bath have been taken in the hope of securing good fortune in hunting, in war, or in love, there also might then appear buffalo or horse tracks or a miniature outline of a woman's moccasin. This was considered a good omen and the sign of a successful ceremony. It was believed to be particularly healthful to culminate the sweat bath by diving in a near-by stream, even if in the wintertime this meant breaking the ice.[2]

Power came to man in dreams or visions. Once it was obtained, it became as much a part of the individual as his physique and his character. Like that of the animals through whom it was bestowed, it was specific and limited to particular areas of achievement. Furthermore, as a trust, it carried grave responsibilities. Nonetheless, the advantages which the endowment wrought in

[2] Brown, *The Sacred Pipe*. Herein is contained an excellent interpretation of the purification ceremony.

success, prestige, and presumed security were so universally recognized that most Sioux men took special pains to secure it.

To a few, power came early and unsolicited. Children of eight
and ten years sometimes had dreams while sleeping. Here some
bird or animal would talk to them, cryptically telling of power
and its responsibilities.

Such was the case of the Double Woman dream. This type of
dream might come to a girl at an early age, and in it the child
received instructions from the Deer Woman or her supernatural
manifestations. The dream often demanded that a choice be made,
and upon the decision of the dreamer may have depended whether
or not one became a true shaman or a woman versed in female arts.

Rattling Blanket Woman dreamed that two naked bears wearing down-feathers on their heads took her to a beautiful cave
lined with parfleches. There she saw another bear and a skeleton.
A withered old man told her in a woman's voice that she must
choose which way she would enter—from left to right, as was the
correct way to enter a tipi, or from right to left. She was warned
that "The three naked bears are your children, one is a boy, and
two are girls. If you fail to take care, your husband will look like
this skeleton. You must choose one side or the other, so be alert.
If you make a mistake, you will become the skeleton and not receive the children." Rattling Blanket Woman chose to enter from
right to left—and as she did, the bears changed to a nighthawk, a
swallow, and a bank swallow, each wearing cattails in place of
their down. When she reached her place again, all had changed
to humans and the old man was herself. Frightened at this, she
awoke.

Rattling Blanket Woman later married and had three children,
two girls and a boy. Each resembled the birds she had dreamed
of—the two younger children "had short chins." Rattling Blanket
Woman furthermore attributed her ability to do excellent porcupine embroidery to the fact that her dream was in actuality about
the Double Woman. If she had chosen, in her dream, the alternate
course to the cave, she felt that she might have become a medicine woman. As a child she had witnessed the Double Woman

Dreamers dancing through camp carrying dolls and buffalo ropes and spitting black stuff—a positive proof of the Double Woman's power. She fainted when they approached, and if she had been allowed to remain unconscious, the people believed that she might have had a dream.

Later in life, she had other dreams cryptically instructing her regarding what work she should do lest she lose her family. Failure to follow precisely the rule caused her to vomit black. Rattling Blanket Woman was considered Wakan, but not a medicine woman. The relationship, however, between those who could do superior quilling and those who had dreamed of the Double or Deer Woman was so close that any difference was a matter of degree.

As with Rattling Blanket, so it was with a boy. Upon reporting a Wakan dream to his father, a child might expect a special hearing. Here the parent would explain the good fortune and seriousness of the visitation and recommend that the child either pay careful attention to any given rules or assume a receptive attitude. Furthermore, in many instances, the child would be introduced to a practicing adult dreamer who had had a similar vision. Thus, if the child had talked with the wolves, his father would take him to a recognized Wolf Dreamer, who would advise him further regarding his blessing.

A young person so fortunate as this might be expected to have dreams of other sorts. Careful parents were quick to see that, if this proclivity were nurtured, their son might one day be a candidate for the highest of dreamers, a shaman. In any case, such a child was considered Wakan, or sacred, and must be shown special attention.

Few men, however, were so fortunate. To gain power they must actively seek it, and seeking it required careful attention to prescribed formulas which included sacrifice. Even the Wakan child, if he were to experience the fulfillment of his blessing, must offer himself in supplication.

Men obtained power in several ways. They might undergo the *hanbelachia* by going to the top of a hill and fasting, preferably for four days; they might drag buffalo skulls attached to their backs by skewers stuck through their muscles; they might publicly suspend themselves from a pole by means of skewers thrust through their chests. No matter what method they selected, each involved a willingness to endure physical torture, for self-sacrifice was the most certain means of experiencing rapport with the supernatural.

After Black Horse had dreamed of the Thunder, he was alarmed, for this was Wakan indeed. Everyone knew that to dream of the Thunder was a sign that could not be ignored lest one be struck dead by lightning. But the dream also brought the obligation of being a Heyoka, and these responsibilities were difficult and frightening. Heyokas were expected to act antinatural, always to play the clown. They must wear foolish clothes, live in ragged tipis, sleep without blankets in winter, and cover themselves with heavy robes in summer. To show their power, they barehandedly dipped meat from boiling skin kettles, for they were unlike other men; they were Heyokas. The Heyoka was often a lonely person—avoided and ridiculed by other people. Only the most able were revered and honored; many were sad and forlorn.

Even after complying with the urgency of the Thunder dream by visiting an old Heyoka and fulfilling the necessary requirements, some men lived in the constant fear of being killed by lightning. Knowing this, Black Horse called upon the Heyoka Horn Chips, told him of his dream, and said that he wished to "go upon the hill" to become a Thunder Dreamer. When Horn Chips was confident that Black Horse's intention was sincere, he agreed to be his sponsor. He knew about Black Horse, and moreover, he knew his father, Ghost Head—a Dreamer of Wolves. It was natural that the son showed such a proclivity, for visions seemed to run in some families.

Black Horse then prepared a purifying lodge for Horn Chips. It was to be an impressive ceremony consisting of four periods in which one hundred heated stones were used to create the steam. Then four other Heyokas were invited, and the cleansing ceremony lasted all night.

Before daybreak Horn Chips gave Black Horse a piece of pemmican and a sip of water, and then the four Heyokas escorted Black Horse to the top of Eagle Nest Butte. When they reached the summit the Heyokas cleaned out the vision pit, a covered hole with an opening to the north, large enough for a man to rest in. This had been used on other occasions by men seeking visions. Now they lined it with a bed of fresh sage. Horn Chips set up sticks with tobacco offerings and colored banners at the four sides. Around the perimeter, enclosing the pit, were strung many tiny tobacco offerings, each tied in a bundle made of a bit of flesh from Black Horse's forearms and thighs, in order to supplicate the supernaturals.

When the site was thus prepared, Horn Chips and the Heyokas descended the butte, leaving Black Horse standing naked and alone, holding the stem of his consecrated pipe to the rising sun. All day he stood there, crying. As the sun reached its zenith Black Horse slowly turned, raising the pipestem toward it. When the sun finally set in the west, Black Horse stood facing it with his pipestem lowered in its direction. When darkness came, he remained facing the west. By now owls hooted and often the entire hill shook and voices called from the sky. Sometime after midnight Black Horse entered the pit and lay on the bed of sage, but he did not sleep.

Long before dawn he arose, and as he faced toward the east, a voice from the sky said, "What is it you want, Black Horse. Why do you stand here like this?" Black Horse answered, explaining his dream of the Thunder, how he wished to become a medicine man to cure his people. Then the voice replied, "You are going through the ceremony which not everyone can do. Only a few men are chosen. The Thunder Dream came to you so that you would undertake this."

As the day began to break, Black Horse heard another voice calling. Then someone said, "You have come to befriend nature's animals—birds as well as beasts." And as Black Horse looked up, there was an eagle to whom he replied, "Grandfather, I came here to be your servant." And the eagle said, "You have undertaken to live a life that is difficult," and with that he flew away.

After sunrise, Black Horse realized that he was in another world. Someone said to him, "Look Black Horse, look to your tipi." And though many miles away, he could clearly see his son and a man named Bad Hand approach him. Then there was much hard talk and suddenly Bad Hand was shot. Black Horse raised his eyes and said, "Grandfather, permit that act to pass to another man. I am undergoing this so that such evil things may not happen to my family." Then Black Horse heard a voice command, "Pass that act to another man," and as Black Horse looked toward his home, his son was entering the tipi as though nothing had taken place, for he was now empowered even to see through the tipi and he knew that all was well.

Later in the day, another voice spoke, "Grandson, you are undertaking something which not all men can do. Have patience, and you will lead a worthy life." As Black Horse looked up, a prairie hawk flew away. By now Black Horse was very tired—and suffering with hunger and thirst, he walked around crying. And all nature was talking.

As he stood there, a voice called from the west, and he saw a tiny black cloud near the sunset. From it streamed a brilliant ray of light directly into his face. The voice called again, and as it did, the little cloud grew larger and approached the hill where Black Horse was standing. Then the voice said, "Your grandfathers are returning."

Shortly the storm was upon him. As he stood there holding his pipe, the Thunder Voices sang and he joined them. The rain was violent, driven by the wind. "Behold, my grandson, the birds of the air are rejoicing to see you following the footsteps of your forefathers. Look, this is the way we live." Whereupon a bolt of lightning struck the butte upon which he stood and shook it as if it were a leaf.

"Look before you, take heed that you do not overdo what you have seen and heard." Ahead was a long, straight trail as far as his eyes could see. And it was lined with men's bodies with blood running from their mouths. "Those men overdid what they learned after undergoing what you are now endeavoring. They went beyond their powers." Four bolts of lightning shook the butte and the Thunder Voices sang. Black Horse held his pipe and sang with them. And as the rain fell, their song faded, yet not a drop had fallen within the square of offerings. "Grandson, stand up, you are about to see your Grandfathers."

Black Horse looked and he was no longer on earth—all the world was in darkness. Rising, his feet touched nothing. There appeared a tipi suspended from nowhere by ropes, swaying in the wind.

Black Horse and the Voice entered the tipi from the smoke hole at the top, and as they entered seven men sat at the rear. The men in the center held a pipe. As Black Horse entered, the seven men cried out, "*Hn-n-n-ned*," in quivery, quavering voices louder than the screech owl's cry, louder even than the medicine men's singing as they shake their rattles.

The man seated to the north was wrinkled with age, and as Black Horse surveyed the men, the one who had accompanied him said, "Behold what is before you. You are facing men few others have seen since the beginning of time." Then the man holding the pipe spoke, "Grandson, the birds and animals on earth will hear you when you ask anything of them. Now you are between the sky and the earth. Your Grandfathers living between the earth and sky will help you in administering medicine to save life on earth. It is to your Grandfathers that you should appeal to help. No matter if you are calling from the depths of the earth, your voice will be heard and your appeal will be answered.

"Should you receive gifts from someone whom you have cured, you shall not keep them, but give them to someone else. You will be empowered to save the lives of many who are on their death beds. Be kind to all men and animals—do nothing to harm your family or the families of others. Now you will return to earth. Remember and do not forget anything you have seen."

"Behold, Grandson," he said, pointing to the ancient, wrinkled man, "this one lived before the beginning of the earth. When you ask for help, remember us, worship nothing above us, don't go beyond us in calling for aid. Look upon us well."

As Black Horse studied them, they were human, but in reality, they were miniature men, covered with fur. Their faces were red; around their heads was a halo of red. Their eyes were as sunflowers, and above their ears were horns. Though they were not winged, yet they flew away as if they were birds.

Before he knew what had happened, Black Horse found himself standing again on the butte holding his pipe. A voice from above said, "Remember what you have seen," and Black Horse sang.

Sick and dizzy, he lay down in the bed of sage. For some time he lay there, and when at last it was morning, Black Horse stood up and looked toward home. There the fire for the purifying lodge was blazing, and Horn Chips was heading from the camp toward the butte. Slowly, interminably slowly, Horn Chips made his way to the hill where Black Horse stood. Horn Chips took the offerings down as Black Horse, trembling, held his pipe. Then Horn Chips gave Black Horse his breechcloth and a robe, and together they descended the hill. With his mentor's help, Black Horse proceeded to the purifying lodge, where he was met by the other Heyokas. Horn Chips presented him with something wet for his mouth. And they went into the purifying lodge, where Black Horse told the assembled Heyokas his vision. When he had finished, they left the lodge. Horn Chips gave him some pemmican and Black Horse slept in the purifying lodge.

The next day Black Horse took three more sweat baths with Horn Chips, who interpreted his vision and told him what herbs should be used and what wotawes he might assume. When this was completed, Black Horse made his way to his camp. His ordeal was over and he was now a Heyoka.

Two days later Bad Hand, in an argument with another Sioux, was shot. His wounds were serious, but he recovered. Black Horse's wish had been granted; the Thunder gods had fulfilled the promise. Black Horse's dread was a reality—his was to be the empty, lonely, forsaken life of the clown destined to save others from death through his power, yet to receive nothing for himself save ridicule. His now was a tattered robe, a rotten tipi, and the ability to dip meat from boiling water with his bare hands.[3] And only if he were highly successful in all this would he be revered by his fellow men. This was the Heyoka's way, the consequence of dreaming of Thunder.

No other dream, no other vision which might be received carried with it quite the ambivalent blessing which the Thunder imposed. The Buffalo, the Bear, the Wolf, even the Elk or the Deer—none of these conferred the mixed rewards which the Heyoka enjoyed. Each vision carried with it handsome responsibilities, but none was tinged with the tragedy which the Thunder demanded.

Men who had been successful in obtaining a vision became known as Dreamers. Their power might enable them to cure certain diseases, to foresee events, to find lost articles, and to make certain war medicines. Thus White Horse, who dreamed of the Thunder and the Deer, made four shields, each valued at one horse, and sold them to warriors. The Heyoka Brave Buffalo was known for his skill in curing snow blindness and for his ability to find lost articles.

The role of the Dreamer accrued to it prestige and influence. In itself, it was not a profession which could support the practitioner, but there were definite emoluments and honorariums that greatly augmented one's economic status. Actually, the number of practicing shamans was apparently quite small; it was, in reality, a profession pretty much confined to older men whose mature judgment and experience instilled confidence in their clients. Successful Dreamers were held in high esteem and were accorded respect which the dignity and responsibility of their power demanded.

On certain occasions Dreamers publicly tested their powers. At these times Dreamers gathered at a specially prepared lodge in

[3] Densmore, "Teton Sioux Music," *loc. cit.,* 168. This writer reports that Heyokas, prior to exhibiting their ability to dip their arms in boiling water, rubbed their arms with *Malvastrum coccineum,* A. Gray.

277

the center of camp. In one instance Brave Buffalo, who had dreamed of the Elk, called upon four other Elk Dreamers to join him as helpers and two young women to serve as assistants. A short distance from the ceremonial tipi a purifying lodge was set up so that its entrance faced toward the west and the tipi door.

The ceremony was inaugurated by the four Dreamers' purifying themselves in the sweat lodge. When this was completed the men entered the tipi. There they painted themselves yellow and blackened their hands and forearms and their legs from knees to feet. Each wore a yellow mask marked with a black circle on the forehead and chin, the whole surmounted with antlers made of branches. Each also carried in the left hand a hoop wound with otter skin and crossed with two strings with feathers suspended from the four points. The girls, dressed in their finest gowns, also painted their faces yellow, with rings on their foreheads, and their hair hung loosely over their shoulders.

On the altar the helpers placed a wooden bowl which contained a granite sphere—a symbol of lightning. They also put a pipe on the "mellowed earth" with the stem pointed toward the south.

When the performers were thus prepared, Brave Buffalo ceremonially placed his *wiconte* or "death" upon the altar and over it the granite sphere. Then Brave Buffalo, after offering the pipe, formally instructed his helpers and female assistants regarding the details of the "test."

Now the Dreamers were ready. One of the assistants began to drum and sing; the young women arose, and as one lifted the pipe, the other held the bowl.

The little procession left the tipi led by the pipe bearer, who first made a ceremonial presentation to the west of the offering pole, then to the north, and so on to the east and south. The others followed, with the bowl bearer close behind. Brave Buffalo was last to leave the tipi, and as he left there mysteriously appeared the hoofprints of an elk upon the altar.

After the group had paid tribute to each of the four cardinal directions, they proceeded to march around within the camp circle. Here all the villagers were lined up to watch, and among them were the rival dreamers, Buffalo Men, Heyokas, Deer Dreamers, and others ready to test the potency of the Elk Dreamers and especially the power of Brave Buffalo.

The virgins, leading the procession with pipe and bowl, circling the camp from left to right, stopped at intervals while the rival dreamers tested Brave Buffalo. They magically shot grasshoppers and fingernails at Brave Buffalo, in an attempt to wound him. But Brave Buffalo defiantly spat them out to show his power. By the time the procession had circled the camp, dancing as elks while Brave Buffalo withstood his adversaries' attacks, they were ready to re-enter the tipi. The Elk Dreamers' test was completed.

Heyokas, Bear Dreamers, and Deer Dreamers frequently held similar exhibitions. The Dreamer of the Buffalo, wearing buffalo hides with head and horns attached, often painted a circle on his back which served as a target. Then his adversaries shot arrows, but a Dreamer whose power was strong could deflect the missiles. These exhibitions were apparently required of all neophytes to prove their strength of power, as a kind of final examination. Displays were also given to re-establish in the minds of the people the mystical potency of their abilities.[4]

The importance of the vision quest—of power through self-sacrifice—to the operation of the entire Sioux system was formally crystallized in the Sun Dance. This ceremony probably more than any other one religious activity symbolized for them their inherent relationship to the supernatural. Where the vision quest had been a personal matter between a man and a particular supernatural, the Sun Dance was a national affair between the people and the universe. Within the Sun Dance were incorporated many rites and many ceremonies involving a multitude of participants. In a sense, the Sun Dance was an aggregation of tribesmen seeking personal advantages through the medium of a commonly ordered series of rites, the sum total of which was of great mutual benefit. As such, it was a unifying group enterprise.

[4] Wissler, "Societies and Ceremonial Associations," *loc. cit.* This author presents a valuable listing of the dream cults. See also Densmore, "Teton Sioux Music," *loc. cit.* With respect to dream cults, this writer includes important anecdotal material.

Men might undertake the Sun Dance for any one of four purposes. Most common was the fulfillment of a vow in return for a favor granted by the gods in time of need or distress. Men promised, if saved in battle, or if the life of a sick child were spared, to offer themselves in the Sun Dance. Failure to carry out a vow inevitably meant tragedy.

Occasionally men danced to secure supernatural aid for someone else, but more often to obtain aid for themselves. Here, whether or not they received a vision, their sacrifice would be looked upon with favor by the people and by the gods. Finally, those who wished to seek a vision or become a shaman danced for the purpose of securing supernatural power for themselves.

The requirements of candidates for shamanism were involved and included full participation in the Sun Dance. These men were in reality seeking the rights and privileges of a priesthood, and in order to obtain that position, they were expected to prove the sincerity of their intent and successfully to complete the fullest measure of training and endurance.

Those individuals who had had early dreams and visions, and whose sustained interest indicated that they possessed the potentials necessary for true shamanism, must reveal this desire to a professional who had himself danced the fourth and highest form of the Sun Dance, and who might be willing to serve as his tutor. Upon agreement, the candidate was expected to give a feast or feasts and pay horses or other goods to the mentor for the course of instruction.

These arrangements generally were completed many weeks, possibly months, before the Sun Dance; for sufficient time must be allowed to prepare the student for his test. He must go on the hill to obtain a vision, and then undergo concentrated tutoring. The course of instruction included not only information about the Sun Dance itself, but far more important, a thorough indoctrination in the tribal organization, the supernatural hierarchy, and the sacred language of the shamans. A qualified shaman must be versed in the ways of his people and their cosmology.

When these conditions had been thoroughly satisfied, the candidate was ready to undertake the Sun Dance in its highest form, "Gaze at the Sun Suspended."

The Sun Dance was held each year during the moon of the ripening chokecherries. The ceremony lasted twelve days. The first four days were a festival period devoted to general preparation of the campsite. There the groups gathered to visit and renew acquaintances. This was an opportune period for young women to look for spears of grama grass bearing four heads which would bring them good luck in love. During this time, too, the shamans selected various individuals from the assembled camps to serve as lay assistants. Appointment as a symbolic Hunter, a Digger, an Escort, or a Singer was a great honor. Virtuous women were chosen to chop the sacred cottonwood tree, and one was given the honor of felling it. Chaste female relatives were all selected to attend the dancers.

The next four days were spent in giving special instruction to the candidates, who were isolated within the council lodge with the shamans to whom they had first revealed their intention to dance. Often one shaman was responsible for the over-all supervision of all the candidates and their instructors. This Mentor was granted complete authority over the ceremony, including the administration of the entire Sun Dance camp. Hence, during this week of religious observance, the Sioux experienced theocratic government.

The final four days were the Holy Days. On the first day the ceremonial camp was formally established. A large circular dance arbor of poles covered with leafy bows was erected in the center of the camp. To the east of this shaded bower the Sacred Lodge was placed. The Sacred Lodge, where the candidates would receive final instructions, was constructed of new materials. While the Sacred Lodge was being put up, the Hunter scouted for the enemy—the forked cottonwood tree which would serve as the hallowed Sun Dance pole. When a suitable tree was found, he reported this to the Mentor. It was on this day that the Buffalo Dance was held—a great processional propitiating the Buffalo and the Whirlwind, patrons of the household and love-making. A

Buffalo Dreamer supervised the pageantry, dancing the Buffalo Dance and blessing the feasting which followed.

The second Holy Day was devoted to the capture of the "enemy" or cottonwood tree. After the camp had been cleansed of the evil gods by the Mentor and other shamans, the women chosen to capture the tree were ordered by the Mentor to search for the "enemy." In doing this, they made three attempts, each time reporting that no sign of the "enemy" had been found. On the fourth try, they found the tree, previously marked with red paint by the Hunter, and surrounding it, bound it securely with thongs. The capture was then reported to the camp amid much rejoicing. A procession was formed which included the Mentor and other shamans, the honored women to chop the tree, and mothers with children who were later to have their ears pierced. The parade was planned in four stages so that halfway between the tree and the camp a stream of water might be crossed. Here the Mentor cleansed the water of evil spirits. At the last resting place before the tree was reached, four warriors were selected to recount their exploits which entitled them to strike the tree.

At the tree, after the warriors had symbolically counted coup on it and thereby subdued its *nagila*, or spiritlike essence, the children were formed in a line and honored with gifts. When this was completed, the Mentor then ordered the tree to be killed and each woman took her turn at chopping so that all selected had an opportunity. When the tree was ready to fall, the woman honored to fell the "enemy" struck the final blows. Everyone sang and cheered with joy.

The pole was next peeled to a point just below the fork, while the top leafy branches were left entwined. Women gathered the cottonwood twigs as a protection against Anog-Ite, the supernatural who tempted women. Then young men lifted the pole with carrying sticks, for the sacred tree might be touched only by shamans or by those who had previously danced the Sun Dance. The tree was carried to camp in four successive stages. At the last stop, the young men ran a race—the first to reach the sacred spot where the pole was to be erected won the right to carry a red coup stick.

When the pole was finally brought to the center of the Dance Lodge, it was painted so that when erected the west side would be red, the north blue, the east green, and the south yellow. To the fork were attached black rawhide figures of Iya and Gnaske, each bearing exaggerated genitalia as marks of their libertinism. A bundle of sixteen cherry sticks enclosing tobacco offerings, an arrow for buffalo-killing, and a picket pin for securing a captured horse were tied to the top of the pole together with a shaman's banner of reddened buffalo skin. The pole was then raised in four successive stages, and on the last it was dropped into the sacred hole.

When the pole was raised, the throngs hooted the images of Iya and Gnaske. However, since the power of these indecent gods prevailed in the camp, men and women jested and bantered about things sexual in a manner which would normally have been highly indecent. An end to this period of sexual license came when the warriors danced the War Dance and shot arrows at the evil gods, who fell to earth to be trampled by the dancers.

The end of the day was spent in final preparation of the Dance Lodge. Rawhide ropes were attached to the hallowed pole from which the dancers would be suspended, beds of sage were prepared for the children who were to have their ears pierced, and the drum was placed on its supporting sticks together with rattles for the singers. At nightfall the shamans consecrated the dancing area as the people remained quietly in their tipis.

Before dawn of the fourth and final day, the Mentor and shamans went upon a near-by hill to greet the Sun, and as they had done on the previous mornings, prayed for a blue day and invoked Sky to give strength to the dancers, and Bear to give wisdom to the Mentor and shamans.

After sunup, the candidates were prepared for the ritual. The shamans painted the hands and feet of their candidates red and painted in blue, symbol of Sky, stripes across their shoulders. If a candidate was to dance the second form, stripes were painted across his shoulders and chest. For those dancing the third and fourth forms, an additional stripe was placed across their forehead. Finally, the sign of the dancer's animal mentor was applied by the shaman. Each dancer wore a long red kilt, arm bands and anklets of rabbit fur, and a fur necklace with a symbolic sunflower medallion. In their right hand they carried a spray of sage and on their head they wore a wreath of sage.

When the candidates were thus prepared, the shaman took a decorated buffalo skull and followed by the prospective dancers and their tutors, formed a procession from the ceremonial tipi along the staked, marked trail to the shade of the Dance Lodge. Here the buffalo skull, with due formality, was placed upon a prepared altar facing the sacred pole.

Now the people gathered, and the candidates rested on beds of sage. Those entitled to sit within the confines of the shade took their places. These included the tutors, singers, and female assistants, as well as women who had chopped the tree, men who had previously danced the Dance, parents whose children were to have the ear-piercing ceremony, and prominent men of the various bands. Strangers were carefully questioned lest in reality they be Waziya the Old Man of the North, or Iktomi the Trickster.

The Mentor then brought harmony to the Dance Lodge by lighting and passing the pipe to all assembled, while assistants made a fire of buffalo chips upon the altar, on which was placed sweet grass to create purifying incense. Now the tutors gave their wards a blue willow hoop as a symbol of Sky, the emblem of the four directions, and an eagle-wing whistle wrapped in porcupine quills and decorated at the tip with a breath feather of eagle down. With these investments, the preparations for the Sun Dance were completed and the candidates were ready to undergo the ceremony.

Those who were to dance any one of the last three forms of the Sun Dance now were entitled to dance the Buffalo Dance. The leader danced to the altar, and after feigning three times, removed the skull to place it in the open. Around the skull the dancers formed a line, and imitating the antics of a raging, pawing buffalo bull, fixed their gazes upon the skull. There were four periods to the Buffalo Dance, and those who completed it satisfactorily were thenceforth honored as Buffalo Men.

Upon the completion of the Buffalo Dance, the children who were to have their ears pierced were placed upon the beds of sage. Their mothers then called upon the men who were to pierce their babies' ears. With a sharp-pointed knife and a block of wood, the men first announced their exploits which confirmed their right to perform the operation, and then advised the parents of their obligation to rear the child in accordance with Sioux customs, for it was believed that pierced ears were a sign of faith in the ways of the Sioux. Then kneeling and holding the infant's head, they pierced the ear lobes amid the baby's screams.

When the ear-piercing was finished, men who had danced the Sun Dance were called upon by the neophytes to act as their captors. The captor, standing beside the one who chose him, then announced the exploits entitling him to perform this role. Next the captors retired to one side, and in a sham battle, attacked the candidates and symbolically captured them by throwing them to the ground. Each captor, singing victory songs, then ritually tortured his victim by piercing his flesh. For those who were to perform the "Gaze at the Sun Buffalo," the skin below the shoulder blade was raised and a slit was cut, through which a skewer was inserted. Candidates for the "Gaze at the Sun Staked" also were pierced through the back and through each breast. For the "Gaze at the Sun Suspended," wounds were made only through the breast. While the captives were undergoing the torture, they could sing songs of defiance as the female assistants wailed and encouraged them and wiped the blood from their wounds with bits of sweet grass. Incense made from burning these sweet grass swabs insured constancy in love.

When the skewers had been inserted in each of the candidates, the captors prepared the dancers for their respective ordeals of captivity. Heavy thongs were secured to the skewers of those dancing the second form, and to them were attached two to four or more buffalo skulls. Those dancing the third form were placed in the center of four upright poles, with buffalo-hair ropes running from each pole to the skewers at chest and back. Those dancing the highest form had ropes tied from the sacred pole to the skewers in their breasts, while those to be suspended had the ropes so adjusted over the fork of the pole that they might be raised and lowered during the intermissions.

The Sun Dance proper began when all the captives were secured, while those who planned to dance only the "Gaze at the Sun" came forward to the open dancing space. The leader then instructed the singers to begin the slow, measured music which opened the ceremony. The men began to dance slowly, blowing their whistles, pretending to break their bonds, and gazing constantly at the sun while the spectators sang encouraging songs. The first half of the dance consisted of two periods of four songs each which gradually increased in tempo after each intermission. During intermissions the dancers rested and were attended by the female assistants. At the beginning of the third period the captors, pretending to discover that the captive dancers were in truth Buffalo Men, now came to their assistance and stayed with them as friends during the remaining periods of the Dance. Again the tempo was increased while the dancers struggled to free themselves, being careful, however, not to do so. After the third major intermission the tempo of the music was intensified still more, and now the captives struggled violently to release themselves by tearing the skewers from their flesh. At intermissions the assistants now aided the dancers, cleansing their wounds and wiping away perspiration with wisps of sage, and a lover might surreptitiously give her dancer a bit of water to quench his thirst.

Often it was long after dark before the men had begun to free themselves, and many were helped to tear themselves loose by their friends. It was considered most honorable to escape by oneself, less effective to receive assistance, while to faint before escaping so that a friend must remove the thongs and skewers was the least meritorious. But in any case, when the captives were finally freed, or the leader had announced that the Dance was over, there was great rejoicing, and much tribute was bestowed upon all the dancers. At the conclusion, amidst the congratulations of relatives and friends, the dancers were assisted to their tipis by their friends and assistants. The Sun Dance was finished—the sacrifice accomplished.

At the completion of the Sun Dance, the ceremonial camp gave way to the ordinary organization of the secular auspices. The tipis were moved from the great ceremonial circle to the usual camping circles, and within the next few days the people dispersed, the various bands leaving in many directions to begin the autumn hunt. The hallowed pole, with its willow bundles and red banner, alone remained until it might be blown down by the winds. Those men who successfully completed the Sun Dance and wished to become shamans now sought a Mentor for further instruction. Those who had not received a vision, either before or during the Sun Dance itself, might endeavor to do so now or in the near future.[5]

The Sun Dance, by interrelating the various elements of Sioux thought, became the epitome of religious expression, culminating in supplication by everyone and active sacrifice by the more arduous. The quality of the participation exhibited by the Sioux is characteristic of their religious fervor—of what some men were willing to give of themselves in order to find the true way of life. In dancing the Dance in any one of the four forms, the individual voluntarily subjected himself to physical suffering for the well-being of others. He publicly demonstrated his selflessness by submitting to capture, torture, and captivity. Only after enduring excruciating suffering could he expect release. In negating the ego, in denying the drive for self-preservation, the dancer might experience in the fullest sense a resolving of one of the fundamental

---

[5] Walker, "The Sun Dance and Other Ceremonies," *loc. cit.* The above description of the Sun Dance is drawn primarily from Walker's brilliantly analytical and detailed report. See also Densmore, "Teton Sioux Music," *loc. cit.* This student's description of the Sun Dance is invaluable.

enigmas of life. The Sun Dance offered the outstanding opportunity to solve the conflict between ego-expression and adjustment to the physical and social forces.

Unlike the Christians who passively revere Christ's example of self-denial through crucifixion and yet profess a comprehension of that denial, the Indian who would purport to understand the implication must himself experience sacrifice physically, mentally, and spiritually. And to be a Sioux, to live life on the best and highest plane, participation in one of the four forms of the Sun Dance was a requisite. The result was that the Sioux shaman, in knowing whereof he spoke, was held in high esteem as a spiritual advisor to his people.

To the man who had been successful in receiving a vision, who accomplished the Sun Dance in its highest form, and who completed the course of theological instruction under the guidance of a shaman, the Sioux accorded great respect. Such a man became responsible for interpreting to the people the Sioux way of life as set forth by the gods. His authority extended to the supervision of all ceremonies; his advice was sought by civil leaders in all matters of serious import. Shamans formed a kind of priesthood and were granted almost theocratic authority in periods of religious observance and during times of national crisis.

Dreamers, men who had actively sought visions and who may have participated in one of the three lower forms of the Sun Dance, were recognized by the people as influential sources of power but were not accorded the priestly position reserved for shamans. Their powers were limited to those instructions received from their particular animal intercessor and the directions given by a man who had enjoyed a like vision. Such cult members had specialties, either for curing certain ailments or wounds or for preparing *wotawes* or protective devices.

The Sioux believed that sickness was the result of the introduction of evil spirits and foreign bodies within the individual. Ill health resulted from failure to adhere to certain taboos, from disregarding prescribed ritualistic forms, or sometimes from the evil influences of a medicine man.

Spirits could cause worms to enter the body; by squeezing the flesh, they caused spasms, rheumatism, or colic. Other worms might bring diarrhea; some caused headaches. Worms also lived in stale water, and persons who drank such water must be careful lest they got pains in the internal organs. Frogs, too, might be swallowed, and they caused serious stomach contractions.

Boils and carbuncles were caused by eating goose eggs. Scabs and black splotches about the face and hands were due to a woman's tanning a bear hide during her menstrual period. Informed women, therefore, tanned bearskins only after menopause.

When butchering a bobcat, a man had to be careful not to tear the joints lest he himself suffer pains in his joints. Contact with menstrual flow caused diseases of the skin and genitals, though it has been said that skillful shamans were able to concoct from it love potions. Fevers were a result of a spirit's building fires near the victim. Should Waziya, the Old Man of the North, blow his breath upon a person, frostbite occurred.

Certain ailments were the direct result of a breach of ethics. A thief was afflicted by warts, while a person given to telling lies suffered peeling of the palate.[6]

The cure of sickness was directed to removal of the cause. Illness that was due to foreign matter could best be remedied by expelling it from the body. Since nature contained elements of both good and evil, the practitioner endeavored to rally the cleansing forces of good against those of evil. He did this with a purifying bath, incense, and song, with rattle or drum, with *wasicun* and with medicine. Songs to the Dreamer's emissary were chanted prayers for supernatural assistance. Incense of sweet grass gratified good spirits, while that of sage was repugnant to the evil ones. The rattle and drum made music which was pleasing to the gods, and when they heard it, they gave attention. The *wasicun* was that object—a round stone, a bird's claws—to which the Dreamer had imparted a Wakan spirit, or *ton*, which became in itself

---

[6] Densmore, "Teton Sioux Music," *loc. cit.*; James O. Dorsey, "A Study of Siouan Cults," *loc. cit.*; Walker, "The Sun Dance and Other Ceremonies," *loc. cit.* Each of these authors has recorded various causes of disease.

a force for good. Medicine or *pejuta* was any one of many plants or herbs used to cure the sick or alleviate pain.

A shaman, when called upon to treat the sick, diagnosed the case primarily to determine whether he was the specialist qualified to effect a cure. Should he discover that the condition was one which he was not empowered to cure, he recommended some other specialist. If, on the other hand, he believed himself able, a purifying bath in the sweat lodge was usually prescribed at the same time the fee was announced. It was customary to pay for professional services in advance, not to the shaman himself but rather to some member of his family. Fees might range from food and articles of clothing to one or two horses.

After the shaman had officiated in the purifying bath designed to drive the evil spirits from the patient, the patient and members of the family retired to the tipi where the curing ceremony took place. Here the physician, painted and costumed in the paraphernalia appropriate to his vision—as an Elk, if an Elk Dreamer; as a Bear, if a Dreamer of Bears—ceremonially prepared such an altar, offerings, incense, and medicines as would correctly propitiate the deities and implement the cure. Then, while singing his visionary songs, drumming and rattling, the shaman administered to the patient, praying to and often touching the patient with his mysterious *wasicun*, as well as giving him herbal medicines. Such a curing rite might last several hours. A certain pattern of performance was also practiced, so that at the beginning of the session a measured dignity was in order but as the curing progressed, the intensity increased so that the shaman himself often reached a frenzied trance and ended the ceremony in a dramatic crescendo.

Expelling evil spirits was no easy task. It demanded the patient's devoted faith in the shaman's complete rapport with the supernatural. Sickness was a spiritual matter which affected the physical, and consequently the proper cure was psychotherapeutic. The shaman's incantations were designed in part literally to frighten the evil forces out of the victim. That the patient may have also experienced a certain consternation at the magic performance had the double advantage of providing a shocklike therapy and instilling an awesome reverence for the practitioner.

Curing the sick and the wounded was the responsibility of the shamans, the Dreamers, and the herbalists. Certain Dreamers were recognized for their abilities to remedy particular conditions. Bear Dreamers, for example, were qualified to set fractured bones. One of these Dreamers, Eagle Shield, first treated the broken limb with a warm salve composed of *"hu hwehanhan pezula"* (Allionia nyctaginea Michx) mixed with grease.[7] This was so soothing that the patient often fell asleep. The bone was then set simply by pulling it into place and splinting it with a laced rawhide sheath.

A wide variety of herbs were utilized as poultices and infusions for various ailments. For pains in the abdomen, the leaves of horsemint or the fruit of hops were boiled to make a drink. A concoction of lamb's-quarters was used to treat dysentery, and verbena tea was for stomach-aches. The root of calamus was chewed for toothache. There were cures for coughs and fever, for head colds and irregular menstruation.[8]

In addition to the medicines, some cures were effected by sucking. With either mouth or bone tube, the shaman sucked the foreign matter from the patient and spit out the evidence in proof of the cure. Thus, while snow blindness might be prevented by putting black paint around the eyes, a shaman could relieve inflammation by sucking out a bit of dry grass from the corners of the eyes. Bleeding, too, was practiced, while emetics and purging also helped rid the body of evil spirits.

Sickness, for the Sioux, was a very frightening thing, for it involved not merely physical discomfort but contamination with evil, loss of rapport with good, and fear of death. The whole physical and spiritual self was endangered. Life was too precious not to resort to every possible means of preserving it—and the shamans were best qualified to undertake its preservation.

---

[7] Densmore, "Teton Sioux Music," *loc. cit.*, 261.

[8] *Ibid.*; Melvin Randolph Gilmore, "Uses of Plants by the Indians of the Missouri River Region," Bureau of American Ethnology, *Thirty-third Annual Report* (1919). Excellent descriptions of curing techniques and pharmacopoeia appear in these writings.

Since not all men were able to gain power, no matter how assiduously they "went to the hill" or fulfilled a vow to dance the Sun Dance, many were forced to get it secondhand. Thus men could purchase from a shaman or a Dreamer the right to administer a particular curative herb, or they could buy some protective charm such as a shield already endowed with power by the maker. Many highly successful men and even Dreamers had to resort to purchase, particularly since a Dreamer's power was limited to specific activities or purposes. Among the Sioux, there were in reality three classes of practitioners—the shamans, the Dreamers, and the herbalists. Herbalists might become Dreamers if they secured a vision, and Dreamers wishing to undergo the Sun Dance in the fourth degree could be eligible for shamanship. Conversely, shamans themselves were frequently members of a cult and likewise practiced pharmacy.

While the ultimate source of inspired power was given forth from Wakan Tanka, the manifestation of that power was granted to man through various emissaries. Shamans were informed concerning the significance of the whole Siouan cosmology whereas Dreamers might know only particular aspects of it. Allegiance to one's supernatural mentor was strong, and the testing ceremonies suggest the character of these loyalties. Competition among the cults was real—partly to establish their mystical prowess in the eyes of the people, partly to ensure their own continued professional status. The lay people, who seemed to possess only a generalized sense of the cosmology and a vague comprehension of its systematic operation, patronized those Dreamers whose powers equipped them to perform specific services.

The shaman's role required him not only to cure individuals but to alleviate group difficulties. When the food supply was threatened, the shaman might well be urged to assist actively through ceremonial intervention or to instill security by predicting good fortune.

In cases where a shaman had foretold the appearance of bison, it was he who prescribed the peculiar form upon which the success of the particular hunt rested. But when the buffalo were sighted, the civil authority assumed its standard pattern.

Apparently it was always a Buffalo Dreamer who assisted with regard to buffalo, for it was his rapport with the Buffalo Nation which enabled him to supplicate these animals for his people's good. In nearly all recorded *hanbelachia* experiences, the Dreamer begged his Helper for personal aid so that he might in turn help his people, for the instructions received specified that his power should be used for the general welfare.

In the first case, it was the people who came to the shaman for assistance; to maintain his prestige he was obliged at least to make an effort. If he was successful, the general faith in the Dreamer and the institution was strengthened. The failure of a Buffalo Dance to secure game is recorded in the Winter Count of 1871, but the reason for this failure was that the "buffalo fooled the people." Criticism was directed at no one, and faith in the ceremony was apparently not shaken. In the second case, the shaman's information resulted in personal prestige if he was successful, though this was probably less meritorious since there was no "test" involved. The fact that cults were small, comprised sometimes of only two persons and rarely of more than ten, directed prestige to the individual for his particular powers rather than for his membership in the cult.

From the point of view of the entire society, the dream cult had a real foundation in the economic and religious needs of the group. There was no schism between the individual need and the group need. A man desirous of success in hunting would call for the services of a shaman and follow the rules outlined by him. The power and authority of the Dreamer were understood by all, and the theoretical and practical aspects were consistent. Nor did the sacred usurp the authority of the secular; it merely supplemented and assisted the civil authority in matters which the latter did not pretend to understand or control.

Nowhere in the Sioux way of life was the conflict of self-preservation versus selflessness more vividly demonstrated than in the character of their relationship with the supernatural. The Sioux seemed to have met the conflict head-on in a violent realization of its enormity. The urgency of comprehending the unknown, of assuring existence on this earth, was apparently so compelling for them that they voluntarily suffered torture and deprivation to attain insight and peace of mind. Their self-denial was so masochistic as to make it appear that they subconsciously sought death in resentment against the gods for the nature of things. Having conceived themselves as the least endowed of creatures, they offered themselves as sacrifice, as if to show how valueless they were. On the other hand, they felt that their propitiation might be made acceptable by giving physically of themselves.

The physical torture of self undoubtedly served as a release from this conflict. Furthermore, self-destruction has been for many a proven method for securing recognition—from one's fellow men as well as from the gods. It was the Sioux male who endured the most severe, self-inflicted torture, and in this masculinely directed society, it was fitting that the men should exemplify its goals.

Unlike many peoples who glibly offer up others, either animals or captives, or who vicariously endure the sacrifice of religious heroes and through a process of rationalization salve their own emotional conflicts, the Sioux believed that only by suffering physically themselves was it possible for the individual to experience the full implication of sacrifice. The Sioux, at least, were forthright.

In a sense, the Sioux were also masochists. In order to obtain the "power" essential to well-being, denial of self through the painful humiliation of torture was the accepted procedure. This was the price that men paid for mental and physical security; this was the most certain way to achieve success.

The self-tortures endured in the *hanbelachia*, or vision quest, or during the Sun Dance were not, for most men, recurring ones. The sacrifice was offered by younger men and served them for the remainder of their lives. The scars left by the skewers were marks of honor and lifetime reminders of their fortitude and self-lessness. Whether the therapeutic aspects of the *hanbelachia* or the Sun Dance were effective can only be surmised, yet the continuance of the customs from generation to generation suggests their enduring value.

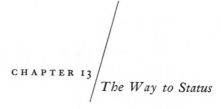

CHAPTER 13

The Way to Status

PRESTIGE AND RECOGNITION, leadership and reverence were accorded those individuals who practiced the principle of self-sacrifice. The ideal of selflessness applied also to personal property.

Property among the Sioux was real and individually owned, and there were definite rights of property. If a man captured a herd of twenty-five horses, those horses were his; if a woman made a tipi, that tipi was hers. Persons bought shields, prescriptions, arrows, and robes. Children were given dolls, pets, and horses over which they assumed complete responsibility—nor was their right of ownership questioned or abrogated.

The accumulation of more property than was actually needed was discouraged. Conversely, the ideal of generosity, and the acclaim accorded those who literally disposed of their possessions made giving imperative.

The man who owned many horses and hoarded them was flaunting convention and was looked upon as selfish. Unless he had compensating virtues, his prestige was less than that of the man who continually gave away horses. Property was for use, not for accumulation, and its chief use was bestowing it on others.

Wealth, therefore, was counted in terms of a man's ability to accumulate for disposal. This principle kept operative by the understanding that to receive a gift implied the responsibility to give a gift in return. It was not entirely necessary that the gift be returned in kind or within a specified time; but, except possibly from the old and destitute, a token payment was expected. Wealth, then, was not an end but a means. The society placed a check upon the natural acquisitiveness of the personality in order that

296

individuals less capable of obtaining basic needs should not suffer undue privation. The generous man was the subject of public acclaim, and the miser was the object of public disdain. The giveaway pattern was crystallized, however, much more rigidly than the mere giving of gifts would imply. Most striking was a formalized set of ceremonies, each of which was terminated by a giveaway and each of which required arduous accumulation of gifts prior to the undertaking. To attain an office of authority, it was necessary to perform ceremonies involving certain life crises, particularly puberty and death. A loose sort of grading operated so that an individual had to perform two out of four initial ceremonies before undertaking the final two. The cost of each ceremony, in terms of gifts, was considerable. Some men could afford to perform only one; few could afford the complete series of four. Nor was wealth—that is, the ability to give—the sole prerequisite. Individuals were selected to give the last two ceremonies by those who had previously performed them. These latter thereby constituted the leading class and became known as Wicasas.

If a man intended to become a prominent member of his group he must first give for his daughter either the *Isnatialowanpi*, "Singing over First Menses," or *Tatanka avicalowanpi* "Buffalo-sing," or *Tapawanka-yeyapi*, "Ball-Throwing." He must also give for either his son or his daughter the *Hunkayapi*, "Waving the Horsetail." If he had no children, he might adopt one for the purpose. Then, if selected, he must perform "Owning the Ghost" and finally the "White Buffalo Ceremony." The interrelationship of this series of ceremonies and the giveaway pattern imposed upon the leaders the beneficence which the ideals of society upheld and conversely protected the members from exploitation by their leaders.

The Hunka ceremony generally involved the adoption of a younger and usually less wealthy individual by the elder one. The relationship required sharing through life on the part of both, but the burden of dividing was generally placed upon the elder. Occasionally a parent, in honoring his son, would perform the ceremony, wherein the son would adopt a less fortunate friend.

The individual sponsoring the Hunka employed the services of a shaman. The shaman then appointed various people to serve as assistants: musicians, two men to wave the "horsetails," and others to hold the ear of corn. A ceremonial tipi in which the adoption rite was to be performed was constructed.

When the time was set, the couple who intended to participate in the adoption were often formally escorted around the camp to the ceremonial tipi. The younger person might then be symbolically placed in the lodge as a "captive," while the elder partner was questioned about whether anyone would take the captive as Hunka rather than see him put to death. When the older man volunteered to save him, the "captive" was "rescued" and the ceremony continued.

At the tipi, the shaman, dressed in the ceremonial regalia associated with his vision, was ready to meet them. Here the guests, themselves Hunkas, were already assembled, wearing their eagle down Hunka feathers and with faces painted in red stripes in token of their status—the men to the right and the women to the left. A buffalo skull painted with the marks of the Hunka was placed on the "mellowed earth" altar, and near by was set up a miniature meat rack.

When the candidates and the assistants were seated, the formal procedure was initiated by the passing of the pipe so that everyone might smoke. When the undertaking had thus been consecrated, persons who themselves were Hunka might lecture the candidates upon the virtues and duties of a Hunka.

When their instructions had been completed, the shaman was handed the "horsetails," two blue painted shafts from which a fan of eagle feathers was suspended near the grip, and from there to the tip a row of red horsetails was hung. The shaman then stood. Singing a song extolling the Hunka relationship, he waved the wands over the candidate's head.

In this manner the candidate learned that the red paint he would wear pleased the Sun, that as a faithful Hunka he would be wealthy, and that his wife would be industrious and faithful. He learned too that he might expect many children, that he would be successful in war and in the hunt.

Next the shaman offered a tobacco consecration to the buffalo skull by blowing smoke into its nostrils. Then, offering the pipe to the young candidate, he informed him that the buffalo would provide meat and hides in sufficiency. This was followed by a similar rite with the ear of corn, and the shaman reported that the corn was brought to the people by the Buffalo Woman, that its children were many.

The shaman then took meat from the miniature rack, and giving a piece to the young man, directed that the remainder be distributed to the audience. As this was being accomplished, the shaman announced to the young man that he was hungry and without meat, that he was cold and without a robe, that he was footsore and without moccasins. Upon hearing this, the young man took from his mouth his meat, from his feet his moccasins, and from his body his robe and leggings and offered them to the shaman. The shaman, when he had accepted these gifts, painted a red stripe on the young man's face as he announced to all assembled that this man had done as a Hunka should: he had given all that he possessed. From thenceforth the red striped paint was testimony that he was Hunka.

As the young man sat naked among his fellows, the older man who was to be Hunka was called upon to sit beside him. Here, hidden from the public's view by a robe, the two were literally bound together with thongs to signify their future relationship. Then the pair were exposed to view. Thereupon the shaman announced to all assembled that, as Hunkas, what was one's was the other's—whatever horses or captive women or children, whatever meat or clothing, they were to be shared. If one were in danger, the other should help, whether in war or sickness or want. The young man henceforth should be as a son, the elder as a father: this was the meaning of being Hunka.

The shaman then arose and announced to all assembled that these persons were now Hunkas. With this, the ceremony ended, the Hunkas left the tipi to dress themselves for the feast and give-away. The shaman destroyed the altar.[1]

The female virtues were solemnized and publicized through religious ceremonies and women's gatherings and feasts, and the building of a woman's prestige was dependent upon her record and her family's support.

A well-to-do man honored his daughter upon her first sign of womanhood by celebrating with the Buffalo Sing, or the Ball-throwing Sing, or the Singing over First Menses. In each case the father organized the preparations and enlisted the services of a Buffalo Dreamer, for the Buffalo was the protector of young girls, the patron of such virtues as industry, fecundity, and generosity. It was the Buffalo who was the deity of ceremonies and sexual relations—it was fitting that one to whom he had given power should officiate.

The Buffalo Sing was held in a ceremonial lodge erected for the purpose. In it were an altar and pipe, a buffalo skull, and a fire of cottonwood branches whose smoke would drive away Anog-Ite, the Two-Faced Woman, goddess of shameful things. A wooden bowl and cherries, an eagle plume, and a new dress were also supplied. The Buffalo Dreamer in his regalia began the ceremony with a song to the Sun, and then the parents, guests, and the shaman entered the lodge where the Dreamer consecrated the equipment while the spectators ceremonially smoked the pipe. When the smoking was finished, the shaman sang to his helper, the Buffalo—the patron of female virtues.

The girl was brought in and lectured by the Dreamer regard-ing her moral obligations. She was then symbolically tempted by the Dreamer, who performed the Dance of the Buffalo Bull in the rutting season, as the Crazy Buffalo tempted women. The mother

---

[1] Brown, *The Sacred Pipe;* Densmore, "Teton Sioux Music," *loc. cit.;* Melvin Randolph Gilmore, "The Dakota Ceremony of Hunka," Museum of American Indian, Heye Foundation, *Indian Notes,* Vol. VI, No. 4 (1929); Walker, "The Sun Dance and Other Ceremonies," *loc. cit.* The primary source for the sum-mary description of *Hunkayapi* Ceremony is Walker's researches, but valuable in-sights concerning additional aspects and variations are to be found in the writings of the other above-mentioned authors.

frustrated these advances by placing sage in the girl's lap and under her arms.

The shaman consecrated the bowl filled with water and cherries and offered it to the girl. She and the mentor drank from it as buffalo, and it was then offered to the guests to symbolize their friendship. The girl was next told to undress and place her clothing upon the skull as an offering to the Buffalo Woman. The mother then arranged the girl's hair as a woman, placing the braids over her shoulders; the shaman painted the parting red and attached the eagle plume. All the while he advised her of her duties and explained the significance of her new investments, telling her that she now had the right to paint the part of her hair and redden her right forehead. Upon the announcement that she was now a Buffalo Woman, the parents gave many gifts to the visitors and populace in honor of their daughter.[2]

The Ball-throwing Sing, like the Buffalo Sing, was performed when the girl announced her first menses. Her mother took her to a small wigwam where all women stayed during these periods. Here the daughter was ceremonially taught to quill and make moccasins for four days.

The ceremony was similar to the Buffalo Sing in that the girl was exhorted regarding the female virtues and received the right to paint a red stripe over her nose and cheeks. The rite was consummated by a formal giveaway in which the Dreamer or the girl threw a red painted ball among the visitors. Each time the ball was thrown, the father gave a horse or gift in honor of his daughter to whoever caught it. When the supply of horses and gifts was exhausted, a feast was given.[3]

Not every family could afford to honor a daughter with these costly ceremonies. Only a few were so privileged. But to the man who could afford it came public acclaim, for his generosity

[2] Walker, "The Sun Dance and Other Ceremonies," *loc. cit.* Walker has presented a detailed description of the Buffalo Rite from which this summary was drawn.

[3] Brown, *The Sacred Pipe.* Brown's excellent interpretation of the Ball-throwing Sing was drawn from Black Elk's report in *The Sacred Pipe.*

was recorded in the minds of the people. The Buffalo Sing and the Ball-throwing Sing were credited to his personal prestige account, for it was obligatory for a man to give at least one of these ceremonies if he expected to become a public figure of sufficient stature to be a leader. In so doing he fulfilled and completed one of the steps on the social ladder, and his daughter became one of the select.

As a member of the elite, it behooved a woman to so emulate the virtues that she would be known for her generosity and truthfulness, as well as for her fecundity and fortitude. Opportunities to exhibit her industry—the ability to produce gifts and presents—were available in the quilling and tanning contests and the records which were kept on tanning tools as well as displayed on the tipi linings. Tests of truthfulness likewise gave women a chance to publicize their virtue, for upon women's high status rested much of their family's reputation.

To "Own a Ghost," properly referred to as "Spirit-keeping," was an undertaking few persons could afford. Spirit-keeping not only involved a great personal responsibility but was a matter of serious tribal significance. Its successful fulfillment brought high honor and proof of an individual's devotion to his family and his people. As an example of Spirit-keeping, the following account by Iron Shell is illuminating:

> When Shot at Many Times died, Iron Shell cut a lock of his first son's hair, in reality his son's "Ghost," and placed it in a tiny quilled bag filled with sweet smelling grass. Iron Shell hung the quilled bag containing the "Ghost" from the rear pole of his tipi where it remained for four days.
>
> As the boy was buried, the men mourned and the women slashed their arms amidst their plaintive wailing. And for four days during their grief, the women ceremonially made clothes, pack bags and other household articles.
>
> On the fifth day, Roan Horse Woman, Shot At Many Times' mother, removed the quilled pouch and with her husband took it to the specially prepared "Ghost Lodge" placed before their tipi. Here among others who had previously kept a ghost, a Wicasa Itacan for-

malized the "keeping" with a red painted pipe by charging the parents to lead an upright life. Keeping a ghost was a sacred undertaking and as if to verify that sanctity, the parents painted their faces red. And they would continue to do so for the following year.

When the Wicasa Itacan had completed his admonitions, he placed food in the "ghost's" bowl, so that it might be brought out before the lodge, and each night it would be returned to its place at the rear of the "ghost lodge." The responsibility for accomplishing this ritual fell upon Roan Horse Woman, mother of Shot at Many Times.

When the feast was completed Iron Shell, his wife, and their relatives ceased mourning. There was no need for grief, for their son's spirit was now present and with them. Moreover, as a spirit, he was given a spirit name and henceforth would be referred to by that name.

During the year the family occupied themselves with the task of making things, so that there might be an impressive accumulation of moccasins and robes, of dresses and leggings. Everyone was busy making those things at which they were most skillful, for the esteem in which they held their ghost would be reckoned by the quality of their handiwork.

Whenever the camp moved, the ghost and its tipi were transported by a specially selected horse. When the new village site was reached, the ghost lodge was put up first, for it became the meeting lodge. Here the old men gathered, and after the owner prepared his tipi, he brought food for the ghost and for the old men in order that they might feast.

After about a year, when the owner and his family felt that they had accumulated sufficient articles to honor the ghost properly, a day was chosen for the release. A Wicasa Itacan was chosen to prepare the spirit and perform the rite, and for this service he received a horse and fine clothing.

On the morning of the chosen day, the Wicasa Itacan painted on a small square of tanned skin a face in representation of the ghost, and to it added those marks of rank, such as Hunka stripes, as the ghost was entitled to wear. The painted skin portrait was then tied at the top of a cottonwood pole approximately the height of the child. This pole was then placed to the left toward the rear of the lodge. The Wicasa Itacan next placed a forked pole, nearly the height of a man, in front of the lodge and rested a tipi pole between the forks in such a fashion that the foot of the pole rested on the earth near the lodge entrance. Around the pole, the mentor entwined vines.

When the spirit post was thus prepared, the family and honored guests, who were former ghost owners, gathered to sit at the left of the lodge behind the spirit post. The robes and articles of clothing which had been accumulated were brought in and placed on the ground opposite.

When all was in readiness, the mentor consecrated the gathering with his pipe, asking Wakan Tanka to bless the proceedings, the people, and the spirit, as the pipe was offered to the owner and assembled guests. When this ritual was completed, the mother dressed the spirit post in clothing appropriate to the occasion.

Prayers and supplications offered to the gods explained the gratitude of the Sioux to the White Buffalo Maiden who had brought them not only the sacred pipe but the knowledge of this important ceremony. After the propitiation, the mother brought the spirit bundle into the tipi and placed it on the earth in front of the spirit post.

Here the ceremonial feast began, and after the ghost and the participants had been fed, food was served to the people gathered outside. The young boys were given a special meal of their own, and in this way they might particularly honor the spirit of their former companion. Had the spirit been that of a girl, the girls would have held a separate feast.

When the feast was finally completed, the robe which was considered most handsome among all the accumulated articles was taken outside and placed over the vine-entwined frame at the entrance of the tipi in a manner simulating that of a live buffalo. On its head was placed a war bonnet, and on and about it were hung and draped all the articles and clothing which had been gathered during the year. When this was completed, the owner, through the herald, announced who among the people were to receive gifts. The names of those who had given the owner presents or performed services during the year in honor of the ghost, or who were poor and needy, were called off. As they came forward, they took their prize from the buffalo. Horses, too, were given away in the name of the spirit. By the time everything had thus been disposed of, darkness had covered the earth and the stars were visible. The participants returned to the lodge for the final rite.

Here the Wicasa Itacan, in four ritual stages, unwrapped the spirit bundle, all the time exhorting the spirit to lead a good life in the spirit world. As the bundle was finally to be opened, the priest walked out the lodge door so that the spirit might be properly released to make its journey on the Spirit Road—the Milky Way.

When the soul was thus released, everyone was joyous. The owner and his wife, having fulfilled their obligation, called upon the people to help themselves to their remaining belongings, urging them to take whatever food and clothing and shelter they might want, leaving the spirit post and opened bundle as their only possessions.

Now destitute, the parents were ready to begin life anew. Friends and relatives set up a tipi for them and brought them food to show their love and respect and pity. Thus was performed *Ihta hepi wakicaga,* "Through with the spirit keeping within a day."[4]

Parents who were highly esteemed and well-to-do might be invited by the Wicasas or leaders of the tribe to perform the White Buffalo Ceremony in conjunction with the Spirit-keeping. If parents were offered such an honor, the Owner must secure the skin of a White Buffalo for use on the day of the spirit's release; for this propitiation, following immediately upon Ghost-owning, was

---

[4] *Ibid.;* Densmore, "Teton Sioux Music," *loc. cit.;* Fletcher, "Indian Ceremonies," *loc. cit.* These writers should be referred to for further aspects and descriptions of Spirit-keeping.

an elaboration in special honor of the White Buffalo Maiden. Few men, however, were worthy to give this ceremony, so sacred was its nature, for with its completion went the title of Wicasa.

When Iron Shell was so honored, he carried out the prescribed Ghost-owning as was customary. The White Buffalo Ceremony properly began after midnight and, as was often the case, several parents had joined to hold their Spirit-keeping Ceremony together. Here in the sacred tipi were the spirit posts of three other owners, although they had already given away their possessions and released the souls of their children. Now in the spirit lodge with Iron Shell remained only the shaman and former White Buffalo Owners. To the northwest side of the lodge lay the white buffalo hide, and upon its head an eagle feather war bonnet was placed. At its feet moccasins were laid, with other articles of clothing round about. In front of the head was a small, square hole in which blackened earth was placed, covered with a scarlet cloth. To the rear of the lodge was a buffalo-skull altar and near the buffalo robe was placed a wooden bowl filled with water, a mountain-sheep-horn spoon, a small robe upon which choke-cherries and *wasna* were placed, and two long carved paddles. Incense of sweet grass was made to purify the area, while the floor of the lodge was lined with sage.

The shaman formally opened the ceremony by consecrating the gathering with his pipe and offering the song of the White Buffalo Maiden:

> *With visible breath I am walking*
> *I walk toward the buffalo nation*
> *and my voice is heard*
> *I am walking with visible breath*
> *I am walking this scarlet relic.*[5]

This was a sacred song, during which no dog might bark or child cry.

With the paddles, the priest ceremonially removed the red cloth from the mellowed earth and carefully spread the blackened

[5] Densmore, "Teton Sioux Music," *loc. cit.*, 67.

soil over and about the area. Then, with the aid of an Owner, the priest placed sixteen tufts of red painted goose down, first on the four corners, and then throughout the center area of the blackened earth—all to symbolize the role of the living things upon the earth. The four corners typified the four directions, while the center area represented the progression of men's lives.

"The old die, the new are born, and the nation of men lives on forever. The White Buffalo is the leader of the nation, and from that nation comes our life-giving food."[6]

Next the priest ritually consecrated the equipment in the smoke of the sweet grass. In the presence of the assembled Wicasas he then ceremonially fed the owner first the cherries, as symbols of fruits of nature, from the great horn spoon, symbol of truthfulness, and then the meat, symbol of life and strength.

When the Owner had thus symbolically expressed his gratitude, the Wicasas also partook of the sacrament of cherries and meat.

At daybreak, the hour at which the White Buffalo Maiden left the Sioux camp many generations ago, the priest supervised the taking of the White Buffalo Robe out of the lodge. Four young boys, brothers of the ghost, each grasped one of the legs of the buffalo hide, and after four attempts, carried the sacred skin from the tipi and hung it upon the frame in front of the lodge.

Here were placed all the objects which Iron Shell's family had accumulated, and from this location gifts were distributed to honored guests and to the poor. When all the gifts had been given, the men removed the white buffalo robe from the rack, and in the presence of the throng, cut the hide in three sections. The outer parts were then distributed to the Wicasas, while the Owner was entitled to the center section.

From these sections each man would make a headband, wide as the palm of his hand. At the four corners they would secure a large shell button, to which two eagle feathers were attached. These headdresses were the badge of the Wicasas, to be worn only in times of peace and never in war.

In this manner, the Buffalo Maiden was honored and assured

---

[6] Fletcher, "Indian Ceremonies," *loc. cit.,* 271.

that her teachings should be indelibly inscribed in the minds of Sioux leaders. This was a propitiation by men who aspired to leadership, men chosen by their peers to assume costly obligations in accordance with the holy instructions of the Buffalo Maiden, in order that they might be fit to guide their people. Rarely has mankind devised a better assurance for dedicated, consecrated leadership.[7]

The concept of power through self-sacrifice, operative in the vision quest and Sun Dance, the giveaway and the graded ceremonies, appeared as a determinant effecting the successful continuance and adjustment of the societal system. The implication of self-sacrifice for the Sioux is strikingly exemplified in the war pattern. While the primary objectives of war seem to have been retaliation, protection, and exploitation, the greatest was not one of these, but rather death. Risk and daring were essentials for prestige, for they tempted death. This does not necessarily mean that the Sioux warrior was intent on suicide. In fact, many undoubtedly recoiled from it. But the Sioux point of view was so strongly directed toward self-sacrifice that men voluntarily and willingly risked their lives solely for the recognition which the risk afforded.

The idea that man might gain power through self-sacrifice may have been not only a mechanism for preventing aggressive individualism but also a device to foster the ideal that it was the individual, not the group, who was responsible for Sioux welfare. On the one hand the society encouraged and honored individual initiative, but on the other hand, it penalized egocentrism by ostracism when it failed to conform to the code of generosity and selflessness.

The emphasis upon self-sacrifice suggests the masochistic, yet this interpretation cannot be wholly substantiated in light of Sioux ability to turn their aggressions upon their enemies as opposed to destroying themselves. Rather, it would seem that their ex-

[7] Densmore, "Teton Sioux Music," *loc. cit.;* Fletcher, "Indian Ceremonies," *loc. cit.* Detailed descriptions containing minor variations of the White Buffalo Ceremony may be found in the writings of these authors.

tremely virile aggressiveness, while incipiently masochistic, was primarily expressed through war, and that neither the individual nor the society itself was harmed, but on the contrary strengthened.

The exhibitionism so prominent in war and the giveaway appears to have been a natural compensatory reaction to the intensified pattern of self-sacrifice. Boasting of one's war and sex exploits and of accomplishments in crafts allowed a necessary ego-expression and permitted a balancing of this personality component against the felt and imagined self-denials. Yet the very act of boasting, superficial self-acclaim for prowess and accomplishment, was in fact an admission of the individual's sense of deprivation, inadequacy and feelings of self-sacrifice. Institutionalized though it was, the conflict of self versus selflessness was very real for the Sioux, and they put their minds and hearts to resolving it.

CHAPTER 14

The Individual and the Sioux Way

THE SIOUX WAY OF LIFE was, indeed, a dramatic one. In its forthright vitality, it was demanding, though not necessarily uncompromising. The effect upon the men and women who followed the pattern can perhaps be first interpreted by observing the life cycle of the Sioux individual.

The birth of a child was an occasion of gratitude for the family and for the people. To bear a child was considered fulfillment of a woman's role, for in so doing the White Buffalo Maiden's charge to be fruitful was satisfied.

There was no question in the minds of the Sioux about the basic causes of conception. They knew all the theoretical implications necessary for procreation. They were well aware that the period of gestation involved nine months, and their term for pregnancy—"growing strong"—suggested their understanding of the process.

During pregnancy either the prospective mother or one of the grandmothers made two "sand lizards," one of which was designed to contain the child's umbilical cord. These little amulets were fashioned in the form of either a lizard or a tortoise. Since both of these animals were revered because they were so difficult to kill, it was fitting that their protective power should be enlisted as guardian of the individual's substance.[1] One amulet would be used to hold the cord after birth, while the other would henceforth serve merely as a decoy to guard the child against malevolent forces. The vigilant protection of one's entity was essential to the Sioux sense of well-being.

When the child began to walk the amulet was worn on the

[1] James O. Dorsey, "A Study of Siouan Cults."

clothing. A child of five and six was known as a "carry your navel." Later this sand lizard was put away, and usually it was kept by the mother.

While the responsibility for fashioning the sand lizard fell upon the mother or grandmother, it was the duty of one of the father's sisters to make the cradle. Loving care and devoted craftsmanship were expended upon the cradle, for it was a tangible symbol of sisterly respect.

Shortly prior to labor, necessary preparations were undertaken. When Doing Good Deeds's baby was about to come, her mother Blue Whirlwind and she were alone in the tipi. Blue Whirlwind first got a clean square of deerskin which would be used to catch the baby. Next she found a sturdy stake, which she drove firmly into the ground at the rear of the tipi so that it stood about as high as her waist. Then Blue Whirlwind collected braided sweet grass, which she soaked in warm water, a bowl of buffalo grease, a puff ball in which a hole had been cut, and a strip of soft deerskin.

When the labor pains began in earnest, Doing Good Deeds squatted at the stake and, holding the top, pressed her knees against it. As the pains became more intense, she knelt on the ground, holding tightly to the stake. When the child was born, Blue Whirlwind placed it on the square of deerskin. She cut the umbilical cord so that about three inches remained with the infant. Next she split the end of the cord attached to the afterbirth in the belief that this hastened expulsion.

Blue Whirlwind then drew the navel cord through the hole in the puff ball and thoroughly dusted the severed cord with the fungus powder. Twisting the navel around several times, she fitted the fungus over it. When this was satisfactorily completed, Blue Whirlwind wrapped the strip of deerskin securely around the infant's stomach to hold the navel in place. She cleaned the baby with the sweet grass soaked in warm water, wiped him completely with the buffalo grease, wrapped him in blankets, and laid him beside his mother. Then Blue Whirlwind arranged the mother on her bed to make her comfortable, wrapping a band of deerskin around her stomach, not too tightly.

When the afterbirth came, Blue Whirlwind placed it in a piece of hide, and taking it far from camp, placed it in a tree. Mothers were given ample time to recover, and it was considered best if they rested in bed for about ten days.

When twins were born, it was fortuitous if they both lived. It was believed that they had argued over which would be born first. The strongest of the two always won the right to be the eldest, but the other, being weaker, pouted after birth, was generally sickly, and frequently died. Hence, twins who lived were thought to be mysterious and Wakan.

At the time of birth, the maker of the cradle presented it to the family of the infant. In some cases many cradles were made, thus showing the love and respect the parent's sisters held for the child. The name of the child might be conditioned by a particularly generous bestowal, as typified by Blue Whirlwind's sister's name, "They Love Her," given in recognition of the twenty-two cradles she received at birth. The cradle gifts showed family solidarity and an ability to meet a situation demanding ostentation. The more cradles, the greater the respect, and in turn the greater the prestige. It further symbolized the respect and fondness held by a woman for her brother or male cousin, and publicly showed the woman's ability at handiwork, for cradles were reckoned as important "counts" in the quilling contest.

Four days after the birth of a child, a herald went around the village inviting everyone to a feast for naming the baby. For a family to postpone the naming feast too long was considered disrespectful to the child. On the day of honoring the baby and its mother, people gathered at their tipi. Here the father and the mother's mother gave gifts to friends, to persons of importance, and to the poor. After this display of giving, a feast was presented in honor of the mother. Many tasty foods were prepared so that all would enjoy themselves and think well of the family.

After the feast the father requested the herald to tell all those gathered the baby's name. "This little one will be known as Kills Enemy, in honor of his grandfather." Infants were generally named after their oldest living grandparents, but might also be named in honor of a deceased grandparent for whom there had been much respect.

In families where other children already had received such names, the father often named the baby according to some warlike deed he himself had accomplished, or in reference to a dream he had experienced. When the herald had reported the name, the father announced that a horse would be given in honor of the child to so-and-so, a poor man. Occasionally a horse was given to a wealthy man who would be capable of repaying in kind at some later date, but this was considered a little obvious. The people then expressed their thanks by wishing that the child might live to have his ears pierced, whereupon the father or grandfather announced through the herald that so-and-so, a brave warrior, would perform the operation. This was a vow, and by it everyone knew that the child would live until it walked, for the ear-piercing took place during a Sun Dance at any time after the child was able to walk. Failure to have the ears pierced resulted in bad luck for the child, partly due to the disregard of a vow and partly because pierced ears denoted acceptance of the modes and mores of the Sioux.[2]

For boys a secret name, less formal yet of equal significance, was the so-called *winkte* name, which ensured long life. The method of bestowal might be through a parent's casual conversation with a *winkte*, or through a parent's direct request. In the later case, a horse was paid the *winkte* as compensation. *Winkte* names were never used when speaking to a person, and rarely used when speaking about a person. Only when the proper name was forgotten or a dig was implied was the *winkte* name used, for such names invariably had pornographic connotation. A *winkte* was considered to live a long life, and his bestowal of a name ensured longevity. Sometimes a second name for boys was drawn from the first words they uttered, but this was less efficacious than the *winkte* name.

After birth, the colostrum was not fed the child. An old woman, called a "sucking woman," or a ten-year-old girl was employed

2 Walker, "The Sun Dance and Other Ceremonies," *loc. cit.,* 115.

to remove this initial milk during the first three or four days, in order that the infant might not suffer diarrhea. During this time berry juices and soups were fed the baby from a bladder with a shaped nipple, much like that used to feed nursing puppies.

The feeding schedule was essentially conditioned by hunger. Great freedom was permitted so that the child might nurse and fondle the breast at will. Either breast was offered, there being no routine, and should one breast be emptied, the other was offered until the baby was satisfied. The child was nursed in a sitting position, either on the bed or on the floor. A certain amount of modesty in the presence of men was considered good form, although in practice nursing did occur in public. Children usually were weaned when they reached three years, though this might vary in either direction by as much as a year. It was believed that a child should be nursed as long as possible, for this ensured good health. Supplementary feeding, however, might begin as early as one year. Meat, pre-masticated by the mother or older sisters and dipped in soup, was given the child to suck. Before the child was two, it was fed soups from a spoon. In order to assure the good health and future development of the child, a husband was expected to abstain from sexual intercourse with his wife so that lactation would not halt. This might be as long as from three to four years for it was important not to jeopardize the healthy development of a child.

A good part of the child's first year was spent securely wrapped in the baby bundle. For the first two months, however, a child was allowed more freedom of movement, it being reasoned that the infant was too small for the bundle. This appears to have been a rationalization, since small blankets and robes were snugly wrapped around the smallest of infants, even though no securing strings were used.

The baby bundle made before the child's birth was the same for both sexes, and no distinction was made in form or decoration. Bundles might be quilled, and in later times they were beaded. Some were in the form of hoods supported by an inverted U-shaped willow frame, while others were fully decorated and attached to wooden frames. When the child was from three to five months old, or by the time it reached the creeping age, it was placed in the bundle. This was packed with cattail "down" in summer and early fall, and buffalo chips in winter; both of these substances absorbed the urine. The feces were removed, but new absorbants were not used at each changing. At night children were often left in the carrier. During the day the carrier was leaned against posts or tipi poles near the mother, and thus the child was never left alone. At feeding times the child was not restrained within the cradle, for at such times practice in walking was encouraged. Some mothers carried their children on their backs supported by a robe with the child facing forward. Young girls often played with infant brothers and sisters in this manner, jouncing them in their robes as they skipped around. Frequently the child was carried in the mother's arms and covered by a robe, the baby's buttocks resting upon the mother's forearm. Infants wore no clothing, except for the protection of the baby bundle.

Despite the seeming constrictions of the baby bundle, children were given a limited freedom when nursing; often subjugated to long periods of fondling and rocking, especially by grandparents; and had to endure being a teased and cuddled pet of older sisters.

The care and responsibility of the infant rested in large measure with the mother. She was, however, ably assisted by the grandmother, various sisters and female cousins, or an older daughter. If the infant were a girl, an older sister might care for her almost completely. If the infant were a boy, the sister's attention was limited to feeding and minding.

Young children from four to seven years old ran naked a good part of the time, especially in summer and frequently in winter within the tipi. According to Rattling Blanket Woman, children became tired of their clothes and took them off for relief. By the age of seven more modesty was required, and the degree of nakedness might depend in part upon the sex of siblings.

Parental disciplining of small children was almost nonexistent, as they were catered to with great deference. Children were not

315

permitted to cry, and to prevent it their wants were either immediately satisfied or they were rocked and cuddled until they ceased.
In those instances where this was ineffectual, the grandmother
cried along with the child to "help it." Young children were
"asked," not "told," what not to do. Sententious lecturing began
at an early age, and by ten or eleven such talkings-to were no
longer considered necessary.

Scaring a child into obedience was never flagrantly practiced,
but the use of culture frighteners such as the owl, the *cici*-man,
and later the *wasicu* or white man, were commonly employed.[3]
Children who could not overcome bed-wetting were threatened
by being told that they would be fed mice. This was considered
to be a very effective remedy.

Physical violence was never resorted to in child discipline. As
Blue Whirlwind commented, "We never struck our children for
we loved them. Rather we talked to them, gently, but never harshly. If they were doing something wrong, we asked them to stop."
Among the Sioux, beatings and thrashings were reserved for their
dogs, for it was believed that adults should not express their aggression upon children.

Both parents assumed an active interest in the child's development, but the father's duties as hunter and warrior forced the
mother to oversee and mind the children to a greater extent. It
was she who made the clothes and fed her children. Despite the
frequent presence of the grandmother, usually the father's mother
(since no avoidance was necessary here), children gave the greatest credit for parental care to the mother. Both she and the father,
however, inculcated family pride and respect for elders, and instilled the code of ethics and rules of etiquette through their constant preachings.

The importance of the father-son relationship was evident,
however, by the father's making for his son bows, arrows, and
quivers and instructing him in shooting techniques. Maternal and

[3] E. Homburger Erickson, "Observations on Sioux Education," *The Journal
of Psychology*, No. 7 (1939).

paternal uncles as well as older brothers might play similarly important roles.

Between the ages of four and five, children were given their own clothing, utensils for eating, tools for use in their activities, and a separate bed. They were expected to take care of these things and keep them in order. Younger children were watched closely by the mother or grandmother, or by an older sister. Careful attention was paid to their selection of playmates, their dress, and their manner, for children should display reserve and bearing in exemplifying family pride.[4] Children who lacked qualities of neatness, deportment, respect, and self-control were publicly ridiculed, for scorn served as a real social conditioner for both child and family.

The educational features in the children's play group had a significant role in child development. Owing to the extended family setup and the family-band camping group, play between brothers and sisters as well as between parallel- and cross-cousins must have been most common. Little girls and boys of eight and eleven played together a great deal. The "Packing Game" and its affiliated "Love Game" received directed impetus by the elders. Parents made little tipis, travois, and bows and arrows with which the child might mimic the activities of their elders. Moving camp, cooking, sleeping, and hunting formed the basis for the child phantasy. The changing of a boy, however, from "travois horse" to "husband" in playing camp-moving seems to have been the greatest degree of imagery demanded. That the entire scheme fit the adult pattern so completely must have been of basic importance in making the adjustment to adulthood a relatively smooth one. The freedom of association here between the sexes is interesting, for soon after the children reached eleven years, a strict sex dichotomy in all games was established.

The pattern of children's games seemed to line up in a pair-

[4] Melvin Randolph Gilmore, "The Old Time Method of Rearing a Dakota Boy," Museum of the American Indian, Heye Foundation, *Indian Notes*, Vol. VI, No. 4 (1929).

relationship, frequently extended through the use of teams as paired opponents, with a corollary paired gambling motif. Speed seems never to have been a dominant feature, but skill, endurance, brute force, or ability to withstand pain were the elements of victory. Each satisfied the highly aggressive tendencies, while the competitive scoring stood as a valuable prelude to the adult coup-counting complex.

Such games as the sham battles, the Buffalo Game, or Kick-My-Tail-Off were obviously appropriate for instilling the qualities necessary for good warriorship. Choosing a leader from among those boys assembled was identical to the method of selection in adult activities.

In girls' games, physical prowess was not a part. Skill, paired opponents, and gambling were characteristics of their games too.

The games themselves were of relatively short duration, but they were repeated time and again, sometimes being carried over for another day. The continuity was also maintained by the gambling feature, so that actually there were a series of games going on all the time.

"Throwing One Up Like a Ball," played by adolescent girls at the expense of some younger boy, would seem to have been out of place in a prudish culture like the Sioux's. Sanctioned by everyone and involving an obvious, though vicarious, sex satisfaction for the girls, the game may have exhibited the emergence of repressed sexual activities for closely guarded girls in a society where premarital chastity was stressed.[5]

Boys' hunting parties were all mimic and were frequently communal. There seems to have been no formal organization. They usually went rabbit-hunting, but also took small game, birds, turtles, and the like. The kill furnished the family a supplementary food supply, and even though it often consisted of delicacies and nonessentials of diet, it gave the child a feeling of good service to

[5] Edward S. Curtis, "Teton Sioux," in Vol. III of *The North American Indian;* James O. Dorsey, "Games of Teton Dakota Children," *American Anthropologist,* Vol. IV (1891); L. L. Meeker, "Sioux Games," Free Museum of Science and Art, University of Pennsylvania, *Bulletin,* Vol. III, No. 1 (1916); J. R. Walker, "Sioux Games," *Journal of American Folk-Lore,* Vol. XVIII (1905).

his family. In turn, hunting techniques were learned by each boy. He could employ methods taught him by his father, observe the tricks used by other boys, and experiment on his own. The entire activity would stand him in good stead. Throughout his life, he learned the essentials for becoming a good provider and a co-operative hunter.

A case reported by Black Horse, of a twelve-year-old boy's ability to "shoot" snowbirds by pointing his finger at them shows the early association of supernaturalism in the activity of children. This boy was considered particularly powerful by his playmates, but received their condemnation because he used his power to kill for sport and exhibition rather than for need.

As soon as a boy was able to straddle a horse, his father, if financially able, gave his son a colt and trappings. This became the boy's pony to do with as he saw fit. He was carefully instructed in its care and use by his father, older brother, or uncle, and he was responsible for its well-being. If the child's parents were unable to furnish their son with his own pony, he was not entirely handicapped. The play-group spent much time riding and caring for their mounts, and no child, regardless of his economic status, was likely to grow up without a pretty thorough knowledge of horsemanship. Horse-loaning, even in adult life, was common, and the group spirit in games of war and in horse-breaking made the poorer children's lot less severe. As boys grew older, one of their tasks was to care for their parents' herds. This job was usually done by two or more boys together, and at such times they had a good chance for observation of horses' ways.

War, that part of life which was to figure most dominantly in the male role, came directly to the boy as early as his eleventh or twelfth year. Throughout his earlier years he had been grooming himself for this activity by participating in the games of skill and fortitude, and by practicing the techniques of shooting and riding which trained him specifically for the goal of warrior.

The boy's first war party was for him the stepping stone from childhood to youth. It did not mean that he stopped any of his more boyish activities, but rather he added a concretely adult achievement. The first expedition was a chance for him to ex-hibit his ability and put in practice some of the lessons he had learned from his parents, from his play-group, and from the casual observation of coup-counting and political harangues. Sometimes he was taken by a relative, but it was considered better if he ran away with comrades on his own initiative.

The experienced warriors made the neophyte's trip rather mis-erable. He was relegated to the job of water-boy and general servant, forced to satisfy the whims of the older men, mind the horses which were taken on the trip, and usually stay behind to care for excess traveling equipment when the actual fighting took place. Any chance for him to exhibit courage or fortitude was severely limited, and the possibility of his experiencing serious harm was likewise small.

The war party, however, gave the boy a chance to get the feel of an expedition. It allowed him to break from his parental fold and enter the man's world through his own initiative. Now he could smoke without fear "that his navel would drop out." But his first expedition also reinforced the Sioux concept that the role of the young was to serve and to listen and be scorned by the older, more experienced men.

After his first war party, he might join others when he so desired and thereby build his war record. Not all boys went in their eleventh year; some waited until their middle teens. They received the same treatment, though less prestige, for the fact that a boy was eleven years old on his first trip gave him a head start in joining the Akicita societies, and a certain aura which even in later life might prove a decisive edge in the ever present coup-counting competition.

All boys, with the exception of the *winktes*, were expected to participate in at least one war party as a social requirement of adulthood, but a boy versed in and adapted to things supernatural could make the required bow and let it go at that, reserving his abilities for a shamanistic career. Visions of real significance could come to a child of ten and twelve years and might affect the course of his life. These early motivations are noted in the biographies of Sitting Bull, Rain in the Face, and others. On the other hand, an early start in going to war or in receiving a vision was by no means an assurance of later success. In some cases a premature war party might have been a particularly bad experience. Here the realization that the requirements for warriorship were unsuited to his temperament might well cause a boy to follow the calling of a shaman. Suffice it to say that boys had two rather divergent choices, both sanctioned with important prestige rewards. The problem of choice was less severe than might be at first assumed, because a merging of the two endeavors was the cultural possibility. A third possibility, though of less prestige value, was to follow a course which emphasized his hunting proclivities.

In general, however, most boys were constantly reminded of their warlike duty by hearing old men recite their exploits, by seeing their mothers and sisters celebrate victories in the Scalp Dance, and by observing the young men proudly displaying their feather badges of honor. In the tipi they might study the war record painted on the dew cloth, might watch an older brother as he sunned his shield at the rear of the lodge. Their ponies might have been stolen for them from the Crows or Pawnees. And when one of their brothers failed to return from the warpath, they would see their parents mourn and wail and cut short their hair and gash their legs in grief. Then they would know that everyone agreed that it was best to die young in battle and in glory.

By the age of fourteen or fifteen, a boy might hope to join one of the Akicita societies. When he was seventeen he might steal an enemy's horse or count coup and take a scalp; by twenty he might lead a small war party. And by thirty his warrior days would begin to close; he would have many war honors and many horses. He might even have two tipis, with a wife in each and several children tugging at his legging fringe.

Now he would devote himself to becoming a recognized elder, and would substantiate his claim with the material evidence of his past achievements—horses. He would encourage other young men to seek the warpath to glory and wealth and thereby perpetuate the system and protect his status.

For a girl, the way of childhood was similar to a boy's during the first ten years. Chiefly instructed by her mother, her education was centered around the rules of conduct, techniques of minor household chores, and child care if there were younger siblings.

Rules of conduct and accepted modes of behavior demanded that a girl be reserved and retiring in the presence of both men and elder women. She should be "loving, industrious and generous, kind to all men and animals." She learned that women ate apart from men, that they took the left side of the tipi as their side, that when she spoke she must use female language, that when spoken to she must understand both male and female tongue, and that she must sit in a posture becoming to women. These, together with the host of less spectacular behavior patterns, were well formulated in the girl's mind at an early age. Some modes and *mores* were so automatic, so ingrained, that little digression from the standard pattern was present. Others, such as generosity and industriousness, which were cultural ideals rather than commonplace traits, were less easily attained; these were attributes which characterized the "good woman." In reality, these qualities became inspiring agents which furthered a smooth, functioning for the group through social conformity. Knowing how to sit correctly and doing it and being neat about the person were common decencies that were highly important but less closely associated with the higher feminine goal.

The young girl was early given duties pertaining to housekeeping. Her mother taught her the essentials of cooking, but her chief jobs were dishwashing, wood-gathering, berry-picking, and the straightening of the tipi. Most of these jobs she did as an assistant, but when she reached ten years or so many of them became her personal duty. Instructions in tanning and more particularly in quilling and beading were directed chiefly by her mother, but occasionally an aunt or older sister acted as instructor.

Should the child have a younger sibling, much of the care of the infant was relegated to her. If it was a sister, a girl of six or eight might take almost complete charge of feeding, changing, and amusing. The mother nursed the infant and supervised the supplemental diet, but the girl was primarily responsible for her infant sister's comfort and safety. Doll-playing was a fantasy pastime for the younger children, especially for those girls who were too small to manage a child capably or for an only child who had no baby-sitting responsibilities. The transition from doll care to adult motherhood was of a gradual character.

After girls reached puberty and were recognized by such rites as the Ball-throwing Ceremony or the Buffalo Sing, they were taught in earnest the arts of tanning and quilling and instructed in the female attributes expected of wives and mothers. Parents were careful to see that their daughters were well informed and well behaved. An outstanding girl brought honor to her parents and commanded a high bride-price.

Like ear-piercing, tattooing was a requisite for assuring a complete life. As Little Day explained it:

> Long Woman, Red Leaf's wife, was the only one in our camp who did tattooing; nearly everyone went to her. She marked a circle or line with clay and with an awl punched the color in. Then she put blue clay over this, and though it bled, when the clay dried and was rubbed off, the color remained. People were tattooed with a blue dot on their forehead or with two lines down the chin so that upon death, their ghost will not be pushed off the Ghost road by Hihan Kara, the Owl Maker.

All well-brought-up children were taught that etiquette demanded one knock on the side of the tipi or a shake of the deer-claw door rattle hung at the entrance before entering. When invited to enter, one walked to the left and, after nodding in recognition, sat on whichever of the beds was offered. Men sat with their legs crossed or occasionally outstretched before them, while women placed their legs to the right side with their feet tucked toward the rear.

If a woman sat with her feet to the left, we knew she was left handed. When we women became tired, we might stretch our legs out crossing our left foot over our right. Women never sat cross-legged as men and the only men that sat as women were winktes, for they tried to be women. When smoking, men often rolled a robe and placed it at their back. Then drawing their knees up and crossing their feet, they drew the robe around and tied it below their knees. This was very comfortable. Men and women both knelt, sitting on their turned in feet, but not on the heels. One could sit this way for a long time, we cut tobacco while kneeling.

It was customary for a man to offer a guest tobacco, and most conversations were preceded by the host's offering the pipe to the Four Winds, the Earth and the Sky and then passing the lighted pipe to the guest, who would take several puffs before returning it. The pipe was then exchanged between the men until the tobacco was consumed.

While persons greeted one another saying, "*How*," there was no formal word of parting. To the Sioux, the conclusion of a talk was obvious and a farewell would have seemed superfluous. When a conversation was finished and the visit over, the guest merely arose and left by the right side of the tipi.

The human proclivity of a parent's experiencing a special attachment to one of his children was recognized by the Sioux to the point of institutionalizing that fondness. Quite frequently a couple would forthrightly pronounce one of its offspring as its "Favorite Child" and thenceforth lavish upon it gifts and honors far in excess of those bestowed upon the other children. Usually this exalted position was reserved for girls, but boys too might enjoy this privilege. No gift was too great, no honor too high for such a child, for this was the mechanism by which the family could themselves gain prestige through the status which they endeavored to build for the favored one.[6]

The effect of this special attention upon not only the individual but upon his relations with his siblings would seem to have

[6] Deloria, "Dakota Texts," *loc. cit.* Additional observations may be found in the records collected by this author.

been strikingly deleterious. And yet such blatant favoritism would almost force upon the recipient responsibility for exhibiting the cultural pattern of generosity toward his peers with a special devotion and grace. The mixed blessing of being a favored one held obligations not to be disregarded. The effect of this relationship upon one's brothers and sisters can only be thought to have been the basis of severe rivalry and conflict, yet since custom demanded the most devoted respect for one's family peers, the incipient tension may have been somewhat reduced by the knowledge that one member was so honored.

On reaching adulthood, the Sioux were physically an impressive people. They were big people in a big country, and their physique somehow seemed appropriate to the rigors of the plains. If any men were physically designed to withstand the tempestuous winds, the crashing storms, the winter's deep cold, or the summer's blazing heat, the Sioux were. Moreover, they seemed to thrive.

The average height for men was over five feet seven inches; though many were less than five feet six, some, like Little Thunder, were known to have been over six feet six. Though tall, the men were not ponderously framed and often were lanky. It was usually only after reaching middle age that the term "big belly" became appropriate.

Sioux women were shorter than their men, but their average height too was remarkable. Like their male counterparts, they were often willowy, with beautifully long delicate figures. In maturity, owing in part to their height, they frequently appeared broad and heavy-set. The Sioux height, however, was due in large measure to the extreme length of their legs so that frequently they appeared short-waisted. Physical types were varied. There were fat men and thin, big men and little. There were dark men and light men, handsome men and ugly. Most of them, however, had blue-black hair, deep brown eyes, reddish-brown skin, and generally large physique.

The Sioux have been widely recognized as a handsome race; certainly their size and proud carriage have contributed to this.

Their faces, too, with wide-spaced eyes, broad and relatively long and powerfully arched noses, carried a sense of dignity. The tendency toward heavy chins and a slight prognathism gave their full-lipped mouths a quality of firmness. Again, there were many variations. In some persons the mongoloid characteristics of narrow almond eyes was present, but this was rather rare. In truth, eye form, the strong, aquiline nose, and the length of the face gave many Sioux, especially males, a slightly Nordic cast of countenance. Women's features were softer and less pronounced; they had more finely chiseled and more carefully polished heads than the males, and occasionally some appeared more mongoloid.[7]

If the Sioux's physical qualities set them apart from other men, so did their personalities. The degree to which Sioux personality influenced their society and vice versa is as impossible to solve for the Sioux as for all mankind.

In discussing the personality of a cultural group, two factors assume importance: the justification of labeling psychological types, and the possibility of analyzing group psychologies. However, by obtaining group norms of personality components through administering to modern Sioux such psychological tests as the Rorschach and by discovering even with such a limitation that they substantiate or give insight to sociological observations, the relative personal and cultural values may be clarified.[8]

Custom, etiquette, and manners—culturally imposed patterns of behavior, prescribed conditions, and institutionalized interpersonal reactions—explain, in part, something of the Sioux personality. The more significant determinants were imposed early. It was required that young people should not speak their opinions before more mature minds, but rather that they should sit quietly and absorb knowledge. Respect for the estimation of elders marked the well-bred person.

[7] Louis R. Sullivan, "Anthropometry of the Siouan Tribes," American Museum of Natural History *Anthropological Papers*, Vol. XXIII, Pt. 3 (1920). This author presents valuable anthropometric data.

[8] Royal B. Hassrick, "Some Personality Traits of Sioux Indian Children," MS.

Similarly, it will be recalled that persons were expected to exhibit complete composure at all times, with certain notable exceptions: bereavement, the vision quest, and the warpath. Expression of emotion through bodily contact was unheard of, and verbal displays were limited to specified situations such as coup-countings and political orations. This over-all composure was especially apparent during normal events of social interaction.

Individuals might, without fear of criticism, come out of their shell in times of crises. As has been pointed out, both sexes found release by participation in ceremonies associated with life's exigencies. Serious illness, departure for the warpath, competitive endurance of intense heat during sweat-bathing, burial rites with their masochistic practice of leg- and arm-slashing and finger removal were deeds with suicidal elements which balanced the individual's self-control. The most extreme release, as reached in the climaxes of the Sun Dance and vision quest with their auto-hypnotic behavior, were largely confined to men. This complex of release from suppression appears as an institutionalized loss of control and, in the final analysis, a turning of their aggression, even in aspects of making war, against themselves. Here was a manic-depressive-like syndrome of an explosive nature.

Sex segregation in group activities and in the normal association of men and women acted as another strong control. As previously mentioned, upon entering the tipis women sat at the left; men, at the right. Women seldom looked directly at the men, but rather bowed their heads and talked in whispers to their neighbor. They kept their robes wrapped tightly around them or their arms closely crossed over their breasts and legs together. This protective pose was typical of their stance, their walk, and even their dancing. The men likewise rarely looked directly at the women, but cast their glances to the ground. It was good etiquette among all people not to look one another directly in the eye. When food was served at a function, the men were served separately and before the women. This was part of the pattern which required the husband and wife to suppress any signs of familiarity at all times in the presence of others. This sexual dichotomy of Sioux society was probably a part of the social control which upheld the ideal of feminine virtue.

Extreme distrust of strangers was characteristic in the early culture. Soon after the initial skirmishes with white immigrants and soldiers, *wasicu* or whiteman, as the most dreaded enemy, was a threat intended to make children mind. This method of child control may have served its immediate purpose well, but its continuance today has brought about unexpected complexities.

The importance of gossip as a control agent among primitive societies cannot be underestimated. In a close-knit group everyone knows everyone else, and "talk" is a valuable and strong influence for ensuring conformity. Thus it was among the Sioux; old and young, men and women, participated in "talk." It helped maintain a sort of national *esprit*, reminded one and all of the ideal pattern, and held in check those who would digress. Living under such rigid surveillance may have created certain anxieties, or at least insecurity with regard to social situations and the individual's position with his fellow men. Gossip was one of the pressures developing constraint in the individual. This pressure was ever present but became increased when band joined band or when the tribe met for its annual camp circle.[9]

While the cultural conditioning produced reserved personalities, the Sioux had an additional series of defense mechanisms which became apparent, particularly in interaction with strangers. These may have been an outgrowth of the cultural control agents, but the total pattern seems to indicate a deeper psychological scheme. One obvious form of defense was the habit of children to run inside or behind the tipi or behind their mother, whence they could safely peek at approaching strangers. This was evidently learned early in life. It probably had the advantage of

[9] Erickson, "Observations on Sioux Education," *loc. cit.*; A. Irving Hallowell, "The Social Function of Anxiety in a Primitive Society," *American Sociological Review*, Vol. VI, No. 6 (1941). Each of these authors makes reference to this general problem.

deeply rooting a security in the home, but in turn it made difficult the development of security among strangers.

Among young men the habit of bowing the head when confronted was common, and among the girls, defense took the more marked form of head-turning and utter silence. Among adult males the so-called deadpan or expressionless, noncommittal look was used to advantage. Closely allied, and common to both sexes was the habit of not looking strangers directly in the face, but gracefully dropping the glance. Usually the stranger had to initiate and maintain conversation. When the Indian did originate it, his statements seemed forced. Females, particularly, had the habit of covering the lower face with their hands, handkerchiefs, or robe so that their conversation, soft as it was, was further screened to mumbling. This same action occurred during moments of embarrassment or surprise, and while it was possibly ascribed to a form of oral neuroticism,[10] it also had a truly protective and consoling feature.

In certain ways Indian parents seem to have failed to encourage children to meet, accept, or control new situations. They did not discourage shyness. Youngsters were never forced into social situations or expected to take part in them, except those expected of their age group.

This universal shyness may indicate a deeper insecurity, an actual anxiety in contact-situations where unaccustomed interaction was involved. It may in part have been induced by the parental attitude that children, as reasonable beings, had adult personalities and should be treated as such. Children were given their choices concerning what they ate and when and where they slept and even their going and coming, to the extent of what relative they should visit and how long they should stay. Such freedom may have promoted a form of egoism which had value from a self-sufficiency point of view. By the same token, the gradual shift from such a loose family control into the wider societal sphere where control was strong through gossip may in reality have been

[10] Erickson, "Observations on Sioux Education," *loc. cit.*

329

somewhat traumatic. The adolescent may have really been insecure in social contacts because of insufficient guidance in a set of new choice situations. Such a socialization process can produce an anxiety which may lead to a general distrust in everyone outside the kinship circle, and it is little wonder that the social contacts were basically limited to the *tiyospe* or extended family band.

Because of the parents' shyness and stoical reserve, by imitation the child learned the same reserve. This was reinforced by the constantly repeated admonitions by elders in regard to proper behavior. Moreover, it is also entirely probable that the defense mechanisms of adults were strengthened by their genuine fear of social censure.

How early the child became aware of external pressures can best be surmised from what takes place today. Now among the Sioux as early as the fourth year, children, especially girls, assist their parents to observe the countless goings and comings of neighbors. Peeking out windows at passers-by, carrying tales and bits of news and gossip, all go to round out the parents' picture of community life. People less frequently get talked about in front of the children. But when does it occur to the child that his naïve reporting is part of a larger whole of which he is a member and a victim? In the second and third grades in school the sadistic flavor of gossip and nagging causes too many children to run away, or at least to stay home, from school. It may have been something a close relative had done, or the funny dress a girl was wearing, or the odd haircut a boy may have adopted. To say the least, these seemingly superficial causes indicate that social censure produces insecurity at an early age.

Correlative to the defense mechanisms and their associated insecurities is the entire sphere of Sioux aggression. It is impossible to say just how aggressive the Sioux formerly were, since this whole realm of their psychology was neatly blanketed by their social pattern and its symbols. Undoubtedly the warpath offered a most satisfactory outlet. The strong cultural incentive for war prowess sanctioned aggression, but it was exerted upon nonmembers of the group. The highest honor went to the man whose war record was best, but his aggression was felt only indirectly by his people because of this strong sanction.

Aggression was further mantled by the supernatural power gained through the Sun Dance and the *hanbelachia*.[11] An evil shaman could be destructively aggressive upon others in a group, but his position became precarious if his subversion became common knowledge. Only during public Medicine Testings, when a shaman exhibited his power by running the gauntlet of other medicine men trying to "shoot" him or professionally break him, was overt supernaturalized aggression within the group sanctioned. The shaman's creed as crystallized by the purposes of the Sun Dance and instructions received during the vision quest left a Dreamer little room for gaining personal control at the expense of members of his society.[12]

Coup-countings and virtue feasts served, in part, to satisfy personal grievances and exert verbal aggression because of their highly competitive nature, but taking the oath through "biting the knife" curtailed the freedom with which one might speak. Thus, while aggression was sanctioned, it was limited by the very nature of that sanction.

Physical violence within the society was condoned to a very limited extent, and even then in connection with specific events. Among boys, the sadistic competition in war games showed the most marked form of aggressive outlet. The games were designed to simulate war and develop warriorlike stamina and toughness, thereby acquainting boys with the rigors of adult activity. The fights were with imaginary enemies, not fellow playmates,[13] and the phantasy served to make the aggression extra—rather than intra—societal. Among men, physical aggression took the form of wrangles over property destruction and wife-beating, and, in the case of infidelity, facial disfigurement. Even here the husband must be careful lest he maltreat too severely a wife whose status was above his. Such action was condoned only by those women

---

11 Walker, "The Sun Dance and Other Ceremonies," *loc. cit.*
12 *Ibid.*
13 Luther Standing Bear, *My Indian Boyhood.*

who could not muster sufficient family support to bring the brutal spouse to task. If the woman's word was as good as or better than his, her family and the wheels of gossip would put a bullying husband in his place. Women seem to have had less chance to exhibit any violent aggression, but their quilling, tanning, and virtue feasts were as competitive as coup-counting.

Again it is impossible to know exactly how the former Sioux child-training functioned with reference to aggression, but present observations coupled with life-history experiences permit an insight to the problem. The aggressive tendencies, in part, arose in the home through the paternal attitude that children were to be considered mature. They were further fostered by condoning strong aggression on the part of the youngest sibling against the older brothers and sisters. The smallest child is still given free sway because he is "so little." But what happens to the older sibling as soon as he becomes no longer the only child, or the baby? The outlet for his former nurtured aggression has been closed. The frustrating shock is bad enough, but he has also been alienated. He is not permitted to fight back; he receives little sympathy when he is attacked; and like an adult, he must likewise condone the baby because the parents say, "Baby is a little fellow; he doesn't know any better." Real family security and integration was formerly maintained in spite of this strong sibling rivalry by the common interests and basic needs of the family unit. Brother-sister aggression was strongly controlled by the avoidance taboo and inculcation of a deep and lifelong respect. Such a strong ideal pattern and the avoidance taboo might have been adequate to produce an externalized control by suppressing individual aggression, but it would in turn limit the ease with which the individual might develop an internal sanction.

Control, as observed today, is rarely exerted by the family as a unit, but rather individually. If the mother scolds, the father takes up for the child, or vice versa. Not only does the other parent sympathize with the child, but he actually feigns attack and physical violence upon the discipliner, much to the child's glee. In this fashion, the child transfers his frustration to aggression and thus limits his ability to acquire self-discipline or internalized control. At the same time, the suppressing value of the discipline is minimized because it is not internalized; the suppression might be said to be only skin-deep.

The Sioux of a century ago might best be characterized as having superficially stoical and reserved personalities which normally suppressed a highly emotional and volatile make-up to produce an almost manic configuration. Their approach to life has been well described as Dionysian.[14] The quality of their aggressiveness was phenomenal, and may well have been a compensatory device for an inherent insecurity in group situations. Here they reacted with either flaunting boastfulness or marked modesty, again a pattern characteristic of their particular psychological adjustment.

No matter how fine or crude an adjustment to the Sioux way an individual might have achieved, no matter how retiring or famous, no matter how brave or industrious, generous or wise, death came to each one. To the warrior and to the Dreamer, to the tipi-maker and the quill-worker, to the Akicita and the Wicasa —to each death brought an opportunity of walking the "Trail of the Spirits" to the land of the ancestors. The description of the death of a patriarch portrays the reverent respect which the living held for the dead.

When Holy Circle was killed in battle, his body was left in the field, for it was good to remain unburied in enemy territory. His brother Iron Shell invited Holy Circle's Akicita brothers, the Sotka Yuhas, to participate in honoring the hero in a ceremony of death, and later to avenge the death by obtaining an enemy's scalp—the reciprocal symbol of the lost brother's spirit.

At the appointed time, the members of the Sotka Yuha met with Holy Circle's immediate family at a tipi erected for the feast. In front of the tipi a rack was set up, upon which robes and articles of clothing, donated by the family, were spread to view. Inside the tipi the mourners prepared themselves for their bereavement. Iron Shell then inserted three sharpened pegs in the

---

[14] Ruth Benedict, *Patterns of Culture.*

leg of each man, through the thigh, the knee, and the calf, and two pegs through the arm at the bicep and the forearm.

When Iron Shell had completed this task, one of the Sotkas returned the favor by inserting a similar number of pegs in the host. Then the men cut short their hair in honor of Holy Circle. The female relatives, rather than running pins through their arms and legs, took knives and made three slashes on their thighs and below their knees, and like the men, cut their hair.

When the ceremonial scarification was completed, the group left the tipi and were met by Shot in the Heel, Holy Circle's father, who had assembled Holy Circle's horses as well as many donated by the family. Shot in the Heel first walked over to the Sotkas and touched each on the head in gratitude. Then, as the Sotkas sat in a row before the rack of clothes, a herald announced that Shot in the Heel was giving away horses to avenge the death of his society brother, Holy Circle. Shot in the Heel stood next to the herald telling him which members were to receive a horse, being careful to select them in the order of their bravery. When all the horses had been given away, Shot in the Heel selected pieces of clothing to be given to those Sotkas who had not received a horse. When each man had thus been honored, the herald called Kills in Sight, the indigent, from among the crowd to pull the pins from the mourners.

Kills in Sight accepted the honor, and as he removed the pins, he placed them in a pile before the men. For this service the old man received a horse.

Next, led by Runs Him, their bravest man, the Sotkas followed the family back into the tipi. There he asked Iron Shell for the knife which had been used to inflict the wounds. Then, passing the knife to the next bravest, he raised the flesh of his left forearm with his fingers and requested his neighbor to thrust the point through the skin. Each man in turn along the row of Sotkas underwent the ordeal as a sign of their mutual grief, all the time singing, "The brave Sotka Yuha, Holy Circle, did not come back."

The two servers and the two fire-keepers passed among the family and the warriors food which had been given by Shot in the Heel. When the feast was consumed, the *wacekiyapi* or worship was complete.

This funeral sans corpse was the Sioux's highest tribute to a fallen warrior. While it was said, "It is better to die young on the battlefield than to live to carry a cane," death to a young man was a national tragedy worthy of the most profound ceremonial.

When death occurred at home, it was customary for the family to postpone the burial until a day and a night had elapsed, lest the person might revive. Nonetheless, as soon as it was apparent that hope for life had vanished, the women began their dolorous wailing which could be heard throughout the encampment.

A proper funeral demanded that all the relatives assist in dressing the body in his finest attire, which included for the feet spirit moccasins with beaded soles. In the dead man's hair were placed eagle feathers, badges of his war record, and upon his red-painted face were placed dark blue stripes of the Hunka and the blue V of the White Buffalo Ceremony, were he entitled to these honors. Next to his body were placed those things he most cherished; his weapons, his war paint and *wotawes*, and his flute.

When the body had been thus properly prepared, it was first wrapped in a robe. Over this was folded a tanned skin, and all was tied securely with thongs to form a great bundle.

Others of the family took it upon themselves to erect on a high hill a scaffold of four forked posts, high enough that the wild animals could not reach it, over which was placed a cross frame of sturdy branches. For those men who had accumulated many coups during their life, the women would peel the bark from the scaffold standards and paint black bands about them.

When all was prepared and the body was properly wrapped, the adult members of the family underwent the *wacekiyapi* or worship ceremony. Here the men ran pegs through their arms and legs, and the women slashed their limbs and often severed their little fingers at the first joint. By cutting short their hair, men and women further expressed their sorrow. Then, one at a time, first the men and then the women solemnly walked around the camp circle, weeping and wailing and singing of their grief.

The family continued this ordeal for four days, going about the camp circle as well as wailing beneath the scaffold. Customarily, a Wicasa visited the family with a pipe, advising them to carry on their mourning as well as urging the women to concentrate their energies upon quilling or moccasin-making and the men to hunt. The Wicasa told them that diligence to these causes during their bereavement would demonstrate their expertness in these fields and be a comfort to them even after the bereavement. This advice, of course, constituted a most profound insight. In being recommended by a Wicasa, it carried a weight of a man whose role combined that of judge and parish priest. Here was a harmonious synthesis of the moral and political philosophy aimed at prescribing an effective solace for the individual.

When the four days had expired, the old women of the family took the body through the door of the tipi and, placing it on a travois, transported it to the scaffold. The procession was led by a close male relative, who took with him the man's favorite horse, painted with red blotches and covered with a robe. Accompanying the group was a man, usually a close friend, who would kill the horse. The women raised the body to the platform, two women standing atop and pulling with ropes while others pushed from below. The dead man's belongings—his shield, his medicine pouch, his drum, and his lance—were hung from the top of a long pole fastened at the head of the scaffold, although there was no set direction in which the body must be placed.

When the burial bundle had been firmly tied to the scaffold, the women descended and the horse was led up. The man selected to kill the horse then announced to the animal, "Grandchild, your owner thought a great deal of you and now he has died. He wants to take you with him, so go with him joyfully."

Then the friend shot the horse at close range, aiming so that the animal would die quickly and painlessly. As the horse fell, the men and women cried. After a few minutes, the friend cut off the horse's tail, fastened it to the top of the forked pole holding the bundle, and attached the pole to the scaffold. When this was completed, the family, giving the robe to the friend, might leave, though often they would remain at the grave in mourning until some friend came to take them home.

During the winter when the ground was so frozen that a scaffold could not be erected, bodies were often buried in the branches of a tree. Around the base of the tree thorny bushes and brambles were often placed to keep away wild animals.

Persons of little consequence or means were frequently buried in a shallow grave near the crest of a hill. Here the women dug the grave with their knives and covered it with boulders to protect it from beasts. Sometimes the well-to-do preferred to be buried in a grave lest in the passage of time the scaffold disintegrate and their bones be scattered over the plains.

When a woman died, her face was likewise painted with the marks of honor to which she was entitled. Her awl case and sewing kit were placed beside her in the bundle. If she had a favorite horse, it would be killed and its tail placed on a pole. Girls, too, were buried with their sewing kit at their side. A boy's horse would not generally be killed, but rather given to his best friend. This was known as an "orphaned horse," and the friend was expected to take special care of it. On the other hand, parents might kill one of their horses in honor of their child and place the tail upon a pole.

When death came to the headman of a camp the family performed the *wacekiyapi* in the customary manner, but placed the scaffold not on a hill but on the plain near the camp. Then after the body was placed on the scaffold, the women set up a new unpainted tipi over and about it, picketing down the lodge as tightly as possible, closing the smoke flaps, and sewing up the door. From the main pole the horse tail was hung as a sign of the inviolateness of the lodge. This *tiokete* or spirit lodge would remain unmolested until it was destroyed by the elements.

At death, it was believed that the spirit or *nagi* left the body to travel the "Spirit Trail" or Milky Way to the "Land of Many Lodges." In making this journey, some believed, the spirit had to pass an old woman who would examine each one for the proper tattoo marks which must appear on the wrist or forehead or chin.

If the old woman—Hihankara, the Owl Maker—could not find the proper marks, she would push the ghost from the trail, and it would fall to earth. Such spirits would become ghosts and wander about the earth forever. It was also believed that the spirit must pass Tate, the Wind, prior to judgment by Skan, the Sky.[15]

The Land of Many Lodges was a fabulous place. Here were pitched the tipis of all one's ancestors. Here were one's friends and relatives living amidst lush park-lands rich in the good things of nature. Buffalo and other animals roamed the land in unending abundance. This was a good land, a land where all things which had ever existed now lived for eternity.

The individual growing up in Sioux society naturally came to a generalized acceptance of and belief in the value of the Sioux way. Otherwise, the Sioux culture would not have sustained itself. The conflict of self-expression and self-denial was set from birth, and the individual's need to find methods for resolving it were already operative in the culture into which he had been born. The variety of roles open to the individual, the sanctioned activities which one might emphasize or minimize, allowed for personal variation of a rather surprising degree. For while it behooved the individual to determine how best he or she might evolve a workable equilibrium, the culture, as it were, took into account that no two persons were alike and that no two of their solutions would be identical. Here was a culture which offered opportunities to resolve the conflict but placed the responsibility for the resolution squarely upon its members.

[15] James O. Dorsey, "A Study of Siouan Cults," *loc. cit.*; Walker, "The Sun Dance and Other Ceremonies," *loc. cit.* Each of these authors has pertinent comments with respect to this topic.

CHAPTER 15

Epilogue

THE WHITE STONES on the hill above the Little Bighorn River which mark the graves of General George Armstrong Custer's troops symbolize the tragic cost of destroying a nation of men. Within a year after the famous battle, the Sioux themselves capitulated. Prophetically, they had lost their way of life in a last victory, for they did believe it best to die on the battlefield.

At the end of the Indian wars, the Sioux nation reluctantly agreed to settle on lands in the heart of their domain, lands which were their home. Under treaties with the United States, they received in exchange for peace and for land the promise of a white-man's education, of health services, of equipment and seeds to farm the 160 acres allotted to each enrolled member of the tribe. They received wagons to ride in and nails to build cabins; they accepted rations of flour and potatoes and cattle. They acknowledged the missionaries who preached the golden rule and gave up the Sun Dance with its sacrifice of flesh. They recognized the President of the United States as the Great White Father, and his representative, the agent, became their protector and provider. When the wars were over and the defeat a reality, the Sioux appeared to embrace the white man's way of life. Yet in 1890, nearly fifteen years after Custer's mistake, the Sioux had not relinquished the vision of a world of yesterday. The Ghost Dance, introduced by the Paiute seer Wovaka, promised its believers the return of the buffalo and the disappearance of the white man. The Sioux were enthusiastic advocates. With equal vigor, however, the dream was destroyed by the massacre at Wounded Knee at the hands of United States Artillery. Since that disaster, the Sioux have never recovered.

Today the majority of the warriors' descendants live in cabins and frame houses throughout six great reservations in North and South Dakota. Others have made their homes in urban centers across the nation. About fifty thousand persons claim a heritage from this once dramatically powerful people.

The federal government, as trustee for the Sioux's real property, both individual and tribal, has over the years been charged by the Congress with additional responsibilities. These have included adequate educational facilities, both boarding and day schools; medical services with hospitals, doctors, and field nurses; and opportunities to receive public-welfare aid. Congress has furthermore provided monies for agricultural extension work, soil conservation, and more recently a relocation program designed to help qualified Indians secure employment in urban centers away from the reservations. With United States citizenship granted American Indians in 1924; the enactment of the enlightened Indian Reorganization Act of 1935, reiterating the Indians' right to self-government; the repeal of the prohibition against selling alcoholic drinks to Indians in 1940; and the establishment of the Indian Claims Commission, permitting tribes to seek monetary restitution in the courts for lands they once sold to the United States at unconscionably low figures—with these and other forward-looking types of legislation, the outlook for the Sioux people in the mid-twentieth century should be bright. And over the years, the Bureau of Indian Affairs, a branch of the Interior Department, has guarded and guided its wards toward such a future.

But Sioux life today is almost as if none of these legislative programs had ever been conceived. The reservations are dotted with worn and shabby cabins; the little communities and tired agency towns are a study in despair. The fields of wheat and potatoes on the allotments still owned by the Sioux are more often the crops of a white tenant farmer whose Indian landlord lives in a shack in town. The rolling plains that once supported bison now are fenced, and the herds of white-faced steers are too often the property of a prosperous white cattleman. Occasionally horses may be seen, often the proud possession of a Sioux patriarch who still believes in their prestige value, for that is the only value they have.

It would be incorrect to say that no Sioux man farms or punches cattle. But alarmingly few do. Many more families are dependent upon lease checks—sent into the agency and paid out from individual Indian accounts. Many men seek seasonal work in the beet and potato fields in neighboring states or find work on road gangs or with railroad crews. Women busy themselves with making beaded moccasins or weaving place mats—anything to sell the tourist for supplemental cash. For the Sioux have taken on the white man's cash economy with a vengeance. Somehow, on not more than eight hundred dollars a year per family, they do exist.

Schools, both public day schools and government and parochial boarding schools, provide classes through the high-school level. Here the Sioux children are taught from curricula approved by the state or federal government. But the incentive for going to schools is weak, and attendance is sporadic. By senior-high school, the classes have become alarmingly small and college attendance is insignificant.

Health conditions among the Sioux are bad. While trachoma has been eradicated, the incidence of tuberculosis, ill health and disease due to malnutrition, and infant mortality is pathetically high. Good hospitals and able doctors are available, yet they can hardly remedy the home conditions that are a source of poor health.

Nor does the modern Sioux home life offer any real substitution for the solidarity of the old *tiyospe*. When the allotment system was established, families were dispersed, for allottees were encouraged (to the point of insistence) to live on their own tracts of land. The family of man and wife, in conformity to the white man's way, has supplanted the consanguine family. But the conjugal family, rather than becoming more firmly established, frequently lacked the stability to sustain itself in a period of cultural disintegration. The result is an abnormal rate of divorce and broken homes. The grandmothers still play the role of keepers for children of such families, so that often the children are reared in an environment of a generation ago.

The tribal governments are the recognized leaders of their people. Equipped with constitutions and bylaws adopted by the people and approved by the Secretary of the Interior, the elected tribal councils formulate laws, appoint judges, and hold meetings. While the constitutions themselves provide checks and balances as safeguards against political chicanery, the approving authority of the Secretary of the Interior or his delegated representative acts as all-pervasive protector. The end result is that the council halls of the Sioux provide excellent space for debates and not much else.

The people themselves reflect these conditions. Despair and resignation mark their countenances. They seem to carry on in a kind of insensitive, feelingless apathy, listless and tired in their discouragement. For them there is no chance of victory and they have suffered their defeat. They have been characterized aptly as "Warriors Without Weapons," for they are men without a vision.[1]

This tragic situation commands attention, for it is a cancer in the breast of our nation. If there is to be a remedy, diagnosis must be based on understanding of the causes. These are complex but not necessarily unfathomable.

The collapse of the buffalo-hunting economy not only meant that the Sioux could no longer feed themselves, but they lost the raw materials for clothing and shelter. They must now depend upon the white man, their former enemy, for the very essentials of daily living.

The white man's attempt to substitute an agrarian economy for a hunting economy was in direct opposition to the traditional male role among the Sioux. Even among the Plains Indians who were agriculturalists, it was the women who planted the crops and tended the fields. Farming was a woman's work and not an activity for a self-respecting man.

Treaties of peace with the white man put an end to war. But without war the internal economy, with the horse as a medium of exchange, could not expand. More significantly still, without war

[1] Gordon Macgregor, *Warriors without Weapons.*

men lost the foremost incentive for self-expression—the *raison d'être* of their being.

With the loss of the buffalo, and the denial of the warpath, men found themselves without a role. Government programs which they felt forced them to be "like women" further damaged the ego.

The Sioux accepted the introduction of Christianity without serious reluctance, even though the missionaries were instrumental in the abolition of the Sun Dance. But Christian teachings could hold little inspiration for men who themselves had actively participated in self-sacrifice in a manner far more real than had the clergy. Christianity was too mild to have much meaning for the Sioux.

Federal trusteeships, as applied to the Sioux, obviated any possibility that the tribe would ever reach a maturity which would allow them to handle their own affairs. The agent, as a father-figure, has never left them, and the trust has never been terminated. Because the trustee has been unable to decide upon a termination schedule, the Sioux have never needed to prepare themselves for emancipation. Attempts to decide upon a date for termination have been thwarted either by well-wishers or by the Indians themselves. Self-determined leadership cannot be realized under the stultifying influence of a trusteeship, no matter how benevolent. And those who would criticize the Bureau of Indian Affairs for inept domination are unaware of the facts.

At the time of treaty-making, the time when the Sioux exchanged peace and territory for the promise of schools and farming equipment and Christianity, they also gave up freedom for security. Their military and cultural denial represented so dramatic a change that the Sioux have not yet recovered. As a people whose way of life was sustained by victories, they have been unable to adapt themselves to defeat. Yet, unless they do, they cannot survive. Their cultural loss has been accompanied by a loss of vision. No longer do they find avenues for self-expression, and so they are cursed with apathy and psychic emaciation. No longer is there anything which they can deny themselves, and so they have sacrificed themselves in pity. No longer are they permitted to resolve for themselves the conflict of self-expression and self-denial, and so the essence of living has vanished. No longer is their excessiveness given a healthy opportunity for display, yet this is still the Sioux method of adjustment.

The fact that the Sioux way of life was destroyed by causes beyond the control of the people themselves—the diminishing buffalo herds, the overwhelming military might of the whites, the utter impossibility of maintaining a warlike hunting economy with the framework of an expanding industrial nation—does not in itself imply that the descendants of the Sioux Nation must suffer extinction. In spite of the fact that some of our forefathers advocated a policy of extermination with vindictiveness, more of them foresaw a utopian rural economy for their red brothers. The legislative programs of Congress attest to this. Thus, while the Sioux were not exterminated, neither were they helped to become prosperous farmers. Sadly, their current situation dangerously approximates a condition between the two extremes.

In a very frightening sense the Sioux are victims of the white man's insistence that others accept his way as the only way of life. This insistence has been characterized by harshly overt actions, founded in the hope of bringing civilization to the Sioux, conceived in the wish to show them democracy. The outlawing of many Indian religious practices, from the Sun Dance to the *Hunkayapi,* was accompanied by conversion to Christianity by zealous missionaries. The banning of plural marriages went hand in hand with the splitting of the consanguine families through forcing individuals to accept and live on separately allotted parcels of land. In schools, the teaching of English was equated with denying the Sioux child the right of speaking Indian. Sioux medical practices were scoffed out of existence in favor of modern doctors and nurses and hospitals. Headmen's prerogatives were usurped by government-appointed agents who saw to the welfare of the people in accordance with federally approved policies. Now, even though any or all of these actions may have been morally justified, each in its way represents a little breach of

344

freedom, a tiny, yet destructive, blow to the principle of democracy.

The contribution which the Indians might have made to the American way has been effectively handicapped, but not completely destroyed. The self-respect which the Sioux may be able to express in terms of their high heritage can prove a mirror for the future dignity and well-being of us all. For there yet exists the chance that the theory of democracy need not be equated with the insidiousness of conformity, but rather with the exhilarating concept of freedom for the nonconformist, whether as an individual or as a group.

Only when the Sioux people demand the right to decide how they shall express themselves, what they shall deny themselves, how they wish to adjust to changing situations, to forfeit security for change—only then can they again become the Vision Seekers.

Iron Shell's Winter Count

Good White Man Came (1807).

Woman Killed by Tree (1808). Kettle's daughter was killed by a falling tree. Cloud Shield's account mentions a Brulé man as having been killed.[1]

Little Beaver's Tipi Burned (1809).[2]

Horse with Eagle Feathers (1810). This event is mentioned in several accounts. The Sioux, having captured many horses, discovered one with two eagle feathers tied to its tail.[3]

Starved War Party (1811). It was during this year that a Sioux war party met a Crow war party and killed the entire group. The Sioux, however, nearly starved to death before reaching home.

Credit Winter (1812). This was the year of the striped yellow buckskin, apparently tallies issued by a trader. Big Missouri's winter count refers to this as the year when a trader peddled goods among the Sioux.[4]

A Man with a Gun (1813).[5]

Crushed Witapahatu's Head (1814).[6]

They Died in the City (1815). Three headmen went to Washington on horseback, but they failed to return.

Shot in the Heel Died (1816).

[1] Garrick Mallery, "Pictographs of the North American Indians," Bureau of American Ethnology, *Annual Report* (1882), 135.

[2] Hyde, *Red Cloud's Folk*, 35.

[3] Mallery, "Pictographs," *loc. cit.*, 135

[4] Lucy Kramer Cohen, "Big Missouri's Winter Count, United States Department of Interior *Indians at Work*, Vol. VI, No. 6 (1939).

[5] *Ibid.*

[6] Mallery, "Pictographs," *loc. cit.*, 135.

Bone Bracelet Died (1817).

Smallpox (1818).

Standing Elk Killed by Buffalo (1819). According to Iron Shell, Standing Elk was so badly gored that his intestines were torn out.

Crow Indian Killed Inside a Tipi (1820). The enemy Crow was killed within the Sioux camp.

Whistling Star (1821). According to Iron Shell, the shooting star whistled as it appeared.

Peeler's Leg Burnt (1822). Battiste Good's count called this "Peeler Froze His Leg Winter." Peeler was a Yankee trader who enjoyed whittling. Big Missouri identified the man as "Slicer."[7]

Mature Corn Camp (1823).[8]

Two Berry Pickers Killed by the Sioux (1824). Battiste Good identifies these victims as Pawnees.[9]

Brulés Held at Bay (1825). A Sioux war party, surrounded by a superior force of Crow Indians, managed to escape under cover of darkness without suffering any casualties.

Move Camp Across River (1826). In moving across a river, the Sioux pulled their belongings over the ice.

A Broken Arrow Was Killed in Tipi (1827). A member of the Broken Arrow band was killed in his tipi by his father-in-law.

Many Miwatanis Were Killed (1828). The Miwatanis or Mandans were long-standing enemies.

Painted Arrowhead Performed a White Buffalo Ceremony (1829).

Killed Many White Buffalo (1830). Iron Shell's count states that all of the albinos were bulls, while Battiste Good's records show the albinos were cows. Big Missouri's count mentions that "four white buffalo were killed, the largest number in history."[10]

Camped with the Gomelas (1831). Although Iron Shell was

[7] Cohen, "Big Missouri's Winter Count," *loc. cit.;* Garrick Mallery, "Picture Writing of the American Indians," Bureau of American Ethnology *Annual Report* (1888), 317.

[8] Mallery, "Pictographs," *loc. cit.,* 111.

[9] Mallery, "Picture Writing," *loc. cit.,* 318.

[10] Mallery, "Picture Writing," *loc. cit.,* 318; Cohen, "Big Missouri's Winter Count," *loc. cit.*

unable to identify this tribe, Big Missouri confirmed the camping with an enemy tribe.[11]

Ties His Penis in a Knot Dies (1832).

Shifting Stars (1833).

An Eagle Hunter Was Killed (1834).

Killed Two Flag Bearers (1835). The Sioux, in a battle with the Pawnees, killed two men, each of whom was carrying an American flag.

Fighting over the Ice (1836).[12]

Killed Many Broken Arrows (1837).[13]

Four Sons of Crazy Dog Killed (1838). Cloud Shield's count reports that Crazy Dog carried a pipe and took the warpath, and Iron Shell's record explains the reason.[14]

They Went on a War Party and Nearly Starved (1839). With many wounded, a starving war party ate a mule. According to White Cow Killer, this was "Large War Party Ate Pawnee Horses Winter."[15]

Five Brothers of Little Thunder Were Killed (1840). The headman's brothers were killed and scalped as they slept. Battiste Good, the sole survivor of the ambush, states that it was the Pawnees who killed the brothers.[16]

Big Horse Steal (1841). This is the year the Sioux captured many horses from the Shoshonis.

Shena Was Taken Prisoner (1842). The Sioux killed many Pawnees and brought home as prisoner a boy who was named Shena.

Stealing Arrows from Pawnees (1843).

Dog Father Died (1844). Dog Father, according to Iron Shell, was so nicknamed because one of his sons had a big mouth and ears resembling a pack dog.

[11] Cohen, "Big Missouri's Winter Count," *loc. cit.*

[12] Mallery, "Pictographs," *loc. cit.*, 139; Mallery, "Picture Writing," *loc. cit.*, 320.

[13] Cohen, "Big Missouri's Winter Count," *loc. cit.*

[14] Mallery, "Pictographs," *loc. cit.*, 139.

[15] *Ibid.*, 140.

[16] Mallery, "Picture Writing," *loc. cit.*, 321.

Smallpox (1845).

Woman Shot in Vagina (1846). A man, discovering his un-faithful wife in the tipi of another, brought her home and shot her.

Crow Eagle Was Lanced (1847). In a fight with the Pawnees, Crow Eagle was about to strike a coup when his horse turned and he himself was lanced in the hip.

Crow Stole Many Horses (1848). The Brulés lost many ani-mals to the Crows, which story is also related in the count of the Lone Dog, who indicated that eight hundred horses were stolen. The Swan's count, however, mentions that two hundred horses were captured from the Miniconjous.[17]

Crows Held Sioux at Bay (1849). During the year a war party of Brulés were cornered in a bank by the Crows. Battiste Good locates the battle at Crow Butte near Camp Robinson, Nebraska.[18]

Smallpox (1850).

Big Issue (1851).[19]

Heavy Snow (1852). The winter snows were so deep this year that only the tops of the tipis appeared above the snow.

Mean Bear Died (1853). Battiste Good mentions this year as "Cross Bear Died on the Hunt."[20]

Much Money (1854). The Sioux held up a stagecoach carrying the payroll to Fort Laramie.

Many Red Flannel Offerings (1855). Streamers of red flannel placed on poles were pleasing to the supernaturals. More offer-ings were given this year than ever before. This count may have reference to a great tribal congregation held in conjunction with General Harney's Council on March 18, 1856.[21]

Whittler Died (1856). This may be the trader "Peeler" re-ferred to in the year 1822.

Buffalo Bull Hunt (1857). An entire herd of buffalo was killed, and all the animals proved to be bulls.

A White Buffalo Ceremony Was Performed by a Member of the Corn Owners Band (1858).

[17] Mallery, "Pictographs," *loc. cit.*, 120.
[18] Mallery, "Picture Writing," *loc. cit.*, 323.
[19] Mallery, "Pictographs," *loc. cit.*, 142.
[20] Mallery, "Picture Writing," *loc. cit.*, 324.

Big Crow Was Killed (1859). Big Crow and his brother were hunting magpie when a Crow was discovered. Both men were killed and scalped. According to the Swan, Big Crow was a Miniconjou chief.[22]

Turning Bear Killed (1860). Renowned as a brave warrior, this man was killed and scalped. This, however, is not the "Whirling Bear" killed in the Grattan Massacre of 1854.

Long Foot's Entire Camp Killed (1861). An enemy war party destroyed this headman and his band.

Few Trees (1862). This year the Brulés spent the winter camped where there were only a few trees.

Broken Up Dance (1863). It is recorded that many Sioux divisions were camped together when suddenly they dispersed. Big Missouri states that all the Sioux divisions had congregated.[23]

Laugh as He Lies Down Burned Up (1864). An interpreter named Laugh as He Lies Down was patronizing a trading post which sold liquor to Indians; it was located on the south bank of the Platte River near the Oregon Trail. Indians burned the post while the interpreter and others were inside. American Horse and Cloud Shield refer to the trader as "Bird," and Cloud Shield suggests that it was the Cheyennes who burned him to death.[24]

Many Deer Came to Make a Treaty (1865).

Brulés Camped on a Hill (1866).

Fought with the Omahas (1867).

Fish's Wife Died (1868). Battiste Good records that the Crows killed fifteen Sans Arcs Sioux in addition to Long Fish, a Brulé.[25]

The Sun Died (1869).[26]

Many Strike Was Killed (1870). This man was killed in a battle with the Pawnees.

Buffalo Ceremony Failed (1871). Because there were very few buffalo, a Buffalo Dreamer performed a ceremony. However, no

21 *Ibid.*, 324.
22 Mallery, "Pictographs," *loc. cit.*, 123.
23 Cohen, "Big Missouri's Winter Count," *loc. cit.*
24 Mallery, "Pictographs," *loc. cit.*, 144.
25 Mallery, "Picture Writing," *loc. cit.*, 326.
26 Mallery, "Pictographs," *loc. cit.*, 125.

buffalo appeared, because, according to Iron Shell's account, the buffalo fooled the people.

Old Woman Horn Fell From a Bank and Died (1872). This woman was highly respected by everyone.

Many Pawnees Killed (1873). A large Pawnee hunting party encroaching upon Sioux territory was routed by the Sioux. Many Pawnees were killed, including women and children.

Utes Stole Horses (1874). Iron Shell records the loss of many horses by the Oglalas while Cloud Shield states that "the Utes stole all the Brulé horses." Battiste Good reports that five hundred horses were captured.[27]

Black Hills Treaty (1875).

Went to Make a Treaty (1876).

Spent the Winter at Ponca River (1877). This year the Sioux wintered at the Omaha camping grounds.

First Wagons Issued (1878).

Children Went to School (1879). According to Iron Shell, a white man took the first group of Sioux children to Carlisle Indian School.

Turning Bear Thrown in Jail (1880). Turning Bear was imprisoned for the murder of a white man.

Spotted Tail Killed (1881). The titular head of the Brulés was murdered by Crow Dog.

Four White Buffalo Ceremonies Were Given (1882).

Red Top Tipi Band Made a Dance Hall (1883).

[27] *Ibid.*, 145; Mallery, "Picture Writing," *loc. cit.*, 327.

Familial Terms and Their Use

"Grandmother" and "grandfather": the parents of anyone whom ego calls "mother," "father," or "uncle."

"Father," and "mother": one's own parents, anyone whom ego's father calls "brother," and anyone whom ego's mother calls "sister."

"Uncle" and "aunt": anyone whom ego's mother calls "brother," and anyone whom ego's father calls "sister."

"Brother" and "sister": the son and daughter of anyone whom ego calls "father" and "mother" (siblings and parallel-cousins).

"Male cousins" or "female cousins": the son and daughter of anyone whom ego calls "uncle" and "aunt" (cross-cousins). (There seems to have been shifting of either terminology or mode of behavior in regard to cross-cousins. The terms *"tahnasi"* and *"hankasi"* for male speaker, and *"sicesi"* and *"cepansi"* for the female speaker are derived from the terms for brother and sister-in-law, where *"-si"* implies "stop" or "go away"; yet the behavior pattern is that for siblings and parallel-cousins—one of respect and reserve. It would seem that the shift has been in the direction of the behavioristic, since there is no indication of cross-cousin marriage or joking in recent times, and thus the present terms represent a lag.)

"Wife" and "husband": one's own spouse.

"Father-in-law" and "mother-in-law": anyone whom ego's spouse calls "father," "uncle," or "grandfather," or "mother," "aunt," or "grandmother." (The term "grandfather" seems to have been derived from "father-in-law," while the term "mother--in-law" appears to have come from "grandmother.")

"Son" and "daughter": one's own children—if the speaker is

male, the children of anyone whom he calls "brother"; if the speaker is female, the children of anyone whom she calls "sister."

"Nephew" and "niece": if the speaker is male, the children of anyone whom he calls "sister" or "cousin"; if the speaker is female, the children of anyone whom she calls "brother" or "cousin."

"Brother-in-law" and "sister-in-law": anyone whom ego's spouse calls "brother" or "sister"; anyone whom ego's "brother" or "sister" calls "husband" or "wife."

"Son-in-law" and "daughter-in-law": the spouse of anyone whom ego calls "son" or "daughter," "nephew" or "niece."

"Grandchild": the children of anyone whom ego calls "son" or "daughter," "nephew" or "niece."

"*Omahinton*": the parents of anyone whom ego calls "son-in-law" or "daughter-in-law." "This is considered the 'head of the family' as it comes down."

1. BOOKS

Benedict, Ruth. *Patterns of Culture*. Boston, Houghton Mifflin Company, 1934.

Bordeaux, William. *Conquering the Mighty Sioux*. Sioux Falls, South Dakota, W. J. Bordeaux, 1929.

Brown, Joseph Epes, editor. *The Sacred Pipe: Black Elk's Account of the Seven Rites of the Oglala Sioux*. Norman, University of Oklahoma Press, 1953.

Catlin, George. *North American Indians*. Philadelphia, Leary, Stuart and Company, 1913.

Clark, W. P. *Indian Sign Language*. Philadelphia, 1885.

Curtis, Edward S. *The North American Indian*. 20 vols. Cambridge, Mass., The University Press, 1907-30. [Volume III (1908) contains "The Teton Sioux."]

Densmore, Frances. *Music in Its Relation to the Religious Thought of the Teton Sioux*. Holmes Anniversary Volume, Washington, 1916.

De Voto, Bernard, editor. *The Journals of Lewis and Clark*. Boston, Houghton Mifflin Company, 1953.

Dodge, Colonel Richard. *Our Wild Indians*. Hartford, Worthington and Company, 1883.

Ewers, John C. *Teton Dakota*. Berkeley, United States Department of the Interior, National Park Service, 1938.

———. *Plains Indian Painting*. Stanford, Stanford University Press, 1939.

Hallam, J. "A Sioux Vision," in *Indian Miscellany*, edited by William Wallace Beach. Albany, J. Munsell, 1877.

Hyde, George E. *Red Cloud's Folk: A History of the Oglala Sioux Indians*. Norman, University of Oklahoma Press, 1937.

Lyford, Carrie A. *Quill and Beadwork of the Western Sioux*. Lawrence, Bureau of Indian Affairs, 1940.

Macgregor, Gordon. *Warriors without Weapons*. Chicago, University of Chicago Press, 1946.

Mirsky, Jeannette. "*The Dakota*." In Margaret Mead, *Co-operation and Competition among Primitive Peoples*. New York, McGraw-Hill, 1937.

Neihardt, John G. *Black Elk Speaks*. New York, William Morrow, 1932.

Parkman, Francis. *The Oregon Trail*. New York, New American Library, 1956.

Radisson, Pierre Esprit. *Voyages of Pierre Esprit Radisson*. Boston, The Prince Society, 1885.

Sandoz, Mari. *Crazy Horse*. New York, Alfred Knopf, 1942.

Standing Bear, Luther. *Land of the Spotted Eagle*. Boston, Houghton Mifflin Company, 1933.

——. *My Indian Boyhood*. Boston, Houghton Mifflin Company, 1921.

——. *My People the Sioux*. Boston, Houghton Mifflin Company, 1924.

Vestal, Stanley, editor. *New Sources of Indian History, 1850–1891*. Norman, University of Oklahoma Press, 1934.

——. *Sitting Bull*. Boston, Houghton Mifflin Company, 1932.

Wied-Neuwied, Maximilian Alexander Philipp, Prinz von. *Travels in the Interior of North America*. 3 vols. Cleveland, Arthur H. Clark Company, 1906. (In Reuben G. Thwaites, ed. *Early Western Travels, 1748–1846*. Cleveland, 1904–1907. Vol. XXII–XXIV.)

2. ARTICLES AND MANUSCRIPTS

Anderson, Harry. "An Investigation of the Early Bands of the Saone Group of Teton Sioux," *Journal of the Washington Academy of Sciences*, Vol. XLVI, No. 3 (March, 1956).

Beckwith, M. W. "Mythology of the Oglala Dakota," *Journal of American Folk-Lore*, Vol. XLIII (1930).

Beckwith, P. "Notes of Customs of the Dakotas," Smithsonian Institution *Report* (1886).

Blish, Helen. "The Ceremony of the Sacred Bow of the Ogalala Dakota," *American Anthropologist*, New Series, Vol. XXXVI (1934).

——. "Ethical Conceptions of the Ogalala Dakota," Nebraska University *Studies*, Vol. XXVI, Nos. 3-4 (1926).

Boas, F. "Some Traits of the Dakota Language," *Language*, Vol. XIII (1937).

——. "Teton Sioux Music," *Journal of American Folk-Lore*, Vol. XXXVIII (1925).

Brackett, A. G. "The Sioux or Dakota Indians," Smithsonian Institution *Report* (1876).

Bushnell, D. I. "Tribal Investigations East of the Mississippi," Smithsonian Institution *Miscellaneous Collections*, Vol. LXXXIX, No. 12 (1934).

Bushotter. "A Teton-Dakota Ghost Story," *Journal of American Folk-Lore*, Vol. I (1888).

Cohen, Lucy Kramer. "Big Missouri's Winter Count," United States Department of the Interior *Indians at Work*, Vol. VI, No. 6 (1939).

Colby, L. W. "The Ghost Songs of the Dakota," Nebraska State Historical Society *Proceedings and Collections*, Ser. 2 (1895).

Culin, Stewart. "Games of the North American Indians," Bureau of American Ethnology *Annual Report* (1907).

Deloria, Ella. "Dakota Texts," American Ethnological Society *Publications*, Vol. XIV (1932).

——. "The Sun Dance of the Oglala Sioux," *Journal of American Folk-Lore*, Vol. XLII, No. 166 (October–December, 1929).

De Land, C. E. "The Verendrye Explorations and Discoveries," *South Dakota Historical Collections*, Vol. VII (1914).

Denig, E. T. "Indian Tribes of the Upper Missouri," Bureau of American Ethnology *Annual Report* (1930).

Densmore, Frances. "The Rhythm of Sioux and Chippewa Music," *Art and Archaeology*, Vol. IX (1920).

——. "Teton Sioux Music," Bureau of American Ethnology *Bulletin No. 61* (1918).

Dorsey, James O. "Games of Teton Dakota Children," *American Anthropologist* Vol. IV (1891).

——. "The Social Organization of the Siouan Tribes," *Journal of American Folk-Lore*, Vol. IV (1891).

——. "A Study of Siouan Cults," Bureau of American Ethnology *Annual Report* (1890).

Dorsey, George Owen. "Legend of the Teton Sioux Medicine Pipe," *Journal of American Folk-Lore*, Vol. XIX (1906).

Douglas, F. H. "The Sioux or Dakota Nations, Divisions, History and Numbers," The Denver Art Museum *Leaflet No. 41* (1923).

Erickson, E. Homburger. "Observations on Sioux Education," *The Journal of Psychology*, No. 7 (1939).

Fletcher, Alice. "Indian Ceremonies," Peabody Museum of American Archaeology and Ethnology *Report*, Vol. XVI (1884).

———. "The Sun Dance of the Ogalala Sioux," American Association for the Advancement of Science *Proceedings* (1883).

Gilmore, Melvin Randolph. "The Dakota Ceremony of Hunka," Museum of the American Indian, Heye Foundation, *Indian Notes*, Vol. VI, No. 4 (1929).

———. "The Dakota Ceremony of Presenting a Pipe," Michigan Academy of Science *Papers*, Vol. XVIII (1932).

———. "Dakota Mourning Customs," Museum of the American Indian, Heye Foundation, *Indian Notes*, Vol. III, No. 4 (1926).

———. "Oath-taking among the Dakota," Museum of the American Indian, Heye Foundation, *Indian Notes*, Vol. IV, No. 1 (1927).

———. "The Old Time Method of Rearing a Dakota Boy," Museum of the American Indian, Heye Foundation, *Indian Notes*, Vol. VI, No. 4 (1929).

———. "Uses of Plants by the Indians of the Missouri River Region," Bureau of American Ethnology *Thirty-third Annual Report* (1919).

———. "The Victory Dance of the Dakota Indians," Michigan Academy of Science *Papers*, Vol. XVIII, Nos. 23–30 (1932).

Goldfrank, Esther. "Historic Change and Social Character: A Study of the Teton Dakota," *American Anthropologist*, New Series, Vol. XLV, No. 1 (1943).

Haines, Francis. "The Northward Spread of Horses among the Plains Indians," *American Anthropologist*, New Series, Vol. XL (1938).

———. "Where Did the Plains Indians Get Their Horses?" *American Anthropologist*, New Series, Vol. XL (1938).

Hallowell, A. Irving. "The Social Function of Anxiety in a Primitive Society," *American Sociological Review*, Vol. VI, No. 6 (1941).

Hassrick, Royal B. "Some Personality Traits of Sioux Indian Children." MS in possession of the author.

———. "Teton Dakota Kinship System," *American Anthropologist*, New Series, Vol. XLVI, No. 3 (1944).

Lesser, Alexander. "Some Aspects of Siouan Kinship," *International Congress of Americanists*, Vol. XXIII (1928).

Lyford, Carrie A. "Sioux Designs and the Origins," *Indians at Work*, Vol. II, No. 13 (1935).

Mallery, Garrick. "A Calendar of the Dakota Nation," United States Geological and Geographical Survey of the Territories *Bulletin*, Vol. III, No. 1 (1877).

———. "Pictographs of the North American Indians," Bureau of American Ethnology *Annual Report* (1882).

———. "Picture Writing of the American Indians," Bureau of American Ethnology *Annual Report* (1888).

Meeker, L. L. "Siouan Mythological Tales," *Journal of American Folk-Lore*, Vol. XIV (1901).

———. "Sioux Games," Free Museum of Science and Art, University of Pennsylvania *Bulletin*, Vol. III, No. 1 (1916).

Mekeel, Scudder. "A Discussion of Culture Change as Illustrated by Material from a Dakota Community," *American Anthropologist*, Vol. XXXIV (1932).

———. "The Economy of a Modern Teton Dakota Community," Yale University *Publications in Anthropology* (1936).

———. "A Short History of the Teton-Dakota," *North Dakota Historical Quarterly*, Vol. X, No. 3 (1943).

Mooney, James. "The Ghost Dance Religion," Bureau of American Ethnology *Fourteenth Annual Report*, Pt. 2 (1896).

Riggs, S. R. "A Dakota-English Dictionary," United States Geographical and Geological Survey of the Rocky Mountain Region *Contributions to North American Ethnology*, Vol. VII (1890).

———, and J. O. Dorsey. "A Dakota Grammar," United States Geographical and Geological Survey of the Rocky Mountain Region *Contributions to North American Ethnology*, Vol. IX (1893).

Robinson, Doan. "History of the Dakota Sioux Indians," *South Dakota Historical Collections*, Vol. II, No. 2 (1904).

Speck, Frank. "Notes on the Functional Basis of Decoration and the Feather Technique of the Ogalala Sioux," Museum of the American Indian, Heye Foundation, *Indian Notes*, Vol. V, No. 1 (1928).

Sullivan, Louis R. "Anthropometry of the Siouan Tribes," American Museum of Natural History *Anthropological Papers*, Vol. XXIII, Pt. 3 (1920).

Swanton, John R. "Siouan Tribes and the Ohio Valley," *American Anthropologist*, New Series, Vol. XLV, No. 1 (1943).

Thomas, Sidney J. "A Sioux Medicine Bundle," *American Anthropologist*, New Series, Vol. XLIII (1941).

Walker, J. R. "Ogalala Kinship Terms," *American Anthropologist*, New Series, Vol. XVI (1914).

———. "Sioux Games," *Journal of American Folk-Lore*, Vol. XVIII (1905).

———. "The Sun Dance and Other Ceremonies of the Ogalala Division of the Teton Dakota," American Museum of Natural History *Anthropological Papers*, Vol. XVI, Pt. 2 (1917).

Wissler, Clark. "Decorative Art of the Sioux," American Museum of Natural History *Bulletin*, Vol. XVIII, Pt. 3 (1902).

———. "Influence of the Horse in the Development of the Plains Culture," *American Anthropologist*, New Series, Vol. VI (1914).

———. "Material Culture of the Blackfoot," American Museum of Natural History *Anthropological Papers*, Vol. V, Pt. 1 (1910).

———. "Societies and Ceremonial Associations in the Ogalala Division of the Teton-Dakota," American Museum of Natural History *Anthropological Papers*, Vol. XI (1912).

———. "Some Ogalala Dakota Myths," *Journal of American Folk-Lore*, Vol. XX (1907).

———. "Some Protective Designs of the Dakotas," American Museum of Natural History *Anthropological Papers*, Vol. I, Pt. 2 (1907).

———. "The Whirlwind and the Elk in the Mythology of the Dakota," *Journal of American Folk-Lore*, Vol. XVIII (1905).

Abortion: 124
Accidents: 255
Acorns: 204
Adolescents: 77–78, 122–23, 330
Adoption: 110–111, 297–300
Adultery: 17, 44, 48
Affection: 35, 109, 115
Age: 17, 107, 115
Aggression: 76, 151, 309, 316, 318, 327, 330–33
Agriculture: 172, 177, 188, 209, 342
Akicita societies: 16, 22–23, 48, 149, 227; joining, 17, 37, 320 f.; dances, 19–20, 131, 160; origins of, 20, 91; role of, 21 f., 30, 46, 172–73, 200 ff., 215; in ceremonies, 28–29, 51, 333
All Father (Rock): 254
All Mother (Earth): 254
Allotment system: 341
American horse: 9, 350
Amulets: 86, 310–11; see also wotawes
Animals: 192–93, 194, 256, 266 f.; see also under individual animals
Anog-Ite (Double-faced Woman): 248, 250 ff., 282, 300
Antelope: 175, 188, 200 f.
Appearance, physical: 325–26
Arapahoes: 177
Arikaras: 9, 22, 65 f., 70 f., 177, 209
Arrogance: 71, 80
Arrowleaf berries: 203
Arrows: 228–30; sending- (wismahi yeyapi), 193
Art: 233–34
Artichokes: 204

Ash tree: 230
Assiniboines: 63 f.
Atonement: 50 f.
Autumn, activities: 175–76
Avoidance taboo: 107 f., 112, 115 f., 118, 316

Badger Earrings: 160
Badgers: 191, 192–93, 196; see also Irukas
Bad Hand: 274, 276
Bad River: 9
Ball-throwing Rite (Tapawanka-yeyapi): 27, 123, 259, 297, 300, 301–302, 323
Barrenness: 53 f.
Battle cries: 34
Beading: 42, 123, 322
Bear (animal): 32, 191, 252
Bear (Hunonpa): 247, 254 f., 283
Bear Dreamers: 277, 279, 290 f.
Beautiful One: see Whope
Beaver: 188, 192
Behavior, modes of: 35–36, 45–46, 107, 113–19, 263, 352; for women, 36, 322–23, 324
Berries: 177, 187, 202 ff., 218, 229; see also under individual fruits
Big Bellies: see Naca Ominicias
Big Crow: 124, 350
Big Horn Mountains: 3
Big Missouri: 10, 346 ff., 350
Big Stone Lake: 64 f.
Bird (name): 350
Birds: 192, 193–94, 254, 266, 238 f.; see also under names of individuals

Birth: 310–14
Bison: *see* buffalo
Biting the arrow: 44–45
Biting the knife: 39, 44–45, 331
Biting the snake: 39
Black Buffalo, Chief: 71
Blackfeet: 3, 6, 177; *see also* Saones, Sihasapas
Black Hills: 9f., 13, 65, 68, 78–79, 173, 176, 189; Treaty, 351
Black Horse: 272–77, 319
Black Horse, James: x
Blotahunka: 83ff.; *see also* war leader
Blue Earth River: 63
Blue Whirlwind: x, 44, 110, 134, 223, 311–12, 316
Boasting: 33, 72, 80, 99, 309
Bobcats: 192, 231, 289
Bone Bracelet: 9, 347
Bone-setting: 291
Bordeaux, Jesse: x
Bows: 230–31
Box elder tree: 175, 187f., 218
Brave Buffalo: 277ff.
Brave Hearts (Cante Tinzas): 16, 21; *see also* policing societies
Bravery: 14, 25, 32–34, 39, 52f., 73, 91, 97f., 247
Bride-price: 42, 126f., 323
Brings the Buffalo Girl: 154
Brings the Horse: 110
Brings the White Buffalo: x
Broken Arrows: 6, 347f.
Brothers: *see hakatakus*, peace ceremony, siblings
Brulés: *see* Sichangus
Buffalo (bison): 12, 57ff., 66, 74, 76, 78, 84, 171, 177, 188f., 266; extermination of, 209, 344
Buffalo (Tatanka): 247f., 254f., 281
Buffalo berries: 202
Buffalo Caller: 200–201
Buffalo Dance: 281–82, 284–85, 293, 300
Buffalo Dreamers: 124, 126, 160, 162, 198, 215, 277, 279, 282, 293, 300f., 350
Buffalo Game: 318
Buffalo Horn-Game: 144

Buffalo-Hunt Game: 145
Buffalo hunts: 64, 70, 177, 292–93; communal drives (*wani-sapa*), 23, 91, 176, 189f., 198–201; family (*tate*), 174f., 189f., 198; fall, 175–76, 190, 197; surround, 198, 201–202; running herd over cliff, 200–201; boys', 302–303
Buffalo Maidens: 37
Buffalo Men: 279, 285f.
Buffalo Nation: 293
Buffalo People: 257ff.
Buffalo Rite (*Tatanka avicalowanpi*): 27, 39, 123, 297, 300–302, 323
Buffalo skull: 155–56, 298ff., 306
Buffalo Who Walks Standing Upright: 258ff.
Buffalo Woman: 130, 259, 299, 301
Bull Bear: 49
Bundles: 304, 314–15, 336
Bureau of Indian Affairs: 340, 343
Burial ceremonies: 34, 37, 333–38
Burnt Thighs: *see* Sichangus
Buzzard: 96

Cactus fruit: 203f.
Calamus root: 291
Calf Pipe: 260
Calves, unborn: 174, 218
Camp Robinson, Nebraska: 349
Camps: summer, 12–13, 28, 173, 189f.; circle arrangement of, 13, 23–24, 29, 174; moving, 28, 172–73, 175; independent, 31; winter, 173, 176
Cannibalism: 176
Cannonball River· 62
Can Oti: 255
Captives: 111–12
Carlisle Indian School: 351
Carver, Captain Jonathan: 65, 68
Cat's cradles: 151
Cave Woman: 155
Cedar Island: 9
Cepansi: 352
Ceremonies: the four, 27, 39, 254, 256f.; from Whope, 259; and giveaways, 297ff., 308; *see also* under names of ceremonies

Changes With: *see* Iron Shell, Chief Arnold
Chaperonage: 45, 124, 137
Chasing as He Walks: 23f.
Chasing Crane, Charles: x
Chastity: 121–22, 254
Chastity belt: 45, 124, 136f.
Cherries: 174, 177–78, 202, 204, 218, 229, 301, 306f.
Cherry-ripening Moon (July): 174f., 281
Cheyenne River: 68
Cheyennes: 10, 64f., 71, 177, 189, 224, 350
Chief God: *see* Wakan Tanka
Childbearing: 39, 41, 51, 53f., 310–14
Children: 33, 35, 53, 177; games of, 72, 77, 122, 143–46, 151, 317–18; ear-piercing, 98, 323; and home, 109–10, 113–15, 119; adoption of, 110–11; captive, 111; secret names for, 134; and supernaturalism, 270, 319ff.; disciplining, 315–16, 328, 332–33; Favorite Child, 324–25
Chippewas: 6, 64, 263
Chokecherries: *see* cherries
Chouteau, Auguste: 61
Christianity: 343f.
Chunkaka: 155
Cici-man: 316
Circle, symbolism of: 256
Circling the Kettle: 157–58
Civil codes: 30, 51
Civil societies: 16–17; *see also* under names of societies
Clark, William: 68f., 71
Claw: 196
Clothing: 189, 209, 224–28, 264
Cloud Shield: 346, 348, 350 f.
Clowns: 254, 272, 276; *see also* Heyokas
Cold Clown: 152
Colors: 26, 255
Conjugal home: 113–14, 115, 341
Contests: of women's work, 42–43, 312; of virtue, 44–45; coup-striking, 199

Controllers: 26, 246ff., 254, 256, 264f., 267
Corn: 299
Corn Owners Band: 349
Cosmology: 248, 261ff., 265
Cottonwood trees: 188, 281f., 300
Councils: 7, 25, 28, 35–36, 342
Coups: 33, 91, 96ff.; counting, 66, 70, 88, 331; for stealing, 47, 185; touching, 65, 88, 98; symbols for, 97; for premarital relations, 121, 136; in dances, 158, 282; -striking contest, 199
Courting: 121, 124–26, 136, 156, 255
Cousins: 109, 118, 352
Coyotes: 188, 192, 196
Cradles: 42, 64–65, 109, 171, 228, 311f.
Crane: 193
Crazy Buffalo (Gnaske): 255, 283, 300
Crazy Dog: 348
Crazy Horse: 27
Crazy Woman (Witkowin): 123, 131
Creation myth: 248–53
Creator: *see* Wakan Tanka
Crees: 22, 62ff., 69
Criminal codes: 30
Cross Bear: 349
Crow Butte: 349
Crow Dog: 351
Crow Eagle: 349
Crow Owners (Kangi Yuhas): 16, 20
Crow (bird): 196
Crows (tribe): 64, 68, 92ff., 172, 177, 189, 321, 346f., 349f.
Custer, General George Armstrong: 339
Cut Meat Band: 109
Cyclone: *see* Iya

Dakotas: ix, 6, 62n., 64
Dance Lodge: 281ff.
Dance of the Buffalo Bull: 300
Dances: 94, 156–60, 175; Tokala, 18–20, 24f.; Akicita, 19–20, 131, 160; social, 156, 160; imitative, 267; *see also* under names of dances
Dance Until Morning Dance: 90

Death: 109f., 254, 256, 277f., 297; fear of, x, 265; on the battlefield, 33, 72, 83, 308; infant, 53; *see also* burial ceremonies, mourning
Deer: 175, 188f., 190–91, 215–16, 252, 266
Deer Dreamers: 231, 277, 279
Deer Woman: 223, 270
Defense mechanisms: 328–29, 330
Dentalium shells: 152, 226f.
Des Grosseliers, Jean Baptiste: 177
Dew cloth: 29, 43, 83, 99, 212f.
Dignity: 35
Directions: 254ff.
Discipline of children: 315–16, 328, 332–33
Disfigurement: 48, 72, 136, 138, 331, 334f.
Divorce: 13, 43, 48, 109, 122, 341; and murder, 45, 131; method of, 130–31; causes of, 131–32
Dodge, Colonel Richard: 191n.
Dog Father: 348
Dogs: 33, 47, 216; as food, 24, 89, 157ff., 177f.; as beasts of burden, 62, 64, 176–83; treatment of, 177f., 316; varieties of, 178
Doing Good Deeds: 311
Doing the Sliding Game: 146
Double-faced Woman: *see* Anog-Ite
Double Woman: 135, 162, 223, 227, 270
Dreamers: 149, 161ff., 231, 233, 268–69, 291f., 331; women, 41, 223; public tests by, 277–79
Dreams: 14, 20, 25, 91f., 269ff.
Drum Bearers: 18, 23
Drums: 156, 158, 160–62, 289
Ducks: 188, 193
Dwellers of the Prairie: 6; *see also* Lakotas
Dye: 223

Eagle Feather Back: 29
Eagle Nest Butte: 273
Eagles: 188, 195–96, 266, 273
Eagle Shield: 291
Ear-piercing: 98, 323

Earth (All Mother, Maka): 26, 323, 254f., 259; offerings to, 86f., 324
Eclipse of 1869: 9
Eggs: 289
Elders: 23, 28, 321–22
Elk: 175, 188, 266, 278
Elk Dreamer: 124, 126, 162, 215, 277ff., 290
Elope (game): 122
Elopement: 121, 126, 130
Essence (*nagila*, Spirit-like): 254f., 282
Etiquette: 46–47, 119, 323–24; *see also* behavior
Evil spirits: 248, 255, 290
Executive: *see* Wakan Tanka
Exhibitionism: 72, 80, 98f., 309

Fall (name): 13
Falls of St. Anthony: 63
Familiarity: 107, 114–15, 118
Family: 11–15, 107–108; conjugal, 108f., 341; consanguine, 110, 341, 344; *see also tiyospe*
Famine: 198–99, 204
Favorite Child: 324–25
Fear: 51–52, 53, 73, 98, 137; ways of overcoming, x, 265; culture frighteners, 316, 328
Feasts: 30, 37, 110, 177, 301, 304, 312; Tokala, 24–25; female virtue, 44, 175, 331f.; for war party, 83, 89; marriage, 129; at dances, 157ff.; funeral, 334–35
Feathers: 96, 196, 229, 298, 307
Fecundity: 254, 302
Fever: 289
Fidelity: 47f., 72, 131, 247, 331; in women, 41, 43–44, 48; double standard of, 48
Fire, symbolism of: 255
Firearms: 9, 22, 62f., 69, 74
Fire-throwing Game: 144
First Love (game): 122
First One (Tokahe): 252–53, 257
Fish: 192, 196–97
Flute: 126, 156, 162–63, 231, 233, 335, Big Twisted, 126, 162f.
Food: 136, 172, 187, 327; at feasts, 24,

89, 157ff., 177f.; preparation of, 171, 176, 210, 215–18; varieties of, 202–204
Forest dwellers: 248
Fortitude: 14, 25, 27, 32, 34–36, 53, 247, 265; in Sun Dance, 34–35; in women, 36, 302; and fear, 51–52, 73, 98
Fort Laramie: 349; Treaties, 10, 14
Four, importance of number: 247–48, 256
Four Winds (Tatetob): 86f., 89, 93, 247, 249ff., 254, 259, 324
Foxes: 191–92
Fraternal societies: 14, 15–16, 17
Freedom: 31, 343, 345
Freeze His Feet Off: 13
Friends (*kolas*): 20, 24, 111
Frogs: 289
Fruit: 174, 177–78, 202ff., 217–18, 256; *see also* under names of fruits
Funeral rites: 333–38
Fungi: 204

Games: 143–51; for children, 72, 122, 143–46, 151, 317–18; for boys and men, 77, 143–46, 147, 149, 151, 318–19, 331; as miniature life situations, 143, 151; wagering in, 143, 147, 151, 318; winter, 143, 146, 149; spring, 144, 147; team, 144–46, 147–50, 318; for girls and women, 146–47, 148, 151, 318; for both sexes, 148–49, 317; of marksmanship, 150–51; scoring, 151, 318; Whope patron of, 255; *see also* under names of individual games
Gaze at the Sun (dance): 286
Gaze at the Sun Buffalo: 285
Gaze at the Sun Staked: 285
Gaze at the Sun Suspended: 281, 285
Geese: 193f., 289
Generosity: 14f., 25, 27, 32, 36–38, 51ff., 99, 109, 247, 254, 296f., 308; for women, 39, 302, 322; in ceremonies, 123, 301–302; of Favorite Child, 325
Gens de la Flèche Collée: *see* Prairie Sioux
Ghost (vitality): 246, 248, 254

Ghost Dance: 339
Ghost Head: 19, 92, 195, 272
Ghost Lodge: 302ff.
Ghost-owning (Spirit-keeping): 27, 37f., 302; ceremony, 39, 42, 90, 259, 297, 302–306
Ghost trail: 323, 338
Gica: 255
Gifts: 36–38, 199, 296–97, 308; at ceremonies, 111, 126, 297ff., 301, 304–305, 307, 312; at Night Dance, 157, 159
Gnaske: *see* Crazy Buffalo
Gods: 245ff.; hierarchy of, 246ff.; Associate, 247, 254, 256; Subordinate (Gods-Kindred), 247, 254, 256; Superior, 204, 256; benevolent, 247–48; Gods-like (Wanalapi), 248, 255; evil, 248, 255; Spirits, 256
Gomelas: 347
Good, Battiste: 10, 347ff.
Good Woman's Dance (Winyan Tapika): 160
Gooseberries (wicagnaska): 177–78, 202f., 229
Gossip: 40–41, 44, 47, 328ff., 332
Grama grass: 281
Grandchild: 353
Grandparents: 109f., 112, 115, 341, 352; term for supernaturals, 112, 274ff.
Grand River: 66
Grapes: 218
Grasshoppers: 196
Gratitude: 264f.
Grattan Massacre: 350
Great God (Wi): 247
Great Mediator (Whope): 247
Great Mystery (Wakan Tanka): 245ff., 266
Great Spirit: 247
Great War Leader: 29
Great White Father: 339
Greed: 76, 80, 262
Grizzly bear: 32, 34

Hair: 90, 228, 302
Hakatakus: 123, 129

Hanbelachia (vision hill): 268f., 271, 293ff., 331
Hankasi: 352
Hanwi (Moon): 247, 249, 254, 256
Harney, General William S.: 349
Hawks: 188, 196, 232, 254, 266, 274
Headmen: 13–14, 16, 27, 30, 78, 337, 344, 346
Heart River: 3
Hennepin, Father Louis: 63
Heralds: 18–19, 20, 44, 172, 305, 312f.
Herbs: 276, 290 ff.
Hermaphrodites: 50
Heyoka Dreamers: 162
Heyokas: 152, 227, 272ff., 276f., 279
Hides, preparing of: 175, 210–11
High Bald Eagle: x, 97, 232
Hihan Kara (Owl Maker): 323, 338
Hitting-Each-Other-in-the-Face Dance: 158
Hoka he: 200
Hollow Horn Bear: 17
Holy Circle: avenged, 83, 86, 88, 90; funeral rites for, 333–35
Holy Men: *see* shamans
Homosexuality: 133
Honey: 218
Honeymoon: 130
Hops: 291
Horn Chips: 272f., 276
Horse Creek: 9
Horse Indians: *see* Plains Indians
Horsemint: 291
Horses: 49f., 62, 74, 87ff., 131, 151, 183–86; in funeral rites, 37, 334, 336f.; stealing, 47, 87–88, 91, 93–96, 97, 185; advent of, 69–71, 177, 183; capture of, 76, 78f., 184–85; significance of, 91–92, 189; and status, 92, 98, 322, 340–41; as medium of exchange, 99, 129, 184, 233, 277, 342; as gifts, 110, 126f., 301; as beasts of burden, 172f., 183; breaking, 175, 185–86, 319; "sacred dog," 183; and wealth, 183–84; in hunting, 191, 201f.; boy's first, 319
Horsetails: 297f.
Hotana cute: 144

How Goes It: 13
Humility: 33
Humor: 153
Hunka: 27, 111, 335; ceremony, 38f., 297–300
Hunkayapi: *see* Waving the Horsetail
Hunkpapas (Those Who Camp at the Entrance): 3, 6, 109; *see also* Saones
Hunonpa (Bear): 247, 254, 283
Hunting: 47, 76–77, 202, 254, 264, 318; methods, 188ff.; religious rites for, 194–95, 198; *see also* buffalo hunts

Ice-sliding: 143
Ignorance: 52f.
Iktomi (Trickster): 155–56, 248ff., 284
Illegitimacy: 124
Incense: 284f., 289, 306f.
Independence: 76, 80
Indian Claims Commission: 340
Indian Reorganization Act: 340
Individualism: 30f., 184, 209–10, 310ff.
Industry: 41f., 254, 322
Infancy: 53, 256, 314–15
Iniowaspe (pit): 267–68, 273
In-laws: 108, 115f., 118, 130, 352f.
Insanity: 255
Insecurity: 329f., 333
Inyan (All Father, Rock): 26, 242f., 254f.
Iowas: 63ff.
Iron Horse: 135
Iron Shell: 113, 134, 347f., 351; participating in ceremonies, 28–30, 83, 302ff., 306f., 333f.; winter count, 8–11, 346–51
Iron Shell, Chief Arnold: x, 8n., 11, 129, 146, 174, 191f., 257; initiation to Tokala, 18–19; on eagle-hunting, 195
Iroquois (True Adders): 6, 62n.
Irukas (Badgers): 16, 20
Isnatialoⁿ ɔanpi (Singing over First Menses): 297
Itazipchos (Sans Arcs, Without Bows): 3, 6, 109, 257, 350
Ite: 248–50; *see also* Anog-Ite

Iya (cyclone): 248, 255, 283
Iyuptalas (Owl Feather Headdresses):
16n.

James River: 64
Joking: 107, 115, 118f., 151ff., 352
Juneberries: 174f., 203, 229
Jurisprudence: 46

Kangi Yuhas (Crow Owners): 16, 20
Keepers of the Rattles: 18, 23
Kettle (name): 346
Kettles: 157f.
Kici yuska pi (Untying Each Other
Ceremony): 51
Kick and Scatter the Tobacco Ashes
(dance): 20
Kick-My-Tail-Off Game: 151, 318
Kicks-up-Dirt: 192
Kiganakapi (postpone the finish): 144
Kills Enemy: 312
Kills in Sight: 334
Kindness: 99
Kinship system: 107, 115f., 119
Kiowas (Witapahatus): 9, 65, 71, 78,
189, 346
Kit Foxes: *see* Tokalas
Knocking the Ball Game: 147f.
Kolas (friends): 20, 24, 111

Labor, division of: 209f., 228
Lake Traverse: 64f.
Lakotas (The Men): ix, 6, 62n., 73
Lance Owners: 18, 21, 23, 86
Land of Many Lodges: 337f.
Language, Siouan: ix, 6
La Salle, Robert Cavelier, Sieur de: 63
Laugh as He Lies Down: 350
La Vérendrye brothers: 64
Laws: 46f.
Laziness: 131
Leader Charge, Chief: x, 109, 126, 131
Leadership: 15, 21, 22–23, 25ff., 30–31,
39, 78, 296
Leavenworth, Colonel Jesse: 9
Lesbianism: 135
Lesser Adder (Sioux): 6

Le Sueur, Pierre Charles: 63f.
Levirate: 118, 132–33
Lewis, Meriwether: 68f., 71
Lightning: 278
Lisa, Manuel: 9
Little Beaver: 9, 346
Little Bighorn River: 10, 339
Little Day: x, 12–13, 177f., 323
Little Thunder: 29, 348
Lizards: 254, 310
Loisel, Registre: 9
Lone Dog: 349
Long Face: 177
Long Fish: 350
Long Foot: 350
Long Woman: 323
Love Game: 317

Maggots (Nini Watu): 255
Magpies: 188, 193, 196, 216
Maka: *see* Earth
Making a Buffalo Woman (cere-
mony): 259
Making as Brothers (peace cere-
mony): 27, 259
Mandans: 177, 347
Mannequins: 248
Manufacturing: 209, 228–30, 231–33
Many Deer: 10, 350
Many Strike: 350
Marksmanship, games of: 150–51
Marriage: 48, 352; preparation for,
41, 122; customs, 108–109, 121; plan-
ning of, 126, 129; feast, 129–30; suc-
cessful, 130f.; *see also* in-laws,
polygamy
Masochism: 52f., 99, 137, 294, 308–309,
327
Maynadier, General H. E.: 10
Mdewakantons: 6; *see also* Seven
Council Fires
Meadowlark: 193
Mean Bear: 349
Meat, preparation of: 215–18
Meat Pack: 79, 189; *see also* Black Hills
Meddling Bear: 12–13
Medicine: 124, 126, 231, 233, 289f., 344;

for war, 87, 98f.; given in dream, 91; horse as, 183; Bear patron of, 254
Medicine Melon: 162
Menses: 41, 137, 289; *see also* puberty
Meteoric shower of 1833: 9
Mice: 155–56, 203, 316
Michilimackinac trading post: 61
Migration: 62–64, 175, 177
Milky Way (Spirit Trail): 305, 337
Mille Lacs: 62
Miniconjous (Those Who Plant by the Stream): 3, 6, 8, 28, 68, 109f., 191, 349f.; *see also* Tetons
Mink: 191
Minnesota: 62ff., 74
Minnesota River: 63, 65
Missionaries: 399, 343f.
Mississippi River: 62n., 63f.
Missouri River: 3, 61, 63f., 66, 68f., 71
Miwatanis (Tall Ones): 16n., 17, 347
Mobility: 291f.
Moccasin Game: 143, 149–50, 151
Moccasins: 97, 109; making, 42, 175; spirit, 335
Modesty: 36, 99
Mongoloid characteristics: 326
Monogamy: 45
Monotheism: 261
Months, names of: 174f.
Moon (Hanwi): 247, 249, 254, 256
Moon of Frost in the Tipi (December): 174
Moon of Strawberries (May): 174f.
Moon of the Birth of Calves (April): 11, 174
Moon of the Falling Leaves (October): 174
Moon of the Hairless Calves (November): 174
Moon of the Ripe June berries (June): 174f.
Moon of the Ripening Chokecherries (July): 174f., 281
Moon of Ripe Plums (August): 174
Moon of the Thunderstorms (May): 175

Moon of the Yellow Leaves (September): 174
Moon when the Grain Comes Up (March): 174
Moose: 252
Moral codes: 31, 264
Morale-building: 34
Mourning: 34, 327, 333ff., 336–37; *see also* burial ceremonies
Murder: 17, 45, 48–50, 131
Musical instruments: 156
Muskrats: 192
Mystery Dog: 70; *see also* horse
Myths: 155, 248–53

Naca Ominicias (Big Bellies, The Short Hairs, Those Who Wear Buffalo Headdresses): 16–17, 23, 50, 77, 86, 89, 172, 175, 227; as council, 25ff.; at Wicasa investiture, 29–30; organizing hunt, 198–99
Nadoweisiw-eg: 6; *see also* Sioux
Nagi (personality): 255, 337
Nagila (essence): 255, 282
Nakedness: 315
Nakedness: ix, 6, 62n., *see also* Yanktonais, Yanktons
Names: 18, 38, 134, 303, 312–13
Nation of Beef: 177
Natural environment: 174, 209, 266
Night Dance: 136, 156–59
Nighthawk: 254
Nini Watu (maggots): 255
Niya (vitality): 255
Nomadism: 65, 70, 171
No Mother Band: 28
North Dakota: 340
North Platte River: 10, 68

Oglalas (Scatter One's Own): 3, 6, 16, 21, 26ff., 49, 68, 109, 351; *see also* Tetons
Ohio Valley: 62n.
Okaga (South Wind): 251, 262
Old Man (Waziya, Wizard): 248, 250, 253, 284, 289
Old people: 112–13

Old Woman Horn: 351
Omahas: 63ff., 71, 209, 350f.
Omahinton: 353
One Horn: 191
Ones Who Decide: *see* Wakincuzas
Onions: 203
Oohenonpas (Two Boilings, Two
  Kettles): 3
Oregon Trail: 350
Ornaments: 227–28
Orphans: 110
Ostracism: 47, 49, 51, 133, 137, 308
Otter: 231
Owl Feather Headdresses (Iyuptalas):
  16n.
Owls: 194, 316
Owns a Big White Horse: 13
Owns a White Buffalo: 27

Pachot (trader): 63f.
Packing Game: 122, 317
Painted Arrowhead: 347
Paiute: 339
Papapuze: 216–17
Paralysis: 255
Parents: 53, 112–13, 115, 352
Parkman, Francis: 49
Partisan Walker, Chief: 71
Pawnees: 9f., 78, 97, 321, 347ff., 351
Peace: 78, 100, 263, 342
Peace Ceremony (Making as
  Brothers): 27, 259
Peeler: 347, 349
Pejuta: 290
Pemmican (*wakpapi*): 83f., 89, 154, 217
People, The: 73
People of the Sun: 248
Peppermint leaves: 218
Personality: 254f.; group, 326f.
Perversion: 134f.
Pets: 177, 196
Pharmacy: 292
Pierre, South Dakota: 64
Pigeons: 193
Pike, Zebulon: 69
Pine trees: 188
Pipe: 50f., 234, 259, 261, 324; of peace,

66, 263; to tell the truth, 86, 89; for
  hunting, 194, 199; from Whope, 259–
  61; in ceremonies, 268, 284, 300, 303f.,
  336; in Dreamer's test, 278f.
Pipe Bearers: 18, 23
Pipe Owners: *see* Wakincuzas
Pipestone Quarries: 65
Piracy: 80, 91
Pit (*iniowaspe*): 267–68, 273
Plain Lance Owners: *see* Sotka Yuhas
Plains Indians (Horse Indians): 72,
  92, 342
Plains Sioux: 6; *see also* Lakotas
Plants: 256, 290
Platte River: 3, 10, 78, 162, 350
Plums: 174, 177–78, 204
Policing societies: listed, 16n.; *see also*
  under names of individual societies
Political organization: 26ff., 30–31
Polygamy: 43, 45, 63, 122, 131–33, 344
Ponca River: 351
Poncas: 71
Porcupines: 188, 192; *see also* quilling
Potatoes: 202, 204
Pottery: 171
Power (Potency, *sicun*): 92, 246, 248,
  254f., 266f., 331; in dreams, 269ff.;
  ways of obtaining, 271ff., 279, 294,
  308–309
Prairie chickens: 160, 193
Prairie dogs: 192
Prairie Hawk: 274
Prairie Sioux (Gens de la Flèche
  Collée): 64
Pregnancy: 310
Premarital relations: 121, 136
Prestige: 30, 52, 76, 78, 97f., 112, 296,
  340–41
Privacy, lack of: 40
Property: 47, 78, 296
Prostitution: 122
Provincial Troops: 65
Psychological types: 326
Psychotherapy: 290
Puberty ceremonies: 37–38, 41–42, 43,
  123, 297, 300–302, 323
Punishment, forms of: 47ff.

Purification rite: 259, 267–69; by sweat bath, 50, 195, 198, 232, 267, 289f.; lodges, 195, 268, 272, 276, 278

Quilling: 123, 223–25, 228, 234, 322f., 332; contest, 42–43, 312
Quivers: 231

Rabbits: 192, 318
Raccoons: 191, 193
Radisson, Pierre Esprit: 177
Raiding parties: 92ff., 175
Rain in the Face: 321
Rattles: 156, 162, 289; Keepers of the, 18, 23
Rattling: 177
Rattling Blanket Woman: x, 41, 42–43, 135, 153, 315; dream of, 270–71
Rattling Tipi: 216
Rawhide Hoop Game: 151
Recognition: 51, 296
Red Around the Face: 50
Red Cloud: 14, 49
Red Council Lodge: 25, 28, 43, 171
Red Eagle: 109
Redfins: 196
Red Leaf: 13, 323
Red Shirt, Irene: x
Red Shirt, Mary: x
Red Top Tipi Band: 351
Rejoicing Over His Horse: 110
Relatives: 108f., 113–14, 116, 118f., 352–53
Religion: 155, 245f., 264–65
Reservations: 340
Reserve: 35–36, 115, 327f., 330, 333
Respect: 107, 114ff., 262
Responsibility: 14, 30–31, 269f.
Retaliation: 76, 80, 91; by family of Iron Shell, 83–90
Rewards: 46, 48, 52, 80
Ridicule: 47, 317
Roan Horse: 124
Roan Horse Woman: 225, 302f.
Rock: see Inyan
Rolling Game: 151
Rorschach test: 326

Rose berries: 187, 202, 204
Rounds: 256
Running Horse: 152
Running Horse, Rose: x
Runs-Him: 83, 85ff., 89, 335

Sacred dog: 70, 183
Sage: 255, 283ff., 289; in ceremonies, 268f., 273, 301, 306
Sahiyela: see turnips
St. Louis: 61
Salt: 218
Sand lizard: 310–11
Sans Arcs: see Itazipchos
Santee: 6
Santee Dakotas: 64
Santee Sioux: ix, 6; see also Dakotas
Saones: 6, 63, 68
Sauk Rapids: 63
Scalp Dance: 90, 159, 321
Scalps: 88ff., 99, 109, 333
Scatter One's Own: see Oglalas
Schizophrenia, catatonic: 52
Schools: 341, 344
Scotts Bluff, Nebraska: 9
Scouts: 97, 172f., 199, 262
Screech owls: 194
Security: xi, 31, 51, 74f., 119, 329, 343; through aggression, 76, 80; economic, 186–87, 204
See Who Shoots the Farthest (game): 151
Self-denial: x–xi, 30, 52–53, 99f., 119, 137f., 151, 265, 287, 293f., 296, 308f., 327, 338, 344
Self-expression: x–xi, 30, 34, 51, 71, 73f., 80, 99, 120, 151, 264f., 288, 309, 329, 338, 343f.
Self-sacrifice: 72–73, 272, 279, 288, 294, 296, 308–309, 334f., 343
Seven Council Fires: 3, 6; see also under names of tribes
Sex: and behavior, 107, 114–16, 117; double standard, 122, 137f., 262; segregation, 327–28
Shamans (Holy Men, Wicasa Wakan): 17, 39, 98, 123, 126, 215,

258, 266, 271; as *winktes,* 134; in cere-
monies, 160, 267, 281ff., 298–300,
306f.; curing the sick, 162, 290–92;
and hunt, 196, 198; role of, 254–57,
292–93; career, 280, 320f.; tests by,
331
Shells, dentalium: 152, 226f.
Shell Straightener: 152–53
Shelter: 209ff.
Shena: 348
Shields: 231–33, 277
Shinny (game): 147f.
Shirt Wearers: *see* Wicasas
Shoot for the Katydid: 148
Shoot for the Loop: 148–49
Shoot for the Side: 148
Shooting Dice with a Basket: 146
Shoot without Holding: 149
Short Hairs: *see* Naca Ominicias
Shoshonis: 83f., 87–88, 93, 348
Shot at Bound Grass: 151
Shot at Many Times: 302f.
Shot in the Heel: 9, 28, 83, 89, 334–35,
346
Shyness: 329–30
Siblings: 12, 109, 117f., 352
Sicesi: 352
Sichangus (Burnt Thighs, Brulés): 3,
6, 10, 12, 16, 68, 109f., 346f., 349ff.;
winter count, 8; political organiza-
tion, 26ff.
Sickness: 255, 288–92, 341, 344
Sicun (power): 255, 266f.
Sihasapas (Black Feet): 3
Singing over First Names
(*Isnatialowanpi*): 297, 300
Sioux Nation (Lesser Adders, Nado-
weisiw-eg): groupings in, 3ff.; gov-
ernment, 28ff.; history of, 61–70
Sioux River: 64
Sissetons: 6
Sisters: *see* siblings
Sitting Bull: 321
Sitting Eagle: 109
Skan: *see* Sky
Ska Yuhas (White Horse Owners):
16n., 17, 175, 200

Skunks: 192, 196
Sky (Skan): 26, 86f., 89, 247ff., 254ff.,
259, 267, 283f., 324, 338
Sledding: 143
Slicer: 347
Sliding Wood Game: 144, 146
Smallpox: 9, 68, 347, 349
Smoke: 49, 255
Smoothed trail: 268
Snowbirds: 193, 254, 319
Socialism: 37
Songs: 156, 159, 289; of societies, 20–
21, 24f., 84; of White Buffalo
Maiden, 306
Sore Eyes Moon (February): 174
Sororate: 118–19, 132
Sotka Yuhas (Plain Lance Owners):
16n., 20f., 83f., 149–50, 333–34
South Dakota: 65f., 340
South Wind (Okaga): 249, 251, 262
Spinsterhood: 135
Spirit: 246, 248, 254f., 337
Spirit-keeping: *see* Ghost-owning
Spirit-like: 246, 248, 254
Spirit lodge (*tiokete*): 337
Spirits (gods): 256
Spirit Trail (Milky Way): 247, 249,
254, 305, 333, 337
Sportsmanship: 99
Spotted Tail: 351
Spring, activities: 175
Squirrels: 192
Standing Elk: 347
Standing Soldier, Mabel: x
Star People: 251
Stars: 248, 256
Status: 14–15, 17, 92, 298
Stealing: 47; *see also* horses
Sterility, induced: 124
Sticking-together Game: 143
Stoicism: 34f., 41, 120, 333
Storytelling: 40, 152–56
Strangers: 328–29
Strawberries: 203, 218; Moon of, 174f.
Struck-in-the-Face: 195f.
Success: 73
Suckers: 197

Sugar: 175
Suicide: 53, 308
Summer, activities: 175
Sun (Wi): 26, 247f., 254ff., 283, 300
Sun Dance: 7, 28, 34–35, 42, 73, 98, 175, 256, 259, 327; musical instruments in, 156, 162; locations for, 172f.; description of, 279–88; significance of, 280, 287–88, 294–95; power through, 308, 331; abolition of, 339, 343f.
Supernaturalism: 154, 319
Supernatural power: 14, 92, 98, 125f., 134f., 231, 245ff., 264, 266, 331
Supernaturals (beings): 20, 35, 39, 91, 99, 112, 123, 155, 194ff., 198, 254, 265, 349
Supreme Owners: see Wicasa Yatapikas
Surround, buffalo: 198, 201–202
Survival: xi, 75
Swallows: 254, 266
Swan (name): 349f.
Sweat bath: see Purification rite
Sweet grass: 255, 284f., 289, 302, 306f., 311
Swing-kicking Game: 143, 145–46
Symbols: 97, 159, 161, 227, 232f., 255

Tahnasi: 352
Takoan: 216
Tall Ones: see Miwatanis
Tampco: 216
Tanning: 322f., 332; see also hides
Tapawanka-yeyapi: see Ball-throwing Rite
Tatanka: see Buffalo
Tatanka avicalowanpi: see Buffalo Rite
Tate: see Wind
Tates: 176, 189f., 198
Tatetob: see Four Winds
Tattooing: 323
Tests: 326, 331
Teton River: 68
Tetons: 6, 69, 204; see also Lakotas
Thievery: 47; see also horses
Those Who Camp at the Entrance:

see Hunkpapas
Those Who Plant by the Stream: see Miniconjous
Those Who Wear Buffalo Headdresses: see Naca Ominicias
Throw at Each Other with Mud (game): 144
Throwing It In: 143
Throwing One Up Like a Ball (game): 146, 318
Thunder: 272ff.
Thunderbird (Wakinyan): 247, 254f.
Thunder Dreamers: 231, 272ff., 277
Thunder Voices: 274f.
Ties His Penis in a Knot: 348
Time-reckoning: 8–11, 19, 256
Timpsila: see turnips
Tiokete (spirit lodge): 337
Tipis: 13, 41, 63f., 171; destruction of, 19, 23, 51, 72, 173, 202, 215; location of, 23, 29, 94, 173–74; making, 175, 210ff.; see also dew cloth
Tiyospe: 11–12, 30, 107f., 113, 116, 119, 330, 341
Tiyo-tipi: 199
Tobacco: 172, 255
Tokahe (The First One): 252–53, 257
Tokalas (Kit Foxes): 16, 18–21, 22–24, 149–50, 160
Ton (Wakan): 289
Tortoises: 197, 310
Torture, physical: 272, 294
Touch: see coups
Traders: 61, 63, 69, 347, 350
Traditions: 153, 155
Transvestite (winkte): 133f.
Treaties: 10, 14, 339, 342, 351
Tree Popping Moon (January): 174
Trees: 230
Tribal governments (councils): 342
Trickster: see Iktomi
Trout: 196
True Addars: see Iroquois
Trusteeships: 343
Truteau, Jean Baptiste: 69
Truthfulness: 39–41, 52, 86, 302
Turning Bear: 350f.

Turnips: 202f.
Turtles: 197, 318
Twins: 312
Two Boilings: *see* Oohenonpas
Two-faced Woman: *see* Anog-Ite
Two Kettles: 3, 6; *see also* Oohenonpas, Saones
Two White Buffalo: 211f.

United States: Army, 10, 98, 339; government, 14, 340; President of, 339; treaties with, 249; citizenship, 340; Department of the Interior, 340; trusteeships, 343
Unktehi: 255
Untying Each Other Ceremony: 50
Using Hoofs (Game): 148
Utes: 351

Vanity: 71f., 80, 99
Vegetables: 172, 174, 202–203
Verbena: 291
Villages: 172, 173–74; *see also* camps
Violence: 72, 80
Virtues, four: 14f., 25, 32, 41, 46, 51, 53–54, 262; for women, 32, 39ff., 300
Vision hill: *see hanbelachia*
Visions: 14, 20, 269f.; to children, 320–21
Vision-seeking: 17, 35, 72–73, 175, 194–95, 259, 279, 294, 308, 327, 331, 345
Vitality (Ghost, *niya*): 254f.

Wacekiyapi: *see* worship
Wagering: 143, 147, 151, 318
Wahpekutes: 6
Wakpetons: 6
Wakan: 134, 162, 183, 194, 267, 271 f., 289, 312
Wakanka (Witch): 248ff., 253
Wakan Tanka: 87, 245ff., 258f., 261, 266, 292, 304
Wakincuzas (Pipe Owners, The Ones Who Decide): 13, 27f., 90, 172–73
Wakinyan (Thunderbird, Winged): 247, 254f.

Wakpapi: *see* pemmican
Wanalapi (Gods-like): 248, 255
Wani-sapa: 189f., 198
War Dance: 283
Warfare: 21–22, 33, 76–77, 78, 92ff.; defensive, 79f., 91; causes of, 80, 92; role of, 98, 100, 342–43; objectives of, 308f.
War honors: 33, 80, 91, 96ff., 185; *see also* coups
Warrior societies: 91, 160f., 199–200
War leader (Blotahunka): 77, 83ff., 88f.
War Parties: 77–78, 83, 92, 176, 319–20
Wasicu: *see* white man
Wasicun (medicine): 289f.
Wasna: 306
Water boy: 77, 320
Water spirits: 248
Waving the Horsetail (*Hunkayapi*): 297, 344
Wazhazhas: 10
Wasiya (Old Man, Wizard): 248ff., 253, 284, 289
Wealth: 76, 97, 132, 183–84, 204; acquiring, 17, 36, 78, 80; meaning of, 37, 296f.
Weather: 254
Western Sioux: 6; *see also* Lakotas
Whip Bearers: 18, 23
Whippoorwills: 194
Whirl and Shoot (game): 149
Whirling Bear: 350
Whirlwind (Yumni): 247, 250f., 254f., 281
Whistles: 87, 156, 162
White Buffalo Ceremony: 28, 39, 297, 305–308, 335, 347, 349, 351
White Buffalo Maiden: 29, 260ff., 304, 306ff., 310; analysis of legend of, 262–63; song of, 306
White Buffalo Robe: 305ff.
White Cow Killer: 348
White Crow: 13
White Horse: 231–33, 277
White Horse Owners: *see* Ska Yuhas
White man (*Wasicu*): 316, 328, 342

White-Marked Ones: *see* Wicinskas
White Mountains: 162
White River: 68
Whope (Beautiful One): 247, 251, 254f., 257ff., 263ff.
Wi: *see* Sun
Wicaknaska: *see* gooseberries
Wicasa Itacans: 26, 302ff.
Wicasa (Shirt Wearers): 7, 26–27, 28, 39, 48, 50, 52, 227, 297, 306, 336
Wicasa Wakan: *see* shamans
Wicasa Yatapikas (Supreme Owners): 7, 28–30, 227
Wicinskas (White-Marked Ones): 16n.
Wiconte: 278
Wife-stealing: 47f.
Wigwams: 172, 175
Wildlife: 188
Wind (Tate): 247, 248–50, 251, 254, 338; *see also* Four Winds
Winged: *see* Wakinyan
Winktes: 133–35, 313, 320
Winter, activities: 176
Winter counts: 8–11, 65, 293, 346–51
Winyan Tapika (Good Woman's Dance): 160
Wisdom: 14, 25, 27, 32, 38–39, 51f., 254
Wismahi yeyapi (sending-arrows): 193
Witapahatus: *see* Kiowas
Witch (Wakanka): 248ff., 253
Without Bows: *see* Itazipchos, Saones
Witkowin (Crazy Woman): 123, 131
Wizard: *see* Old Man
Wolf Dreamers: 77, 92, 271f., 277
Wolves: 92f., 154, 188, 192, 252f.

Woman Who Lived with Wolves: 154–55
Women: 34, 84, 116, 121–22, 192, 302, 332, 337, 341; bravery among, 32, 39; virtues for, 32, 39ff., 300; behavior of, 36, 47, 324; childbearing, 39, 41, 51, 53, 310–14; generosity in, 39, 302, 322; truthfulness among, 39–41, 52, 302; dreamers, 41, 223; fidelity in, 41, 43–44, 48; industry in, 41f., 322; making trips, 41, 210–13, 214–15; role of, 41, 210ff., 218, 228; accomplishments of, 42, 218ff., 234, 322; contests, 42–43, 44–45; as adversaries, 47, 121, 135–36; wife-stealing, 47f.; and double standard, 48, 122; farming, 62, 342; captive, 111–12; and divorce, 131; and perversion, 135; games of, 146–47, 148, 151; in dances, 160, 281; preparing food, 176, 202, 210, 215–18; attire for, 225, 228; physical appearance of, 325
Worms: 289
Worship (wacekiyapi): 83, 256, 335, 337
Wotawes: 86f., 94, 98, 231, 276, 288, 335
Wounded Knee: 339
Wovaka: 339
Wyoming: 68

Yanktonais: 6, 63; *see also* Nakotas, Seven Council Fires
Yanktons: ix, 6, 68; *see also* Nakotas
Yumni: *see* Whirlwind

1. *Forgotten Frontiers:* A Study of the Spanish Indian Policy of Don Juan Bautista de Anza, Governor of New Mexico, 1777–1787. Translated and edited by Alfred Barnaby Thomas.
2. Grant Foreman. *Indian Removal:* The Emigration of the Five Civilized Tribes of Indians.
3. John Joseph Mathews. *Wah'Kon-Tah:* The Osage and the White Man's Road.
4. Grant Foreman. *Advancing the Frontier, 1830–1860.*
5. John H. Seger. *Early Days Among the Cheyenne and Arapahoe Indians.* Edited by Stanley Vestal. Out of print.
6. Angie Debo. *The Rise and Fall of the Choctaw Republic.*
7. Stanley Vestal. *New Sources of Indian History, 1850–1891:* A Miscellany. Out of print.
8. Grant Foreman. *The Five Civilized Tribes.*
9. *After Coronado:* Spanish Exploration Northeast of New Mexico, 1696–1727. Translated and edited by Alfred Barnaby Thomas.
10. Frank G. Speck. *Naskapi:* The Savage Hunters of the Labrador Peninsula. Out of print.
11. Elaine Goodale Eastman. *Pratt:* The Red Man's Moses. Out of print.
12. Althea Bass. *Cherokee Messenger:* A Life of Samuel Austin Worcester.
13. Thomas Wildcat Alford. *Civilization.* As told to Florence Drake. Out of print.
14. Grant Foreman. *Indians and Pioneers:* The Story of the American Southwest Before 1830.
15. George E. Hyde. *Red Cloud's Folk:* A History of the Oglala Sioux Indians.
16. Grant Foreman. *Sequoyah.*
17. Morris L. Wardell. *A Political History of the Cherokee Nation, 1838–1907.* Out of print.
18. John Walton Caughey. *McGillivray of the Creeks.*

19. Edward Everett Dale and Gaston Litton. *Cherokee Cavaliers:* Forty Years of Cherokee History as Told in the Correspondence of the Ridge-Watie-Boudinot Family.
20. Ralph Henry Gabriel. *Elias Boudinot, Cherokee, and His America.* Out of print.
21. Karl N. Llewellyn and E. Adamson Hoebel. *The Cheyenne Way:* Conflict and Case Law in Primitive Jurisprudence.
22. Angie Debo. *The Road to Disappearance.*
23. Oliver La Farge and others. *The Changing Indian.* Out of print.
24. Carolyn Thomas Foreman. *Indians Abroad.* Out of print.
25. John Adair. *The Navajo and Pueblo Silversmiths.*
26. Alice Marriott. *The Ten Grandmothers.*
27. Alice Marriott. *María:* The Potter of San Ildefonso.
28. Edward Everett Dale. *The Indians of the Southwest:* A Century of Development Under the United States.
29. *Popol Vuh:* The Sacred Book of the Ancient Quiché Maya. English version by Delia Goetz and Sylvanus G. Morley from the translation of Adrián Recinos.
30. Walter Collins O'Kane. *Sun in the Sky.*
31. Stanley A. Stubbs. *Bird's-Eye View of the Pueblos.* Out of print.
32. Katharine C. Turner. *Red Men Calling on the Great White Father.*
33. Muriel H. Wright. *A Guide to the Indian Tribes of Oklahoma.*
34. Ernest Wallace and E. Adamson Hoebel. *The Comanches:* Lords of the South Plains.
35. Walter Collins O'Kane. *The Hopis:* Portrait of a Desert People.
36. *The Sacred Pipe:* Black Elk's Account of the Seven Rites of the Oglala Sioux. Edited by Joseph Epes Brown.
37. *The Annals of the Cakchiquels,* translated from the Cakchiquel Maya by Adrián Recinos and Delia Goetz, with *Title of the Lords of Totonicapán,* translated from the Quiché text into Spanish by Dionisio José Chonay, English version by Delia Goetz.
38. R. S. Cotterill. *The Southern Indians:* The Story of the Civilized Tribes Before Removal.
39. J. Eric S. Thompson. *The Rise and Fall of Maya Civilization.* (Revised Edition.)
40. Robert Emmitt. *The Last War Trail:* The Utes and the Settlement of Colorado. Out of print.

41. Frank Gilbert Roe. *The Indian and the Horse.*
42. Francis Haines. *The Nez Percés:* Tribesmen of the Columbia Plateau. Out of print.
43. Ruth M. Underhill. *The Navajos.*
44. George Bird Grinnell. *The Fighting Cheyennes.*
45. George E. Hyde. *A Sioux Chronicle.*
46. Stanley Vestal. *Sitting Bull, Champion of the Sioux:* A Biography.
47. Edwin C. McReynolds. *The Seminoles.*
48. William T. Hagan. *The Sac and Fox Indians.*
49. John C. Ewers. *The Blackfeet:* Raiders on the Northwestern Plains.
50. Alfonso Caso. *The Aztecs:* People of the Sun. Translated by Lowell Dunham.
51. C. L. Sonnichsen. *The Mescalero Apaches.*
52. Keith A. Murray. *The Modocs and Their War.*
53. *The Incas of Pedro de Ciezo de León.* Edited by Victor Wolfgang von Hagen and translated by Harriet de Onis.
54. George E. Hyde. *Indians of the High Plains:* From the Prehistoric Period to the Coming of Europeans.
55. *George Catlin:* Episodes from "Life Among the Indians" and "Last Rambles." Edited by Marvin C. Ross.
56. J. Eric S. Thompson. *Maya Hieroglyphic Writing:* An Introduction.
57. George E. Hyde. *Spotted Tail's Folk:* A History of the Brulé Sioux.
58. James Larpenteur Long. *The Assiniboines:* From the Accounts of the Old Ones Told to First Boy (James Larpenteur Long). Edited and with an introduction by Michael Stephen Kennedy. Out of print.
59. Edwin Thompson Denig. *Five Indian Tribes of the Upper Missouri:* Sioux, Arickaras, Assiniboines, Crees, Crows. Edited and with an introduction by John C. Ewers.
60. John Joseph Mathews. *The Osages:* Children of the Middle Waters.
61. Mary Elizabeth Young. *Redskins, Ruffleshirts, and Rednecks:* Indian Allotments in Alabama and Mississippi, 1830–1860.
62. J. Eric S. Thompson. *A Catalog of Maya Hieroglyphs.*
63. Mildred P. Mayhall. *The Kiowas.*

64. George E. Hyde. *Indians of the Woodlands:* From Prehistoric Times to 1725.
65. Grace Steele Woodward. *The Cherokees.*
66. Donald J. Berthrong. *The Southern Cheyennes.*
67. Miguel León-Portilla. *Aztec Thought and Culture:* A Study of the Ancient Nahuatl Mind. Translated by Jack Emory Davis.
68. T. D. Allen. *Navahos Have Five Fingers.*
69. Burr Cartwright Brundage. *Empire of the Inca.*
70. A. M. Gibson. *The Kickapoos:* Lords of the Middle Border.
71. Hamilton A. Tyler. *Pueblo Gods and Myths.*
72. Royal B. Hassrick. *The Sioux:* Life and Customs of a Warrior Society.
73. Franc Johnson Newcomb. *Hosteen Klah:* Navaho Medicine Man and Sand Painter.
74. Virginia Cole Trenholm and Maurine Carley. *The Shoshonis:* Sentinels of the Rockies.
75. Cohoe. *A Cheyenne Sketchbook.* Commentary by E. Adamson Hoebel and Karen Daniels Petersen.
76. Jack D. Forbes. *Warriors of the Colorado:* The Yumas of the Quechan Nation and Their Neighbors.
77. *Ritual of the Bacabs.* Translated and edited by Ralph L. Roys.
78. Lillian Estelle Fisher. *The Last Inca Revolt, 1780–1783.*
79. Lilly de Jongh Osborne. *Indian Crafts of Guatemala and El Salvador.*
80. Robert H. Ruby and John A. Brown. *Half-Sun on the Columbia:* A Biography of Chief Moses.
81. *The Shadow of Sequoyah:* Social Documents of the Cherokees. Translated and edited by Jack Frederick and Anna Gritts Kilpatrick.
82. Ella E. Clark. *Indian Legends from the Northern Rockies.*
83. *The Indian:* America's Unfinished Business. Compiled by William A. Brophy and Sophie D. Aberle, M.D.
84. M. Inez Hilger, with Margaret A. Mondloch. *Huenun Ñamku:* An Araucanian Indian of the Andes Remembers the Past.
85. Ronald Spores. *The Mixtec Kings and Their People.*
86. David H. Corkran. *The Creek Frontier, 1540–1783.*
87. *The Book of Chilam Balam of Chumayel.* Translated and edited by Ralph L. Roys.
88. Burr Cartwright Brundage. *Lords of Cuzco:* A History and Description of the Inca People in Their Final Days.

89. John C. Ewers. *Indian Life on the Upper Missouri.*
90. Max L. Moorhead. *The Apache Frontier:* Jacobo Ugarte and Spanish-Indian Relations in Northern New Spain, 1769–1791.
91. France Scholes and Ralph L. Roys. *The Maya Chontal Indians of Acalan-Tixchel.*
92. Miguel León-Portilla. *Pre-Columbian Literatures of Mexico.* Translated from the Spanish by Grace Lobanov and the Author.
93. Grace Steele Woodward. *Pocahontas.*
94. Gottfried Hotz. *Eighteenth-Century Skin Paintings.* Translated by Johannes Malthaner.
95. Virgil J. Vogel. *American Indian Medicine.*
96. Bill Vaudrin. *Tanaina Tales from Alaska.* With an introduction by Joan Broom Townsend.
97. Georgiana C. Nammack. *Fraud, Politics, and Dispossession of the Indians:* The Iroquois Land Frontier in the Colonial Period.
98. *The Chronicles of Michoacán.* Translated and edited by Eugene R. Craine and Reginald C. Reindorp.
99. J. Eric S. Thompson. *Maya History and Religion.*
100. Peter J. Powell. *Sweet Medicine:* The Continuing Role of the Sacred Arrows, the Sun Dance, and the Sacred Buffalo Hat in Northern Cheyenne History.
101. Karen Daniels Petersen. *Plains Indian Art from Fort Marion.*
102. Fray Diego Durán. *Book of the Gods and Rites and The Ancient Calendar.* Translated and edited by Fernando Horcasitas and Doris Heyden. Foreword by Miguel León-Portilla.
103. Bert Anson. *The Miami Indians.*
104. Robert H. Ruby and John A. Brown. *The Spokane Indians:* Children of the Sun. Foreword by Robert L. Bennett.
105. Virginia Cole Trenholm. *The Arapahoes, Our People.*
106. Angie Debo. *A History of the Indians of the United States.*
107. Herman Grey. *Tales from the Mohaves.*
108. Stephen Dow Beckham. *Requiem for a People:* The Rogue Indians and the Frontiersmen.
109. Arrell M. Gibson. *The Chickasaws.*
110. *Indian Oratory:* Famous Speeches by Noted Indian Chieftains. Compiled by W. C. Wanderwerth.
111. *The Sioux of the Rosebud:* A History in Pictures. Photographs by John A. Anderson, text by Henry W. Hamilton and Jean Tyree Hamilton.

The Sioux: Life and Customs of a Warrior Society has been set on the Linotype in eleven-point Janson, with two points of space between lines. This widely used book face is a recutting of type cast from the original matrices, which were probably of Dutch origin. Like most things Dutch during those years of the seventeenth century which knew Rembrandt and Vermeer, Janson type is of a rich, sturdy design which influences all who know and use it.

UNIVERSITY OF OKLAHOMA PRESS

NORMAN